**"VIVIDLY WRITTEN
AND VERY THOUGHT-PROVOKING"**
Library Journal

"I'm just going to Voorhees Street," the hitch-hiker said as he climbed in the maroon and white pick-up truck.

As the truck approached a stoplight near the neon lights of the fast-food strip, the driver motioned toward a ditch off the road and in a soft voice asked, "Why don't you come down here with me?"

The hitchhiker had no intention of doing that. As he reached for the door handle, the driver pulled out a knife. Mark Henry found himself staring at an eight-inch blade.

**"A SOLID NONFICTION PROCEDURAL . . .
HANDLED WITH
COMPASSION AND DIGNITY"**
Chicago Magazine

**"GRIPPING, INTENSE . . .
COMPELLING . . . HARROWING . . .
YOU WON'T FIND THE NERVE
TO PUT IT DOWN."**
Windy City Times

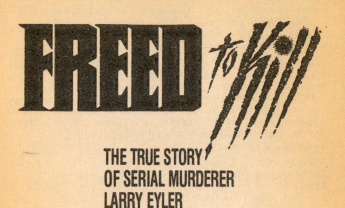

FREED to Kill

THE TRUE STORY OF SERIAL MURDERER LARRY EYLER

GERA-LIND KOLARIK
WITH WAYNE KLATT

AVON BOOKS ◆ NEW YORK

Freed To Kill is a journalist's account of an actual serial murder investigation and the conviction of Larry W. Eyler for the 1984 murder of Daniel Bridges in Chicago, Illinois. The events recounted in this book are true, although some of the names have been changed. The scenes and dialogue have been reconstructed based on tape-recorded formal interviews, police department records, and published news stories. Quoted court testimony has been taken from trial transcripts and is verbatim.

AVON BOOKS
A division of
The Hearst Corporation
1350 Avenue of the Americas
New York, New York 10019

Copyright © 1990, 1992 by Gera-Lind Kolarik
"Constitutional Comment" copyright © 1990 by George Anastaplo
Front cover photograph by *Gaylife*, courtesy of *Gay Chicago Magazine*
Map by Phil Thompson
Published by arrangement with Chicago Review Press, Incorporated
Library of Congress Catalog Card Number: 90-40954
ISBN: 0-380-71546-5

The Chicago Review Press edition contains the following Library of Congress Cataloging in Publication Data:

Kolarik, Gera-Lind
    Freed to kill : the Larry Eyler story / Gera-Lind Kolarik
with Wayne Klatt. — 1st ed.
        p.   cm.
    1. Eyler, Larry.   2. Murderers—United States—Biography.
    3. Serial murders—United States—Case studies.   I. Klatt,
    Wayne.   II. Title.
    HV6248.E78K65   1990   90-40954
    364.1'523'0973—dc20   CIP

First Avon Books Printing: February 1992

AVON TRADEMARK REG. U.S. PAT. OFF. AND IN OTHER COUNTRIES, MARCA REGISTRADA, HECHO EN U.S.A.

Printed in the U.S.A.

RA   10   9   8   7   6   5   4   3   2   1

This book is dedicated to all the law enforcement officers who were involved in these twenty-three cases, only to meet with frustration from what they regard as "the system."

Freed To Kill is also dedicated to the judges, prosecutors, and defense attorneys who staked their careers on upholding their interpretation of the law.

The subject matter may be shocking for some readers, and a book such as this might not have been written until now. The officers, lawyers, judges, and people involved in the investigation cooperated fully.

As the author I have retraced every inch of ground covered in the hundreds of miles involved in the story, from courtrooms to "macho bars" and lonely roads in the middle of the night.

As a newswoman in Chicago I was involved in the case from the beginning.

Of the nearly two hundred people who spoke to me about this complex investigation, my special thanks go to Carmen Pauli, Wilma McNeive, Dan Colin, and Daniel Lee Allen, who gave me many hours of encouragement.

Gera-Lind Kolarik

CONTENTS

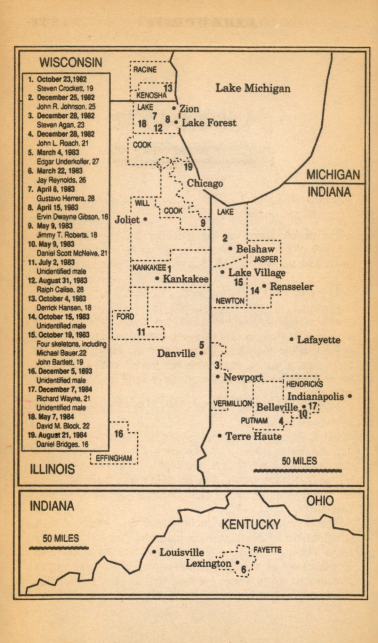

WISCONSIN

1. October 23, 1982
   Steven Crockett, 19
2. December 25, 1982
   John R. Johnson, 25
3. December 28, 1982
   Steven Agan, 23
4. December 28, 1982
   John L. Roach, 21
5. March 4, 1983
   Edgar Underkofler, 27
6. March 22, 1983
   Jay Reynolds, 26
7. April 8, 1983
   Gustavo Herrera, 28
8. April 15, 1983
   Ervin Dwayne Gibson, 16
9. May 9, 1983
   Jimmy T. Roberts, 18
10. May 9, 1983
    Daniel Scott McNeive, 21
11. July 2, 1983
    Unidentified male
12. August 31, 1983
    Ralph Calise, 28
13. October 4, 1983
    Derrick Hansen, 18
14. October 15, 1983
    Unidentified male
15. October 19, 1983
    Four skeletons, including
    Michael Bauer, 22
    John Bartlett, 19
16. December 5, 1893
    Unidentified male
17. December 7, 1984
    Richard Wayne, 21
    Unidentified male
18. May 7, 1984
    David M. Block, 22
19. August 21, 1984
    Daniel Bridges, 16

ILLINOIS

RACINE

KENOSHA

LAKE

COOK

WILL

COOK

KANKAKEE

FORD

EFFINGHAM

Lake Michigan

13

Zion
7   8
18   Lake Forest
   12

19

Chicago

MICHIGAN
INDIANA

LAKE

Joliet

9

2
Belshaw
JASPER
Lake Village
15
14   Rensseler
NEWTON

Kankakee

11

5
Danville

3
Newport

Lafayette

HENDRICKS
Indianapolis
VERMILLION   Belleville   17
PUTNAM   4   10
Terre Haute

50 MILES

INDIANA

OHIO

KENTUCKY

50 MILES

Louisville
Lexington   FAYETTE
6

PROLOGUE

Thursday, August 3, 1978
Terre Haute, Indiana

Some people thrive in the quiet of the night, with the whisper of tires mile after mile, the artificial lights sweeping across the windshield. The world is smaller; everything is less confused. You can feel more of a person.

Larry Eyler brought his restlessness with him along the highways. Now he was heading for Terre Haute in his cluttered maroon-and-white pickup truck, looking from side to side along a row of aging bungalows on 7th Street at two in the morning. There under the glow of a street light was a young man with his thumb out. Larry, his butcher knife stowed in the clutter behind his legs, pulled to a stop.

"I'm just going to Voorhees Street," the hitchhiker told him as he climbed in.

Mark Henry was a slender young man with a pitted face and the muscles of a Marine even though he had been discharged the year before. He kept in shape doing carpentry work for his father, but he didn't like walking when he could just as easily ride. Besides, hitchhiking was friendlier.

The driver was a few inches taller than Mark, with a small mustache distinguishing his round baby face. Larry liked wearing T-shirts to show off the muscles he built up in gyms, and he wore a baseball cap even on sultry nights like this to cover where his hair was thinning toward the front.

As his truck approached a stoplight near the neon lights of the fast food strip, Larry motioned toward a ditch off the road and in his soft voice asked, "Why don't you come down here with me?"

Mark had no intention of doing that. He reached for the door handle, but Larry pulled out the knife. The hitchhiker found himself staring at an eight-inch blade.

The light turned green, and the Chevrolet pickup shot through the intersection. The truck was reaching fifty miles an hour now, passing the Terre Haute Regional Hospital just off the four-lane highway. Larry still held the knife at Mark's shirt, and his blank expression gave the hitchhiker no hint of what might happen next.

The tires screamed as Larry turned sharply onto a dark road, throwing Mark against his arm. The truck skidded into another turn, heading north on a gravel road. It bounded across some railroad tracks, stirring up gravel dust in front of its headlights. Another skidding turn took them to a road used just for farm machinery. As they bounced over the ground, Larry never let go of the knife.

"I don't have any money," Mark said, his throat feeling like dry clay.

"It's not your money I want," Larry told him. "I'm not after your money." They had reached a grassy clearing against a small hill. Larry slowed to a stop and turned off the engine, then lowered the knife to Mark's side. "Just cooperate with me and you won't get hurt," he said. He ordered the hitchhiker to get out and take off his shirt.

Under the moonlight, Mark fumbled at the buttons of his short-sleeved shirt. As he was pulling it off, a handcuff snapped around his wrist. The ex-Marine jerked his hand away and asked, "What are you doing?"

"Hold still," Larry answered, "and don't move."

Larry brought Mark's arm behind him and handcuffed the other wrist, then ordered him to climb into the back of the pickup. The young man moved awkwardly and couldn't make it over the bumper. Larry grabbed Mark's legs and pushed him into the truckbed.

Next he ordered Mark to lie on the cot, a thin mattress on an aluminum frame. Larry did not speak as he reached for Mark's belt and unbuckled it. He removed the man's jeans and boots slowly.

Larry waved off mosquitoes and ordered Mark to lie facedown on the plastic-covered mattress. Then he tied both ankles with clothesline, using a knot to separate the legs and to make it harder for Mark to get them loose. The young man strained to look over his shoulder and saw that Larry was naked now. This couldn't be just a sadomasochistic act. That's when two people are partners in a fantasy. Mark realized the danger he was facing, and he had to wait until the right moment.

Larry was stroking Mark's body lovingly with the flat of the wide knifeblade in a ritual of the dark. Mark twisted and rolled to his knees, startling Larry as if waking him in middream. The ex-Marine pushed his way over the wheelwell in the back of the truck and flipped backward to the ground.

Larry shouted for him to come back, but Mark kept hobbling along the dirt and grass as his ankles worked against the knots. The rope was loosening, giving him a chance to try reaching the utter darkness of the woods.

Mark was nearing the fringe of elm trees as he felt Larry's running-breath on his naked back. Still handcuffed and with the rope around his ankles, Mark turned around and screamed into Larry's blank face, "You fucking queer!"

The butcher knife plunged into his chest. "Oh, Jesus," Mark gasped, staggering and bewildered. He dropped hard to the ground, and Larry stood over him, the blood dripping from the blade. Larry seemed at a loss for what to do now, how to act outside his dreamworld.

Mark could feel his chest sucking air and knew his lung was punctured. Play dead, he thought. He closed his eyes, and Larry stayed above him with the power to kill. But he didn't. His eyes still closed, Mark heard him walk away.

Lying in pretended death, Mark knew he wouldn't be able to get far unless he found a way to close the wound. Every step he took would make him weaker from loss of blood. He had to get his hands in front of him. Mark pushed his buttocks against his handcuffed wrists, then he pressed his knees against the midline slice through his chest, smearing his body with blood. He forced his wrists around his feet even though for a moment he felt that he might blank out. Once his hands were in front of him, he yanked the rope off one of his ankles. Next he used fingertips, wrists, and even the cold metal of the handcuffs to press two waves of skin against the spurting wound. Then he began searching for help.

Mark reached the gravel road that ran along a field. The stones bit into his naked feet. He ran across the railroad tracks and reached the blacktop, still trying to close the three-inch cut. The young man staggered along the road and made out a faint light in a railroad shanty. He cried out but was too far away for anyone to hear.

Next Mark stumbled toward the lights of a trailer camp just past the railroad tracks. He reached the top step of a trailer but didn't want to lose more blood by taking his hands away from the wound to knock. "Help, I'm hurt bad!" he shouted. He could hear voices from inside, but no one opened the door. He pounded on it with the back of his head.

"Give me a rag, anything, just to stop the bleeding," he called out faintly. Too weak to stand, he slid down the steps and fell to the patio. With the pressure of his manacled hands compressing the throbbing wound, he lay on the concrete and screamed.

Amid the sirens and flashing lights Mark looked up, barely conscious, and saw the face of a sheriff's deputy over him. The man went away and came back with a first aid kit. The deputy covered Mark's nakedness with a thin blanket, which soon became soaked in blood.

"Keep talking," the deputy yelled, moving the top of the blanket to keep the wound open. "Don't go to sleep." Mark wanted sleep; then it would be over. . . . "Stay conscious," the deputy shouted. "Wake up!"

The deputy, Kevin Artz, put his hand over the slice in Mark's chest and called for a towel. The trailer owner gave him one, and Artz was able to staunch the bleeding.

By then people from the camp were crowding around, getting in the way of police and an ambulance crew.

One of the men from the trailers pressed his way forward. Artz was about to tell him to step back, that this was an emergency, when he saw that the man was holding a small key. "A boy came to my door and said he stabbed somebody," the man told him. "He says I should give this to you. It's for the handcuffs."

"What?" Artz asked in disbelief.

"We went back to help him, but we couldn't find him."

"Where's this boy?" Artz asked.

The man gestured toward the pickup truck that had just pulled up behind one of the police cars. A Vigo County sheriff's sergeant arrested Larry while Artz accompanied Mark on the ambulance ride to Regional Hospital.

Mark was moved from the stretcher to an emergency room table. A doctor in hospital green and a surgical mask placed an oxygen mask over Mark's nose and mouth; then he applied a compress to stop the bleeding. The butcher knife had cut through the right side of his chest between the fifth and seventh ribs.

Mark was unaware that from his shoulders down his body was covered in blood until the doctor told the nurse to clean him up for surgery. The nurse removed the rope tied to his left ankle. In a moment, she brought a suture table and started an IV. The surgeon used up swab after swab as he lifted blood from around the wound.

Police at the trailer park did not know just what had happened, but Eyler seemed willing to give them a statement when they brought him to the station. They seized his messy truck and in it found a security guard's badge, the kind you can buy in town. There were also a hunting knife, a metal-tipped whip, a butcher knife, a sword in a green velvet case, another pair of handcuffs, a knife with a folding blade, and a container of paralyzing tear gas.

In the hospital, the surgeon worked under a fixed magnifying lens to close Mark's wound with a dozen sutures on the lung and twenty-four on the inner and surrounding tissues. Afterward he inserted a tube that drained the blood that had accumulated in the lung, and he assured Mark that he would be all right.

Mark was in the intensive care unit when Larry was brought into Vigo County Superior Court, where a judge set his bond at fifty thousand dollars. Larry returned the following day, and the judge lowered the amount to ten thousand dollars. A friend came up with the thousand dollars in cash necessary to release him. Larry could always count on his friends.

Mark was released from the hospital a week later and was ready to testify on August 23 about his night of terror. But Larry's lawyer met him in a corridor of the courthouse in downtown Terre Haute and offered him a check for twenty-five hundred dollars, ostensibly for hospitalization and work-time lost.

When the lawyers reported to their client that Mark had accepted and agreed not to pursue charges, Larry changed his plea from guilty to innocent of aggravated battery. On November 13, Judge Harold Bitzegaio dismissed the charge "with prejudice" and ordered Larry to pay $43 for court costs.

This would not be the last time Larry would beat the system.

I

THE PATTERN

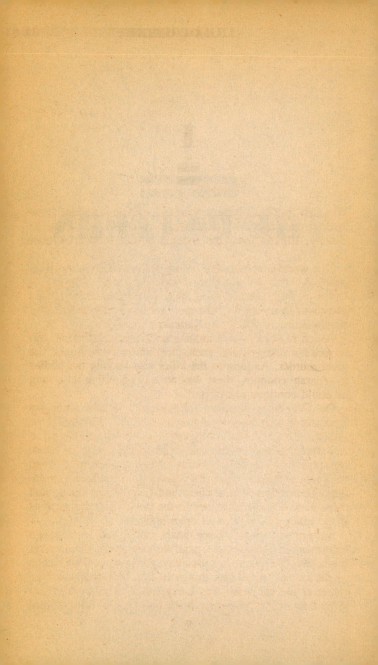

1

The first victim, nineteen-year-old Steven Crockett, was discovered stabbed to death in a cornfield in Kankakee County, Illinois, near the Indiana border in late October 1982.

One week later, the day before Halloween, twenty-five-year-old John R. Johnson disappeared from Chicago's Uptown neighborhood of Appalachians and drifters. His body was discovered Christmas Day along a road in Lowell, Indiana, not far from Kankakee County.

Police in Illinois and Indiana had been conducting two separate investigations, each jurisdiction unaware of the other murder. As long as the killer was leaving the bodies in separate counties, there was no way of telling how long he could continue undetected.

On December 28, Dr. John Pless had two autopsies to perform at the Bloomington Hospital in Bloomington, Indiana. The first was on Steven Agan, who was found in a wooded area near Indiana Highway 63 not far from Newport in Vermillion County. Never in his more than ten years in forensic pathology had Pless seen such mutilation. The abdomen and chest had been sliced open, and there were horizontal gashes in the throat and abdomen as if the killer had wanted to open him up.

Steven was twenty-three years old, lived in his own apartment in Terre Haute, and worked at his father's car wash. He had hopes of someday going to college so he might enjoy "the better things in life." A frequent customer at the car wash was Larry Eyler, who worked just three doors away at a dirty brick building on South Third

Street that held a number of public offices for Vigo County. Larry was in charge of the Project Safe program of the Equal Economic Opportunities Commission, determining the neediest elderly applicants for aid in paying electric and gas bills. Public funds were drying up in December, and word had it that the office would be closed by spring. Although Larry worked there full-time, he regarded the job as a temporary position. He was still going to Indiana State University.

Steven was at his family's home for Sunday dinner on December 19. "Mom, we're going up to town," he told his stepmother. "The boys and I are going to a show." The boys were some of his young friends.

He never returned home. The family was concerned, but Steven had been away from home before, and they told themselves he would be back for Christmas. When he didn't even make a phone call on Christmas morning, they knew something had happened to him. On December 28, Steven's father, Bob, heard over the state police scanner that a man resembling his son had been found. There was rope around his ankles. The family at first thought he was killed "by a junkie," but Dr. Pless knew as he looked down at the body that tremendous rage had been directed at this victim.

Police studying the scene doubted that Steven had been killed where he was found. They went back through the woods and carefully examined an outbuilding on an abandoned farm, where plaster had fallen away to reveal skeletal laths. Several nails were hammered partway into the walls, and there were traces of flesh on one of them. The officers speculated that Steven had been suspended upside down and then cut open as a deer is dressed. Rumors circulated that the killing was a consequence of a party.

After Dr. Pless completed the autopsy on Steven, attendants brought out the body of twenty-one-year-old John Roach, who had been found that day off I-70 in Putnam County. It was a coincidence that the two men should be found the same day and brought to Bloomington because Putnam and Vermillion counties lacked a forensic pathologist of their own. Pless looked at the body of the muscular

Indianapolis man, who had disappeared three days before Christmas, and saw striking similarities to the Agan murder. John had been stabbed repeatedly in the abdomen rather than sliced open, but once again there were signs of rage.

Pless had just finished the autopsies when he received a call from reporter George Stuteville of the *Indianapolis Star*. Stuteville, who calls the *Star* "one of the last police beat screamers" had picked up the pattern in this rash of murders but wasn't making any progress because so many different police jurisdictions were involved. Pless said the only common denominator for the three Indiana cases would be the state police, who should be the ones to coordinate an investigation.

"How do you get a central investigation going?" Stuteville asked.

"Well, I guess maybe I can do that," the pathologist answered in his dry, matter-of-fact way.

He called the state police, but no one did anything about the call and the murders continued.

Larry Eyler was one of the most popular workers at the Equal Economic Opportunities Commission. That's where down-on-their-luck farmers, transplanted Appalachians, and old people who couldn't stay on top of their bills found help. Larry's friendliness was warm, as if he had a special relationship with everyone he met and wanted to be absorbed in the person's life. Once he drove well out of his way on his own time so that an elderly woman wouldn't have to make the trip downtown to fill out a form.

There was a spontaneity to him. On a whim he took a coworker, Karen Burke, to his home at the other end of town to make her quiche for lunch. The spacious condominium townhouse was far beyond the means of Larry's salary. He was staying with a library science professor and made sure he cleaned up so the kitchen was as spotless as the rest of the house.

Burke was in charge of the foster grandparents program. When she held a Christmas party for the senior citizen volunteers, Larry played the elf. This muscular, six-foot-tall young man sat on Santa's lap in a silly costume and teased the guests as if they were children.

On December 30, David Block, a recent Yale graduate, disappeared while in the Chicago area to visit his parents in the affluent suburb of Highland Park. His Volkswagen, only a few months old, was found locked on the Tri-State Tollway near Deerfield in Lake County, Illinois, which is separated by Cook County from Lake County, Indiana.

That January there was tension passing through the Indianapolis gay community. No matter what police said, the men knew that there was a serial killer driving along the highways. The fact that the bodies were being found in separate counties suggested a calculating mind and that the killer had every intention of striking again. But police seemed more intent on looking for differences than recognizing similarities and considered a serial killer just one possibility. For one thing, John Roach was a patron of the Indianapolis gay bars, but as far as anyone could tell, Steven Agan was "straight." For another, John apparently was killed by one person, but Steven's mutilation suggested that two or more people may have been involved.

With John, police had no clues. Under Steven's head they found the tip of an orange plastic glove, and near the body was a Jack Daniels cigarette lighter. On the ground under the beam where the body had been hung police discovered a key—just an ordinary key. What door would it open? they wondered. That little piece of metal could be the most decisive piece of evidence in the case, but it was a clue that could work only in reverse. Instead of leading police to a killer, it would be worthless until a suspect was found and the key tried in all his doors.

Stuteville—a tall, lean man with a young face yet graying hair—felt that he and Pless understood more about the murders than the police did. At a time when newspapers in larger cities were reducing their crime coverage, the *Star* would follow a developing story rather than wait for the police to wrap it up. Until police would admit that a single killer was involved, Stuteville continued using phrases such as "Police have not ruled out a possible link . . ." to force the connection, since police never rule out anything early in an investigation.

All that changed on May 9, 1983, when a farmer found the body of Daniel Scott McNeive in a field on State Road 39 in Henderson County, a mile south of I-70. The body was taken to Bloomington Hospital, and Dr. Pless saw that this was a carbon copy of the others.

Danny lived with his two brothers in Indianapolis. Word on the street was that he was a hustler. Pless took one look at the corpse and doubted the family's theory that he was killed in revenge for giving police information about two street gang members who beat up an elderly man. You would expect wounds in the neck, back, and chest in a gang killing, but the blade in this case also went through the twenty-one-year-old man's liver and kidneys. His blue jeans had been pulled down to his feet, yet there were no signs of sexual attack.

Eleven wounds were to the neck, five to the back, and eleven more to the abdomen. Many were superficial, as if in torture, but one wound was so deep that a great deal of small intestine protruded. There were also several binding marks on the wrists and ankles.

After washing up from the autopsy, Pless called Coroner John Phillips and told him to look for a serial killer. He also called the state police again, and this time they took his recommendations.

2

March 1983

The buildings on an abandoned farm in Lake Village, Indiana, had faded to a gray-green and become part of the landscape. The killer would park his truck a few yards away and carry out his victim. This was not "dumping" a corpse—that could have been done anywhere. Rather, he lay out the bodies methodically, three feet apart and always facing north, with the care of a little girl arranging furniture in a dollhouse.

One body, that of a black man, he had been brought to the other side of a tree as if it didn't belong with the others. The killer had decided to bring it to what a psychiatrist might call a "totem place," part of the ritual of love and hate. A killer with cunning would never place four bodies where they would be discovered at the same time. Why leave clues to the pattern?

The killer shoveled a few scoops of dirt over the fourth victim to be brought to this abandoned barnyard, then gathered leaves left over from autumn as a blanket for the body's coldness. The master of life and death was less concerned with camouflaging the body; some parts of the victims showed through. The four mounds were barely more than a hundred yards off U.S. 41. As the killer drove back and forth between Illinois and Indiana he could not see them, but he could see the tall weeds and the tree that served as the marker for his secret place.

Week after week the killer took Route 41, the tiresome

road from Kentucky, along the flattest portion of Indiana, and up through Chicago to northern Wisconsin. There are no mountains, no great rivers, just small towns and a sprinkling of farms. Except for the portion that is Chicago's Lake Shore Drive, there is nothing to remember about this long highway spanning the contrasts of the Midwest.

On March 22, 1983, Jay Reynolds, the owner of a Baskin-Robbins in Lexington, Kentucky, was found stabbed to death at the bottom of an embankment alongside U.S. Highway 25, south of the city. Reynolds, who had a wife and nine-week-old son, had been on his way to lock up his store.

Summer 1983
Indianapolis

Indianapolis is hardly a city in its own right; it is more the hub of small towns around the state and takes on their rural Midwestern conservative attitudes. Yet in 1983 this city of seven hundred thousand had a large homosexual population. During the fall of the previous year, police had launched a campaign against sodomy and whatever. They raided the parks and homosexual bookstores, then began videotaping customers going in and out of bars such as Our Place and the 21 Club. To an extent, the harassment was successful. A number of men stopped going to gay bars, including Larry Eyler. By January, when the community realized there was a serial killer well before the police did, it was assumed that the crackdown had driven the killer into straight bars, making the investigation even more difficult.

A gay newspaper, *The Works*, set up a hotline and published a profile of the killer to help police, whether they wanted help or not.

"This man is not openly gay yet," publisher Stanley Berg speculated, "but he knows that he is, and when the urge hits him he can only absolve this tendency by committing a murder."

When police did drop by the bars to ask about the highway victims, they found that talking to men in gay bars was like interrogating prisoners of war. Detectives called it "total resistance."

From the bathhouse on North Senate Avenue, Berg made suggestions that the police were unwilling to accept. These included that he review files on each death and that someone knowledgeable from the gay community be called to the scene whenever a body was found to help detectives understand certain clues, which might include tattoos and body adornment.

Berg, who looked like a lifeguard, couldn't even get police to release photos of Roach and McNeive for his paper, even though copies were given to the *Indianapolis Star*. For all practical purposes the "offices" of *The Works* was Berg's desk; he was the only reporter, editor, and ad salesman.

The circulation of his booklet-style newspaper couldn't compare to a daily, but he was sure that *The Works* was seen by more people who needed to read the articles: acquaintances of the killer as well as his potential victims. So Berg dialed city hall and told Mayor William Hudnut, "I want you to call the Chief and shake them up over there."

The photos were delivered by messenger in a few hours.

George Stuteville of the *Star* could not say so in print, but he was hoping his articles on the murders would show that homophobia was standing in the way of developing strong leads.

The McNeive murder was a catalyst. Until then, there had been four individual investigations in Indiana. Now there was only one. Under pressure from the victims' families, the gay communities, and the *Star*, Indiana state police held a meeting of all the departments involved on Wednesday, May 15, to discuss the possibilities. Thirty-five detectives attended the meeting in a former high school that had been converted into the Marion County Public Safety Center, in a residential neighborhood separated by highways and woods from downtown Indianapolis.

An unusual decision came out of the meeting. Rather than designating one department as the principal agency for the investigation or establishing a committee to review police reports, officials formed a task force to conduct investigations of all future cases, independent of jurisdiction. To avoid interdepartmental rivalries, there would be two detectives from the state police, two from the Indianapolis police, and two from each county involved. When Stuteville heard that, he cracked, "What are they trying to build—an ark?" All the officers would be experienced veterans of their departments, commanded by Lt. Jerry Campbell of the Indianapolis police department. The organizers hoped that gays would be more open with the task force than they had been with the city police.

Although Campbell was in charge of strategy planning, he could spend only about half his time in the task force headquarters and at the scenes of new victims. The day-to-day operation was in the care of Sergeant Frank Love of the state police, a bearish man with a kindly voice.

Love presided over a meeting on June 14, this time involving more than fifty officers from eight jurisdictions. They were considering more than twenty deaths of young men and teenage boys and needed to separate the ones with the pattern—stabbed or strangled, usually with deep abdominal stab wounds and their pants pulled down several inches or to their feet, then dumped near highways. The investigators assumed the others were isolated cases, such as drug deals, to be investigated by local police. Such lists are always arbitrary, but police needed to coordinate their resources or they would be back to individual investigations.

There was one other element in the pattern that was elusive for weeks: How were these victims recruited for murder? Some were known to have been homosexual, but several others did not appear so.

Danny McNeive's mother was certain he was not gay or a hustler. "Danny was raised as a Christian, and I know he's disgusted with that lifestyle," Wilma McNeive insisted. "He had a problem drinking, but he was a clean boy." She even hired a private detective for five hundred dollars to determine whether the boy was gay, but the detective reported back that he couldn't verify one way or the other.

But one of Danny's brothers told police privately that the boy had been a hustler. The task force was now confident that the killer wasn't taking his victims at random. But whether hustlers brought out his sexual confusion or he merely thought that anyone involved in prostitution was expendable, there was no way of knowing.

Many hustlers are not homosexual. For spending money, they do sexual favors such as fondling or oral sex. Often this never interferes with their heterosexual life, but sometimes hustling erupts into violence when one or both of the men have conflicts about themselves.

With the assistance of Dr. Pless and a psychology teacher from Indiana, the task force did "a little victimology" to develop a profile of the killer by studying the men he sought out. But the investigation was bound to stagnate unless authorities received fresh leads. The John Roach family offered a five-hundred-dollar reward, to which *The Works* added five hundred dollars and the gay community contributed another five hundred.

The task force, officially called the Central Indiana Multi-Agency Investigation Team, took over a windowless classroom on the second floor of the police training academy, a former high school in a remote part of Indianapolis. Eight desks and some swivel chairs were moved in, the phone company set up four lines, and an IBM computer was hooked up to the statewide police system. On the first day, the task force sent a message through the FBI National Crime Information computer network asking police across the country for information on any unsolved murders of male prostitutes. There were no promising replies.

The task force officers had to contend with the jeers and sarcasm of policemen working in other offices at the academy, who fluttered eyelashes and spoke in falsetto voices. The only way to stop the kidding was to take part in it, so one day Sergeant Love and Detective Sam McPherson skipped down the hall hand in hand.

In the next few weeks, the task force developed leads on five or six possible suspects, including a pig farmer in central Indiana who tried to tie up a man.

The Pattern

On June 6, Tom Henderson of Indianapolis ca[l]
police headquarters and told the dispatcher, "I think
know who's doing these killings." He started to tell about
a man he knew, Larry Eyler.

"Don't give me the information," the dispatcher said,
and he relayed the task force number.

That Monday, one of the other officers reported the
call to Love, who phoned Henderson at work in the early
afternoon. The man admitted he hardly knew Eyler but
said that Eyler had been involved in some sort of stabbing
in Terre Haute in 1978.

"You don't know anything more recent?" Love asked,
disappointed.

"No, but he has a temper, and he's into bondage."

"What more can you tell me?"

"He lives in Terre Haute on weekends and works at a
liquor store in Greencastle. It's called Andy's."

Love took down Henderson's information but thought it
sounded no more promising than half a dozen other tips,
most of them spurred by jealousy or revenge. Since Eyler
had taken this man's lover, James Williams, there was
reason to be skeptical about the tip. This was just one
more name to throw into the hopper.

By then the task force had so many tips that computer
analyst Cathy Berner was working on a link analysis from
what was called the computer menu. This was a directory
of categories that might be needed for cross-references,
such as "Route 41," "john" (patron of prostitutes),
"license plates," "stab wounds," "pants," and the
names of the bars and motels the victims may have gone
to.

Cathy was the heart and sometimes the brains of the
investigation, all five feet four and one hundred and eight
pounds of her. After all, how many computer wizards
have backgrounds in psychology? She had just married a
stockbroker and was assigned to the task force by her
state police supervisors as soon as she returned from her
honeymoon in Hawaii.

Some of the officers in the unit had never handled a
case of psychological violence and could not see how all

the information to be compiled could fit in, but Cathy knew. With enough data, the properly arranged computer storage cells would be an abstract model of the killer's mind.

Anything could be a lead. She studied the police reports as they came in and recorded everything possible about the victims: physical features, the names of friends, height and weight, even the color of shoes. That at least 99 percent of the work was bound to be wasted didn't bother her. The excitement lay in finding that 1 percent. Her new husband was learning to get by without seeing much of her, even on weekends.

As investigators tried to reconstruct the last two weeks in the life of each victim, Cathy would design flow charts that placed each victim in the center, surrounded by dates, times, and locations. Serial killings are acts of fantasy, not madness, and so every case is unique. This means you can never be sure what is important.

While the officers in leisure moments would joke with one another and use locker room language, Cathy would quietly click away and bring order to all the data that was coming in. "She has a steel-trap mind," Sergeant Love said in admiration.

Unlike some of the officers in the unit, Cathy thought Eyler was the strongest suspect. Although the Mark Henry stabbing occurred five years before, all the details pointed to the attack as a rehearsal for murder. She didn't try to convince the others. She knew that time would tell.

Some of the task force members were new to Love, but he was familiar with one: Sergeant William "Billy Bob" Newman of the Marion County sheriff's department. He was given the nickname years ago, because every rural sheriff's department in movies seemed to have a Billy Bob. He was a digger for information and could lay it on heavy when interrogating a suspect. He often took the role of "bad cop" as he and Love played with suspects. He had a good sense of humor away from the interrogation room, and his piercing laugh was contagious.

Only two days after the task force sent a message out asking police in other states for information, police in

Kentucky called to report that Jay Reynolds of Lexington had been found that March. Detectives Newman and Jim Rhineberger flew down there the next day to look over police reports, evidence, and photos of the victim. There were no clues, but the Kentucky victim would fit the pattern.

A few days later the task force received a call from a Cook County sheriff's policeman who said that on May 9 his men found the body of Jimmy Roberts, a Chicago teenager, stabbed to death and floating in a creek south of the city. At first the Indiana officers considered setting that case aside because none of the other victims were black or found in water. But there were two disturbing telltale traits: Roberts' trousers were partially pulled down, and he had been stabbed more than thirty times.

With many serial murder cases, police can determine a geographic area for the killings and stake it out to watch for someone acting suspiciously. But how can you pin down a killer who strikes only in the dark and stalks hundreds of miles of interstate highways?

Love, who was in his early fifties, was less formal than some of the other officers, but he was thorough. As the investigation was centering on two or three men, including the pig farmer, he went over his notes and decided to see if the caller who turned in Eyler's name might be able to tell more about him. After all, knowing that Eyler was a liquor store clerk with a temper was not much to go on.

"He travels 41 and goes to Chicago a lot," said Tom Henderson, who viewed Eyler as a rival for the affection of a mutual friend. Henderson also told of the time two years before when Eyler was arrested for giving a fourteen-year-old boy, Fred Harte, Placidyl pills that put him in a coma, then dumping him in a woods in Greencastle. The boy was hospitalized for several days, but his family dropped charges.

Love started making calls about these assaults. With other suspects, an alibi or an explanation eliminated them one by one. Not so with Eyler.

In late July, someone tacked Eyler's mug shot on the bulletin board. No one said so, but he was quickly becoming the prime suspect. When the officers filed into their chairs every morning in the windowless room, that picture seemed to taunt them in a game of catch-as-catch-can.

On July 29, Sergeant Love and Detective Sam McPherson talked over a baseball game as they climbed a flight of stairs. McPherson was lean and tall and could pass for a Texas ranger, drawl and all. This fifteen-year veteran of criminal investigations in the Indianapolis police department loved action but hated the bureaucracy. He was already thinking about an early retirement to get away from bosses.

Frank Love was a gentler sort of officer, with a Hemingway beard and a sense of humor. Years of fast food restaurants showed at his waist, and from time to time he chewed pinches of tobacco from his palm-sized can of Skoal. By now, these detectives were investigating at least a dozen murders of young men, and seven of them closely fit a pattern.

McPherson pressed numbers into a computer control panel and switched on the lights without pausing from his story about last night's baseball game. A green chalkboard lined the back wall. Instead of the math problems of a few years ago, it held a dozen names, the dates these victims were found, and their locations. All the information was in the computer, but the board served as a reminder. On a side wall was a ceiling-to-floor map of Indiana and bordering states, with pins at each crime scene. What had once been school lunch tables now supported file folders, photos, stacks of report forms, and the four phones.

McPherson put a match to his fourth or fifth Camel of the day and glanced at the signal light blinking on the overnight answering machine. Love picked up a pot of day-old coffee on the percolator, and McPherson said, "Maybe we got lucky." The tall investigator opened a desk drawer for a legal pad as Detective Fred Jackson arrived with what everyone was looking forward to—a bag of brownies and Danish pastries.

With pen in hand, McPherson rewound the message tape and hit the start button. A man's soft, frightened voice came first. "My boyfriend is missing and I'm afraid he may have been one of those victims. Please call me. I have pictures and things like that. My phone is . . ."

A cold, harsh voice came next. "I have information about a man that may be doing all those killings," he said on the fringe of anger. "I lived with him for six years. I will call back and give you his new address and the number of the man he is living with now. He is a lawyer, too."

Soon after the task force was set up, one of the officers remarked that if it weren't for lovers' quarrels they might all just as well go home.

One of the other calls came from an apparently older man. "Why don't you guys let those fags just kill each other," he bellowed. "Why waste our tax money; let them all kill each other."

Next came something sadly different, a woman's quiet voice. "This is Wilma McNeive, Danny McNeive's mother. I'm calling to see if there's anything new. I might drop in tomorrow. I found another address book of his. I'll call back. Thank you."

Then McPherson played the last message, but there were no words, just the click of a receiver. That kind of call bothered him the most because he never knew if the caller had a good lead but was too afraid or too loyal to divulge it.

The room started to fill with detectives slipping into the small chairs for their daily assault upon the unknown. Except when the members needed to conduct formal interviews, there was no dress code for the unit. Most of the men wore jeans and colored shirts or T-shirts, and tennis shoes replaced their highly polished leather shoes or boots.

The officers were assigned to the task force for a number of reasons. Some, like Love and McPherson, were tops. Others were sent because they were the only people free at the time. One or two were misfits that their supervisors wanted out of their hair for a few months. A natural choice for the team was Sergeant Steve Garner, who spent years in vice investigations in Indianapolis. Many people in the gay and lesbian community disliked Garner, but they didn't let that get in the way of an investigation this important.

"OK, OK now," Love said to start the briefing. "Three murders from Kentucky—can we connect them?"

"I don't think we will," one of the men mumbled. After all, there weren't strong similarities, and the Kentucky police considered their job done when they mailed a photocopied set of reports to the Indiana police.

"There's still a possibility that more than one killer is out there. Anything on that?"

Again, not much of a response. Two agents who came in from the FBI's Behavioral Sciences Unit in Virginia had looked over the task force work and went to the scene of two of the murders, then concluded that there probably were separate killers involved. That left some members of the unit thinking that the killers were working in pairs or that two killers were attacking young men separately. Further investigation removed one of these victims from the list.

McPherson put his elbows on the back of his chair and said, "I bet that Eyler guy knows a lot about these killings." No one said anything. "He is into that bondage stuff and that macho image; and, like that guy who called us said, he's got a violent temper."

"We've got three better suspects," one of the other officers muttered.

"I know we have three, but I'll put my buck on Eyler."

At the front of the room, Love raised his hand as if to say "All right, let's consider him." He knew that McPherson had good instincts when information was scarce.

"Sam may have a point. We know a little more about these other men; and, while we wouldn't want our sons going off with them, they're pretty much the same person all the time. With Eyler, we're dealing with two men. You've all seen the pictures we took outside the liquor store where he works. We see Larry change from a normal clerk to a Macho Man. But where does he go, what does he do when he changes? We still don't know, and maybe it's time we found out."

"We're not going to ask him," said one of the officers.

"No, but I think if we tail him good, if we ˒
out, we might get a good lead on him," the sergean˒

Love turned to the green blackboard and picked u˒ ˒
piece of chalk. "All right. We're back in school now.
Let's run down what we know about him."

Officer by officer, the scanty information was repeated:
Eyler drives a silver-gray 1982 Ford pickup truck, usually
well past the speed limit. He works as a clerk at Andy's
Liquors in Greencastle, usually from 4 P.M. to closing.
He lives in Terre Haute with Robert David Little, a library
science professor at Indiana State University.

"Record?" Love asked.

"A 1978 arrest for stabbing Mark Henry, but the case
was dropped," one of the detectives answered.

"But he handcuffed him, tied his legs, took off his
shirt, and stabbed him," Love said, trying to prod their
thinking. "So he is a good suspect. Many of our victims
were missing shirts, and many appeared to have been
handcuffed. But we can't place Eyler with any of the
twelve. We know he picks up hitchhikers, but what does
he do?"

Vice Officer Steve Garner had something to say. "What
we need is to see a hitchhiker picked up right in front of
us, and then, just as the guy we're looking for is ready
to kill him, we jump in." Garner himself didn't seem to
know whether he was joking.

"We're not going to give a killer a thirteenth victim,"
Love said.

Sam McPherson stamped out a cigarette and raised his
hand.

"What, Sam?"

"I'll be the hitchhiker." Everyone looked at him. Not
only did the idea seem peculiar, but McPherson was old
enough to be the father of some of the victims. Perhaps
it wasn't a brilliant piece of police logic, but he was tired
of working with the telephone. "Let Eyler pick me up.
We use three vehicles to follow him, so he doesn't get
wise. As I see it, one vehicle has me in it, and we get a
mile or two ahead of him. Hell, he travels like a demon,

but we can get ahead of him. You guys drop me off, then you follow me after he picks me up."

"All right, Sam, what happens next?" Love asked.

"He takes me wherever. You follow me, and if I get my gun out fast enough, I win." He looked around. "Any other bright ideas?"

Love leaned against the desk. "OK, then you're the decoy tomorrow night. We'll take the van and two cars. A total of seven men."

Officer Don Henry looked at the handful of photos that were being passed around. The first shot showed Eyler as a typical young man: a little taller than average, a baby face with a small mustache, summer shirt. Then he is seen a few minutes later. Not only is he wearing a Marine fatigue hat, a red Marine T-shirt, and combat boots, his expression is harder and his posture is more aggressive. Tomorrow night Sam could be face-to-face with Dr. Jekyll and Mr. Hyde.

An hour later, Garner tried not to bore his partner of the day, Sammy Maldonado, with talk about his new baby. They had driven seven miles from the task force headquarters to downtown Indianapolis.

Garner knew the underside of the city like no other officer and was hated for it. His squad always came in tops or at least second place in the number of arrests each month, and on his own initiative he had compiled a dossier of female impersonators for crimes they might do in the future. His investigation into the robberies of middle-aged homosexuals had contributed to complaints of harassment at gay bars and other gathering places.

He was now a familiar figure on the street with his full beard and broad forehead, and he was devoting most of his time to supervising and training at the police academy. By now he could sense happenings in the hangouts as if by the pricking of his thumbs.

"What do you feel like doing today?" Maldonado asked.

"Let's go see our buddy Stan and show him these pictures of Larry. Maybe he knows something."

They pulled up to a stone building housing the Body

Works, Stan Berg's bathhouse. Whatever color the building was when it was built, it was a dull, pollution color now.

Garner pressed the buzzer as a man looked suspiciously at them through the window. The officers were let in and the man standing in front of a shelf of towels said, "I already called Stan. Just stay here and don't wander around, please." The presence of the police could hurt business.

The man who came down to talk to them had turned his heaviness into a trim, muscular body. He was in his forties and was letting his age salt his dark hair. He was wearing jeans, sneakers, and a short-sleeved shirt stretched at the biceps. Under his right sleeve was the bottom half of a green and blue tattoo.

"You know why we're here," Garner said. "We think we're on to someone."

As Berg leaned over the counter from his chair, Garner laid out the photos before him. Larry Eyler, the store clerk; Larry Eyler, in military gear and about to go to town.

"Isn't that something?" Garner asked.

"No," Berg answered. "You know, you guys are tripping over each other, and you come in here and we just sit amazed at your conception of what we are. Now you think because somebody dresses like that, he's a killer. Maybe this is your man, but these pictures don't show it."

To Berg it seemed the two officers were fidgeting just being in a place where avowed homosexuals streamed by. He kept back a smile and told them, "I sometimes get dressed up like a Marion County police officer with handcuffs, fake badge, sunglasses, and a large deputy hat, and walk into gay bars and scare the shit out of my friends."

"You don't know anything about Mr. Eyler?"

For an answer, Berg went through some issues of the monthly newspaper he published. He opened one to a sketch that could be almost anyone, but not Larry Eyler. "Ever since May we've been running this composite. It doesn't look like him at all, like most composites. See, we don't have any more information than you do.'' He handed the pictures back. ''I'll ask around and call you if I hear anything.''

''You know, there wouldn't be so many murders if you could get these hustlers off the street,'' Garner told him, with an edge as if wanting to hold Berg accountable for anything that happened in the gay community.

''I wish we could, but how are we or you going to do that? Most of them are untrainable for steady jobs, and there are always clients. But I'll tell you something that would work. You guys need someone who can sift through all this crap, this data on victim after victim. You people don't know what to look for. You need a couple of gays working on your task force.''

''No,'' Garner said, closing the folder. ''We have enough people on the team.''

''Don't you want to solve these killings?''

''That's a stupid remark,'' Garner answered.

''There could be things at the scene that are ritualistic, something that could give you a clue to certain behaviors that could really help you.''

''Don't you think we know what we're doing?''

For the sake of the armistice, Berg didn't reply.

From there, Garner and Maldonado drove down Washington Boulevard in an area known for hustlers and saw a red-headed boy about fourteen hitchhiking onto the highway. He put his arm down as he saw the squad car pull up.

''We aren't going to pinch you,'' Garner said from the car. ''All we want is to talk to you.'' The detective opened the door of the Ford and the boy sat in the back.

''How old are you?'' Maldonado asked.

''Eighteen,'' the boy lied.

Garner closed the door and began a slow drive down the street. ''Have you heard there is some guy out there picking up kids and killing them?'' the vice officer asked. ''Ever hear what happened to Danny McNeive?''

''No, and no one is going to get me. I'm too smart for that.''

Yeah, sure, Garner thought. The morgues are full of

smart people. Maldonado showed him the photos and told him about the reward. Garner stopped the car and handed him a business card.

"Hey, man, for fifteen hundred bucks I'll be your eyes out there," the boy said and walked back into his world.

There would be more street questioning, more warnings, more people to show Eyler's photos to. The work was dull, but who knew what it could lead to. Besides, maybe it helped people like that fourteen-year-old kid get a little smarter.

Garner drove to Our Place, a leather bar at Sixteenth and Alabama. From the outside, it looked like a storefront office in a green building in the middle of the block. The air conditioner hummed over the door but could only be heard between the wails of the jukebox. It was only 5 P.M., but the bar was filling up as it usually did on Fridays.

The bar itself dominated the tavern, and a pool table in back was hardly noticed in the little sunlight that came through the blinds and the smoky windows. The investigators walked among the patrons, some wearing leather pants and silver-laced motorcycle vests. The detectives sat down and ordered two Cokes. Maldonado wasn't as comfortable in the place as his partner, who knew some of these people from his vice cases. When the bartender brought the Cokes, Garner said, "I have some photos to show you."

"Not now, not here," said the bartender. "I go on break in twenty minutes. I can meet you outside."

Maldonado held the Coke glass as if it were alive and said barely above a whisper, "Hell, I hate all this."

The officers left two dollars on the bar and waited in their car.

When the bartender joined them he said, "This is one hell of a busy afternoon in there, honey. I could just go crazy sometimes. What do you have for me?"

Garner showed him the pictures. "Ever seen him before?"

"Gosh, yes, yeah," the bartender said and paused. "Let me think of his name. I don't remember any trouble with him. Yep, he is part of the leather scene all right.

Terry or Larry. I'll keep a lookout for him." The man leaned toward Garner and asked confidentially, "Is he our guy?"

"You're right about the name Larry at least," the officer said by way of avoiding a direct answer. "We're running down a tip."

The bartender stared at the pictures as if memorizing them.

"Now, don't go wild on me," Garner said. "We don't have much on him."

The bartender put his hands on his chest to suggest total innocence. "Who, me? Don't worry, I don't open my mouth."

Garner slipped some money into the bartender's apron, and the man opened the door. He turned back to the officers and said, "It's scary whenever there's another body. They're just young boys. It's so senseless."

Love and McPherson drove down a dead-end road that afternoon to Wilma McNeive's ranch-style home in the southern end of Indianapolis. It was late Friday afternoon, and Wilma had just arrived from work. She was a small woman with a lined, determined face and spoke with a country drawl.

Funeral home cards with a religious message lined the television set, and a smiling photo of Danny on the wall seemed to fix him forever. Wilma was still suffering from a double shock—the murder of her boy and the suspicion that he was homosexual. "I want to crawl under the carpet, that's how bad it is," she confided. Her eyes were bloodshot, and her skin was almost clay white. She let the officers in without greeting and handed them a small address book. "Here, I found this with his stuff," she said.

She offered them a soda as they sat on the blue velvet couch. Sergeant Love's heart went out to her, and he told her something he knew he should not have. "We think we know who killed your son."

Mrs. McNeive covered her mouth and wept. Then she raised her face and asked, "Who is it, and why did he kill Danny? It's those boys and that burglary, isn't it? They killed Danny because he got the police on them.''

"No, Mrs. McNeive, that isn't it,'' McPherson said.

"Danny was gay,'' Love said. The sheer size of him made his bluntness seem like an accusation against her and her family.

She turned to the white-bearded policeman. Her tone was brittle hard. "Danny was a good boy. I told you he was with a friend at a country bar and he got drunk just before he disappeared. You can go there yourself and see. It is not a gay bar.''

"We're sorry, Wilma. We don't mean to hurt you or your family, or Danny's memory,'' Love said. "Just don't worry. We know who killed Danny, and we are going to catch him.''

"Get out of my house if you are going to talk about my son like that,'' Wilma said.

Love put his hand on her shoulder. "I know it's hard, but you must help us.''

"You're going to leave my house unless you want a lawsuit,'' she demanded.

The officers left her alone and drove back to their headquarters. Wilma never forgave Sergeant Love and often in her bitterness called him "that big bad man.''

The following night, Detective Sam McPherson was ready for decoy work. He wore faded jeans with a thin jacket over his T-shirt. A day of not shaving had given him a rougher appearance than usual, and he even made sure his cowboy boots were gray with dust. There was no way to hide his age, his sunburnt forehead drawn down from the top of his head like an awning, but with his curving mustache and informal gait he could easily pass for a drifter.

Waiting for the briefing to begin, he turned this way and that in a swivel chair and asked himself, "Why do I think this is going to be a long night?''

Detective Bill Newman, who was assigned to the unit from the Marion County Sheriff's Police, looked him over and said, "Where's your gun?''

Lifting his T-shirt, McPherson pulled out the grip of a

.357 magnum revolver from his crotch. His expression said "No jokes."

Sergeant Love explained to the seven men chosen for the stakeout how they would be deployed. "We've got our walkie-talkies, and we're taking state police radios, too, just in case," he added. "I wish we could wire you up, Sam, but we don't have enough time."

McPherson waved that off and let some of the other officers make their inevitable jokes about how he might get to like hustling as a second career.

An hour later the officers drove into Greencastle and saw Eyler's pickup truck in the lot of Andy's Liquors. Some of the casually dressed officers drifted into the Monon Grill as if they were typical Hoosiers. McPherson smoked one of his Camels as he sat at a table with Love. The aging restaurant was indistinguishable from thousands of others strung along the highways, expecting only truckers and drifters.

Love looked out the window of the restaurant and said, "Better than the last time."

He was referring to a night, weeks ago, when McPherson had been in the back of the van with a 35-millimeter camera on a tripod, trying to take photos of Eyler without letting him know that he was under suspicion. Love had parked the van just outside the door, but the trouble was, as McPherson would tell the story, "It must have been a typhoon that night; you couldn't see two feet in front of your face." The storm was keeping Eyler inside the store, and there was no way of telling when he might come out. So Love went in, pretended to be a customer, and when checking out, said offhandedly, "Look at it rain. It looks like a flood." Not knowing when Eyler would come in full view, McPherson snapped what must have been thirty pictures while Love turned his head so that he wouldn't be in the frame while Eyler looked out the window.

Yes, that was some night, all right.

Love paid the bill, and they all went out to the van and cars. Eventually Bill Newman's voice came over the walkie-talkie. "Frank, our boy's shutting off some of the lights. Maybe he's closing early tonight."

They didn't have long to wait. Eyler came out of the liquor store and opened the door of his pickup truck to remove a gym bag. Love knew that McPherson would like nothing better than to do everything on his own, so he said into his walkie-talkie, "Remember, stay in contact."

Eyler returned to the store. When he came out again, his steps were quicker, as if he really were trained in the military. He kept adjusting the visor of his Marine cap, trying to get the tough look he wanted. His tight red T-shirt showed off his pectoral muscles and his biceps in contrast to his baby face and almost pouty expression. Until now, Eyler had an almost distant appearance about him, a fragility despite the weight lifting. His hair was closely cropped as if he were from the military, but his long eyelashes lent him an almost feminine appearance.

The future decoy watched his every move, studying him for when they might be just inches apart. Sitting behind the wheel of the van, Garner asked McPherson, "Where do you think he has the knife?"

"I bet you ten dollars he keeps it in the combat boots he just put on. I'd love to know what he's got in that bag besides clothes," McPherson said.

Unaware that he was being watched, Eyler didn't turn around as he unlocked the door of the pickup and climbed in. He put the truck into reverse, shifted gears, and sped out of the lot.

"Our modern-day cowboy is on the road," McPherson said into the walkie-talkie from the front seat of the van.

"I'm right behind you," said Newman from his car.

They were over the speed limit as they shot out of Greencastle and headed toward Indianapolis, and it wasn't enough. Garner toed the accelerator to seventy, seventy-five, eighty miles an hour.

"This is Frank to Sam," Love's soft voice said over the walkie-talkie. "Where are you guys?"

"Steve's foot just went through the floorboard," McPherson answered. "It took a while, but he's on our tail. Forget it. He just passed us."

It was now one o'clock in the morning, and Eyler's truck and the stakeout vehicles were in their own universe.

Whatever buildings they were passing were invisible in the darkness, and the van was speeding so fast that McPherson couldn't see the mileposts that might have given him an idea where they were. Garner had to hit ninety miles an hour to give them a half-mile lead.

"Sam to Frank—do you see Larry?"

"We see his headlights."

"OK, a mile or so and we're going to pull over so I can get out."

The van slowed down, and McPherson told Garner, "Pull off anywhere."

Over the walkie-talkie, Love kept up his running commentary. "Larry is pulling over; be careful. He's backing up. We're going to pass him soon, and you'll be on your own. Son of a bitch! He just picked up a hitchhiker."

McPherson had been about to climb out of the van, but now he grabbed the walkie-talkie from the seat. "Are you sure, Frank? We never saw a hitchhiker back there."

In a moment, they could see for themselves as the pickup truck sped past them. They could make out the form of someone on the passenger's side. McPherson let out, in almost a gasp, "I don't believe it."

Garner knew what to do. He hit the gas pedal again to stay within a minute of the pickup truck to make sure that this hitchhiker lived. They barreled down Highway 40 for another twenty minutes until they reached the outskirts of Indianapolis. The pickup truck slowed down and entered a side road to a residential neighborhood.

"OK, guys," Love said, "it looks like he's going to take that kid to the creek by the bridge. Park behind, out of view. We'll have to sneak up on him. Remember, do not interfere unless that boy's life is in danger. If we're too soon, we can screw up the case. If we're too late . . . Let's not wait until it's too late."

The van and two cars pulled off the road. Through backyards, over fences, and around driveways the officers scrambled to reach the bridge. McPherson found himself separated from Garner in the darkness but kept running. He thought about what he would do if he saw Eyler about to use a knife on the boy. The adrenaline was pumping through him at the notion that this could be the end of the case.

Some officers hid behind a pizza restaurant, and the others crouched low along the bridge. They watched tensely, but Eyler and the boy were just talking in the truck. Then the door opened, and the teen got out—alone.

The detectives were caught by surprise when Eyler screeched into a U-turn in the restaurant lot and headed toward downtown Indianapolis. McPherson and Garner raced toward their van, and Sam, nearly out of breath, said into the walkie-talkie, "We see his taillights. Anyone there?"

No answer. The other men were still running to their cars. McPherson and Garner laughed, surprised that they had reached their vehicle first. They were exhausted. After a few more breaths, McPherson tried the transmitter again. This time he got Love. "We're on our way," McPherson said.

The van followed the pickup truck to the Our Place leather bar, where Garner had been the day before to talk to the bartender-tipster. McPherson said into the walkie-talkie, "It's now 2:30, and the bar closes at 3. Do we wait, or does someone want to go in?"

"No thanks," Love replied. "One decoy a night is enough."

McPherson easily became impatient waiting. He nudged Garner after a few minutes and said, "I'd love to see what's in that truck. Come on, let's get a peek."

Some patrons were standing outside the leather bar when the two detectives walked up to the pickup and looked in. In the truck bed was an old, thin mattress covered by crinkled plastic. In the driver's portion, there was something like laundry but no sign of the bag that Eyler had carried earlier.

McPherson and Garner returned to their van as Eyler came out of the bar, accompanied by three men who were laughing with him and still drinking.

"Hi fellows," McPherson drawled into the walkie-talkie. "We're on the road again."

Soon the pickup truck entered the parking lot of a White

Castle, and a car filled with men pulled up. The men
joined Eyler's group inside. They sat and had hamburgers
and coffee for fifteen minutes as the officers watched from
the outside. Pathological killers are not supposed to be so
ordinary.

It was close to four in the morning when Eyler and his
friends left the hamburger restaurant and drove down side
streets to the southern end of the city, toward Indiana
Central University and Garfield Park. They pulled into a
driveway and entered a house, still laughing. The undercover vehicles were parked down the street. Love's voice
sounded tired over the walkie-talkie. "We've had enough
adventure for tonight, don't you think? We can try it again
next weekend."

Later McPherson was asked if he would have followed
Eyler past the state line that night. "We'd have followed
him to hell if we had to," he said.

Sergeant Love decided that police had enough on Eyler
to keep an informal track of his whereabouts but not
enough to order an actual surveillance. Cathy Berner made
calls to state police posts in the area to ask that any officer
seeing Eyler call Love. He didn't want the truck stopped,
he just hoped there would be some way to prove whether
Eyler was the killer without someone else being butchered.

Saturday, August 27, 1983
Greencastle, Indiana

There was one more stakeout, the last one the task force
ever made. This time Frank Love and Sam McPherson,
the most experienced members, were together in a squad
car. The beefy sergeant picked up the walkie-talkie and
said to Garner in a car across the street, "Well, Steve, I
see he's getting his uniform for his tour of duty tonight."

Eyler adjusted the visor of his cap in the side mirror of
his truck and jumped in. Garner, with Billy Bob Newman
beside him, pulled out of the restaurant driveway, then
Frank and Sam followed. Soon they were tearing down
Indiana Highway 240 at seventy-five miles an hour in the
midnight darkness, then eighty-five miles an hour, slowing

down only after they reached the city. As Sam drove, Frank tried to hold an Indianapolis map steady and said, "He's headed for Sixteenth and Alabama."

"Ah, Our Place," Sam remarked. "I'm getting to know it like a regular customer."

The pickup shot into the gravel lot and stopped suddenly. Eyler wasn't in so much of a hurry that he would forget his appearance. He adjusted his cap once more and walked into the bar.

Two hours went by as Frank and Sam waited in a car parked across the street, and Steve kept surveillance from a church parking lot. Wanting to make sure Eyler hadn't slipped out, Steve climbed out of his car and walked by the large plate glass windows of the bar. Eyler was there all right. He was drinking a beer like the most ordinary man in the world.

No sooner did Steve return to his car than Eyler walked out laughing and talking to a good-looking man with wavy blond hair. Eyler opened the passenger door of the pickup for him, then walked around the front of the truck.

The pickup soon was racing to Highway 465. When it pulled off at U.S. 40, Sam leaned over the wheel a little as if from the sheer pleasure of his job. "Well, Frank, looks like he's headed for those woods again. Maybe tonight we'll get our man." By then all that could be seen of the truck were two tiny red dots.

"Don't lose him," Frank called out.

"Hell, I haven't lost one yet."

The pickup slowed down as it approached the Oasis Restaurant on U.S. 40. Frank said into his walkie-talkie, "He's driving slowly at the Oasis. Either he's hungry or he's interested in that motel over there."

The officers stopped their cars near the motel and watched Eyler register with the blond young man and take a key from the woman at the desk.

"This is strange," Sam said. "Why would he pay for a room when he has his truck and the great outdoors?"

"Who knows," Frank answered. He yawned and shook his head from side to side to keep awake. "I don't think this guy is our typical pickup for Larry."

"He's safe, then?"

"Could be. But I wouldn't put any money on it."

Eyler and his companion walked down the rows of rooms facing the parking lot, stopped and double-checked the number with his key, then unlocked the door. The light went on, but the officers couldn't see any movement. "You know," Sam said after a while, "it could be all over."

"Who knows what the maid will find in the morning," Frank mused, even though he doubted that anything would happen. If this were the woods, that would be something else again.

Sam opened the car door and said to Frank's surprised expression, "Hell, let's take a peek. I'm going up there and look into the room." He went to Garner's car and said to him and Newman, "Cover me, guys."

Sam walked with his cowboy strides to the side of the motel and looked around to make sure he wasn't drawing any attention before he lowered himself to the window. He peered for a moment or two through the blinds, then strode to the squad car. It was 4 A.M.

"Well?" asked Frank.

Sam slipped behind the wheel and stayed loose. "Heck," he said, "I don't think anyone is going to get hurt in there."

They stayed until dawn was lifting, then went home.

3

**Wednesday, August 31, 1983
Oak Park, Illinois**

In the Chicago suburb of Oak Park, Carmen Calise Pauli lay twisting in her sleep before dawn, having a dream that was more than a nightmare. She wasn't the one in danger—it must have been her older son, Ralph. She was fighting some unseen evil, trying to escape but something was holding her arms back.

Mrs. Pauli awoke and sensed that her son was dead.

She told herself she was being foolish. Ralph was a big, strong young man; what could happen to him?

She caught a little more sleep, then tried to make the morning as normal as she could. She stepped out of bed at 7:45 A.M., plugged in the coffee pot, took the butter out of the refrigerator, pushed thoughts of Ralph from her mind, and made the beds.

At 9 A.M. she received a call from Jolene Red Cloud, the woman Ralph lived with in Chicago. Jolene said Ralph had left their apartment at 11 or 11:30 the night before and hadn't returned.

On any other morning, Carmen would have said, "Maybe he passed out at a friend's house; give him time." Now she told Jolene, "Start calling his friends, something might have happened."

Then Carmen sat down in her kitchen and waited for someone to bring her the news.

ednesday, August 31, 1983
North Chicago, Illinois

Detective Dan Colin of the Lake County, Illinois, sheriff's police, was to be the officer most involved in the investigation of the highway murders. On this humid day of a dying summer he chewed on a taco restaurant toothpick and turned his unmarked squad car onto Twenty Second Street in a north suburb. His partner for the day, Portia Wallace, was beside him, and in the back were two instructors from the FBI. They were heading for the bureau's firing range after lunch. For Dan and Portia, this seemed one of those easy days they could go through in their sleep.

Colin was a firearms instructor, but for him the real police work was the "whodunnit" part—weaving cold, hard logic through a case and pulling together all the evidence, motives, and hunches. He was of average height and thin, with a head a little small for his body. His broad forehead, small chin, and unlined face gave him a perpetual look of innocence. Chewing something, whether it was a pipe stem or a straw or a match, helped Dan think, even while driving.

The slim, black woman detective beside him turned up the police radio, but all that came over were routine traffic stops and license checks. She opened the window a crack despite the air conditioning and blew out a trail of smoke, then cranked the handle back.

Lake County didn't have much crime. When it did, the results tended to be bizarre or spectacular. The public aid neighborhoods were more than made up for by the affluent expanses of Highland Park and Lake Forest.

The FBI practice range was next to the officers' quarters of the Great Lakes Naval Training Center. Colin drove across the railroad tracks and past the guard post at Foss Park Avenue. He had been a detective for eight years, ever since he was twenty-one. When he was in charge of an investigation, it became a part of his life, and sometimes his friends in the department kidded him about it. Colin was generally quiet and good-humored, yet every now and then he put his professional objectivity aside to tell someone what he thought of him.

As the officers pulled in front of the firing range they heard on the police radio that a body had been found in Lake Forest south of Route 60 near the tollway. The North Shore suburb was one of the most exclusive communities in the Midwest, with picture-perfect homes behind private driveways. Colin immediately thought of the two victims who had been found not far from there in the last few months. With one hand he reached behind him for the red Mars light, and with the other he grabbed the radio transmitter. "553; I'll be en route with 518." That was all he needed to say.

He and his partner dropped off the firearms instructors and rushed back over the tracks. Not so much to Wallace as to himself, Colin muttered, "Somebody's using us for a dumping ground."

Sheriff's Police Detective James Rowley was already talking to the tree-trimming crew that had found the body. The beefy detective was a specialist in evidence. If anything was left, he found it; then he kept watch over it as if he were personally responsible.

Colin climbed out of the car and looked around, hands on hips. "What do we have?" he asked in his usual undertone. Then, as he listened, his pale blue eyes took in the scene as if photographing it.

"A kid, maybe twenty-five. Stabbed. Dan, his guts are hanging out."

Colin withdrew the munched-up toothpick from his mouth. "This one is close to the other two; I make it a circle."

"This time we got something," Rowley said. "Come on, I'll show you."

While Wallace talked to the tree trimmers, Colin and the heavy detective walked down a dirt road at the edge of the woods that muggy afternoon. The temperature was only in the eighties, but the buttermilk sky dripped with humidity. Colin pushed aside some brush and saw the form of a well-proportioned man with slightly wavy black hair, a thin mustache, and a two days' growth of beard.

He was naked from his shorts up, showing fairly hairy arms and chest. He looked Italian or Hispanic. His belt was unbuckled, and his corduroy pants were pulled slightly down, just past the hips. There was silence except for the bees hovering over the body.

"Whoever did the others did this one," Colin said flatly. "Shit, it's the same."

No department wants to admit there's a serial killer on the loose. Only he knows when he will strike next and what he is killing for. There is no way to console the families. Besides, it's the creepiest kind of police work there is.

"Over here," Rowley said, using his raised foot as a pointer. Tire tracks, footprints, and seven feet of drag marks. "He or they left something for us, isn't that nice? The tracks stop here. The victim wasn't dumped, he was thrown there. He's a pretty big hunk of meat to throw eight to ten feet. I don't know if I could do it, could you?"

"So maybe our killer lifts weights. It would fit. The wounds show he's strong," Colin said.

"Or mad as hell."

The other killings had been just as ghastly, but there had been some comfort in the presumption that the murders were isolated instances. On April 8, a construction worker found the body of Gustavo Herrera, another dark-haired young man with a good build and a mustache. He was buried under debris at a building site three-quarters of a mile away. Herrera had been difficult to type. He worked out at gyms and occasionally hung out in gay bars, but he also went out with women and had two children. Colin guessed that this latest victim was pretty much the same. Friendly, perhaps living with a woman, unemployed or working in a factory or on construction jobs, and probably someone who liked bars or hitchhiking.

Herrera lived in Uptown, a transient section of Chicago, and perhaps this man lived there too, or at least nearby. He certainly didn't come from Lake Forest. But there was one troubling difference: Herrera's right hand had been cut off and eventually found in the general area. Why was there no dismemberment with this victim? Colin wondered.

A week after Herrera was discovered, the body of a teenage boy was found over the corpse of a dog and covered with plywood, garbage, and brush in a woods two miles west of the latest victim. There was no dismemberment then either, but the boy's overalls had been pulled down and he was stabbed numerous times, especially in the abdomen. Both bodies, like this one, had been near an exit off I-94.

Colin crouched near the body, wondering what it could tell him. The light hazel eyes were cloudy with death, and the skin and clothes had streaks of dried mud and blood. Jockey shorts that used to be white were now pink with blood. Unlike the unidentified boy, this man had been dead for only a few hours.

Rowley, the evidence expert, slowly removed a flip-top box of Marlboros from a pocket of the pulled-down pants and put it into a transparent evidence pouch. Carefully he slid his fingers into a pocket on the other side and pulled out a set of wallet inserts, but they didn't seem to belong to the man. Rowley handled the inserts carefully, since they might have useful fingerprints, and saw that they had photos of the man, a few handwritten phone numbers, and an identification card for Jolene Red Cloud of Chicago.

"Is that Uptown?" Rowley asked.

"Near there," answered Colin, who grew up in the city. He began wondering who was Jolene Red Cloud: a wife, a sister, a girlfriend?

After police took photos of the body, Detective Roy Lamprich helped Colin put it into a coroner's station wagon. Portia Wallace remained behind with Deputy Chief Investigator Willie Smith—"Smitty"—and a few officers.

Smitty was in his middle thirties and had the look of a cowboy, complete with weather-beaten face and mustache. He brought some imagination to the department and was willing to try anything, even if his style was low-key. He could relax anywhere but was known to snap at his men if they bungled an investigation. Smitty was in a suit and polished shoes now, but he preferred Western shirts and snakeskin boots.

He had read how dental plaster could be used for improved evidence casts. Plaster of Paris tends to seep in its slow drying, blurring the edges of its impressions. When Smitty told Detective George Martin to get the plaster from the evidence truck, his men knew he was having one of his brainstorms again.

Since the first batch was experimental, Smitty didn't pay much attention to how much water he used. The mixture flowed easily from the bucket, like pancake batter. There were still more important impressions to cover. The second batch seemed too thick, even after he asked Corporal Kurt Proschwitz to pour in a little more water. Martin returned from his scavenger hunt for a stirring tool, finding only a narrow stick. Smitty tried it but became impatient and tossed the stick back into the weeds.

He began mixing the dental plaster with his fingers, but each turn around became more difficult. "More water," the investigations chief called out. "It's getting hot as hell on my hand." The water only made the binding worse, and Proschwitz looked up with his guileless smile as if to say "Any fool could have told you that would happen."

Smitty's men snickered as he tried to pull his hand free from the bucket. In exasperation, he said, "Oh, fuck, get this shit off me!" He raised his elbow, and the bucket hung down like an extension of his arm.

Someone suggested a sledgehammer, but the bucket came loose after the officers pounded it a few times with their hands.

Cooler heads prevailed as the detective made another batch. There were tire tracks and three sets of footprints to cover. One set seemed to match the shoes of the victim. Another was made by someone in stockinged feet. The other was made by someone in lug-soled boots, probably size ten. Colin thought that perhaps Rowley was right about there being more than one killer.

The dental plaster hardened quickly. Smitty removed his pocket knife and dug into the ground just under the cast to lift it. "You know," one of his men said, "you only get one shot on something like this."

"Don't remind me," Smitty replied and gently eased up the first impression.

Even Smitty could hardly believe how well the cast turned out; it was as if a sculptor had been hired to carve the bottom of two shoes and the intricate tread of relatively new tires. The Lake County sheriff's department had just turned state-of-the-art.

The Lake County, Illinois, morgue is a tiny, squat building of sallow brick under a mansard roof across Washington Street from the modern courthouse in downtown Waukegan.

Detective Roy Lamprich brought an ink pad to the autopsy table after nail clippings were removed for microscopic study. This tall, stocky man looked like an old-time street cop. He now rolled the cold fingers of the corpse one by one onto the black pad and pressed them against the cards that would be sent to the Chicago police, the Illinois state police, and the FBI laboratory in Washington, D.C. Then he crossed the street to the underground garage for county vehicles and took a small elevator to the private entrance for the first-floor sheriff's police offices. He had time for a coffee before Smitty arrived. By then the day was cooling off, and a breeze from Lake Michigan fluttered the blinds.

Smitty and a few detectives entered the conference room from the front way, past the belly-high swing door and the bank of secretaries at typewriters. He carried three folders. One was marked "G. Herrera," another "Unidentified Boy," and the third was brand new. "Everybody take a seat," Smitty said. "We have to talk over what we have."

"Another Gacy," one of the detectives muttered.

"Gacy was easy," said another. "We could have another Atlanta." In that case, not even an arrest answered all the questions.

With Smitty everything was informal. He was so relaxed in the chair behind his desk that he looked as if he were at home. "I think either the killer is gay or hates gays, or maybe both. Anyone think otherwise?" No one said anything. "Dan, how about you take over this case? You're not working on anything major; besides, you're from Chicago, and chances are so was he."

"I'm from Chicago too," Rowley said.

"The South Side doesn't count. Dan, talk to that Red Cloud woman, whoever she is. See if she can ID anything."

Smitty handed him the gold-colored Phoenix watch Rowley had slid off the corpse, police photos, and the new manila folder. That's how all cases begin—an empty folder. All you have to do is fill it.

Colin and Rowley went to Chicago. They made their first stop the Area 6 detective headquarters, on the Mid-North Side in a neighborhood of small factories and aging bungalows interspersed with three-flat apartment buildings. Colin knew the area well; he had gone to sprawling Lane Technical High School a few blocks up Western Avenue.

The Lake County officers said hello to the desk sergeant, identified themselves, and went to the detective section upstairs. From there Colin called his office to learn whether there had been any developments in the hour they spent traveling to the city. Smitty told him the prints checked out to Ralph E. Calise, born November 5, 1954, with an arrest record for marijuana possession and petty theft.

"Gay?" Colin asked.

"We don't know; that doesn't show up on our rap sheets."

Colin learned from Smitty that by coincidence Calise's girlfriend, Jolene Red Cloud, was downstairs in the lobby of the building they were in. She was asking whether police knew anything about the young man. No one had told her that Calise had been murdered.

Colin went downstairs and knew the young woman waiting nervously was Jolene as soon as he saw her. She was half Indian, and it showed in her straight black hair parted in the middle, her dark skin, and cheekbones that highlighted her plain, open face. Colin introduced himself and asked if he could talk to her privately for a few minutes, then led her to one of the small off-white interview rooms. While Jolene told him how unusual it was for Ralph to stay out all night, Colin opened his new folder and removed two plastic evidence bags, intending to set them aside until after breaking the news to her gently. As he played with the folder on the desk, two Polaroid photos slipped out, and Jolene saw them at the same instant she noticed the gold band of the Phoenix watch he was holding. The photos showed Ralph's face streaked with mud and blood and his ripped-open abdomen.

Clasping her hands to her mouth, Jolene cried, "He's dead!"

Minutes passed before Colin and Rowley could calm her down. When she could speak clearly again she removed five photos from her purse to show the detectives something of their life together in the small, third-floor apartment a few miles away. She let Colin keep one of the photos to show to witnesses who might turn up.

From the snapshots, it would seem that Ralph cared more about people than things. The photos showed him with long stringy hair and a grin relieving his almost triangular face, as he and Jolene sat barefoot on a dark-orange couch. In no way did he appear the sort of man to be involved in ritual violence. The sparseness of the apartment in the photos suggested to the detective how Ralph might have met with his killer. He needed money.

"What did you live on?" Colin asked.

"Welfare," she said hesitantly.

"That's all?" the Lake County detective asked in a tone that showed he knew she was keeping something from him. "Look, Jolene, the past is past. We can't find the killer unless you help us out. How else did he make money?"

"Sometimes people would call him to get some drugs," she said. "He wasn't a dealer himself; he'd just know the dealers, and they'd give him a finder's fee."

"What did he use himself?"

"Ts and Blues," she said of the the heroin-like combination of Talwin and the baby-blue pyrobenzamine pills.

"And sometimes cocaine. He wasn't an addict. He said he had some trouble before, but that was all over now."

"He had eleven joints on him. That was for himself?" Colin asked.

"He wanted something for us to eat, so he rolled them," she explained. "He was going to the lakefront to sell them. A dollar each."

"When did he leave?"

"About 11 or 11:30 last night," she answered. "He said, 'Wish me luck . . .' " Her sentence just hung there. Those were his last words to her.

Ralph was wearing a Grateful Dead T-shirt, and in his pants pocket was a red wallet with just two dollars in it. He had planned to stop at the Clark gas station at Ravenswood and Foster, then contact a friend at the Green Mill nightclub at Broadway and Lawrence—one of the busiest corners in Uptown—to talk to someone about money. He was carrying the "windows" from her wallet for safekeeping because Jolene had been playing under an opened fire hydrant with some neighborhood children earlier in the day, and he had put them in his pocket for her.

The young woman paused for a moment, her face beginning to look haggard. "Can I call Carmen, Ralph's mother?" she asked. "I want to tell her what's happened."

"We can do that," Colin told her.

"No, shouldn't it come from me?" Jolene asked. Colin shrugged, and she went downstairs to the public phone.

Mrs. Pauli didn't say much when Jolene blurted out that Ralph had been murdered; she had been half-expecting such a call since her dream that morning. She asked Jolene to bring her Ralph's dog, Shags, so that it wouldn't be left alone.

The detectives drove Jolene to the courtyard building made of pale yellow bricks and green clay roof tiles that looked like oversized macaroni. A narrow flower garden running along the sides relieved the vastness of the building. This neighborhood was called Ravenswood; it had its share of misfits and public aid cases, but families here generally kept to traditional values, more so than in Uptown just to the east.

Jolene stayed in the apartment just long enough to put a leash on the mixed Pekingese and poodle. Colin said, "Let's see if we can trace Ralph's steps. Do you think you can do it?"

She nodded and followed the officers to their car. She told them to drive to the end of Hermitage Avenue, which forms the stem of a T, and turn left. As Jolene sat in the rear seat, she hugged the little mutt and cried.

An attendant at the gas station down the street said Ralph had tried to borrow money at around 11:30 the night before and bought a pack of Marlboros. That was as far as the officers could go without more information—just two blocks for a man whose body was found fifty miles away.

At Rowley's suggestion they returned to the apartment to look through Ralph's personal effects for anything that might help them understand what happened. Shags ran down the familiar corridor as if this were a game, and Jolene flicked on the light. Roaches scuttered across the bed, and she pounced on them with loathing and anger. In embarrassment she said, not very convincingly, "This never happened before."

She handed the men an address book, and from a center drawer in a dresser she removed a few letters. Now that Jolene felt that she could be more honest with the detectives, she said, "Ralph had a lot of private numbers but he kept them in his wallet. Even away from me."

"Drugs?" Colin asked.

The half-Indian girl just shrugged.

Carmen Calise Pauli was a heavyset Hispanic woman with a pleasant face giving way to age. Her ringlets of black and white hair were cut close to her head, almost like a cap. Usually she had a trusting glow that drew people to her, but now fear darkened her features. She had been so disturbed by her nightmare of that morning that she lost her temper with her younger son when he said his expensive bike was stolen at school. When Jolene called to tell her that Ralph was dead, Carmen was almost glad the boy's bike had been stolen; it took away some impact of the senseless murder.

Ralph had been a good enough student at Oak Park/ River Forest High School and loved playing on the football team. His mother and stepfather had wanted the best for him and maybe stressed education and careers too much. He was accepted at DePaul University in Chicago but wanted to scale down his plans and go to nearby Triton College instead. He had known he was kidding himself. All the intelligence in the world doesn't mean much when your heart isn't in studying. He became involved in drugs and seemed to drift away from his family and friends, everyone telling him to apply himself and that he could do anything if he put his mind to it.

One night Ralph came home high on drugs. His mother was alarmed at how her own son had become a stranger, and Oak Park police arrested him for marijuana possession. At times he was treated for drug problems at the Madden Health Center in Maywood.

One day when he was in his early twenties, Ralph was found setting fires in the backyard. At other times he became violent without provocation. Police suggested that he be put into a mental institution until he was cured or that he be moved out of the neighborhood. There might have been a few years before when understanding what Ralph was really like would have helped, but he was beyond that now. Unable to afford long-term treatment, Carmen and her second husband, George Pauli, had asked a friend to bring Ralph to the Salvation Army's Pacific Garden Mission in the run-down neighborhood just south of the Loop. Within a few days, the Salvation Army and the city found Ralph the apartment on Hermitage Avenue.

All Ralph had to do was walk a few blocks east to his world of drifters and misfits. For a while he had lived day-to-day, sharing liquor and drugs with men just like him. Then he met Jolene, and the two were so grateful for turning back the erosion of their lives that they believed they were in love. The couple cut out photos of Hawaii and put them in picture frames. They lived on welfare and dreams.

Their apartment had a tattered rust-colored couch, an orange crate bookcase for stuffed toys and knick-knacks, and a four-dollar wind-up alarm clock. In their bedroom a foot-and-a-half-tall ceramic night-light Christmas tree Mrs. Pauli had given her son years ago was kept on a dime-store plastic table year-round.

Mrs. Pauli had never considered herself pushy, but Ralph hinted that if he wanted to see her or his stepfather he would call or take a train to Oak Park. The only time she had been in her son's courtyard apartment building was this morning, after Jolene called to say that Ralph hadn't come home. Her daughter, Zorie, went with her and kept assuring her that Ralph was all right, but Mrs. Pauli knew better. She never had a premonition before, and she felt that her son had been trying to reach out to her for one last time.

When they returned home, Mrs. Pauli's sixteen-year-old son, George Junior, was in his bedroom doing homework. She walked upstairs and opened his door. He looked at her and said, "What's-her-name [Jolene] called to say the police found something and she was going to the police station."

Carmen went downstairs and waited by the phone in the kitchen. After receiving Jolene's call, she called her husband at a bridge game and said, "George, Ralph is dead. Don't stop for a sandwich or a drink. Come straight home."

Then she sat down in her spotless kitchen to face life without her son.

It was just after midnight when the detectives reached Oak Park, a little west of the city. Carmen came down the stairs from her enclosed front porch, and Jolene ran to her as the dog followed. Carmen prided herself on her emotional strength, and sometimes that meant cutting other emotions a little short. She seemed to want to hug Jolene to share the grief, but instead she turned back and went up the stairs. The little dog followed.

Carmen let the officers inside and went to make coffee and feed the dog, anything to keep herself busy so that the reality of her son's murder would not set in so soon.

She went to the living room, where there were some friends she had called over to get through this. In front of them she asked the detectives, "Was he shot or stabbed?"

"Is there somewhere we could talk?" Colin asked.

She took them to the enclosed porch as Jolene stayed with the neighbors. Carmen looked nervously at the detectives. She had to know the details, and yet she didn't want to know them.

"I'm very sorry about the way you heard about your son's death," Colin began.

"That's all right," she replied. "Jolene's young. She gets hysterical."

The screen door opened, and Ralph's stepfather came in. George Pauli, who ran a wholesale meat business, had the strong, thoughtful face of someone decisive. He shook hands with the officers with a firm grip and sat next to his wife.

"Mrs. Pauli," Colin resumed, "we don't think it was drugs. We think it was something else."

"Do you know who killed him?" Carmen asked the other detective.

"No," Colin replied.

"Then you'll never find the killer," the mother said, almost in tears.

With an almost hard voice Colin told her, "Don't ever say that." It was almost a scolding. Without hanging on to hope, families become even more victimized.

Rowley asked whether Jolene and Ralph had any problems. The mother told him that Jolene left her son for about five weeks but had recently moved back in. Questions like this were not likely to produce many leads, but they made the tough questions easier to ask.

When Colin felt that the parents were ready, he looked at them directly in the dim lighting of the enclosed porch and asked, "Was Ralph gay?" He let a pause set in. "Did he ever, to the best of your knowledge, get paid for sex with men?"

Mrs. Pauli was shocked that he should say such a thing. "My son was not and is not gay," she shot back. "Ralph is not gay; he's been dating women all his life."

"Ralph is not gay; no, he's not," his stepfather echoed, and Zorie shook her head.

Perhaps Ralph Calise wasn't, Colin thought, but who knows. He learned long ago that few parents know that their son is homosexual, or admit it.

Now that the hard part of the questioning was over, Colin could be more relaxed with the family. "I'm sorry, but I had to ask," he said. "We've had two other murders in Lake County and because of the similarities, we think they are sexually motivated."

"You mean, all young men?" Carmen asked.

"Yes, and all stabbed to death."

She and her husband just looked down at their hands.

When the questioning was over, Colin handed the stepfather his card. "The autopsy is tomorrow," Colin said. "You can call the Lake County coroner's office in the afternoon to make arrangements for the body. Here's my number; please call us if we can do anything or if you remember anything at all that can help us—even if it seems foolish to bring up, because you never know what can be important."

As Colin slid behind the steering wheel of the police car, he glanced back at the Pauli home. At 2 A.M. it was the only house on the block with lights still on. Through the windows of the enclosed porch he could see Carmen, her husband, and her daughter watching them leave and looking too numb for emotion.

That Monday, the Pauli family car stopped at the main driveway in the Oak Ridge Cemetery in Hillside. The others remained in the car as Carmen, dressed in black, walked into the main office. A few minutes later she came out with a bronze-colored urn the size of a coffee can. She carried the urn on her lap during the short ride to the hole that had been dug by the grounds keepers. She kissed the lid of the urn and placed it in the freshly dug ground. On top she laid roses and daisies cut that morning from the family garden in Oak Park.

Her family told her to let Ralph rest in peace, not to carry her grief with her wherever she went; but as long as the young man's killer was free, she would not let the police forget this case. This wasn't just one of those dozens of unsolved murders whose files get set aside after a few weeks, this was her son.

4
=

September 1983
Chicago

The storyboards at WLS-TV, the ABC-owned and -operated station in Chicago, were blank at 9 A.M. except for the commercial spots timed in. The daily problem was finding the right local and national news to fill the spaces, sometimes thirty stories for a one-hour newscast.

Two show producers and their assistants were reading overnight copy from the United Press International, Associated Press, and City News Bureau wires. These came in sheets yards long and were scrolled up like ancient Roman documents, only to have certain stories ripped out for reworking and the rest thrown into the three-foot-high garbage cans. The producers were also studying the daily Chicago newspapers. Sometimes a fact in the fifth or twelfth paragraph of an article will spark someone's imagination for a fresh story.

The station workhouse was on the ninth floor at State and Lake Streets. The studios were three stories above. The large office building was put up in 1925 and was never intended as a broadcast facility. Since the office was jerry-built, there was a lot of sidestepping and almost bumping into people. The newswriters were on each side of a long table, with phone books and other reference material in a common heap. The smell of brewing coffee wafted over all.

The Assignment Desk newsroom was a cubicle of fiberglass. There, Gera-Lind Kolarik made the phone checks to bring in fresh stories, followed up breaking events, and developed stories already aired while someone else was in charge of covering scheduled events. Familiar with the Chicago police and fire departments, Gera-Lind often monitored the thirty zones of scanners for the region from southern Wisconsin to northwestern Indiana.

On this slow news day before the Labor Day weekend, she made her morning beat calls to the morgues in five counties to learn whether any deaths since last night had any news value. A reporter has a list of sources to call each day to keep from being scooped, and the successful ones personalize their calls so that it seems as though they're talking to a friend.

She now dialed the Lake County coroner's office and spoke to Coroner Barbara Richardson. A woman heading a pathology department is rare, but the white-haired, stately Richardson was an old pro in the art and the science.

"Hi, Barbara," Gera-Lind said. "Any murders, accidents, or heat-related deaths we can turn into a good story?" She took notes above the sounds of a South Side police chase. "A Latino, Ralph Calise—a Latino with a silent *e*—age 28, Chicago. Stabbed and tossed in a field. Do you mean tossed and not just dumped from a car? Who would do something like that? Hey, how did you identify him?" Through his fingerprints. "Where would those prints be on file—with the Chicago police narcotics, by chance? Yeah, I thought so. He probably held out on someone."

Even as she spoke, she began having doubts. Some of the details were a little too familiar.

"Say, Barbara, anything unusual—shoes taken, fingers cut off? Remember that Herrera guy? Can't believe you never solved that. And that other kid—was he ever identified? Aren't all these three bodies sort of close together? You must be having a good-sized drug war going on. Wasn't Herrera from the North Side, too? How many times was this Calise guy stabbed? Yeah, I'll wait for the autopsy. No wallet in his pants?"

"His pants were pulled down," the coroner told her.

"Are you sure they didn't come undone when he was maybe dragged after he was stabbed?"

Richardson was being as helpful as she could, but she never wanted to make a comment on something that might be changed. All the reporters knew that, but it didn't stop them from trying to get something extra while the case was still fresh.

Gera-Lind hung up the phone and walked over to the 6 P.M. assignment board. The producer of the show, who was sipping hot coffee this warm September day, was Dan Allen. It was 9:20 A.M. Soon he would be entering the morning news meeting where the main stories and assignments for the evening newscast would be discussed. Dan was a stocky man with more than twenty years in the business. He could be stubborn, and he liked to take reporters like Gera-Lind under his wing. He was in his late forties and had seen it all as a reporter and foreign correspondent. Sometimes the earth had to move for him to lift an eyebrow.

Dan pulled at his mustache and sat back in his chair as Gera-Lind outlined what stories she had rounded up, including the "drug stabbing." The ground did not shake.

"We better hope for a good fire," Dan said. "I have nothing but a network piece about a goose with a plastic six-pack holder caught around his neck."

Gera-Lind returned to her desk feeling a little uneasy. The more she thought about the Calise murder, the less it seemed like a drug killing. This wasn't déjà vu, but it came close. In January Coroner Assistant Mark Allen of Indiana's Lake County had asked her for help in identifying a young man found along U.S. Highway 41 near Lowell. Allen thought a small item in the news might encourage friends of missing men to come to the morgue in Crown Point or at least have the parents send copies of their son's dental records. But Lowell is out of the coverage area for the Chicago station—it's near Kankakee—and Chicagoans aren't interested in rural settings.

Gera-Lind hadn't been able just to drop the matter, not after hearing the tone in Allen's voice: a sigh of sadness from someone who cares but can't do anything about the circumstances. But WLS wasn't interested, and neither was any of the other stations or the newspapers. The victim seemed destined to be just another unidentified body, meaning that the killer probably would never be found.

In January Gera-Lind had tried to revive the story when she read of five similar killings in Indianapolis. Her station turned down the idea, but this time she called Bill Williams of *Gay Life*. The paper, distributed largely on Chicago's North Side, had run the story, and within a week the victim was identified as John R. Johnson.

Now it wasn't a story about rural Indiana any more. Police had learned that the 26-year-old bartender and dancer came from Uptown. That might have interested the editors at Chicago's regular daily newspapers, but readers in late January couldn't care less about someone found eighty-five miles away on Christmas day.

Gera-Lind didn't know that she was the only person who realized that the Lake County bodies might be linked to the eight or ten bodies found in Indiana.

Lake County, Illinois

Detectives Dan Colin and Roy Lamprich walked behind Dr. Helen Young, a forensic pathologist, down the short corridor of the morgue. Dr. Young was one of those people whose considerable skills are masked by eccentricities. The woman, in her late fifties, had stringy fly-about red hair and for reasons known but to her had one long, gold fingernail.

Once they entered the autopsy room where the body of Ralph Calise lay, she quickly set to work. "All right, gentlemen. The body is that of a normally developed adult white male appearing to be the stated age of twenty-eight years. The body and clothing are partially covered by dried blood and dirt. Several loops of small bowel protrude from the abdomen. Rigor mortis is present and complete."

"Doc, can we get to the wounds, please?" Colin asked.

Seeing their impatience, the pathologist decided to show them the need for thoroughness and that there could be something more important to learn than the depth and number of wounds. "Look on the wrist," Dr. Young said, lifting the lifeless arm. The two detectives stepped closer to the table.

"The left arm shows the presence of a faint pink, horizontal, one-quarter-inch 'zone' across the back of the upper arm," Dr. Young continued. "There are white and slightly red pressure marks on the wrist. The right arm shows two linear 'zones.' " She looked directly at the officers again and said a single word: "Handcuffs."

Lamprich nudged Colin and half-whispered, "Like Herrera."

Colin was less sure of a link. By nature he always tried to consider alternate possibilities. Herrera's hand had been cut off. Why hadn't Calise been dismembered in some way, if they were killed by the same people? For all he knew, those wrist marks could have been caused by something else.

"Roy, hold out your hands," Colin said.

Lamprich felt a little silly, but he let Colin snap the metal braces around him and stood by as Young continued her autopsy. After a couple of minutes Colin inserted a small key into the lock and the cuffs clicked open. He raised the wrists to within a few inches of his eyes and saw the same parallel indentations that were frozen on the wrist of the corpse. He even put one of Lamprich's wrists next to Calise's body. They matched.

"As for the knife wounds, I see seventeen incised wounds," the pathologist continued. "There are three wounds of the right back. There are nine wounds on the left side of the chest. There are four wounds to the abdomen and one to the left neck. The wounds all go all the way in and pierce internal organs, so we have a hunting knife or a butcher knife being used—a long blade, about eight inches. The lung is punctured, the liver cut. God, this kid was really sadistically stabbed."

Colin decided to bring up an idea he couldn't shake off from the time he saw the body the day before. "Doc, do you think it's satanism? Could this be a dumping ground for some cult?"

"Hard to say, Dan. I never saw a devil-worshipper

body, but I'll look into this. I'll mark and measure every stabbing case to see if they have any patterns, and I'll check Herrera. Do you men want to stand by the table as I now open up his gastrointestinal tract to see what his last meal was?'' Dr. Young asked with a polite lifting of the gold fingernail.

''Hold on, we're moving back,'' Lamprich said.

This part of the autopsy showed the detectives only that Calise was killed several hours after eating a great American meal: french fries, corn, tomato slice, ground beef, onions, and a pickle, and he swallowed some spearmint chewing gum. Imagine making inquiries at every McDonald's, Burger King, Wendy's, and hash house in the six-county Chicago area.

Since there are fewer crimes in the north suburbs than in Chicago, the hours that suburban detectives work are less structured. They are freer to follow their instincts and take fifty-mile trips to settle nagging thoughts, such as those three sets of footprints. If Calise were killed by satanists, he might well have been a member of the cult rather than someone lured to his death at random. Lamprich was less interested in the theory than Colin, but they decided to return to Jolene Red Cloud's home to see what they might learn about Ralph's friends. Colin was glad he was going along. With Lamprich's prodigious memory, it would be like having a computer at his side.

It was close to noon when they turned off North Lake Shore Drive at Foster Avenue, leaving the beautiful lakeshore behind and heading west for the seedy area of Uptown. Colin had been reared just a few miles away, but he was unaware of how Foster Avenue Beach had changed.

Any time of the day or night, drivers park their cars or vans along the curving, scenic road just behind the artificial beach to look at the lake and wait. In time, some good-looking young man is likely to show up and in a usually roundabout way offer to sell small amounts of drugs or go off with the driver for a good time. Nothing was flagrant, and many people who used the beach and park were unaware that the lover's lane had become more specialized. This, quite likely, was where Ralph Calise met his killer.

A few more turns and they were in the quiet block of North Hermitage Avenue where Calise had lived. As the detectives left their air-conditioned car they removed their suit coats and loosened their ties in the ninety-degree afternoon. Down the street, children were laughing as they ran in and out of the spray from an open hydrant.

"We never have open hydrants in Lake County," Lamprich said.

"That's because the homes come with their own pools," said Colin.

Jolene, five friends, and three officers were in the small apartment. The detectives had no intention of conducting interviews *en masse* and talked to each one separately in the bedroom.

A man named Dwayne said, "I used to be Ralph's roommate, and he wasn't gay; no way. He was a nice guy—mellow, low-keyed. I ain't never seen him in a fight with anyone. Hey, he liked his dope, but he'd only do deals for friends."

One of the other men said, "Ralph had nothing to do with gays. There was no reason to kill him. None. He also had nothing to do with motorcycle gangs, street gangs, or the occult."

When it was Jolene's turn, Colin told her, "I want you to remember everything about that day from the time you woke up to the time he left. Please, everything."

The dark-skinned young woman leaned her head back and ran her fingers through her long, straight black hair as a nervous habit to help put her recollections in order. As she told it, the day had been no different from any other before Ralph disappeared. They got up at 10 or 11 A.M. and were hungry. They left the apartment, and Ralph walked across the railroad embankment to use a pay phone at a 7-Eleven to call a friend, John Lindsey, to borrow ten dollars.

Lindsey had told Ralph he would bring the money later, but the couple didn't want to wait. They walked to a friend's home across the street from their apartment and borrowed three dollars.

They walked for twenty minutes or so to Foster Avenue Beach, then turned around and returned to Lindsey's apartment. They borrowed ten dollars and one marijuana joint. Afterward they went back to their neighbor to return his three dollars. Then they went to a restaurant a few blocks away at Hermitage and Lawrence. As Jolene spoke, she began to cry.

"What did you do at the beach?" Colin asked.

"We would walk up and down trying to sell joints for a dollar."

"You're not that close to the lake; did Ralph ever hitchhike?"

"No, Ralph was a walker. He did hitchhike once—all the way to California and back again, about a year ago. But that was different."

Calise should have stayed on the West Coast, Colin thought; his kind seemed happier there. By now the detective felt that he knew Ralph, but this didn't help explain what happened to him or how he wound up in Lake County.

For the next four hours the detectives talked to people in the neighborhood and on the beach, showing the photo of Calise and leaving business cards with numbers to call if any information turned up.

The streets of Uptown come alive at twilight on summer nights. The neighborhood has declined rapidly from its heyday in the 1920s, when major dance bands played at the Aragon Ballroom and Al Capone frequented the small Green Mill nightclub a block away. By the 1950s the neighborhood had gone from middle-class to Appalachian with a number of American Indians. These drifting families from North Carolina, Tennessee, and Kentucky made no effort to disguise who they were. A large sign in a music store read "Hillbilly Music," and a bar near the aging Aragon was called Hillbilly Heaven.

In the 1960s the neighborhood changed with the squeezing out of Skid Row on the West Side and the closing of mental institutions across the state. Uptown became a unique area, not a physical slum but a mental one. The street teemed with bag ladies, men with knife-scars on their faces, and runaway teenagers.

Behind the green drapes taking up much of the front window, the Green Mill gave no hint of its bootleg glory. This is where the detectives found John Lindsey, the son of the owner, at 6 P.M.

"Ralph was a nice guy, very likable," he said.

"If he was so likable," said Lamprich, "then why would anyone kill him? Maybe over drugs?"

"Nah, Ralph was no dealer," the husky man said from his bar stool. "You hear about how he was always out of money. Does that sound like a dealer? He was a small operator. He supplied me with a little grass now and then, and I'd lend him ten. There was a gal who left him, before Jolene. She was real mad at him, claimed he got her pregnant. Once she pulled a knife on him, but nothing came of it. Ralph found out that the baby wasn't his."

"That's all you can tell us?" Colin asked.

"What else is there? It's a shame he was killed."

As Colin and Lamprich headed back for Lake County they passed Parkland Street at Foster Avenue Beach, where drivers pulled up and waited.

That evening Gera-Lind Kolarik arrived in the Mayor's Row restaurant across the street from the Daley Center just before a waiter cleared the pizza, cheese, and crackers from the hors d'oeuvre table.

She sat at a table with lawyer friends and unslung her purse with her tape recorder, pager, and books of contact numbers. She put the purse next to her bulging leather briefcase. That was her traveling office, with more beat books; maps of Wisconsin, Illinois, and Indiana; and a clutter of newspaper clippings, notes, and memos. "I think I'm onto something," Gera-Lind told her roommate Barbara and the others.

"Here we go again," said Barbara.

"Let me run this by you," said Gera-Lind. She told of how police had found Calise's body in Lake Forest two days before and the Indiana victims. "I'm thinking we have a homosexual serial killer who found out things were getting too hot for him in Indiana, and he's starting to dump his victims in Illinois.''

''Why aren't the police jumping all over these new cases?'' Annelie asked.

''To be frank, I don't think they know.''

Gera-Lind could see their interest evaporate, and she felt foolish for bringing up her suspicions. Suppose she called her friend Sheriff Mickey Babcox in Waukegan and he laughed at her? Yet just talking about the cases clarified some connections for her, and she was convinced of her theory more than ever. There were more than a dozen murders, and she couldn't just shrug them off as somebody else's problem.

The next day, Gera-Lind was reluctant to make the phone call to Lake County. She didn't even want to call from her desk, with reporters and editors moving all around her. She excused herself and went to Dan Allen's cubicle while he was at a meeting. ''Mickey,'' she said, ''don't laugh at me, but I think there's a homosexual serial killer from Indiana who's now killing his victims in Lake County.''

''Ahh, Gera-Lind, I don't have all day.''

She told him about the murders and the pattern and started to give him the phone numbers to call for the task force and the state police.

''You're full of shit,'' Babcox growled.

''Mickey, what will it cost you—a dollar to make the call?''

After a pause the sheriff said, ''Well, maybe I'll give this to Smitty, and I'll get back to you.''

At around eleven o'clock that night, Babcox gave Gera-Lind a call at home. Instead of ''Hello'' he said, ''Agatha Christie, you've got it. They got similar murders down there. I don't know what we are going to do with this now, but you have hit on something. All I know is we're the only ones who have fresh evidence. Hey, thanks.''

The Calise case followed Dan Colin to his home in Round Lake, a dozen miles from the sheriff's office in Waukegan. When he was a teenager, his family moved from Chicago and he underwent culture shock from the open spaces and crickets, but now he felt the bedroom community of a little more than a thousand was becoming too crowded.

This was a fisherman's town, but he never had the time to relax completely. Instead, he unwound nightly in a ritual that helped him think. Colin knew that Pam, his petite blonde wife, would be waiting for him and that ten minutes after locking up his car he would be climbing into sweatpants and slipping a burgundy robe over his V-necked T-shirt. If something perplexed him, he and Pam would bounce ideas back and forth and things would seem clearer. Colin seldom noticed that his wife didn't distract him with talk about her own day.

What nagged at his mind this night were the possibly satanic elements: the severed hand, the unidentified boy on top of a dead dog, the protruding intestines.

Colin had called home early enough for his dinner to be warm. Pam was cramming into her life the old-fashioned values of cooking and shepherding her family while living the busy schedule of a working mother, which often meant four hours' sleep after a day of getting her children off to school, working as a jewelry manager at the K-Mart in town, and talking with her husband past midnight.

On this night, Colin smoked a pipe on a living room sofa, and his wife sat with her legs curled up in a chair. From what she heard, it seemed more likely that a single killer was involved than three or four people.

"If there's a pattern," said Pam softly, "it's the hands."

"Only one had his hand cut off."

"What if it's a different avenue, Dan? It doesn't sound satanic; to me it sounds like bondage."

Bondage—just regular sadomasochism, but deadly? John Wayne Gacy, the amateur clown, had snapped handcuffs on his victims by pretending he was showing them a trick. Herrera and Calise had looked fairly strong. The killer, if it were a single person, would need a way to keep them from striking out at him. Suppose all three were hustlers and they submitted to bondage, only to discover that the man who offered them money had no intention of letting them go?

"About that guy whose hand was cut off," Pam added. "That I wouldn't know about."

But Colin did. Perhaps the killer didn't want to leave his handcuffs at the scene as a way of identifying him or because leaving a corpse bound was not part of his fantasy, and he discovered he couldn't find his key.

"You know," Colin said, "you may be right." He left the living room to make a call to Smitty's home, then sat thinking over and over the facts he knew of the three cases, as Pam went to bed without him.

Colin and Lamprich returned to Chicago the next day and interviewed Calise's previous girlfriend, Marie, a thin, attractive woman with dark hair down to the small of her back. Speaking to the officers while in a faded smock, Marie said her husband once knocked out two of Ralph's teeth, but that was the end of it.

"Do you know if Ralph street-hustled?" Colin asked. His wife's suggestion of bondage kept coming back to him.

"Ralph never—or at least he never told us," Marie answered. "But I do remember some times when he'd disappear for a few hours and then come back with a lot of money."

"When he was living on Hermitage?"

"No, this was before, when he had a roommate—Rocco somebody. The address . . . the address . . . I think it was 4017 North Kenmore."

Lamprich drew his partner aside and said, "Dan, 4019 is where Herrera lived in 1979. If Calise lived at 4017 Kenmore, then they were next-door neighbors. It's kind of weird." No one needed to look through notes when Lamprich said something; he was a walking filing cabinet.

"So they lived next door; maybe they didn't know each other," Colin said. "You know how Chicago is."

"Then maybe they hung out at the same places."

Lamprich didn't need to complete the thought. If the two victims had frequented the same places, then the killer probably did, too. The detectives looked at each other and took a deep breath. They were finally onto something.

From Marie's home, Colin and Lamprich went to Area 6 headquarters to talk to other police about where hustlers hang out. Besides, rap sheets on Calise and Herrera might give them a lead.

They walked into the modern, boxlike building with their suit jackets over their shoulders. Seeing a familiar face, Colin went to where Detective Thomas Keane was hammering at a typewriter.

"Hi, Tom. We need some help on two rap sheets concerning a homicide we had on Tuesday—"

"Calise, right? I remember you, you're from the rich suburbs." Colin could match the poverty of Waukegan's slum and Zion's racial tension with anything Chicago had to offer, but there was no way of dispelling the impression city police usually had of Lake County.

Keane gave the sheets to Lamprich and put his cigar back in his mouth. Colin asked him, "Have you heard of any suburban murders or in rural areas where young men were found with their pants pulled down?"

"Queer murders, you mean? Like yours, stabbed real hard in the belly?" Keane thought a moment, or perhaps he just wanted to take another puff on his cigar. There weren't any such killings in Cook County suburbs that he could recall, but sheriff's police from Kankakee came up one day to ask about an Uptown kid found dead there. Anything more than one county away from Chicago was regarded as remote bordering on myth. "Yeah, there was one," Keane said. "I think it's still open. Let me get it for you."

Keane, a stocky man, walked to the wall of metal drawers and thumbed through the records. He pulled out a file as Colin looked over his shoulder. "Here it is— Crockett, like Davy. They ID'd him through a laundry tag on his pants, like the old days. The kid was stabbed real bad. Lived on Malden somewhere."

Colin slid the folder from the older man's hands and quickly opened it.

"It's the pants that stick in my mind," Keane said.

"There's another case like that—now who the hell was it? Jay Jay." He spent a minute or two looking up that case. "J. R. Johnson." He gave the folder to Colin and said, "Have fun."

My God, Colin thought. Herrera lived at 4019 North Kenmore but was found in Lake County. Calise lived at 4017 North Kenmore a couple of years ago but was discovered in Lake County. Steven Crockett lived at 4501 North Malden, also in Uptown, but was found in Kankakee County. John R. Johnson lived at 3241 North Broadway in Uptown but was found in a rural area in Indiana's Lake County. Someone was killing off a whole neighborhood of hustlers and making sure that the Chicago police weren't the ones who found them.

"It's them pants," Keane said as Colin only half listened while scanning the reports. "A smart killer wouldn't leave something obvious like that. If he kept their pants up, the cops'd figure drugs or something."

Colin's pager went off, and he called the sheriff's office. Smitty told him to talk to the Cook County sheriff's police about a body found in a creek last May. The deputy chief didn't believe that the lead was promising, since the killer they were after preferred leaving his victims near highways. Smitty added, nearly as an afterthought, "Then maybe there are a lot of other guys we should look into."

"Hold on," Colin said and gestured for Lamprich to come to the phone at Keane's desk. "You're not going to believe this," he told his partner and handed him the receiver.

Smitty continued. "There's a whole task force down in Indiana doing the same thing we are, only with their own victims. They got—get this—they got eight to twelve, all with the same pattern we have. The highways, the pants, the stabbings, all hustlers. But all of theirs are from Indiana, and they never thought of calling us, even when they had a survivor from Uptown."

"A survivor!" Lamprich exclaimed, and Colin came closer.

"He wasn't stabbed, just drugged," Smitty added. "No one can find him, but he could be our link."

Colin took the phone. "This is Dan. Where did you hear about this?"

"Someone from Channel Seven, a friend of Mickey's."

This morning they were working on a list of three murders. Now they had one from Kankakee, a possibly linked case in Cook County, and eight to twelve from Indiana—seventeen. Colin could hardly believe that no one on either side of the state line used a multimillion-dollar computer or a twenty-five-cent phone call to learn how extensive this case was.

Back in Indiana, the task force wasn't idle, but for all the leads the unit was turning up it might just as well have been shut down. The officers were conducting an "elimination investigation" on two possible suspects besides Eyler. One was a man who lived with his parents in a rural area near Indianapolis and used a van extensively in the produce business. The other worked for a pharmaceutical company. Both were homosexuals with violent tempers. By then, investigators had ruled out the pig farmer.

Love's team felt that the other two suspects weren't as likely as Eyler to be the highway killer, but there was the disturbing feeling that one of them might have killed boys or young men who were not included on the list. Perhaps the detectives were right. The other possible suspects were never ruled out, and those murders remain unsolved.

5

September 3, 1983
Chicago

When Colin and Lamprich returned from the Area 6 station in Chicago, Colin went to Smitty's small office, where sharpshooting awards hung on lime green walls. He sat down in front of the desk and said, "I think it's time for a meeting of all the cops with similar cases. That means Indiana and any other state with bodies."

The deputy chief had been thinking the same thing since receiving the call from Sheriff Babcox sharing Gera-Lind's suspicion. "We'll have to keep the media out," Smitty cautioned. "They'll just blow this thing out of proportion."

"That's not the worst thing," Colin said. He didn't want the killer knowing that the police had formed a link. "You set up the meeting, and I'll call some people over in Indiana to make sure they keep things quiet."

The meeting was set up for Wednesday, September 8. It's such a long drive between Waukegan and Indianapolis that both sides agreed to a middle ground: Crown Point, Indiana.

In the two weeks before the conference, police in the two states continued to investigate their own cases without pooling their information. Colin made repeated trips that early autumn to Uptown and the adjacent Ravenswood neighborhood to show people three photos. They were of Gustavo Herrera, Ralph Calise, and the man who had survived an attack in Indiana, Craig Townsend. Police still had no idea what happened to Townsend after he fled from

70

a hospital in Crown Point, but they had his mug shot from a narcotics arrest in Chicago.

Colin had shown the photographs around so often he felt he had known these men. Calise, with his stringy black hair and happy grin; Herrera, a weight lifter who kept his hair long and had a flowing mustache curving down past his upper lip; Townsend, with his wide, wide eyes, sunken cheeks, and a look of helplessness; and Crockett, with the lost look of a boy from Uptown and a smile, frozen by the camera, that was almost tender.

The landlord where Calise had once lived on North Troy Street before he met Jolene remembered seeing Townsend around but not Herrera. A friend of Calise's on North Collum had seen Herrera but not Townsend. So had a friend who dropped by. And a young woman in the building was sure she had seen Herrera in Calise's earlier apartment on Troy. For Colin, the important thing was knowing that all the victims had moved about in the same circles.

He felt closer to the killer, but an invisible barrier was keeping him back. None of these men had steady jobs. Their days and nights were spent drifting to places on the North Side and drifting back. He had to know where they went and how strangers entered their world of casual friends. Until he knew more about Uptown and the homosexual world, Colin felt that he would never get anywhere in the investigation.

It didn't matter that Colin told Indiana police to keep the impending meeting in Crown Point a secret; someone apparently thought the precaution was unimportant. After months of criticism, police could finally show that they were doing something. Word reached the Indiana media, but Gera-Lind Kolarik heard of the meeting just hours before it was to begin.

Kolarik had been doing something the police had not; she was cooperating with her Indiana counterparts and already had a tape of where John Roach was found and of Steven Agan being carried away in a body bag. With background coverage called b-roll, a station can expand a story and revive it at every development.

She was sure her immediate boss, Mort Meissner, would be eager to fly someone to Crown Point and rush him back for the six o'clock news. In her breathless way she declared, "This is a Chicago exclusive."

There was no twinkle in Meisner's eyes. "Is this the same story we didn't do last winter?" asked the compact middle-aged man, sitting back as if to enjoy the sunshine of her enthusiasm, a reminder of her early years in the business.

"*Gay Life* knew it was a story, and they got Johnson identified," she reminded him.

"Oh, it's a story. But a little kinky." He smiled at her enigmatically. "Tell you what. I'll try to sell it at the morning meeting, but we're down to two reporters today. See if you can get Bill Nigut to work a couple of hours early."

Driving two hours down there and two hours back would tie up a reporter too long, and the proposal nearly died at the morning winnowing. It wasn't easy, but Kolarik lined up a helicopter for Nigut and a crew. "Remember," she said, "all we need is a little stand-up. We've got all the b-roll we need."

Despite the chopper that throbbed over midday traffic, the crew didn't get to the meeting until after most of the officers had arrived. Nigut found himself competing with Indiana reporters trying to wring quotations from officials so that they could pack up and go back to Indianapolis and Terre Haute.

Crown Point itself is merely a country town ignoring the nearby steel mills of the Calumet district. There had not been such a convergence of lawmen and reporters since John Dillinger broke out of the old jail with a wooden gun.

The meeting began after a lunch provided by Indiana police in the jail cafeteria. Inmates with paper hats and see-through gloves served food as officers from two states slid plastic yellow trays down the line. Detective Kurt Proschwitz of Illinois's Lake County was hoping for steak, but what they dished out was liver and onions.

Colin noticed the reporters getting ready and wondered

out loud, "What happened to our secret meeting?" His tone didn't show bitterness. He knew of cases that were lost because reporters learned too much before an arrest was made. The Indiana sheriff even played up to the reporters, holding a news conference in one of the corridors that linked buildings in the nine-year-old complex.

The newspeople were being led to believe that there was a concerted effort and that an arrest might be made soon. The truth was that the Illinois police were nearly exhausting their leads on Calise, they had nothing to go on with the unidentified boy and Herrera, and they knew nothing about the Indiana crimes except for the names of some of the victims. The Indiana police were not much better off, despite their task force.

The strongest lead they had was the pattern itself: the victims were men usually eighteen to twenty-six years old; they suffered numerous stab wounds, especially in the abdomen; most were hustlers or hitchhikers; all had their pants pulled down; most had ligature marks on their hands; and most had mustaches. Usually their shirts and wallets were missing, many had on white tube socks, and combs were found near several of the bodies. At least three of the victims had traces of the "hypnotic" prescription drug Placidyl.

After lunch the officers went to the second-floor training room and filled most of the fifty steel chairs with attached arm-rest platforms for taking notes. It was like being back in school. Just one officer, Detective Frank Kajari, represented Chicago police. He would report back to Area 6 what progress had been made. None of the crimes were known to have occurred in the city, but the department knew it would soon be involved.

Sgt. Frank Love of the task force with his neatly trimmed white beard and robust form looked like the father figure of the investigation. He stood up in his gray suit and outlined the work of the more than twenty members of the Central Indiana Multi-Agency Investigation Team. Other officers, sometimes speaking from their chairs, told of bodies that might belong to the list attributed to the unknown serial killer. The new cases included Jay Reynolds, found in Kentucky in March that year; Robert Foley, found around Halloween the previous year in Will County, southwest of Chicago (later removed from the list); Edgar Underkofler, a twenty-six-year-old man found in March near Danville, Illinois; a skeleton found July 2 in Ford County, Illinois; and Mark Riley, who was found in Hancock County on June 6 (later removed from the list).

The task force detectives told the others about Daniel Scott McNeive, and Illinois police gave details about eighteen-year-old Jimmy Roberts, the black man from Chicago's South Side who was found in Thorn Creek, in the southern suburbs. Sam McPherson of the task force told of how two FBI agents arrived in May and spent the day in the Marion County Public Safety Training Center in Indianapolis, talking to officers and seeing what they had in their computer. He mentioned in passing that the task force was keeping an eye on several possible suspects, including a liquor store clerk named Larry Eyler, something of a born loser who stabbed a man a few years ago.

Colin listened intently, hoping for a single element to jump out. When Eyler's name came up, Colin wondered if the man ever lived in the Chicago area; then everything would make sense. Nothing the Indiana officers could tell about any of the suspects would suggest that he was the killer, but Eyler came close to the FBI profile.

The FBI experts from Quantico, Virginia, said that the killer—assuming only one person was involved—was most likely a white man in his late twenties or early thirties, a common laborer who didn't mind getting dirty. In fact, he might like mess as part of his macho persona. He needed to present a rough exterior because he was worried about his feeling an attraction for other men.

Being with other macho men was important to him to feel he belonged, the FBI agents speculated. This meant that he might be a heavy beer drinker who frequented "redneck bars." The agents didn't say whether he went to gay bars or not.

They added that the killer was probably always on the edge of homosexual panic, forever afraid that someone would regard him as "queer," a "faggot." As a result, he might show hatred for gays. But, as Sergeant McPherson relayed to the other officers, when the killing was over the man would try to erase the act by covering the victim with leaves and dirt.

Later the FBI fed additional information into its computer as more bodies turned up in Indiana and agents visited some of the locations where the bodies were found, McPherson said. They determined that the killer must have made considerable efforts to build up his torso, particularly his chest and arms, and he might be considered a night owl.

The FBI's Behavioral Science Unit contended that its profiles can be "uncannily accurate," but there are so many factors that they must be used only as a general guide, not as a way of excluding any possible suspects.

At the end of the meeting most of the officers stood up as if glad to return to their own jurisdictions, but Smitty led his men to Love and McPherson in the back of the nearly empty classroom. Smitty's men had physical evidence but no suspects; Love's men had suspects but no evidence.

"This suspect you mentioned—Eyler. What does he drive?" Colin asked.

"Pickup truck," McPherson answered.

"Maybe you can use these," Colin said and handed him photos of the tire tracks Smitty had made with dental plaster. "And see if he wears boots that would leave this pattern." He showed the Indiana men photos of the shoe prints.

"Waffle stompers," Love remarked, referring to the waffle-like design of the heel. "They're kinda common, but we'll see."

The Indiana detectives, in return, showed the Illinois police their surveillance photos of Eyler: thirty-one years old, nice looking but not quite handsome, muscular, with a round baby face offset by a small mustache. Not much to go on, but of all the people being considered so far, he was the only one who made frequent trips to the two cities where most of the victims lived, Indianapolis and Chicago. The Illinois police said they would watch for him, but they returned home without the feeling that they had just reached the turning point in the case.

There wasn't much the task force could learn without tipping off this liquor store clerk and sometime house-painter that they were zeroing in on him. But Love and his men discussed the possibility of getting permission from Eyler's boss to plant a listening device in the phone some Saturday morning before Larry came to work, then dropping by around eleven o'clock that night to ask him to go to a police station for some questioning. It would be interesting to hear whom he called and what he said.

What they did know was that Larry was a walking con-tradiction. He disguised his emotional vulnerability and sentimentality by going to gyms and lifting weights, until most of his one hundred eighty pounds was muscle stretched out on his six-foot-one-inch frame. He looked tough, and he often acted tough in public, yet he spoke softly with a faint lispy sing-song.

On September 17, Love called the state police post in Lowell, since that was where one of the bodies was found, and asked about any traffic citations against Eyler. He contacted the post at the lunch period and instead of reach-ing the commander was referred to a clerk. She told him she could not help him. Rather than waste a call, Love asked her to take down Eyler's name, date of birth, and a description of his truck "and perhaps put it on the bulletin board."

He had nothing formal in mind; this was just a follow-up recommendation for the message Cathy Berner of the task force had sent out earlier. Love had been a state policeman for nearly twenty-two years and knew the inves-tigation had not reached the point where the police should tip their hand. Besides, the loose organization of the unit did not lend itself to strategic planning.

Then Love went on to other business, unaware that this call could lead to the undoing of the investigation by police in both states.

12:20 A.M., September 30, 1983
Chicago & Lowell, Indiana

By now Detective Frank Kajari was developing a sixth sense about this case. The officer had been the only Chicago policeman at the meeting in Crown Point. The Lake County police were aware that Uptown was a common thread in many of the cases, but they were unfamiliar with the gay hangouts a little south of there.

For decades North Clark Street had been the main artery of the gay and lesbian world. Then Little Jim's opened on nearby Halsted Street in 1975. Over the next few years more gay bars set up shop along the four blocks of Halsted. That was the area where Eyler would hang out; Kajari was sure of it.

Kajari was always watchful. On this early morning, something seemed familiar about the 1982 Ford pickup truck parked on a side street half a block from Loading Dock, one of the gay bars. Without a word to his partner, he made a U-turn and drove by again, glimpsing the Indiana license plate. "Paul, that's the guy. I just know it," Kajari said.

They parked nearby and Detective Paul Carroll turned down the police radio, as if most of the barhoppers couldn't spot an unmarked police car even in this dark. "Let's sit on him for a while and see what he's up to," Kajari muttered.

A moment later, Kajari straightened from his surveillance slouch as the taillights lit up. The truck then went on its prowl, going up Halsted to Addison and then east to nearby Broadway, all at just ten miles an hour, cruising speed. The Area 6 detectives could see Eyler's face now and then as he poked his head out to look at teenage boys along the sidewalks. And so it went for twenty blocks to Bryn Mawr Avenue, then the pickup truck turned around and cruised the same twenty blocks to Broadway and Addison. There it stopped at a young man holding a six-pack under a lightpole. A second later the truck door swung open and the young man disappeared inside.

We've got him, Kajari thought. But now he and Carroll

had to follow and watch. There is no law against giving someone a lift. All the pickup meant was that Eyler didn't know he was being followed and possibly that he still didn't know he was a suspect.

The rolling surveillance continued for at least half an hour as the truck headed for the anything-can-happen neighborhood of the Near North Side, where liberals, homosexuals, upscale traditionalists, and bums live in an uneasy truce. The truck that had been moving so slowly stopped suddenly, and the door flung open. Kajari feathered the brake as the young man climbed out. Eyler sped off, and Carroll called the kid over. "We're police," he said. "What happened in the truck?"

The young man walked over. "He wanted to have sex with me and I said no," he answered. Then he held up the six-pack as if that explained everything. "I want to party."

The detective left him there without explanation, still holding up the beer. Kajari had to speed up to make up the lost time. They returned to their surveillance distance and watched the pickup truck turn east at Chicago Avenue and drive to Clark Street.

They slowed down in front of the Gold Coast bar, where three men in leather jackets and black leather pants sat on motorcycles. Eyler turned west on Hubbard from Clark and went north on LaSalle, just short of the Loop, and then disappeared. Those streets were in silent anticipation of dawn, and Eyler wouldn't want to go down the canyons of dark, empty skyscrapers. Who knows where he went.

Sometimes police instincts go wrong. "Come on, let's circle the block," Kajari said, assuming Eyler had gone into the bar to catch a drink or a friend before closing. He hadn't thought that Eyler might now be headed for an expressway that would take him out of the city and return him to the rural spaces that formed the canvas of his fantasies.

The detectives searched the quiet streets of the Near North Side until a foggy dawn was starting to look like a dirty cobweb. They returned to the Area 6 station and went to the commander's office for an outside line rather than use the Pax (police auxiliary) intradepartment system. Kajari took out a notebook with numbers and made a call to the task force in Indianapolis. "I just want to tell you people we saw Larry Eyler in Chicago, but we lost him an hour or so ago. Don't get excited; he was alone."

Soon after Kajari lost sight of the truck, Larry picked up a hitchhiker on the Ontario Street ramp to the Dan Ryan Expressway. Darl Hayward of Arkansas tossed his brown shoulder bag to the cluttered floor and said he was going to Indianapolis for the funeral of his grandparents.

Darl had the look of someone meant for the highways. He brushed his long, dark hair carelessly across his forehead and his eyes were watchful under their arched brows. He had been around, that was clear, but he didn't know what he was getting into.

Larry told Darl that he was going to Kentucky but that he was cutting off near Indianapolis, so he could take him there. Darl unzipped the light jacket he wore over his T-shirt and settled back on the red seat. "Tonight's my lucky night," he said.

It must have seemed as if this driver with the baseball cap and dash of mustache lived his entire life in the truck. Under the seat were bags and bottles and papers and old clothes. The Ford was less than a year old, yet the odometer had more than thirty thousand miles on it.

As the pickup sped down the expressway, Darl noticed a yellow-orange emblem on the driver's blood-red T-shirt and asked, "Are you in the Marines?"

"Just got out two years ago," Larry answered.

Maybe it's true, Darl thought, but the driver didn't seem the military type. Someone that messy wouldn't have got out of boot camp. A lot of guys claim they were in the Marines or saw action in 'Nam; it does no harm. Darl had been around and seen all types. He had a couple of arrests for prostitution even though he claimed he was no hustler. From the side his face looked dumpy, but when he turned to Larry his arched brows and chiseled, narrow upper lip made him seem attractive.

Larry handed him a stick of gum. "I'm going to see my parents," he said. "I work for the government. I can't tell you what I do, but I work for the government." A hitchhiker hears all sorts of things, not so much lies told as dreams revealed.

They were nearing the Ninety-Fifth Street exit in the heart of Chicago's black South Side. Larry looked away from the ribbon of lights and smiled at Darl with the familiarity of a stranger who understands the other. "I have a fantasy," he said. It wasn't a statement; it was an invitation.

"What's your fantasy?"

"Tying people up."

Larry returned his attention to the expressway; his face was blank. A few seconds passed. "I will give you one hundred dollars if I could tie you up. I get off like that." When Darl didn't reply immediately, Larry added, "Then I'll untie you."

"I'm not into bondage," Darl said. "No one ties me up."

"I saw how they do it," Larry told him in a tone intended to suggest that he had never tried it himself. "I saw it at the Bijou," he said of the homosexual movie theater on the North Side, "and it turned me on. I come to Chicago regularly and pick up hustlers. I usually go through an escort service, but the kid I like went to California. So when I saw you, I just thought . . ." He let his meaning go unspoken.

"I do it sometimes, but not tied up," Darl said. "All you want to do is tie me up?"

Larry answered by reaching into a purple Crown Royal bag on the dashboard and pulling out a hundred-dollar bill. Darl turned his head away and wouldn't touch the money. Larry folded the bill and slowly returned it to the small felt bag with the gesture of someone expecting to take the bill out again. They had entered Indiana.

When the two men had been together for twenty-five miles, Larry said, "I won't hurt you. I promise. You can trust me."

Darl kept thinking of that hundred-dollar bill. Larry was smiling again. Somewhere in the last couple of miles, he had won—and he knew it.

"Can you take off your shirt?" the driver asked, resting his arms on the black steering wheel. Darl slipped out of his jacket, and Larry looked him over, playing over something in his mind. Then his eyes went back to the road. "I do this once a month. I usually go through an escort service and get someone drunk."

"I said no."

"It's just someone being helpless for a while, being tied up; that gets me off." Larry offered him another stick of gum.

Darl looked at something that jostled toward his feet during the ride. It was a flimsy beige Jewel Foods bag with a piece of rope protruding. He picked up the bag and saw that all it held were surgical tape and two lengths of rope, one for the hands and one for the feet.

He was weighing the possibility as the pickup went south down Interstate 65 toward Indianapolis. The early morning fog was settling on the wetlands and laying dew on the fields.

The highway neared a creek that was hardly more than a ditch with two feet of water. Larry parked and Darl grabbed his shoulder bag of personal effects. Larry picked up the beige plastic grocery sack with the ropes. The drifter from Arkansas hadn't said he would go along with the game, but he wasn't resisting.

Larry wasn't much of a drinker, and the whiskey bottle he had was one of those four-inch miniatures sold at Andy's Liquors. He stood near the tall weeds and threw it down the creek, then he turned to Darl. "Here," he said in his almost whispery voice, "why don't you lay down here? Lay flat, so traffic can't see you."

The hitchhiker lowered himself to the wet weeds a few feet from the stream as Larry stood over him, master of the moment, not touching him, just looking. For Larry, having sex within the sound of a highway heightened excitement.

"Pull your shirt up," Larry said. Darl rolled his T-shirt over his shoulders and dropped it behind him. Larry looked over the drifter's chest and abdomen, smiling. "Let me tie you up, and I'll put the hundred dollars in your shirt pocket.''

The rush of cars and trucks just out of sight made the drifter a little uneasy. ''Why don't we go where nobody can see us?'' he asked.

''OK, there's a quiet place I go to. A barn.''

''Near here?''

''It's on our way. No one will bother us. Come on.''

They were walking up from the creek and climbing back into the truck when Trooper Kenneth Buehrle passed by in a tan Dodge. He was young but cautious. Buehrle often had seen long-haul truck drivers pull off the side of the road to catch a few hours' sleep, but this didn't look so innocent. Not when murder victims were turning up county by county.

''Mile marker 238, investigating a gray pickup truck with two men,'' he said quietly into his hand-held transmitter. The time was just before 7 A.M.

Buehrle, whose name is pronounced ''Burley,'' had worked in the department less than two years and was to be the least experienced officer directly involved in the case. Every step he took was by the book and was never questioned. What he was about to do was called a Terry stop, after the *Terry v. Ohio* decision that officers who have a reasonable suspicion of criminal activity may detain a suspect and frisk him if considered necessary and conduct limited questioning. Larry watched the trooper in his rear-view mirror, and the calmness of the last few hours slipped away. ''Just don't, don't, don't say nothing to anyone—and don't say nothing about money.'' Larry pushed some of the miniature liquor bottles under his seat.

Buehrle examined the pickup truck as he neared. The vent window on the right side was broken, meaning that the truck might have been stolen. The trooper unsnapped his holster and put his revolver behind his leg to be ready for anything yet not alarm the men needlessly.

''Let's see some IDs,'' Buehrle said, giving the interior of the truck a darting glance. ''What were you two doing back there?''

Larry spoke up. ''I was taking a shit.''

"What's in the brown bag you took down there?" the trooper asked the passenger, referring to the small Jewel Foods bag.

"Toilet paper," Darl answered.

"Can I look at it?"

"Sure," Darl replied. But instead of giving him the grocery bag with the rope, he handed the trooper his own plastic tote bag. He had in it just what a drifter might need: razor, a can of shaving cream, some coins, a comb, and not much else.

"I don't see any toilet paper," the officer said.

"I used it all up."

Buehrle checked Larry's license and registration. Even if the truck wasn't stolen, the men were acting guilty of something. The bag of personal items he had just been shown was not the bag he saw as the men were walking up from the creek, and he also thought he saw the man with the baseball cap throw something into the weeds.

Careful not to let his suspicions show, the trooper said, "You aren't allowed to park a vehicle along the interstate. Mr. Eyler, could you come with me to my squad car so I can write out a warning and check this information?"

As Larry stepped down from the truck, Buehrle returned his revolver to its holster. Larry and Darl never knew he had his gun out.

Larry sat next to Buehrle on the front seat as the trooper picked up his handset and radioed dispatcher Max Hunter to check the registration. Hunter asked what the exact location was. That meant he was sending a backup car and that this was no simple traffic stop. Buehrle reached over and turned his radio down so that Larry would not hear any further messages.

As soon as Hunter heard the name Larry Eyler, something clicked. He turned over the clipboard of the day's assignments and looked at a note the secretary had written. The description ended with "Wanted for possible suspect in murder cases." Cases!

Everything matched—the height, weight, balding in front, driving a gray Ford pickup, "looks somewhat military"—yet the name was different. The message gave it as "Larry M. Eyle," but Buehrle spelled out the name as "Eyler." Could it be that the secretary had made a mistake? That would explain why no one at the Lowell state police post could find out anything about the suspect "Eyle" on the computer.

"We got 'im!" Hunter called out.

All the officers at the Lowell post rushed over and started looking for reports. They were eager to jump into their cars and see this Terry stop turn into the arrest of a lifetime; all they needed was authorization.

At this moment, Indiana state police Sgt. John Pavlakovic was leisurely preparing for work. Some people shoot out of bed and hurry to their jobs, but not John. He would rather set his alarm for 5:30 and take his time. Besides, no one with a wife and two children can be entirely sure of having a bathroom free at 7 A.M. His hair turning steel gray, he was a contemplative man and liked putting things in order, whether it was his office or his home.

Pavlakovic lathered for a shave but was interrupted by the phone. The sergeant put the razor on the sink and ran to the bedroom, catching the receiver on the third ring. Max Hunter was on the other end and briefed him on the stop. Then he asked, "What do you want done?"

Pavlakovic was the shift supervisor and had been with the state police for more than twenty years. He was a good cop, and he was from the old school. From what he understood, the man with Eyler could be an accomplice in the murders or, more likely, a potential victim. Under standard procedures they would have to let Eyler go on his way. But for what—to make this rider or some other hitchhiker the next victim?

"What do you want done, Sergeant?"

Pavlakovic didn't have to think twice. "Have them brought into the post for interrogation, and have the vehicle impounded."

Pavlakovic knew of the highway killings from one victim found in his jurisdiction, John R. Johnson, but he had not spoken to anyone in the task force about what their duties were or what his men should do if a suspect were stopped for a routine violation. The task force, working on its own, failed to make periodic briefings that would avoid miscommunication in times like this. Even now when Pavlakovic said "Have them brought in," he did not necessarily mean that his men should charge Eyler. He was not entirely sure what he meant. He assumed the situation would settle itself once everyone got to the station.

The sergeant walked into the kitchen and made a cup of coffee as his Doberman followed him around for a pat on the head. Normally Pavlakovic read a Chicago newspaper in the morning, but he knew he should be down at the Lowell post as soon as he could. He walked out to his car and drove to the station, turning on the police radio to listen to the car-to-car transmission of the officers at the scene.

At mile post 238, Trooper Buehrle was sure his case was important when his backup turned out to be his squad leader, Sgt. Peter Popplewell. Eyler uneasily stayed in the police car as the slender young trooper conferred with the stocky veteran of sixteen years.

"This was posted at the station, Ken," the sergeant said as he handed the trooper the note from Sergeant Love's phone call nearly two weeks before.

Sgt. William Glenn Cothran, a nineteen-year veteran, pulled up next and Popplewell radioed dispatcher Hunter from his squad car. "Everything's under control." Then he nodded to the two other officers, letting them know they should proceed.

"What do we have?" Cothran asked as he walked toward the truck.

"I'm not sure," the trooper replied.

Cothran saw Darl sitting confused and afraid. "Young man, would you step out please?"

The drifter complied, and Cothran patted him down for weapons. Turning to the trooper, the older officer asked, "Now, what seems to be the trouble?"

Buehrle pointed to the brown shoulder bag that was on the floorboard. "That's what they told me they had when they were in the weeds, but I saw a different bag. It was smaller, lighter, maybe plastic."

Buehrle had been careful not to touch anything, but Cothran was less concerned with the fine points of police procedure. He reached inside the truck and brought Darl's bag forward, against the pedals. Behind it he noticed a zippered vinyl bag with a lock on it. He brought it from under the seat then pulled the seat forward and upward to look at the small storage area. There were all kinds of things there, but the bag was all he lifted out of place. He dumped it onto the passenger's seat, and out spilled the two pieces of nylon rope. The only other items in there were two rolls of adhesive tape.

EYLER'S ATTORNEY DAVID SCHIPPERS SPEAKING DURING A HEARING ON THE EVIDENCE: *Did you have his consent to search into that truck, or to look into that truck?*

COTHRAN: No, sir.

Cothran kept the bag inside the truck but showed it to Buehrle so that the younger man might see what kind of people they had come across.

Buehrle went to his squad car and motioned for Eyler to step out. "Put your hands up and against the car and spread-eagle," the officer said.

"Can you tell me what's wrong?" Eyler asked.

"Never mind," the trooper told him.

Snap went one handcuff. Snap went the other.

The two older officers at the scene had a common thought: at last the murders have stopped.

II

THE EVIDENCE

6

7:15 A.M., September 3, 1983
Lowell, Indiana

The sun was burning through the hazy sky over the farm-land. Traffic passed along the highway, ignoring the parked pickup truck and two police cars. Eyler sat blankly in the trooper's auto, as if he were a schoolboy in detention.

Darl, naked from the waist up and holding his white T-shirt in one of his hands, said, "Hey, I didn't do anything wrong." Popplewell handcuffed him and led him to his car.

Buehrle told the more experienced officers, "I think we should go back to where I spotted them coming out of the ditch."

Eyler was transferred to Cothran's car so that the trooper might play his hunch. Because of the handcuffs, the sergeant buckled the seatbelt for Eyler and put the shoulder harness across him.

DEFENSE ATTORNEY SCHIPPERS: *Did you feel that you had been arrested?*

EYLER: Definitely.

Climbing into his car and putting a little of his paunch over his belt buckle, Popplewell asked Darl, "How long have you known this fellah?"

"Since Chicago—a couple of hours. Is there trouble? He seems pretty decent to me. Whatever he's done, ain't got nothing to do with me."

Cothran backed his car a quarter mile to the ditch over-

89

pass, then watched Buehrle and another trooper searching the weeds. They gave up in a few minutes.

Popplewell put himself in charge of impounding the pickup truck. When the tow truck arrived, Popplewell went inside the Ford only to put the gear in neutral and turn off the ignition. Then he locked the door and kept the key.

He returned to his car where the hitchhiker was handcuffed in the back seat. After reading him his rights, the sergeant sounded more friendly. "OK, what do you do for a living, Darl?"

"I travel around. Right now I live in Chicago, in the bus station.

"Did Mr. Eyler proposition you?"

"He just gave me a ride, man."

The tow truck with its flashing yellow lights led the caravan to the Lowell state police post. Eyler remained with his wrists handcuffed behind him in the back seat of Cothran's squad car. No words were spoken; there were just the sounds of the police radio.

When the tow driver unhitched Eyler's pickup, Popplewell went into the processing room and brought back tape marked "EVIDENCE EVIDENCE EVIDENCE" to seal the doors and the broken window. In addition he wrote in big letters on two sheets of paper "EVIDENCE DO NOT TOUCH" and taped one to each side of the truck.

The state police post was a modern, squat building in the flatlands. Beyond the wide window of the communication center, the station was nothing more than narrow corridors turning every which way to connect all the small offices. The wallpaper had the rough texture of a gunny sack.

Eyler was brought in through the large garage in the back. Usually officers continue working as a prisoner arrives, but now they formed a wall of eyes. Eyler kept his head down and walked with his submissive lope as Sergeant Cothran led him down the short hallway. On their left was the alcove the officers called their processing room, and on each side were the two holding cells. The time was 7:25 A.M.

In the processing room, Buehrle unlocked the handcuffs and routinely had Eyler remove his belt and empty his pockets into a tray. At the time no one thought twice about asking Eyler to remove his boots. They were taken just to avoid their being used as a weapon and the laces from becoming a noose.

"In you go," Cothran said as he held the cell door open.

The cell hardly seemed real. It was barely more than a closet, and the bars were light brown rather than prison gray. The door closed without a clank but with finality just the same.

SCHIPPERS: *By the way, at that time, in your own mind, had Mr. Eyler been arrested?*

COTHRAN: No, sir.

When Pavlakovic arrived, Popplewell briefed him on what the officers had and didn't have. They didn't have anything except the physical presence of a man and a truck and whatever grab bag of belongings might be inside.

"What about the other guy?" Pavlakovic asked about the drifter.

"That kid is scared," Popplewell said.

"Does he have a reason to be?"

"He looks like just a hitchhiker. He says Eyler offered him a hundred dollars to let him tie him up and have sex. We've got Eyler in the cells. Do you want to interview him?"

"Hell, I wouldn't know what to ask. We'll get those task force people to do it; they're the experts. At least we got him. Propositioning isn't much, but it's something."

Eyler was trying to stay calm. At first he was hoping everything would be over in a few minutes, but the state police seemed in no hurry. He sat on the cot in a six-by-nine-foot cell that had just the cot and an open toilet. He was having a stress headache and couldn't think about much else.

Pavlakovic looked him over and wasn't impressed. The tall, muscular prisoner, just starting to put on a little fat, looked more like a potential victim of the highway slayer than he did a killer. "What's going on?" Eyler asked. "Nobody wants to talk to me. Could you tell me why I'm here?"

"You're here because you are a suspect in a major felony case," Pavlakovic told him.

"Can I have a couple of aspirin?"

Pavlakovic thought it over for a moment before leaving the corridor. He conferred with First Sgt. Larry Beach as if this were a weighty matter. Now that the prime suspect was behind bars, the police were realizing that anything they did or said might have repercussions. Pavlakovic saw no harm in two aspirins, but Beach tried to consider all the possible consequences. There was neither a physician nor a psychiatrist in the station, and they couldn't be sure what emotional condition he might be in. The men decided it would be better to play it safe. The decision over two aspirin took considerably more time than the one determining to bring Eyler in.

Pavlakovic returned to the cell and said, "I'm sorry, Mr. Eyler, but we can't do it."

Larry went closer to the bars and asked, "Isn't anybody going to tell me why I'm here?"

The sergeant felt he had to do something to make up for not being able to give him the aspirins. "You are being held for questioning in some homosexual murders. Do you have any information about them?"

"I have no information to give you about anything, that I know of," he answered, stepping back a few inches. "What time is it?"

"Around 9:30."

"Can you tell me about when, you know, I'm going to be questioned, or whether you're going to let me go?"

"No. If I want I can hold you for pandering, prostitution. So just relax, all right?"

SCHIPPERS: *Did you feel at that point you were free to leave whenever you wanted to?*

EYLER: No.

SCHIPPERS: *Did anyone tell you you were not under arrest?*

EYLER: No one told me I was free to go.

Pavlakovic ground out his cigarette. Having Eyler in a cell was more than an anticlimax; there was an unsettled feeling. He pushed a few buttons on his desk phone and called the task force to ask that someone drive up to Lowell and talk to Eyler. Unfortunately this was the morning of the fall inspection, one of the two days of the year when even the paperclips had to be in order. That meant no one would be able to make it until noon.

The sergeant tried to do his other work, but that incomplete feeling was disturbing. He walked down to the small office of the post's legal officer, Jerry Ezell. The spit-and-polish black ex-Marine looked up from his papers and sat ramrod straight at his desk.

"Say, Jerry, do we have a problem holding Eyler?" the more experienced officer asked.

"Don't worry," Ezell answered as decisively as he said everything else. "Is it our fault the task force is taking its time? We are just holding him for them."

That seemed reasonable, and yet . . . "Well, I'm going to get what we can from the other guy," Pavlakovic said, bothered by the thought of how Eyler's detention might appear to people who were not involved.

He put another cigarette into his mouth and fed a fresh cassette into the post tape recorder as Trooper Buehrle brought in Darl Lee Hayward, who knew his way around bus stations from Ohio to Arkansas. By then no one considered him an accomplice, yet he looked considerably more scared than Eyler did. Pavlakovic took Hayward's statement and decided to keep him only as long as the task force wanted him around.

At 12:15 P.M. the state police helicopter lowered to the late summer stubble of a field outside the post. When the overhead blade stopped, Love, McPherson, and Newman climbed out of the bubble. During the ride from Indianapolis, McPherson and Newman had spoken excitedly about the custody as if they had just won a football game, but Love wasn't so sure the case was wrapped up. He expected that they would just look Eyler over to make the state police happy, since there didn't seem any reason for Eyler to be in the station.

Love shook hands with Pavlakovic outside the post and asked in his kindly voice, "Where's Larry at?"

"We got him in one of the cells."

"You what?"

"Where else were we going to put him?" Pavlakovic asked. "He'll be all right."

SCHIPPERS: *You were rather concerned that he was . . . being detained without being charged for an improper length of time and . . . without probable cause, right?*

LOVE: (Nods.)

The task force men let Hayward go after fifteen minutes of halfhearted questioning, for they saw daylight shining through the holes in the case. What did the state police expect them to do—keep poking around until they could find some justification for what happened this morning?

Pavlakovic had told Love that Ezell approved the detention, but he wanted to speak to the lawyer-policeman himself. "You're still going with solicitation, aren't you?" Love asked with something of a command in his voice. "You *are* going to charge him—failure to gawk, anything?"

Ezell didn't see the need for urgency. "I researched it," he said. "There is case law substantiating this."

Case law! My God, Love thought, you can't make a judgment on a major case based on an isolated ruling. The Indiana law on detention had recently been changed, and Love couldn't be sure how a judge would rule. Couldn't these men realize what was at stake? He looked at Ezell and Pavlakovic, standing at his side, and felt like choking someone.

Love's face reddened and he stomped out. Following him down the corridor McPherson said, "I thought you were going to hit him in the mouth."

"I thought about it," Love replied. "Damn hayseeds. Can't do a thing about them hardheaded . . . hayseeds."

The Lowell post officers caught up with them, and Love vented a little more of his feelings. "We didn't say stop him and impound his truck, we said notify us if you see

Eyler driving by," he snarled. "We wanted to pinpoint just where he'd been in case there was another body. We planned to start questioning Larry next week by just asking him to talk to us when he got off work at the liquor store."

Pavlakovic didn't want to justify himself to these men. All they were thinking about was their case. They didn't have to decide whether to let the prime suspect drive off with a man who seemed like all the victims.

Pavlakovic went over to the cells and told Eyler that men from the task force wanted to talk to him, and let it go at that.

It was around 1:30 P.M. when the sergeant led him into a carpeted office without windows and with filing cabinets against the wall. Love leaned against a desk, and McPherson pulled up a chair for Eyler. The suspect seemed calm but not relaxed.

Love wasn't looking forward to this questioning. He hadn't been prepared to interrogate anyone—no notes and no mindset for the work—but as long as Eyler had been kept six hours in a cell he might as well have something for the record so that Eyler would not accuse the police of harassment. Love knew that if McPherson were in charge, he would grill Eyler as hard as if he were caught killing someone. But Love was afraid that Eyler would go to court, since at this moment there wasn't a shred of evidence. What was left but to play Mr. Niceguy or, as he put it, to "kill him with kindness"? McPherson didn't say a word.

"We've been working very heavily since May of last year on some homicides involving the gay community in Indianapolis," Love began as the tape recorder wheels turned. "We found a guy out east of Indianapolis, and he had been tied up and killed. We got an anonymous phone call mentioning your name."

Love let that sink in. Eyler kept silent but fidgeted in his chair at the realization that a friend or lover thought he might be the killer. Eyler looked away, but McPherson kept watching him.

"I'm aware of the Harte situation, that boy," Love added and paused.

"Uh-huh," Eyler answered. Fred Harte was the Green-castle boy who was picked up, drugged, and left in a field. The boy hadn't been molested; there seemed no motive except to test the effectiveness of an overdose of the prescription drug.

"So you're a good suspect at this time, and we'd like to eliminate you. As of now, we've done a pretty extensive background on you."

Eyler said he hoped the police didn't talk to him at Andy's Liquors, where he worked Saturdays. "He's gonna think, regardless of—"

"I understand," Love told him.

"Regardless of what the outcome is, he's gonna say . . . well, you know . . . 'Larry, you know . . .' " Softly he added, "You have a stigma." That was spoken so low that the tape recorder didn't pick it up, and the officers later had to add it from their memories to complete the transcript.

"To be up-front—are you homosexual, Larry?" Love asked, sounding as casual as he could.

"OK," he replied, bristling. "I don't mind answering any of your questions pertaining to a homicide, or anything else."

"OK," Love said.

"I really don't want to answer anything personal about my preference. 'Cause that would just, you know. Anything pertaining to the homicides, feel free to ask."

Love mentioned the Roach and McNeive murders, and Eyler said he had read about them in the *Indianapolis Star*. The sergeant then asked, "Are you involved in any way with any homicides?"

"No."

"None whatsoever?" Love drew out the word.

"None."

"Would you have any objections if we process your truck?"

"If you what?"

"Process—like take fingerprints, tire samples, this sort of thing."

"Uh, no," Eyler said, easing back.

"No objection whatsoever? Would you have any—I'm trying to make this as pleasant as I can, Larry. Like I said, I'd like to eliminate you 100 percent, as far as being a suspect, because we've got other things to do. Would you have any objections next week sometime to taking a lie detector?"

"No."

"OK," Love said, and moved to another point. "Were you ever in the service, Larry?"

"No."

"Do you frequent—see, it's hard to get around asking about homosexuality because we are dealing from the gay community, understand? I'm not trying to . . . I don't care what you do."

"Yeah," Eyler said with a gesture of let's get on with it.

"I've been a cop for twenty-five years, so, and all of us have been here for a long time. I'm not trying to embarrass you, but we are dealing with the gay community. Do you ever frequent gay bars?"

"Well, if I answer that, then that's saying, you know . . . that's back to your original question. About my sexuality."

Love cast a glance at McPherson as if to say "I'm getting nowhere this way."

McPherson stepped forward with his Texas ranger confidence and in his country drawl asked, "Can I show you some pictures, Larry? These are the victims. The reason I also ask about this is, some of these victims that have been killed frequent gay bars."

"Yeah," Eyler said.

"If you're not involved in this, maybe you can help us. Look at these pictures and see if you know."

They were hoping for an overreaction, but Eyler just glanced at the photos and answered in his shambling way, "I have never seen any of these people. If I've seen them, then it's not knowingly seeing them. I mean, I've never spoken or met any of them personally.''

He handed the pictures back, and the questioning turned briefly to his home in Terre Haute and how long he had the truck. When McPherson asked if he had "done a situation like this before," offering a man a hundred dollars to tie him up, Eyler again begged off. "If I say that, then that's back to admitting that. It's back to your original question," about whether he was homosexual.

It was strange to see a man at ease when answering questions about multiple murders and yet unable to complete his sentences when referring to his sex life. His feelings were so deep, so rooted to every part of him, that he could not even lie about them.

Even when giving the officers permission to search his truck, he wasn't concerned about what might be regarded as evidence. His only objection was "I could have a letter from my lover or something."

"That's no problem," Love said. "We don't want that. Just anything that we feel may be pertinent to this investigation."

SCHIPPERS: *Did you feel that you had the right to refuse the consent for the search of your truck?*

EYLER: No.

They brought him a glass of water, and he agreed to take a lie detector test in Indianapolis. If the officers didn't know better, they would have taken him for being naive. There was no guile, sarcasm, or request for a lawyer as the questioning continued. Eyler said his memory failed him when they asked about a man he spent a recent night with in a hotel in East Plainfield after leaving the Our Place bar. The rope found in his truck this morning, he explained, was from when he helped his sister move to Indiana from Florida.

"Does blood bother you?" McPherson asked.

"As long as, uh, you know, I don't deal with it, it doesn't bother me. I mean, knowing it's there doesn't bother me. I don't like to look at it."

"If you had a lot of blood on your body, would that bother you."

"It would bother me, yeah. I would think there's germs or whatever, if it was somebody else's."

There was no point in trying to draw a reaction from Eyler. He was responding as if he were someone taken off the street. As they were wrapping up the questioning, Love asked, "I hate to be redundant, but you will definitely take a lie detector?"

"Yeah, I'll take a lie detector."

"It'll be on nothing but the murders. We don't have to ask about your sexual preference 'cause we already know what it is, so there's no sense dwelling on that point."

"OK."

McPherson put in, "We know and you know." He said it almost as a threat.

As Eyler was being led out of the room, the tape recorder was off and McPherson didn't have to be restrained. "I think you're a cold-blooded murderer, and we're going to do everything we can to prove that you did this!" Love gestured for him to leave Eyler alone, but McPherson was still poised for attack.

"That's ridiculous," Eyler said, fumbling for words. "Obviously you've decided I'm the person you're looking for, so what I say's not going to make any difference."

SCHIPPERS: *Did anyone suggest to you . . . that you could make a phone call?*

EYLER: No, never.

Eyler was taken to another room to wait out "the hour or so" that eventually would stretch out to three times as long as officers outside took potential evidence from his truck. Love, McPherson, and Newman were nearby—leaning against walls, sitting in chairs, and looking out the window—just waiting for any problems.

At midafternoon an officer intended to bring Eyler the belt, shoelaces, and other items taken before he was put into the holding cell that morning. To the state police they were just routine personal belongings, but they drew the interest of the task force men.

McPherson was particularly curious about the lug boots the trooper was holding. Eyler stepped back and let him come closer. To McPherson it didn't seem likely that a killer would be wearing the same boots a month after a murder but he wanted to see whether they matched the clear photos police in Lake County, Illinois, had taken of footprints beside the body of Ralph Calise. If these were the boots that made the impressions, they would have a starburst and waffle pattern on the bottom.

"You want to see them?" Pavlakovic asked, and he turned the boots over so that McPherson and Love could get a better look. Not only was the pattern the same, the tip of the soles had considerably more wear than the heels, just as the photos showed.

"Do you think they're them?" Love asked quietly.

"I can't be sure," Sam said, still holding the boots and moving them this way and that to see how they appeared in the changing light. There was nothing but memory to compare the boots to. The Illinois photos had not been distributed to the Indiana state police, and the ones given to the task force at the Crown Point meeting were back in Indianapolis.

"Well, we'll fix that," Pavlakovic said. He turned to Eyler and called out, "We're going to take these boots, too, Larry. OK?"

"OK," Eyler replied with a shrug.

A little while later one of the evidence technicians working on the truck reported that the hunting knife found in the back had blood on it. "If it's got human blood, it's mine," Eyler said. "I cut myself and went to County Hospital in Chicago. You can look it up."

For the task force officers, this afternoon kept dragging. They didn't know why they were there, and they hadn't eaten anything since breakfast. And watching Eyler sitting around and occasionally pacing by the windows in his stockinged feet, neither a prisoner nor free, was clawing at Love's sensibilities.

"Come on," he said to McPherson, "let's see if we can talk to these guys."

The task force officers and Pavlakovic went over the situation in one of the small, square offices. "You've got to charge him," Love insisted. "Soliciting for prostitution isn't much, but it's all we've got."

"Bond's one hundred dollars, and Eyler's got a one-hundred-dollar bill," Pavlakovic said. "What would be the point?"

"The point is, you don't have a leg to stand on for keeping him here."

"We're just waiting for them to get through with the truck," Pavlakovic said. "Who's going to be your witness? That Hayward kid is on his way to Arkansas; he's not going to come back here. And do you know how hard it's going to be to get a judge at this hour?" It was only about 3 P.M. "When noon comes around on a Friday, judges start thinking about going fishing. If we do get a judge, he's not going to like holding a hearing just so it looks better for another judge."

"Are you saying you're not going to charge him?"

"Hold on there," Pavlakovic answered. "Who knows what the officers back there will find in the truck. Just take it easy. No one's hurting him."

Love almost had to wrestle with his temper to keep from saying what he really felt. "Look, if you want I'll take him to court." He found himself looking into a stony face. No officer wants an intrusion by another jurisdiction.

McPherson opened the door and said, "Thanks a lot," not without sarcasm.

As they left the office Love said, "Sam, we better call Lake County and tell them to bring some of their evidence up here." Once they were out of earshot, he added, "You can't tell these police anything. It's like another country down here."

For Pavlakovic, charging Eyler just to charge him made little sense. Why go through all that paperwork and drive around looking for a judge still in his chambers when soliciting wouldn't hold up? Besides, Eyler was so cooperative he was actually being nice to police. Then came an unprofessional thought: the only thing Eyler had asked for was a couple of aspirins, and even then he didn't get them. He let police search his truck and keep his boots. Why not let him go and just forget about it?

No one told Love that Eyler wouldn't be charged, but he knew it and didn't press the matter. He was so disgusted with the state police by now that he didn't want to talk about it any more. Love almost hoped the troopers wouldn't find anything significant in the truck. Suppose they did, and a judge threw it out? That would mean that the evidence, which might have been found some other way, could never be used again.

SCHIPPERS: *The inconvenience to go out and get charges filed . . . so you figured, well, we'll just keep him here for another seven or eight hours and see what happens. Is that right?*

LOVE: (No response.)

After a couple of hours waiting for the Illinois police to arrive, the task force detectives decided to drive somewhere for dinner and asked Eyler if he wanted them to bring him back something. He said he wasn't hungry, even though he hadn't eaten all day and had just a glass of water during the interrogation. No one told him about the vending machines in the station.

As the detectives were going out the door, Eyler asked Sergeant Newman if he might be able to go home. "You can leave, but they're not quite done with your truck yet," Newman answered. Eight hours had passed since he was put in a cell and four hours since he consented to the truck search.

A few minutes after the detectives left, Eyler tentatively opened the back door near the holding cells, waiting for some trooper to shout "Hey, you can't do that!" But no one cared where he went, and he strolled to the garage section to watch evidence technicians James Bonfield and Matt Jaworski work on his truck.

Under the front seat the technicians, wearing plastic gloves, found: half a dozen liquor bottles, a large atlas, a muscleman magazine, two six-packs of beer, two pillows, plastic cups, a pocket cassette player, two newspapers, several latex gloves (one with a fingertip missing), a mallet, several T-shirts, a bag of shorts, hair brushes, two baseball bats, and a hammer.

In the truck bed was a small key for unlocking handcuffs.

After the truck was gone through, one of the technicians

inked a tire with a small roller, placed an eight-foot-long sheet of paper on the concrete, and pushed the truck forward slowly with a grunt, just far enough for the tread to leave an impression. Then he used the same procedure for another tire. Smudged paper had to be thrown away for another try.

Eyler watched them without saying a word.

In contrast to the take-your-time attitude of the Indiana police, Dan Colin in Waukegan, Illinois, could hardly wait to get down there.

He was working on another case when his pager went off. He called his office, and Smitty told him about the traffic arrest and said that Lamprich didn't see the urgency. This was Lamprich's quitting time and his birthday; his family was at a restaurant waiting for him. Smitty suggested that they go to the Lowell post by plane, but Lamprich—a big, strong Vietnam veteran—didn't want to be in any aircraft not piloted by someone trained on jumbo jets. Besides, as he saw it Eyler was just stopped for illegal parking.

"Dan, I want to talk to him," Smitty said. "How about you?"

Colin's answer was to drive through Friday evening expressway traffic at eighty-five miles an hour with Smitty sitting beside him, saying more than once, "I hope they don't let him go."

No one discussed the case as task force members had dinner at a restaurant near the Lowell post. This case was going down like a bad taste, all because someone said "Bring them in." When Love and his men returned to the post it was 6 P.M., and the Illinois police still hadn't arrived. Love felt that they would have been there by then if they really were interested.

Rather than make this day a total loss, Love decided to do one thing more since Eyler was so cooperative. The sergeant went alone to him and said, "We want to fingerprint and photograph you." He had forgotten to make this a question, but Eyler didn't seem to notice.

Love led him to the small processing room. A few

minutes later one of the evidence technicians came by and said, "The truck is finished."

"All right, Larry, you are free to go now," Love said. There was defeat in his tone.

"Can I make a phone call?" Eyler asked for the first time that day.

"Yeah, sure, no problem," Love answered and pointed to the free phone.

Eyler made his call and walked into the garage, then turned on the ignition of his truck. The Ford was a part of him; it was the home of his heart. Now someone had put white fingerprint powder all over the dashboard and seat.

After Eyler drove off, Sergeant Pavlakovic felt good about himself. His men might have saved a life, Darl Hayward's; and perhaps—who knows—if Eyler was the killer maybe he wouldn't try it again for a long time.

SCHIPPERS: *So this young man was never arrested, was he, in your mind?*

PAVLAKOVIC: Not technically, no.

SCHIPPERS: *No, just held in custody twelve hours?*

Shortly after 7 P.M. the Lake County officers arrived after shooting through traffic. Colin flashed his badge at the main desk, with Deputy Chief Smith behind him.

McPherson and Love stepped out of an office a little confused. "I thought you were coming by plane," Love said during the exchange of handshakes.

"We couldn't get one," Smitty answered.

"Well, we talked to Larry, and we have something very interesting to show you," said Love with a self-satisfied stroke on his stomach. "Did Sam tell you everything? We've got his boots, and they match your pictures, and a handcuff key, and a knife with blood on the handle. We practically made your case for you."

"Have you charged him with anything?" Colin asked.

"We didn't have enough evidence."

"How about soliciting? That's what Sam told us on the phone."

"Pavlakovic said it would be a waste of manpower."

Colin stopped in his tracks and looked at Love. "Wait

a minute," he said, "then why are we here? Where is Larry Eyler? We drove like hell to talk to him."

Love didn't say anything, leaving McPherson to tell them, "We had to let him go."

"Aw, shit," Colin said. "Do you people know all we had to do to get here to talk to him?"

"What could we do? We didn't have a cause."

"All right," Colin said, "where's the boots and tire tracks? I have the photos to show how they match."

Love led them to a table, and Colin picked up the boots, immediately recognizing the waffle pattern from the casts his department made. "Do you have casts made from the truck tires?"

"Casts?" Love asked. "You're kidding." He left the Illinois officers for a moment and came back with a rolled up piece of light brown paper.

"What's this?" Smitty muttered.

"This is our tire tracks," Love answered and showed them.

To Smitty it looked like something left over from a children's party, but Colin was less amused. "You had Eyler here from seven o'clock this morning, and you don't have casts? This is just butcher paper put together end to end. You can't tell where the marks begin and end. This won't hold up."

"I'm sorry," said Love in an unapologetic tone. Neither he nor McPherson liked the way the Illinois detectives were thinking they were so much better.

"OK, we aren't totally lost," Colin said. "Just bag the boots. The knife, let me see this, too." A thin red-brown trace was at the haft. "We'll take it."

"Sorry, we can't do that," McPherson said. "This is our evidence, and we have to check it out here. This is our jurisdiction. You have to get a court order."

"You're kidding," Smitty yelled. "This far for no Eyler, no charges, and no evidence? I'll be damned."

"OK," Colin said, knowing that losing control would be meaningless. "We will get that order, and we will be back. Soon."

Smitty still couldn't get over letting the prime suspect

in more than thirteen murders go as if he had done nothing more than steal from a cookie jar. The Illinois investigators returned to their car; there was nothing they could do.

Once they were in the parking lot, Smitty gave a hollow laugh. "I can't believe it," he said. "Anyone knows if you're going to hold someone that long you're going to lock their ass up."

But after the gut reaction phase they didn't have much to say. Colin broke the silence as their car passed the tiresome fields along the Interstate. "What's their law on probable cause?"

"The hell with that legal shit," Smitty growled. "Let's just get a subpoena so we can get our evidence."

"They think it's their evidence."

"The hell it is."

There was a championship mood in the Indianapolis headquarters of the task force that night. The officers who had stayed behind learned from a call from Love and McPherson that they seemed to have all the evidence they could hope for—if not for any of the Indiana murders, then at least for the Calise killing in Illinois. Someone walked over to the blackboard that had been haunting them for weeks, picked up the chalk, and across the description of the man wanted for the killing wrote, "THANK YOU, LARRY EYLER."

7

Dawn, Saturday, October 1, 1983
Terre Haute, Indiana

The pickup was in the driveway after last night's 120-mile drive due south from the Lowell post to Terre Haute. The police cars pulled up with little more than a whisper of tires, and none of the officers slammed a door shut as fog rolled in with the morning. Handsome Lt. Jerry Campbell, the head of the task force, gestured for Billy Bob Newman to follow him in covering the rear of the condominium, which overlooked a thicket. The fog silenced the birds that usually made noises like squeaky hinges from the copse and Deming Park across Keane Lane. The task force had known where Larry lived for weeks but never went inside. Newman and another officer, Jack Hanlon of the Putnam County sheriff's office, had kept an eye on Larry's pickup truck outside for three hours one day, but Larry never came for it.

These homes of the west end ignored the sprawl of the university town and tried to capture the feel of the country in just a few hundred feet. Each had a different color and design and faced its own direction despite the common walls. The town house of library science professor Robert David Little was a pinkish beige traditional home with a cross-gabled roof; the design cried out, Comfort! Respectability!

Love and McPherson weren't expecting trouble, but they were ready with guns drawn. As the men were returning to Indianapolis the night before, they had discussed the nagging thought that there was nothing to stop

Eyler from getting rid of everything incriminating now that he knew he was a suspect. A little after four in the morning they woke up a Vigo County judge for a search warrant. The men had only had a couple hours' sleep, but they were wide awake with the energy of a breaking case.

Sergeant Love rang the doorbell five times before Eyler opened the door with the puffy look of interrupted sleep. He was wearing just a T-shirt and white boxer shorts.

"Good morning, Larry," Love said. "Sorry we're here so early but we'd like to look over your home to see if there's anything that can help us. Any evidence. Is that all right with you?"

"Yeah, I guess so," he said sleepily. "But this isn't my house, you know."

Love and McPherson put their revolvers back into their holsters and walked into the three-bedroom condo. The rooms were as neat as if the owner were expecting photographers.

"Where do you stay?" McPherson asked.

"On the couch, and I have a room where I keep my things," he answered as he led the way. So this is the monster we've been chasing, McPherson thought.

The officers could have told which was Eyler's room at a glance—everything was a mess. Clothing was in boxes or piled in a corner, and there was an empty beer can on a desk that had some old copies of magazines and the Chicago newspaper *Gay Life*.

By then Campbell and Newman had come in the back door, and Dr. Little was coming down from his room with hurried steps as he belted his robe and put on his glasses, his gray hair a mess from sleep.

After the task force officers identified themselves to Little, McPherson asked, "Do you want to know why we're here?"

"No," the professor said.

The officers had some information about Little but not enough to have an idea how well he knew Eyler.

Love found a stack of phone bills in the kitchen and took from Eyler's room a few credit card bills, knowing that such routine pieces of paper can trace someone better than fingerprints.

Eyler simmered as he watched McPherson and Newman dump socks, shorts, pants, and personal items into a plastic bag. "You said you were looking for evidence. Since when are my shirts evidence?" he asked.

"Look, Larry," McPherson said. "We'll return all these things as soon as we have looked into them."

After driving back to the task force headquarters, the officers laid out what they had onto a table. "This is like a puzzle," Cathy Berner said after a little study of the bills. "Look at the phone calls in the middle of the night to Dr. Little's home."

Love came over and stroked his white beard as he studied the data. There seemed to be a pattern, yet he couldn't grasp it. "I want a calendar for the whole year and put in the times and locations for everything. Let's see if we can trace Larry from day to day."

Why would Eyler make so many calls at odd hours? Perhaps whenever tension built up in him he needed to talk to his mentor for emotional reassurance.

On Monday morning McPherson made a call from the task force headquarters in the west end of Indianapolis to Dan Colin in Waukegan and gave him a list of three phone numbers from Illinois to check. The first call was made from a pay phone in Cook County Hospital shortly before dawn on April 8. Colin didn't have to be reminded why this date was important. The call was made a few hours before Herrera was found in Lake County near Lake Forest, with his right hand cut off.

Following procedure, Illinois Bell spokeswoman Rosemary Thomas told Colin to get a subpoena. After he obtained one from across the way in the courthouse building, Colin drove with Detective Roy Lamprich to the phone company offices in downtown Chicago. Mrs. Thomas was ready for them and said that one of the numbers couldn't be traced because the phone had been disconnected. The call besides the one from Cook County Hospital was to the home of John Dobrovolskis at 3249 North Greenview, in Chicago's Mid-North Side.

"Who is he?" Lamprich asked his partner.

"Let's find out," Colin said.

The time was 4:30 in the afternoon, and the sky had turned gray with the threat of rain. As they drove down the narrow street in the folksy old neighborhood, they saw a silver-gray pickup truck. Colin said, "Guess who's here."

The one-time coachhouse was one of the dumpier buildings in an area dominated by aging small apartment buildings just off the corner of Lincoln and Belmont avenues. The two-story home was the color of pea soup and oddly narrow. The white door opened directly to the sidewalk, without any steps.

Lamprich called Assistant State's Attorney Raymond McKoski in Waukegan for authorization to impound the pickup truck. They hadn't expected to find it, but now they didn't want to let it go. As a courtesy, Colin called Chicago police for a backup in case there was any trouble over the pickup. All this would have been avoided if the Indiana police had made casts of the tires instead of treating them like fingerprints.

Before long, a brown unmarked Chicago police car stopped near the sheriff's auto. Colin told the two North Side detectives, "We've got a tow coming from Lincolnshire."

"From Lincolnshire?" one of the officers asked. "We'd just back up our own tow truck and take it."

"That's Chicago style," Colin said. "We do things by the book."

Just what went on in that slate-sided, aging home? That's what Colin wondered as he waited. At the time, police knew only that a John Dobrovolskis paid the bills, but this lead had brought them to the nerve center of the investigation. Dobrovolskis was a married man with a family, but he also spent many of his nights in gay bars and became Eyler's lover. This was no love triangle, just three people living compromised lives under the same roof.

John was trying to live the lie that he was heterosexual; his affection for his wife Sally went little further than gratitude for the illusion of "normalcy" she provided.

Sally knew that John was gay when she dated him, but she wanted a handsome husband even though it meant that her feelings for him would never be returned. As for Larry, when in their home he acted like no more than a drinking buddy of John's so that nothing would disrupt the family.

Despite her penchant for wrong decisions about her life, Sally was an intelligent young woman. She was working at an insurance company when she met John, and she found him to be conscientious and attentive. She had been carrying his baby for seven months when they were married in City Hall. Sally knew that their relationship had built-in problems, but she explained, "John makes me do things completely out of character."

John could never relax. He was always watching people, waiting for them to make mistakes that he could set right or wondering what they might be thinking about him. For John, living up to his own standards of a father and a man was all that truly mattered. Whatever jobs he worked were immaterial to him.

Also in the family were Sally's son from her first marriage and three foster children. Larry paid a third of the rent and fit in as if he were a member of the family. He would drive Sally's mother to the store because she had trouble walking, and he often played ball with the children when they returned from school. Usually he slept late unless he had a house painting job. Larry and John would make appearances at one gay bar after another on weeknights, and on weekends Larry still made the long drive to work at a liquor store in Greencastle.

When the couple took on the twin sons and the daughter of Sally's cousin as foster children, Sally had to quit her job to care for them and for her own two children. John was a self-driven man who wanted no sign of weakness to show, and his brittleness kept him from keeping a job. For a while he was a security guard at the Marshall Field's store in the Loop. Later he had a job in a hardware store but quit. His temper and insistence that things go his own way worked against him. Sally once found her husband cleaning the bathroom tiles with a toothbrush.

Larry saw no threat in Sally's lopsided love for her husband, but it was different with the attention that John received at the Halsted and Clark street bars. He once modeled bikini shorts and was "Mr. Broadway" in a pageant. His flamboyance in the bars was in sharp contrast to his stark conservatism at home. Most of the attention he received at the bars was just friendliness, but Larry seldom took it that way. He seemed to need jealousy.

Most of the time everything was fine in the rented house on Greenwood Avenue. Larry provided the easy humor and vulnerability lacking in his lover, but once or twice a month the two men would quarrel in a volcanic interlocking that knew no logic. Larry was possessive but refused to act that way, behaving at times like a recalcitrant eight-year-old. John would tell Larry to do something around the house, and Larry would answer, "Yeah, in a minute." This would lead to shouts and threats, and sometimes John would strike Larry. But no matter what, Larry never fought back. He prided himself on controlling his temper. Usually he would go outside to his truck and sulk. When he was really angry he would leave the house and spitefully not say where he was going. Then he would return a few days later as if nothing had happened.

At the time the police arrived at this house, Eyler was watching "Scarecrow and Mrs. King" with Sally and the children. Her mother, Rose Marie Kyle, and some neighbors were with them. The tow truck finally arrived form the north suburbs, and the problem was to bring Eyler out of the house without a warrant.

Colin liked things simple. He told the driver to turn on his flashing lights to see if Eyler would step outside. A moment later the white door opened, and Eyler headed for the tow driver, saying, "What are you doing to my truck?"

Colin identified himself and watched Eyler's reaction; it was as if someone had poured ice water down his spine.

"We want to take your truck to Waukegan, if that's all right with you," Colin said.

"Look, I've already gone through this in Indiana. I don't understand why I have to go through it again."

"We were in Indiana too. We just missed you the other day. The ink impressions they took of the tires are not suitable. We need the actual tires to make comparison plaster casts from."

"Well, I really don't want you to take my truck to . . . Why Waukegan?"

"Look, Larry," Colin said, "we could have been assholes about this and just jerked your truck up on this flatbed, and that might have messed up your transmission. Instead we sent an officer to the corner tavern to get someone to move his car, and we want your keys so we won't have to hurt your truck."

Sally came outside and asked what was going on.

The plain woman kept her reddish blond hair pulled back and was starting to become plump. Her deep-set blue eyes gave her a sad, self-conscious look. Eyler told her not to worry and to go inside for his keys. Then he asked Colin again, "What's in Waukegan?"

"That's where Lake County sheriff's police headquarters is. We're investigating the murder of Ralph Calise. We're up north about an hour away. We want to talk to you, too, but not here."

"Are you guys going to lock me up in a cell like they did in Indiana?"

Colin almost smiled. Eyler seemed to have no knowledge of police practices. "No, Larry, we just want to talk to you. It's hard to talk to you in the street, do you mind going with us to Area 6?" That was the nearest detective headquarters.

Dobrovolskis then came walking down the street. Eyler's lover was a slender man with brownish-yellow hair and a full mustache. He was also self-confident to the point of being arrogant, and he asked in a clipped tone what the problem was.

"Something about my tires," Eyler told him. "Go ahead," he said to Colin, "take it; that's what you want."

John asked, "Do you want me to call a lawyer?"

"No, I can handle this," Larry said.

As the suburban officers helped load the pickup truck onto the flatbed trailer, Eyler went in the Chicago police car to the station at Belmont and Western. Colin returned to Dobrovolskis in front of the house and asked if he and Eyler were lovers.

"No," Dobrovolskis answered sharply.

"Well, how long has he lived with you?"

Dobrovolskis replied with a shrug and let the officers into his home.

"Who are these people?" asked Mrs. Kyle, a short, obese woman whose small mouth was almost hidden by her cheeks.

"Never mind, they're the police."

"Why would the police come all the way here because Larry sold some liquor to a kid?" Mrs. Kyle asked. Eyler told the family over the weekend that the Indiana police had stopped him because he didn't check the age of a teenager who had bought alcohol at the liquor store in Greencastle. "Anybody can buy a tin badge," Sally's mother said contemptuously as the officers passed by her. Police get used to not having universal admiration.

Dobrovolskis led them to Eyler's second-floor room and turned on the light in the master bedroom shared by Larry, John, and Sally. He pointed to a box on the floor next to the king-size bed. John told the children to stay in their room for awhile, and closed the door. He turned on the light and pointed to a box on the floor.

"Is this all?" Lamprich asked.

Dobrovolskis showed them some shirts in the closet and added, "Larry had two suitcases of things, but they were stolen."

"Do you know for a fact that they were stolen?" asked Colin.

"That's what he told me."

Many of the corpses were missing shirts and wallets: those things had to be somewhere. Maybe in the two suitcases, burned or buried or thrown into some dumpster.

Not needing a warrant because he was receiving permission to search, Colin put the box on the bed and went through it with Lamprich. During the conversation, Dobrovolskis had an almost parental worry about Eyler and asked to go to the Area 6 station to be with him. Sally changed to accompany her husband, and in a few minutes the detectives drove them to the undistinguished modern police building near the ugly rising of an overpass.

The Lake County detectives were at the station just long enough to persuade Eyler to accompany them to Waukegan, where their case files were. Dobrovolskis spent some time in the parking lot trying to persuade Chicago police to take him to Lake County, even though Sally wanted to return home.

The suburban officers stopped for hamburgers and Cokes at a North Side drive-through Burger King with Eyler before reaching Waukegan shortly before 10 P.M. They led the suspect through an underground garage to an elevator and took him the back way to the conference room in the sheriff's office. Half a dozen chairs were around a table with oak veneer, and there were a couple of filing cabinets along the walls. A phone was on one of the metal cabinets.

The detectives relaxed for what could be several hours of questioning. Eyler sat up straight as Colin lit his pipe.

"I want to ask you some personal things," he began. "I want to get to know you better. Some questions I am going to ask are very personal, I know, but I have to ask them. Larry, how long have you been gay?"

Eyler became uneasy and sighed. He turned away, looking out the window and at the occasional cars passing along Washington Street. "I don't know," he said.

"Look, Larry, I don't want to go into that a lot. Lots of people are gay, good people; it doesn't bother us. I'm just asking."

"I feel uneasy talking to you about my sexual preferences, OK?" He turned his eyes toward Lamprich as if hoping to find someone more sympathetic. He was wrong.

"I understand," Colin said, "but you do have a lover, and isn't that John?"

"Yes, it is."

"Are you into bondage?"

"Yes, I am."

"Do you like to be tied up, Larry, or do you like to tie up or handcuff the other person and then suck them off, and then have them tell you how it was good? You like that stuff?''

"You sure do get personal," Eyler said and turned away in his chair.

"Well?"

"I prefer rope or handcuffs on the other person, but I like them to tell me it wasn't good enough so I can suck them off again."

Lamprich cleared his throat and sat back uneasily. This wasn't his kind of investigation.

"Do you and John ever get into big physical fights? You know what I mean."

"Yes. John hit me so hard that I had to get stitches. That was just once."

"What was that fight about?" Colin asked.

"Just things."

"You're bigger than he is. Do you hit him back?"

"What good would it do?" Eyler said.

"What happens after a fight?"

"John tells me to go away and I do, and I don't tell him where I'm going."

"On September thirtieth Chicago police saw you pick up a guy on Clark Street, but you let him off. If John is now your lover, what were you going to do with that guy?"

"I prefer not to talk about it because I don't want John to find out. I don't want you telling him that I was cheating on him. Nothing happened, anyway."

"OK, Larry, no problem. Now let me refresh your memory to a month earlier: Tuesday, August thirtieth, and Wednesday morning, August thirty-first. Do you remember where you were and what you were doing at that time?" That was when Ralph Calise had been murdered.

"I can't remember specifically what I was doing, but if it was a Tuesday night or in the middle of the week, I was probably home with John and Sally."

Colin stopped for a rest, and Lamprich took over. "Larry, you had a red Chevy pickup truck a couple of months ago. You sold it. Do you know who you sold it to?" Some of the murders might have been committed while Eyler was driving the Chevy, and perhaps there was something of interest inside that escaped his attention.

"I'm not familiar with the Chicago area. Someone in the suburbs. John would know better than I do. John remembers everything."

"Larry, that knife Indiana police took from your new pickup truck has what we believe to be blood on it. Where would that blood come from?"

"It's my knife; I don't remember where I got it. If that is blood, I have no idea how it got there or who used my knife." He had told the Indiana police he had cut himself with the knife.

There was a knock on the door, and a deputy whispered that a man named John was calling from Chicago and "says it's urgent." Lamprich told the deputy "In a moment" and soon left the room so that the questioning might continue without distractions.

Colin had Eyler look over the photos of the tire tracks and footprints and told him they matched the evidence Indiana police seized. "They are not my footprints, and they are not my tire tracks; I wasn't there. I don't know how they were found at the scene."

"Well, then, whose are they? Do you lend your truck and your shoes to people?" Colin asked.

"On occasion I lend my truck to John, but I never lend out my shoes."

"Look, Larry," Colin said, "John wants to come up here, so I'll call Area 6 and ask them to pick him up, all right?"

Eyler didn't say anything, and Colin made the call from the phone on the filing cabinet. Then he began a slow walking around the room. "Larry," he resumed, "how does Sally feel about you living there and being John's lover, all in the same house?"

"I really don't want to get into my private life. She accepts it, OK?"

"I just wanted to know, Larry. Don't get angry; I'm just asking." He put his pipe down and showed Eyler a black-and-white photo of Ralph Calise. "Did you ever see this guy? Maybe around Clark and Foster?"

"No, I really can't tell if I have."

"I have some more photos to show you." He laid before Eyler the color Polaroids of Calise's body. "Go ahead, pick them up, Larry. Look at them. Look at the blood coming out. He was stabbed seventeen times." With the stem of his pipe, he pointed to the wounds. "Look at this one here, to his back, and this one. Look, we have them numbered." His voice was slightly rising. "Look where the knife entered here, and here."

The normally quiet detective tossed the photos in front of Eyler and seemed to be challenging him now. Colin had been living this case for weeks and the only motive that made any sense to him was that Larry killed men as stand-ins for John. Now he decided to throw his idea at the suspect.

"Larry, we know something about you," Colin said, "you'd get into a fight with John and pick someone else and stab him because you think it's John."

Colin pointed his finger. Eyler winced but said nothing. He pointed his finger at him and jabbed him in the ribs. "You took that knife, and you stabbed him *here*."

Eyler winced, not at the treatment but at the change in Colin's tone.

"You were in such a state of frenzy, once you got this man out there you took that knife and stabbed him *here*, then you stabbed him *here*."

"Don't yell at me," Eyler said without changing his inflection. "Don't point your finger at me, and don't raise your voice at me."

Colin turned and looked blankly out the window at the two o'clock darkness. "We're all tired, Larry. Maybe we should take a break." He should have known better than to try to provoke Eyler. Eyler was the kind of man who lets anger build up and releases it at some other time and, perhaps, at some other person.

Colin went to Smitty's room and poured a cup of coffee from a pot on a filing cabinet. Smitty, leaning back, was ready to sit this night out for as long as it took. He had the knack for looking relaxed in any position.

"How's it going?" Smitty asked.

"He's a tough one. No expression. I showed him the pictures, and it's like he saw the body for the first time."

Two Chicago detectives arrived with John Dobrovolskis and headed back for the North Side. The young man made no demands and was willing to talk to the sheriff's detectives, but his self-consciousness took some getting used to. When Colin took him to a separate room and asked how long he had known Eyler, Dobrovolskis gave the exact date and time of night they met.

"Where were you on Tuesday, August thirty-first, and with whom?"

John said he and Larry were in the home on Greenview with a mutual friend, James Williams, a computer consultant. They left at 11 P.M. to go to the Loading Dock, one of the Halsted Street gay bars, and were home within an hour. Williams stayed with them and went home to Indianapolis after Labor Day.

Lamprich had been listening to the questioning and broke in. "Can we ask you about your sexual preferences in participating in acts of bondage with Larry?"

"I'm not into bondage. Larry and I never perform acts of bondage."

Colin asked, "How does Sally feel about you and Larry being lovers?"

"She tolerates the relationship. She's understanding. Tell me now, why is Larry a suspect in these murders?"

Colin outlined what the Lake County department had and about the twelve murders in Indiana and how many of the bodies lined Eyler's route when he went to Indianapolis or Chicago.

Dobrovolskis looked almost without expression at the detectives and said, "If at all possible, I want to talk to Larry about this."

While Colin was talking to Dobrovolskis, deputies Charles Fagan and Michael Blazincic took over for him in the sheriff's police conference room. "I am not involved in any homicides," Eyler told them. "If I was, would I let you take my truck?"

"Can you tell us about you and John?" Fagan asked.

"I am very, very, very much in love with John."

"Have you ever cheated on John?"

"Sometimes we would argue and I would go to gay bars and pick up a stranger. You know, spend a night with him."

"Did you feel guilty?"

"Not during, but after. You won't tell John, will you?"

"You and John—that has nothing to do with us," Fagan answered. "Larry, that knife from your truck—where did you get it?"

Blazincic, who had been standing off to the side, now walked over to the table before there was an answer and said, "Larry, we know how you stabbed Mark Henry. Do you pick up a lot of hitchhikers? Why, Larry? What happens to them?"

Eyler looked out the window. He rolled a tuft of hair between his fingers, a sign that he was becoming nervous.

"You know, Larry," Blazincic said, "if you got problems we can send you to a doctor and make you better."

"I'm fine," Eyler told him softly. "This is ridiculous. I want a lawyer."

"Now? It's 3:30—four o'clock," Blazincic said.

Fagan went to the filing cabinet and handed Eyler a Waukegan–North Chicago phone book opened to the lawyer's section. "Go ahead, see if you can get somebody to come out this time of morning."

"I don't know anybody from that book."

Fagan went to the cabinet and returned with a thick Chicago yellow pages directory while saying, "I'm a police officer. I can't refer you to an attorney."

"I just want to get out of here."

"Did anyone tell you you couldn't?" Fagan asked. "There's the door, no one will stop you."

"I just want to talk to John."

"Don't worry, you'll see him all you want. They're just not done talking to him yet."

During the questioning, Sheriff Mickey Babcox was standing in the hallway to be of help if there were any questions but mainly to snoop around on his own. Babcox was a tall, heavy man with a rumpled face and a habit of wearing glasses where they look as if they're about to slip off his nose. He was fifty-five now, with a double chin and a forehead that could wrinkle all the way to the fringe of hair between his ears.

Colin briefed the sheriff and Babcox went into the conference room with three deputies. He eased himself into a chair and tried to sound understanding but his penetrating voice worked against him. "Larry," he said, "I really think it would be best if you cooperate and confess to the murders. We know you did them. Until you do there isn't much I can do for you. But if you want to cooperate, I'll see to it that you are protected."

"I didn't do them," Eyler said. They blinked at each other, and Babcox gave up with a shake of his heavy jowls and a gesture of dismissal from his cigarette-yellowed hands.

Sheriff Babcox conferred with Colin and Lamprich, and they agreed to let Dobrovolskis join his lover so everyone could go home. Eyler had undergone hours of questioning without so much as changing his tone. "Aw hell," Smitty said, "he'll be back." With a serial killer, there is always another victim.

Lamprich called his wife to say he would soon be on his way. The time was 4:30 A.M. Then he asked around, "What should we do about Larry—drive him home?"

"Hell no," Colin answered, his irritation showing through his tone. He had been up for nearly twenty-four hours, only to see the leads come to nothing. "There's a 5 A.M. train to Chicago; put him and his lover on it."

A few minutes later Colin sat on the edge of a desk in front of the sheriff's office as Eyler and Dobrovolskis waited for officers to pick them up. "Hey, Larry," he called out. When Eyler turned, the detective said, "You caused us to stay up late tonight, and you're going to make us do a lot of footwork. You asked me to stop yelling at you; I did. You asked me to stop poking you; I did. But the next time, I'm not going to be so nice."

Colin's cold stare said even more. It warned "I'm going to get you, Larry; if it takes three weeks or three months, I'm going to get you."

Just a few hours later that October 4, two mushroom

hunters in Petrified Springs Park in Kenosha County, Wisconsin, came across a large garbage bag not far from Highway 31. Inside was a human torso. The head, arms, and legs had been severed with a fine-toothed blade, such as a hacksaw. Stranger yet was the fact that the body was completely drained of blood. The rest of the body was never found.

Normally there would be no way of identifying such a victim, but the pathologist doing the autopsy notified police that the young man had undergone a number of operations when he was a boy to correct a concave chest, a spinal defect. A comparison of X rays showed that the victim was eighteen-year-old Eric Hansen from the town of St. Francis, Wisconsin. He had a reputation of doing anything for money and was last seen around September 27 at the intersection of Chicago and Buffalo in Milwaukee's gay bar area.

When sheriff's police Lt. Lee Copen looked over the autopsy photos, a chilling thought ran through him: "Someone is learning to cut up a body." He contacted police in neighboring Lake County, Illinois, for information about the serial murder suspect they were investigating even though the torso did not have the abdominal mutilation or torture marks of the others. Colin sent him a packet including Eyler's photo.

A few men in the area said Eyler "looked familiar," but so did the photos of some others they were shown. Officially the case was still open, but Copen had no doubt who the killer was. Hansen was the fourteenth victim placed on the list.

8

=

Tuesday, October 4, 1983
Chicago—North Side

Not much happens for a lawyer far from downtown. Kenneth Ditkowsky sat behind a pair of bronzed baby shoes and a small American flag in a holder, waiting for business. His elderly secretary was handling checks and other mail, and near her two love seats served as the waiting room for anyone who might drop by. At last a client walked through the door off Touhy Avenue.

"Can I help you?" Ditkowsky asked. No answer. "Is it a traffic ticket or something?"

"Murder," Eyler answered. The word came out almost as a whisper. To fill the silence that followed, he added, "They think I did a lot of murders."

Ditkowsky offered a chair and needed to sit down himself as well. The lawyer considered himself a windmill fighter but never imagined a case like this would fall into his lap. He straightened his suit jacket over his silk vest and wondered for a moment just how to phrase what he was about to say. "I'm not a criminal lawyer, you understand. You really might want someone else. How many murders?"

"Some in Indiana and Illinois."

"You're here, so you haven't been charged." Ditkowsky was trying to approach the situation. "How do you know you're a suspect?"

"The police told me. They stopped my truck, and they took some things of mine. Last night some guy poked me, and they didn't let me go until four in the morning."

Ditkowsky thought this might be his kind of case after all. "How did you hear my name?"

"A friend of mine, his father got caught buying cigarettes in Indiana and bringing them here. He says you did a nice job for him. The police have been harassing me. They took my things in Terre Haute, and I didn't see a warrant, and they poked me in the ribs in Waukegan—things like that."

For a lawyer in his early forties, Ditkowsky had an almost adolescent bundle of undirected energy and became excited at the possibilities. "Your name, please?"

"Larry Eyler," the client said, and he spelled out his last name.

"Larry, were you beaten, threatened?"

"Oh, the cops were real nice to me, but I don't think they should be doing what they did and following me around wherever I go. They just want to pin these things on someone. Can you stop them?"

Ditkowsky was still uncertain whether to take the case, but he was already seeing how a defense could be mounted on questions of civil liberties. What was intriguing for him was that Eyler didn't say "defend me"; he said "stop them."

The lawyer took a breath and started in. "Look, Larry, I'm going to think this over for a while, all right? In the meantime I want you to give me a list of people and their phone numbers."

"Like references?"

"Just like references, like you're applying for a job. If you can remember the names of the officers who bothered you, put those down too. Then we'll discuss whether you want me or someone who handles felony cases."

After Eyler left, Ditkowsky made a number of calls to people on Eyler's list. Everyone assured him that his client was a gentle man, even timid. The lawyer wasn't familiar with the case, but two aspects troubled him. One was that Eyler was a suspect because someone turned his name over to police, no doubt a former lover or rival. That meant the case might be based on spite. The other disturbing aspect was that Eyler's name appeared to be put down for every unsolved murder of a young man in four states, as if police wanted to clear their books.

The lawyer spent the rest of that Tuesday verifying, between other cases, what Eyler had told him of the Lowell stop, the evidence raid on his home in Terre Haute, the seizure of his truck in Chicago, and his questioning in Waukegan.

On Wednesday he called Lake County Deputy Chief Investigator Willie Smith and let his anger show. Ditkowsky pinned down the usually easy-going Smitty and got him to admit that detectives didn't have enough evidence to charge Eyler. The lawyer demanded that the truck be returned, and Smitty promised to have it ready by four o'clock that afternoon. But soon after hanging up, Smitty called Assistant State's Attorney Ray McKoski and asked for a search warrant that would let police hold the truck for as long as they wanted to.

When Ditkowsky called about the truck that afternoon, Smitty put on an apologetic tone and claimed he knew how the lawyer felt but that there was nothing he could do. "I'd like to help, but the state's attorney wants it."

Detective Jim Rowley kept going in and out of the office that day. His job was to gather all the evidence to be brought to the FBI in Washington, D.C. From the evidence section of the sheriff's department he picked up a sample of Calise's hair in a plastic bag. Next he went across the street to the tiny morgue and grabbed a styrofoam cooler containing a plastic bottle of blood drawn from Calise's heart, packed in ice. Then the heavyset detective drove to the Northern Illinois Police Crime Laboratory on the second floor of the police station in the North Shore suburb of Highland Park. The technicians still had the casts of bootprints and tire tracks Smitty had made with dental plaster.

The next morning, the evidence bodyguard went with Colin and Lamprich to serve police in Indiana with a subpoena for 36 items removed from the truck. They included a Jewel-Osco bag with clothesline; debris vacuumed from the floorboard; several rubber gloves; rope; a hunting knife; three hairbrushes; and underwear of several sizes.

There were also a handcuff key, the lug boots, cigarette butts of various brands, nine matchbooks, and just plain junk.

Sgt. Frank Love and a couple of the Indiana officers accompanied them to the airport. For the Illinois detectives this was a wasted morning because the long trip would not have been necessary if their Indiana counterparts had handed over the evidence on their own. Tempers were smoldering.

"You're not going through with that," an airport security guard said at the sight of Rowley holding a large cardboard box and a styrofoam container. "That goes through X ray," she said.

Love held up his pocket badge. "This man is with the Lake County, Illinois, sheriff's police, and he's on his way to the FBI lab. The FBI has advised him not to expose this blood to X rays."

"What else do you have—anything metal?"

"A knife," Rowley told her.

"I'm sorry, but you will have to ship the knife. It can't go by air."

Love disputed this with her, she called her supervisor, and the officers had to repeat everything—but this time not so politely.

"Look," Love told the supervisor, "this is evidence in a murder case—a multiple murder case. They don't kill people with ice cream cones. If you screw up this evidence, you will have to go to court and tell why and how."

The Illinois detectives joined the task force men in badge flashing, and finally the supervisor let them through. "Dumb fucks," Love muttered as he walked away.

After seeing Rowley off, the Illinois detectives and two members of the task force left the airport and headed for the Antelope Club, one of the gay hangouts in Indianapolis. They had arranged a meeting there with James Williams, Eyler and Dobrovolskis' mutual friend, to keep their trip to Indiana from being entirely wasted. James Williams was waiting for them. It was still around noon, and there wasn't much action. A bartender was drying glasses with a towel and pretending not to pay attention to the detectives.

Williams was jumpy and needed to be assured that his answering questions about homosexuality would not affect his job with the Indiana Department of Public Instruction. He said he had known Eyler for ten years and up to four years before had lived with him in Terre Haute. Williams described him as a laid-back guy who wouldn't fight back if he got into a quarrel. He told how John Dobrovolskis had hit Eyler once the previous summer, sending him to a hospital with a cut lip.

"Then what happened?"

"Nothing. Nothing ever does. Larry keeps coming back."

Williams added that Eyler didn't take drugs except for an occasional sleeping pill. He also described Eyler's close relationship with his mother, "a tremendous person," and his sister, Theresa Moell. She had helped get him his job at Andy's Liquors, where she worked.

The last time he saw Eyler, Williams said, was the week around Labor Day. Williams arrived in Chicago on August 29, a Monday, and stayed with Eyler and Dobrovolskis until Sunday, September 4. Calise was murdered on the night of August 30 or early the next day.

Williams said that when he was in Chicago the three men would stay out late at gay bars, sleep late, drink a lot, and play games.

"Games?" Lamprich asked.

"You know, parlor games. The night I got to Chicago, we played Boggle."

Williams said Eyler was with them on and off that weekend, and he couldn't be sure where Eyler was late Tuesday.

In Washington, D.C., that afternoon, Rowley handed the box of evidence and the container of blood to technicians at the FBI laboratory and took a return flight. He was met at O'Hare Airport at 9 P.M. by sheriff's police Captain Donaldson, who told him that his long day wasn't over yet. The warrant had come down for Eyler's truck, and they needed to hand it to Eyler.

They reached the house on Greenview Avenue half an hour later. When Eyler came to the door the detectives handed him the warrant, and Eyler read it over with the slowness of someone unfamiliar with legal documents. "Does this mean I can't ever have my truck back?" he asked.

"You'll have to contact Chief Smith at the Lake County sheriff's office tomorrow, sir," Rowley answered.

There were no shouts or threats; the young man just took the paper back inside with him. Naive, agreeable; that was what Rowley liked about Eyler.

Driving back to the northern suburbs, Rowley and Captain Donaldson decided to take a look at the truck. It was up on blocks in the garage of Ernie's Towing in Half Day, a town that is hardly more than a couple of restaurants and bars at a crossroads.

"The guy must live in this thing," Donaldson said.

Rowley, the evidence expert, couldn't believe what the Indiana police had overlooked. Didn't those rural officers realize that something as small as a hair could be critical evidence? A receipt for the tires, a loan agreement from a bank, a business card from a gymnasium, oil company credit card statements, slips of paper with names scrawled on them, a drug store receipt, and a phone bill. And two pillows with reddish-brown stains on them.

Larry stepped out of the sunlight that Friday and into St. Alphonsus Church near Dobrovolskis' home. He had been there several times besides Sunday masses, but usually the church was locked during the day. He normally didn't assert himself but asked the pastor to keep it open for anyone needing solace. It didn't work.

After Mass the following Sunday, middle-aged Father James Ryan came up to the young man and asked quietly, "Is there something wrong?" Larry looked up at him, surprised at the directness. The cleric explained that he recognized him as the man who stood outside a few days before, annoyed that the church was locking him out.

"I'm being investigated," Larry replied.

The priest took him to a room in the rectory and Larry told him that the police were hounding him and he didn't know what to do about it. The priest believed every word of it, and Larry made another friend.

We cannot know what Larry felt about his action, but for him there seems to have been no hypocrisy in keeping ties to the church. All his adult life he tried to be good; everyone said that. Perhaps he was hoping his sexual urges and unpredictable violence could be prayed away.

Deputy Chief Willie Smith was feeling the gnawing frustration of a stalled investigation. A boxload of evidence is worthless without something decisive. So when Gera-Lind Kolarik of WLS-TV called for an update, he gave her enough to have a general understanding of where the investigation stood at that moment: there was a possible suspect named Larry, and on September 30 Indiana police pulled over his pickup truck and found rope and a knife with what appeared to be human blood.

"Does anyone else have this story yet?" she asked.

"Nope, you're the first."

"Smitty, give me his name and address," she said excitedly.

"You know I can't do that, Ger. We had to let him go. But his lawyer called to get his truck back; maybe he'll talk to you."

She wrote down Ditkowsky's number and called it as soon as she hung up. Kolarik didn't really think she would get anywhere; lawyers are notorious for shielding their clients from reporters. A secretary put her on to Ditkowsky.

"Look, if your client's innocent, why not let us do a silhouette interview with him," she said. "We can keep your client's name out of it."

Ditkowsky paused and said, "I will talk to Larry, and I'll give you an exclusive . . ."

"Now, you mean?" she asked, almost fumbling with her pen.

"We are filing a federal lawsuit tomorrow against the Lake County sheriff and the Indiana state police for harassing my client."

What? Kolarik wondered. A suspect in multiple murders suing police even before he is charged? That was unheard of.

"Hold on, will you?" the lawyer asked.

She ignored the phones ringing on the assignment desk.

"Hello," came another voice, a softer tone.

"Hello, who is this? This is Gera-Lind Kol—"

"This is Larry Eyler. What do you want to know?"

For the second time in ten minutes Kolarik was stunned. She had no idea Ditkowsky's client had been sitting across from him. She was actually talking to a serial murder suspect. She spoke slowly as she had trained herself to do in important circumstances. "I heard how the cops are harassing you and that they took your truck and all. Look, we can do a silhouette interview with you. It's like your shadow and nobody sees your face. Otherwise, it'll just be the cops' side, not yours. What do you say?"

"Well, silhouette . . ."

"We can do it today, before Mr. Ditkowsky files your suit."

"OK."

Kolarik hung up and threw her pen in the air as a gesture of triumph. Reporters around her smirked without knowing what she had. She had been excited but didn't want it to show over the phone. She clapped her hands and ran into the newsroom.

"Dan," she told the producer, "I have a real ballbuster for you today. No, I mean it. Come on, listen."

Listen he did—resting his face on the springboard of an index finger. When she walked back toward her assignment desk, she was grinning.

At 6 P.M. the nearly bald Sheriff Babcox sat in front of a television set in the detective office in downtown Waukegan. He and Smitty watched glumly as Eyler's profile came on and they heard his quiet voice accuse police of persecuting him. Jay Levine's interview with him had been edited down to a few seconds, but it was enough to make him seem innocent if only for the audacity of accusing his accusers. What these officers knew, and most listeners didn't, was that serial killers always sound and look innocent. That's how they get away with murder.

Eyler appeared on the screen as a phantom: the vague form of a man without cunning. The shadow spoke: "If I was going to murder someone I certainly wouldn't just leave things back there," he said, referring to his truck. "I certainly would be smart enough not to let them sit there like that. It doesn't take too much of a genius to know if you did kill somebody you wouldn't have a knife with blood on it just sitting in the back of your truck for the police department to take you away."

That was it. The director called for punching up the camera aimed at the news deck, and the viewers were hit with more fires and politics and faraway unrest.

Because of the homosexual nature of the murders, the news media never bothered to tag the killer with an official-sounding nickname, such as "The Hillside Strangler," "Son of Sam," or "The Toolbox Killer." The newspapers and rival stations reversed their lack of interest once the interview aired and Ditkowsky announced on WLS-TV his intention to sue the police. Six television crews and three newspaper photographers staked out the three entrances to the Dirksen Federal Building.

For Ditkowsky, this was the day police would be asked "to fish or cut bait." He was the son and nephew of doctors, and he had almost become a physician. In his quixotic way he viewed the laws as a means of healing the wounds of society. He saw his suit as a way to make police leave Eyler alone as long as they couldn't file charges against him. If they brought action against him now, with nothing more than questionable evidence, there was a good chance they would lose all thirteen of the cases.

Until this moment, the newspapers and television stations other than WLS had only vague information about the serial murder suspect, and Eyler was able to walk past the reporters unnoticed in a dark suit and red tie. A WLS field producer emerged from an elevator and pointed him out to reporters as a courtesy. Eyler answered no questions and walked expressionless down the corridor to the court clerk's office. Ditkowsky paused in his habitually rapid strides long enough to announce that the suit charged violations of the Fourteenth Amendment and sought two hundred fifty thousand dollars in damages from officers in both states.

In a few minutes the tape crews wrapped up their coverage, and newspaper reporters filed their story. Then nothing happened for days on end.

Was Eyler a suspect or wasn't he? The accused man wasn't acting like a defendant; he was responding as an outraged citizen. And the police weren't acting like police. To reporters—unaware of all the work still to be done to tighten the case because of the Indiana interruption—it seemed as if everyone had simply "forgotten" about the investigation.

9

October 15, 1983
Lake County, Illinois & Chicago

Gera-Lind Kolarik was up at four o'clock that Saturday morning, putting on her jeans, cowboy boots, and bright orange hunting vest. Once a year she accompanied Sheriff Babcox on the first pheasant hunt of the season. Gera-Lind was not an outdoors person, but Babcox was a good source and something of a friend.

He was a political animal but completely approachable because murder was his hobby. In the 1950s the "boy wonder" deputy sheriff was elected coroner. Even when he withdrew from public office a dozen years later, he stayed close to the work as a mortician. He missed the action and became the coroner once more and then sheriff, sometimes chafing when confined to the niceties of the law.

Gera-Lind had an hour-long drive from her home in Chicago to the Canvasback Club on Nippersink Road in Ingleside. The private clubhouse was filled with old-timers dressed in camouflage fatigues and vests with pouches for carrying freshly killed game. Going on a hunt brought back the adolescent in them.

As sheriff and head of the Lake County Republican Party, Babcox moved among the men with an easygoing, take-charge attitude. He made sure the cooking staff served everyone pancakes, sausages, and freshly brewed coffee. His blue suit and pearl handled revolver were replaced by green pants, a flannel shirt, and orange hunting vest. The word ''sheriff'' was inked into his matching hat. Walking with him along the tables was his Labrador retriever, as dogs more eager for the hunt barked in cages or on leashes at trees outside the clubhouse.

''Hi, Ger; say hello to Hoover,'' the sheriff said with an extended hand. ''This is our Agatha Christie, Hoover.'' Gera-Lind petted the black dog. She pretended to be amused, or Mickey would never let up.

He led her to a weapons cabinet in the back and handed her a shotgun. Then he gave her a license. ''I as sheriff of Lake County make you a four-hour hunter,'' he announced. ''How does the gun feel?''

She lined up the sight on the kitchen light. ''It's not loaded, is it?'' she asked.

''Shit, Ger, I'm crazy but not that crazy.''

By then the barking of the dogs outside was so insistent that there was nothing to do but let them loose. Mickey, three of his poker friends, and Gera-Lind tramped out to the parking lot. The sheriff declared that the pheasant season had just begun and that each hunter could bag only three birds.

Retrievers and spaniels disappeared into the weeds and soon there was the sporadic popping of shotguns. Mickey handed Gera-Lind two shells, saying ''Remember, you can shoot me but don't hit Hoover.''

As she walked into the marsh with the gun pointed downward, Gera-Lind asked the sheriff, ''What's the story with Eyler? Are you going to charge him or what?''

''Hell, yes,'' Mickey answered with the unfinished tone of someone who intends to explain his meaning at a more convenient time.

Hoover rushed into the tall grass, scaring a pheasant into an awkward flight. ''My target,'' the sheriff called out and fired into the sky. The Labrador came back wet from the pond, with the bird in his mouth.

''Go on, Ger,'' Babcox said, ''it's yours next. Flush them out, Hoover!''

She waited a moment, then fired at where she felt the birds would soon be. One pheasant fell from the sky. She was becoming suspicious of the proliferation of birds and diplomatically asked, "Am I bringing you luck?"

"Ger, I just released the birds a couple of hundred feet from here; you can't miss."

"That doesn't seem sporting."

"I'm a busy man. I can't tramp around like this all day," he said lightly, not mentioning his age or ample waistline.

"Why aren't you arresting Eyler?" Gera-Lind asked.

"That damned Foreman and McKoski are being very hard," Mickey explained as he patted Hoover for retrieving the second bird. Fred Foreman was the state's attorney, and Ray McKoski was the chief prosecutor. "It's that damn lawsuit. It has everyone scared to move off their ass. If we charge him and the charges don't stick for one reason or another, we lose our case and we lose our political ass and we open ourselves up for a really big harassment suit."

"You believe he killed Calise and the others, don't you?"

"Sure I do, but what can I do? Don't worry, the minute Foreman approves the charges I plan on arresting our friend myself, personally. I want to see his eyes when I tell him."

That was Robert "Mickey" Babcox. He was honest, and he rigged pheasant hunts. He lived in a simple house and stocked it with antiques he acquired from his inside track as coroner. When he had an exhumation case, he had Kolarik come up from Chicago because he wanted to watch her expression. He brought Hoover with him to the scene of crimes until the large dog once urinated on the evidence. The man was one of a kind.

On Monday Detectives Dan Colin and Roy Lamprich returned to Chicago in hopes of learning more about Eyler's personal life. Their first stop was to interview Phil Rogers, a flight attendant they learned about through *Gay Life*. Rogers had moved to Chicago the previous October and was walking down Clark Street when Eyler drove by, turned around, then stopped and struck up a conversation. They had gone to a restaurant on Halsted Street, roughly paralleling Clark Street in direction and reputation. Over the next few weeks the men met a dozen times, and three of these dates had led to sex.

Eyler occasionally asked if he could tie him up, but Rogers told him he didn't get into bondage. Rogers also informed the detectives that twice Eyler had said he would like to take him to a field up north for sex. "Up north" may have meant Wisconsin, Rogers added. Both times Rogers turned him down. He didn't do the outdoor scene, and he didn't trust Eyler all that much. Now what he was reading in the newspapers made him realize how right his feelings were, even though most people who knew Eyler believed he was passive and even gentle.

Rogers told them that Eyler became violent during sex and seemed to fantasize that his partner was a woman. That is, he would scream "bitch" and "whore" at him and not really seem to be seeing him.

"How common is this?" Colin asked. For all he knew, this was typical of some kinds of sexual encounters.

"Common?" the flight attendant repeated. "I've never heard of it before. It's scary."

Rogers eventually realized that he was being used, that Eyler would call him only when he wasn't getting along with Dobrovolskis and seemed to want to involve him in some form of three-way relationship. Rogers said he might have allowed himself to get drawn into that sort of thing if Eyler hadn't let himself get violent at times. That was all that Rogers could tell them.

For Colin it seemed that Dobrovolskis' name kept coming up whenever police asked about Eyler's background, as if that young man were never far away from Eyler's thoughts.

The detectives didn't learn much from Dobrovolskis' mother-in-law, Rose Marie Kyle, even though she seemed honest with them. The woman told them in her simple apartment on North Rockwell Street that she had known John was bisexual ever since Sally started going out with him. "You get mixed feelings about John," Mrs. Kyle said. "In some ways he can be so good; other times you want to hang him." He would be a good father and play with the children on the floor, then he would go out with friends to the gay bars late at night.

"How well do you know Larry Eyler?" Colin asked.

"He comes here sometimes. When he and John have a fight."

"Why here?"

"Maybe he wants John to think he's out with someone."

As the detectives were leaving, Lamprich glanced at a photo in the hallway of Sally and John smiling like a happy couple. "That was when they were first married," the obese woman said, hobbling toward the door. "Know where they went right after they got married? To a Wendy's. That was their reception. Do you know who went with them? Their best man, Jeff—that was John's boyfriend at the time." The officers couldn't tell from her tone whether she found that amusing or sad.

From there the detectives drove to the Dobrovolskises' converted coachhouse on Greenview Avenue. When they told Sally they wanted to ask her a few questions, she answered, "I don't mind. I have nothing to hide."

She led them to the kitchen, where John sat at a table. He looked, as always, like a clothing store model. Although he commanded the house, he was less open with the detectives than Sally was. There was no suggestion of jealousy or resentment when she spoke of Larry. Her husband's lover was a dear friend.

"I liked him immediately," the blonde woman said in a break from her rapid chain-smoking. He loved to play games with the children, especially Uno, a simplified version of gin. When the children weren't around, he would watch television or read every page of a newspaper. John looked as if he wished his wife would not tell the officers so much.

She spoke of how the two men would squabble frequently. Once, last June, John hit Larry in the face and split his lip. Sally accompanied Larry to the hospital.

"Was that the only time he had to go to the hospital?" Lamprich asked.

A long time ago, she said, Eyler called to say that he had been driving down the Dan Ryan Expressway on the South

Side when he was attacked in a traffic fight. He told her he went to Columbus Hospital, on the North Side, but was transferred to County Hospital because he didn't have insurance.

Lamprich asked John if anyone had told him not to talk to the police. Yes, Larry's lawyer had said something about it, but the lawyer couldn't tell him what to do.

"Have you ever used Larry's truck?"

"Yeah, a few times. About twelve times," John said. "But Larry always knew about it."

"Did you ever wear Larry's boots?"

"I tried them on once, but they didn't fit."

Both detectives felt relieved. Just because Eyler's truck and boots left impressions in the mud near Calise's body didn't necessarily mean he was the one who used them.

The Lake County detectives had arranged their stops of the day so that they would arrive in the Halsted Street gay district in the evening, when the bars were starting to fill up. There was nothing of the flamboyance of hangouts in some other cities, for Chicago is still part of the prairie. Aging bungalows and apartment buildings of dark, rippled brick predominated, with a few stores here and there. Halloween skeletons decorated some windows. A woman with graying hair dared traffic as she walked slowly across the street with an empty shopping cart.

In three and a half blocks, there were a half a dozen bars. Each had a different tempo, a different style. In the blue lighting of Side Tracks, nine teenagers and a young man stood along the back wall while the video equipment drowned out any attempted conversation. At Little Jim's the mood was serene, with soft lighting and the quiet click of a billiard game in the back.

The detectives didn't want to scare off anyone with their case folders and notebooks, so they used cardboard bar coasters to jot down names and phone numbers. The bar-keepers seemed willing to cooperate, but they couldn't help much. To them, Eyler was just another regular—no quarrels, no outbursts of temper. The Illinois officers felt they wouldn't learn much more about Eyler until they made more trips to Indiana and filled in the blanks.

This had been another long night for Colin. When he was in charge of an investigation, it became part of him and his family had to adjust to it. One night last month, before the autumn weather settled in, he pulled up to his house in Round Lake Beach around midnight and saw his wife in the backyard. Flashlight in hand, she was making sure the coals in the grill were red hot as she cooked their steaks. Now the novelty of her husband's eating, sleeping, and living this case had worn off, and Pam sometimes felt like throwing his pager into the toilet.

As a policeman's wife, Pam had learned to be "independently dependent." She got the children up, saw them off to school, drove to the store for groceries, and made sure the house and the household were in order so her husband had a wall between his home life and his work.

When he came home at 9 P.M. the previous Friday, Colin was sure his two children would be in bed. But he was wrong, and he didn't understand. Pam gave him some explanation for why the children would be eating with them, but he was not entirely convinced.

Pam flitted about the table as she laid out the dishes. Five of them.

"We're having company?" Colin asked.

"Oh, didn't you bring him?"

"What do you mean?"

"Why Dan, didn't you bring Eyler with you?"

With the trace of a smile, Colin replied, *"Touché."*

The day after Colin and Lamprich visited the North Side bars, they drove to Indianapolis to augment their Illinois investigation. Lamprich stayed at the former high school to absorb the latest reports the task force received and study the computerized leads, most of them dead ends. Lamprich was better than a computer; his memory didn't develop glitches.

Colin picked up Detective Don Henry of the Indiana unit for his partner. They made their first stop at the First Citizens Bank in Greencastle where Eyler had taken out a loan for the truck, which Sally had described as "his baby."

The detectives located Eyler's sister, Theresa Moell, at work in the town bowling alley before noon. She was frank

with them and said that her brother had been gay ever since
he was a teenager. That was one of those things you just
know; it piles up. She knew he liked bondage but said she
didn't know of any time he hurt someone.

"What about stabbing Mark Henry five years ago?"

"He told me it was self-defense," Mrs. Moell said.

"You believed him?"

"He never went into details," she answered.

All Mrs. Moell could provide were externals about her
brother. But police would never know the Larry Eyler of the
people who grew up around him. That person was warm and
caring, not shy but private.

For example, in the third grade at St. Joseph's School in
Lebanon, Indiana, his friend Mabel Endres had come back
after being sick with the measles for a month. She was worried that the other children would make fun of her, but Larry
offered her a package of M & M's, sealing their friendship.
Even then, Larry was the tallest boy in the class and handsome with his brown wavy hair. His family had less money
than some of the other children's, but he was always dressed
neatly "for a boy" and made sure that his hands were
washed and his hair combed.

Once he and Mabel made their own play money in ten-,
twenty-, and hundred-dollar denominations and pretended
they could buy gifts for everyone in class. The two of them
exasperated the nuns by creating a long paper chain of notebook paper stapled together and giggling as they added more
links every day until it reached about forty feet.

Larry played Red Rover and kickball but stayed with just
a small group of children, and sometimes the other boys
would pick on him. His sister, Theresa, was sensitive to this
and would look out for him. He was the youngest of the four
children and perhaps the one affected most by family
problems.

He was only two and a half when his parents divorced.
Shirley, his mother, worked in a factory and as a waitress
but didn't bring in enough money to support the five of
them. Out of desperation, Shirley had one family take care
of Theresa and another take care of Larry while she was raising her two older sons. Shirley even nearly gave her two

younger children to an orphanage but didn't have the heart. The separations and reunions kept drawing the family emotionally closer.

Shirley had felt that all the children needed was a strong father. She married again, then a third time. Both unions were a disaster, and Larry was getting out of hand. At the beginning of sixth grade, Mabel rode a bus from her farm to St. Joseph's School and couldn't find Larry at his desk. He wasn't there the next day, or the one after that. Talk around school was that a priest had drawn the boy aside and reprimanded him about his mother's divorces. Another rumor was that the boy had a mental breakdown.

The truth was that he had been asserting himself at home, and his mother couldn't handle it. She placed him in a home for unruly boys, and he found that being apart from his family was devastating. The brother who operated the facility asked Shirley to have one more talk with Larry. The boy said tearfully that he would do his chores and be good forever. Shirley hugged him, joined his tears, and took him back.

Mabel didn't see Larry again until seventh grade. He was different now. Not very much different, just enough to show that something had happened to him. He was more of a loner and quieter, but they laughed together as friends and fellow conspirators in occasional pranks.

In eighth grade Larry became interested in another girl, and Mabel told him that she hoped to enter a convent when she was old enough. Around this time he began talking of wanting to be a priest even though he had not been particularly religious before. Boys in a Catholic school often will talk about the vocation for a few days if only to hear how it sounds, before the reality of the discipline and study hit them.

Mabel's cousin Vince became Larry's best friend when they were around twelve or thirteen. They played ball and learned chess together. Larry was more aggressive with pawns and castles than he was at gym, and he still was a lot of fun.

"He was such a likable kid, so giving," she recalled. "If he had it, he'd give it to you."

As for Mabel at that age, she was becoming self-conscious about her appearance as she suffered through the awkward stage. She thought she was too short to be attractive, and at the graduation dance no one asked to take her arm. She stood embarrassed in her sister's semiformal lavender dress and wanted to hide. Then Larry stood next to her and softly touched her hand.

"Do you want to dance?" he asked.

He was so tall, and she was so short, that in their first steps they giggled. Then he told her quietly, "You look beautiful, Mabel," and she felt like crying.

That was the last time they had been part of each other's life, but she could never forget a moment like that. They attended different public high schools and lived across town from one another. They exchanged letters about courses, but when they were sixteen Larry stopped answering. When Mabel married a few years later she tried to invite him to the wedding, but no one in Lebanon, Indiana, knew that he was living in Terre Haute. Mabel did not hear of him again until his arrest for the murder of Ralph Calise. She still kept childhood photos of her friend tucked away in a shoebox, including a wallet-sized picture with "The Pest" written on the back.

Larry left college to work as a guard in the Indiana National Bank and spent six months as a Pinkerton guard in the Marion County General Hospital in Indianapolis. He also had jobs at a shoe store and a trucking company and spent a long period on welfare. Now he lived on odd jobs when they came available and he was in the mood for them.

The detectives were beginning to know Larry better than his own family did.

Larry didn't seem to care what he did in the daytime, when he was little more than an easygoing waste of intelligence. He brought all his intensity to his nighttime private life. The *Terre Haute Tribune-Star* learned that when he lived in that college town he would call a sex hotline used by men and women to make appointments with strangers. A typical call from homosexuals would be "Any muscular young men." Most of the time the callers found themselves waiting at corners and parking lots for men who never showed up.

Larry would have sex with men he met in a bar but preferred staying within his small circle of friends despite the little pools of contentions from overlapping lovers. Then he met John Dobrovolskis on August 8, 1981, and his rootlessness was replaced by something far more than just love. Larry needed to feel at all times that he was the one and only man in John's life. And yet, from what Colin could learn, Larry appeared to have resented his dependence on John and wanted to be free for his own casual relationships.

What followed was a paranoid jealousy, where love is chewed up by hate and apprehension. Although Larry himself was unfaithful, interviews with his friends showed that he was seeking out hints of infidelity in John even if it meant twisting the facts to justify his fears. And yet nothing that Colin had heard showed that Larry was in any way different from what could be thousands of other men like that. There was a missing element, but the detective thought that it might never be found.

While Colin was in Terre Haute, he wanted to talk to Mark Henry, the first of the known Eyler victims. Colin and Detective Henry met him at work in the Morris Trucking Company, and he directed them down the streets to the woods where Eyler had handcuffed him and plunged a butcher knife into his chest as he tried to escape. The clearing was just off a road, but the entrance was covered by underbrush and a fallen tree. The information fattened the manila folder, but it didn't help Colin understand the killings any better.

Dr. Little was out of town that day, so Colin and Henry drove to Indianapolis to interview another professional they had heard was a long-standing friend, Dr. Frank Smith, a physician at St. Francis Hospital. Sitting in his apartment in Rowley Towers, which housed a number of professionals, the thin man in his thirties said he had met Eyler at a party in October 1981 and had an affair with him until January when he broke off his relationship because Eyler had no goal in life and the other factor. "What factor?" Colin asked.

The violence.

Smith said he had about ten sexual encounters with Eyler and that the two remained friends. He had met Dobrovolskis and knew of a few quarrels the two men had had. Eyler was a very jealous man, the doctor said.

As for the cut on Eyler's hand, Smith was the one who removed the stitches. Eyler claimed he had fallen out of a truck and onto a broken beer bottle. (Just the day before, Sally had said Eyler told her he was cut in a traffic fight on an expressway.) Smith said that when the doctor at Cook County Hospital in Chicago sutured the wound, he neglected to stitch the tendon, permanently damaging Eyler's hand.

"Is there anything you can tell us about Eyler and sex that's, if you don't mind, a little unusual?" Colin asked.

Smith mentioned that Eyler liked to call his sexual partners names like "bitch" and "whore," as if they were women. The doctor said he permitted this only once. He also said Eyler had mentioned bondage to him, but he refused.

To Smith it seemed that Eyler had a difficult time accepting his homosexuality. He added that Eyler had a strange temper. It could be triggered by minor upsets but not by major ones, as if minor ones caught him unprepared. He also recalled seeing Eyler with a knife with a four-inch blade that was almost razor sharp, like a scalpel.

Colin decided to call it a day and headed back with Henry to the task force headquarters. The trip to Indiana had seemed uneventful, but it wouldn't be for long.

That evening two mushroom hunters walking through the tall yellow weeds behind an abandoned farmhouse in Newton County, Indiana, saw something odd. There were two or three small mounds near a tree a little off the highway. The man and the woman stepped a little closer. For a moment there was such a silence that the whoosh of traffic going north to Illinois or south to the heart of Indiana seemed twice as loud as before.

One of the mounds was dirt with brown, curled leaves over a skeletal body. The mushroom gatherers turned back and started looking for a house where they could call the police.

No one in the task force was more excited about the discovery than Cathy Berner. Some of the officers jumped in cars, and others made phone call after phone call; but the petite young woman settled down opposite her computer and let her mind race. There was a connection between where the bodies were found and something that was in the hundreds of facts she had been analyzing, but it wasn't entered into the computer. Then she had it. One of the collect calls to Dr. Little's house had been made from Lake Village, a short distance away from the barnyard.

"You onto something?" McPherson asked.

"Maybe it's nothing . . ."

"All right, out with it."

"I think he made a call out there, but I have to check the records."

She started going through her stack of phone records and saw McPherson leaving with Jim Rhinebarger and Billy Bob Newman. McPherson would rather make an hour-long trip than sit still for fifteen minutes waiting for something to happen.

In time she received a phone call. "This is Sam. Guess where I'm calling from. It's a pay phone right at the crossroads in Lake Village, and as I talk to you I can see the barn and right where those graves are. Now I wonder just who made that call in the wee early morning hours to Dr. Little's home from here."

Berner turned around in her chair and shouted to the officers in the task force headquarters, "Bingo! We've got another piece!"

The county and task force officers crisscrossed their flashlight beams inside the sagging barn just to get a "feel" of the scene before the evidence technicians began removing everything of interest. On an overhead, written in ink or paint, McPherson saw a pentagram and another symbol of satanism, an upside-down cross.

Newman bent down to get a closer look at something on the dirt and straw. "Say, Jim, weren't there a whole bunch of gloves found in Larry's truck?" he asked Rhineberger.

"A few. One had a tip missing."

"Look at this. Doesn't this beat all?"

Near their feet was the fingertip of a glove, down to the first joint. It was the size and color of the tip that was missing from the latex glove police had seized during the twelve-hour Lowell detention, but there was no way of proving that this tip came from his glove when thousands just like it were in use across the country.

The killer was leaving clues, all right, but nothing that would hold up in court.

One of the other officers who rushed to the scene was Roy Lamprich, who had heard about the mounds while he was with the task force investigators. Another was state police Sgt. Ted Knorr, who was from a task force on organized crime.

The highway murders fascinated as much as they repelled Knorr, and he realized that police could use the discovery of the killer's totem place as a way of putting pressure on Eyler. Knorr used to operate a small auto racetrack and knew the value of organizing publicity. He recommended that the bodies remain there overnight, giving Indiana reporters time to arrange their coverage. At the time, police did not know whether there were three or a dozen mounds in the field.

Colin had expected to be driving home in the evening but instead went to the Indiana state police headquarters now that the case was taking on greater urgency. He had wanted to question Tom Henderson, the man who turned Eyler's name in to police on June 5, and it was decided to take him to McPherson's office in the criminal investigation section.

Henderson told the officers almost immediately that he was a roommate of James Williams and that they were about to move into Rowley Towers, the building Colin visited earlier in the day. He said his first contact with the case had come when the task force called him because they knew he was gay. Later he thought that Eyler matched the psychological profile offered by *The Works*, Stan Berg's newspaper, and decided to call the hotline.

"You were angry with Larry, weren't you?" Colin asked.

"I hardly knew him."

"What about him and Williams?"

"That wasn't the reason."

"But you were, weren't you?"

"Larry wasn't the matter," Henderson said. Colin had to hammer away at the motive because some defense attorney was bound to. "It was John," Henderson admitted. "I was angry with John."

The night before he called the hotline, Henderson quarreled with John and afterward shattered a window of Larry's pickup truck with a crowbar. So that was the explanation of the damage that had drawn Trooper Buehrle's attention to the truck near Lowell, thinking it might have been stolen.

"You said Larry fit the profile," Colin said. "In what way?"

Eyler and Williams had been lovers for six years, and Williams told Henderson that Eyler had a violent streak. On one occasion Williams let Eyler tie him up, but Eyler beat him with his fist and got into rough sex.

Colin tried to comprehend all the relationships within these clusters of people in Terre Haute and Chicago. There were John and Sally. John and Larry, Larry and Williams, Williams and Henderson, Henderson and John, John and Williams. Bonds of love, bonds of need, and sometimes bonds of hate—the emotions were all jammed together.

For Colin the disturbing element was that the hate was diffuse or directed away from someone. Eyler becomes angry with Dobrovolskis, so he dates Rogers or goes out and sulks, or else he picks up hitchhikers. Henderson becomes angry with Dobrovolskis, so he smashes the window of Eyler's truck and turns in Eyler's name.

Where was Little in all this? Henderson said the relationship was platonic. Little paid Eyler's bills and took him on a trip to New York in August. Lots of middle-aged men give young men money just to accompany them to places. Once Little and Eyler went to San Francisco, and the professor paid for everything.

Colin wanted to learn how deep these relationships were. Henderson mentioned that Dobrovolskis had tried to commit suicide in Williams' apartment. Indiana police confirmed that they received such a report on August 9. Dobrovolskis had used the name Crawford, the name of his wife's first husband. The suicide attempt—and this Colin found interesting—came two days after Eyler had left for New York with Little.

The next morning the field in Newton County took on the bustle of a Vietnam encampment with news media helicopters from major Indiana stations arriving and departing for more than four hours. Sergeant Knorr and the sheriff agreed to let crews and newspaper photographers come as close to the mounds as possible. Detectives in floppy fisherman's caps and state troopers in their Smoky-the-Bear hats and blue uniforms carefully went over the ground section by section.

Since only the Indiana media were notified, Gera-Lind Kolarik in Chicago did not learn of the grisly discovery until she made her first call of the day to the morgue in Lake County, Indiana. The coroner told her that the coroner in Newton County had some bodies by a farmhouse on Route 41. An attendant in Newton County would say only that the coroner was at the scene. U.S. 41—God, that's Eyler again, she told herself.

The on-air reporter for the story would be Joan Esposito, the black-haired news anchor who managed to look like both a model and a no-nonsense executive. She had just walked into the newsroom in her high heels from a speaking engagement when her pager went off. She found editor Mort Meisner excitedly running to the producers' offices with an ice cream bar in hand to tell them the news. Esposito walked to Meisner's vacant desk and read Kolarik's memo about the burial place. "Yeah, and I had to wear my heels today," she muttered.

A courier was waiting to rush her to the helicopter at Meigs Field, the small airport just off the lakeshore. Kolarik was unable to reach Eyler or Ditkowsky by phone to see if police had contacted them; that meant the only information would be coming in from reporters going to the abandoned farmyard.

When the crew of the WLS Skycam flew fifty miles southeast of Chicago, they could see the parked police cars and men in uniform walking around an aging barn with shovels on their shoulders. By then all the Indiana choppers had left, and the Chicago crew felt that it owned the sky.

Technically, the crew was in limbo, since Kolarik was still on the phone trying to get permission from state police for the blue helicopter to land nearby. If the Skycam had to land elsewhere, the bodies and all the officers might be gone by the time the crew reached the barn.

The police had held off removing the skeletal remains until the Indiana media had their fill, and they were in no mood to postpone the work any longer. The whirring blade waved the tall grass and swirled debris. Over the roar of the Skycam, a state police sergeant pointed to the chopper and shouted, "God damn TV station, they're ruining our crime scene!"

As Kolarik spoke to the dispatcher she could hear the transmission of a sergeant to communications: "Someone call Channel Seven and tell them to move their helicopter. Tell them if they don't move, we will shoot them out of the sky."

The dispatcher told the sergeant that WLS was on the phone and wanted to know where to land it. "Far away!" the sergeant screamed into the mike.

Kolarik grabbed the two-way radio and told the pilot the situation. Esposito took over the receiver and said, "Gera-Lind, we've got to land."

"Joan, there should be a squad car driving away. Is there?"

"Yes, why?"

"Follow it. He's going to stop where you can land. Maybe he'll give you a lift back to the barn—show him your high heels."

"Thanks, Gera-Lind. Appreciate that. Skycam out."

On that day, a fourth body was found in the abandoned farmyard. Three had been carefully lined up on one side of the oak tree that served as their marker. The other, the remains of a black man, was rather crudely buried in a shallow grave on the other side of the tree. As with the others, his trousers had been pulled down. While police placed the remains in a body bag they could see knife marks on the rib cage. The killer had been powerful and motivated by something unfathomable to everyone else.

Standing in weeds past his knees, Newton County Coroner David Dennis watched the work and said, "Ritual."

The body bags were driven to the Indiana University medical laboratory in Indianapolis, the sheriff's police threw their shovels back into their car trunks and the evidence van, and the blue Skycam headed back for Chicago.

Edgar Bauer, whose son Michael had been missing since March, was watching the evening news with his wife when he saw the abandoned farmyard and a skeletal hand behind the weeds. "That's Michael!" he said with a shudder. "The coat, look at the coat." But by then the image was gone from the screen. Bauer went to the phone and called his older son, John, who had been making periodic checks at the morgue and the Cook County Jail. John always held out hope, and yet from the beginning he had the cold feeling that his brother was dead. All he could do now was call the police, send them Michael's dental records, and wait.

The killer's secret place wasn't secret anymore.

10

Mid-October 1983

Eyler's family remained in shock at the disclosure that Eyler was the suspect. His brother Alan claimed he was "still shaking" weeks after police talked to him. Larry's mother, Shirley DeKoff, was so distressed she could hardly get through her days afterward. Her once-attractive face looked tired and aged behind her tinted glasses, but she still dressed well, as if to deny the suffering that kept getting in the way of her thinking. Her husband, Irving, an administrator at the Indiana State Hospital in Richmond, had her consult a psychiatrist for treatment and some badly needed sleep.

What the stepfather couldn't understand was why there was all this publicity when Eyler had not even been charged with anything. From the time his lawyer filed suit, Eyler's name was used on national news. That happened again when the four bodies were found on October 18. DeKoff, an understanding and rational man, was wondering whatever happened to the U.S. Constitution.

Some of this attention Eyler brought upon himself, since it was attorney Kenneth Ditkowsky's strategy to take his side to the public. Normally, reporters don't learn the name of a suspect until he is charged, and then he is inaccessible to them. With Eyler, all they had to do was call his Chicago home as if he were no more than a witness. He told reporters his life had been "hell" ever since the Lowell stop and he was wrongly accused. As for the handcuffs found in his pickup, he said they had been given to him by a friend as a joke.

"If I was the murderer," Eyler said in his velvety tone, "they would have had the evidence by now."

Sounding convincingly like an innocent victim of police overreaction, he explained that he was financially ruined by the seizure of his truck. He couldn't even make his appointment for a lie detector test in Indianapolis without it and was unable to work (not that he ever did much work). "I know my mother stays up nights and cries about this," Eyler told reporters. "This is going to be with me for the rest of my life."

Officially, police in both states were going by the book and were investigating all other suspects who might turn up. Unofficially, they were doing whatever they could without jeopardizing the case, often on their own initiative and sometimes on their own time. Officials deny that Eyler's pickup was kept on blocks for months in a garage an hour's drive from his North Side home to help keep him out of trouble, but it worked out that way.

There were very perplexing aspects to the case, including socks.

Perry Hollowell, the deputy sheriff of Vermillion County, worked with the task force on the Agan case and kept up with reports from Illinois police investigating the murder of Edgar Underkofler, who had been found near Danville. Both victims had on their feet white tube socks with yellow and blue markings, yet their families said the men never wore socks like that and none could be found in their homes. Hollowell went to Indianapolis after the October evidence "raid" on Little's home, but none of the socks seized were the ones he was looking for.

Sam McPherson wondered about socks too, but from a later investigation. He had noticed that all four victims in the Newton County barnyard had on white socks, but two of them had a single sock with a blue-and-red stripe. To McPherson, that meant that although the bodies were found clothed the killer had had them at least partially undressed and perhaps naked at the same time, something the autopsies could not determine. Or perhaps the killer had just removed his victims' socks as souvenirs and replaced them with new ones so no one would know.

But the mystery of the socks remained unsolved, along with why the killer might have undressed his victims and what he did with them until dumping their bodies or laying them in shallow graves.

Unlike Indianapolis police, investigators in Illinois had a good working relationship with the homosexual community. When WLS-TV news anchor Jay Levine asked for human interest information to round out the story he was putting together on the killings, Gera-Lind Kolarik decided to contact the same source. She left Levine's office with all its golf paraphernalia—including a one-hole desktop putting green—and called *Gay Life* editor Bill Williams. He gave her the names of two men who knew Eyler, and one of them agreed to talk to her. She set up a meeting at a Near North Side pizza restaurant, Gino's East, after they were both through with work.

Kolarik waited for half an hour, lingering with her scotch and soda. Finally a tall, very well dressed man went to her table. She shook his hand and tried not to make him uneasy by direct questions or looking him in the eyes.

"I was a little nervous coming here," Jim admitted. "I'm a lawyer and a businessman with a pretty big firm in town—I won't say which one. You see, they don't know I'm gay, and I don't know what they would think."

"Do you think Larry Eyler is the killer?"

"Whoever it is, he's still out there, isn't he? I want to help others and maybe help the police."

Jim said Eyler had picked him up in a leather bar in February and given him some pills that made him pass out. "I remember handcuffs on my hands and him pounding me."

"He wasn't trying to kill you, was he?"

"No, but I don't know what he was trying to do."

"How did you feel? Afterward, I mean."

Jim lowered his head. "Ashamed. And scared; even after it was all over, I was scared. Then I started reading about all these killings. God, I could have been one of them, but something made him change his mind, don't you think? All those years in law school could have been wasted, just because I was alone in a bar.''

The time was already 9 P.M., too late to arrange an interview for the ten o'clock news. She rose and shook his hand. "Talk to the police, Jim; help them. I need your interview to make our story better, but I think you would feel exposed.'' She fingered the piece of paper she had used to write his phone number. He seemed a little surprised when she handed it back to him. Jim didn't say anything. She put on her trenchcoat and caught a cab, leaving him alone with his drink.

The shocking discovery of the killer's hiding place near an abandoned barn led to a letter from West Virginia. Ed Healy notified the task force that when he was staying in Indianapolis June 1, 1980, Eyler had handcuffed and beat him for an hour and at one point seemed about to kill him with a shotgun.

Two detectives flew down to West Virginia and brought Healy to Indianapolis, where the task force videotaped his interview so that he could return home. What he had to say drew the attention of all the officers because what had happened to him might have been similar to the ceremony that ended in death for the others, but there was nothing that could be considered evidence in a murder case against him.

Healy said he was sitting on the steps of the downtown Soldiers and Sailors Monument on a hot evening when Eyler drove up. Healy had no sooner climbed into the truck than Eyler asked if he turned tricks.

"Are you a cop?" Healy asked.

"No," Eyler replied.

"Maybe we can work something out."

They started talking of something for twenty dollars, just to start the conversation. As they spoke, Eyler headed down Washington Street, away from the Capitol, and asked his passenger if he were into S & M. Healy said no. Gradually Eyler returned to the subject, assuring Healy that nothing would happen that he didn't want to happen. The driver offered him one hundred dollars.

Healy was still thinking about the offer as they went to a country and western bar, where the jukebox sang of lost loves and hard times. The two men returned to the truck, and they headed for the home of Eyler's sister in Greencastle. Healy didn't know why Eyler had wanted to have sex near the home of his sister, but the drifter hadn't thought much about it. He had not agreed to anything rough, but he wasn't trying to get out of the truck either. For him it was one of those "let's see what happens" situations. Or so he said.

They lay in the back of the truck and had sex. When the officers asked him to be specific, Healy said they had anal and possibly oral intercourse. One thing was a little unusual; Healy didn't think Eyler had climaxed. This alone wouldn't mean much, but there were no semen traces in any of the bodies.

Suddenly Eyler handcuffed Healy and shoved a gag into his mouth. Eyler then tightly wound a gauze bandage around Healy's eyes and bound his ankles with rope, saying, "This will last exactly sixty minutes."

Holding a flashlight with one hand and a knife with a razorlike blade in the other, Eyler dug nicks across his victim's naked chest. Healy thrashed at the pain but there was no escape. Next Eyler slammed a fist upon the chest, again and again—pounding, pounding, and saying every few minutes how much longer Healy would have to endure this. "You only have half an hour more . . . only twenty minutes more . . ."

Healy could endure the pain, but he feared that he might suffocate from the gag. He gestured until Eyler pulled the wet cloth from his mouth. "I won't holler, I swear," Healy said. "Please leave that out." He told the officers he was the kind of man who could think clearly even when others might panic, and Eyler had trusted him.

Eyler stopped pounding but now sat on Healy's chest and ejaculated into the cuts. "You bitch," Eyler shouted— and yet not *at* him. "You slut, you whore!" When the hour was up, Eyler stopped and grabbed a shotgun, but something had changed his mind. He brought Healy back to a transient hotel in Indianapolis without showing any realization of what he had done. Eyler even asked him for a date, but the drifter slammed the truck door and didn't feel safe until Eyler drove away.

After the officers let Healy go, they talked among themselves about what they had. McPherson thought the tape made their case—the hundred dollars, the handcuffs, the torture cuts, everything. To Sgt. Frank Love, they had nothing. "Consensual" was all he needed to say. A defense attorney was bound to suggest to a jury that anything short of murder was part of sadomasochism.

In Chicago at this time, Colin and Lamprich interviewed Jim Griffin, a short, athletic baker. He identified Eyler from a photo as the man he met in a parking lot on November 30, 1981. "I told him I wasn't into anything heavy-duty," Griffin said. "I asked him how he was hung, and I said I wasn't into sex unless there was the equivalent of what I had to offer."

"Go on," Colin said to get him over his reluctance to talk about it.

"He said he could meet the bill. I was going home, and I told him if he wanted to come on by, he could. He wanted us to go to Indiana, but no way would I do that."

"There was no threat on his part?"

"Nothing like that. Just the usual kind of talk."

Griffin's role was always the passive partner. For a while he tried being the "top man" in a service run through a gay magazine, but he wasn't good at it. That takes someone angrier or more manipulative.

Griffin drove home, and Eyler followed to the Victorian-era apartment building on North Dearborn Street. There were twelve-foot ceilings, and Griffin had doubled the space of his room by installing a loft that could be reached by a short ladder. His two black Great Danes stayed below, suspicious of strangers but trained to intervene only on command.

Griffin didn't pay any attention to an eighteen-inch-long black bag Eyler had brought with him. The baker stripped, but his guest kept on his shorts and T-shirt and the baseball cap he used to conceal a balding spot. He had also brought up the ladder his black bag and neatly folded pants, saying he didn't want to get dog hairs on them.

Griffin had agreed to being tied up, but then there was a dull pain on his back that almost knocked the breath from him. "Stop it, will you?" he blurted out. "Stick to what we agreed to, all right?"

Eyler didn't say a word as he brought his fist hard against the naked back, time and again. The baker arched against the pain, and fear jolted through him when he saw in the mirror just above his bed that Eyler had laid out two knives and an ice pick.

"Were you in fear of your life?" Colin asked.

"Yes, I was."

The question always had to be asked in S & M cases. "Those knives you saw—would there be any other use for a knife in a bondage-type situation?"

"The only time in my experience that knives have been used is when somebody panics or, in most instances, when the person doesn't know what he is doing and he usually ties too tight or ties a knot he can't get undone."

But that wasn't the case with Eyler. Griffin felt that he had done this before.

From his experience Griffin knew that you should never show panic when a sadomasochism situation gets out of hand; fear might become an excitement to the partner and lead to something serious. After Griffin had been struck again, he tried to keep his voice in a monotone and said, "Larry, this isn't my thing. We still have time to go to a bar. You want to do that, go to a bar? Maybe you can get into it with somebody else."

The pounding didn't stop. Griffin had almost been at the point of summoning his dogs when police arrived nearby with their sirens blaring because of a coincidental report that a woman had been raped in a nearby alley. Eyler put the weapons back but, as Griffin noted, he seemed in "a state of frustration or anger." Even so, there hadn't been a "bitch fight." That's when bad sex leads to bitter sarcasm and put-downs. Eyler merely left, saying

"You are in no danger" three times before closing the door behind him.

Not only were Illinois and Indiana police now trading information, they were sharing hunches. The task force in Indianapolis had an idea that fell somewhere between a stroke of genius and being off the wall. It occurred to someone over there that while we sleep and drive to work and brush our teeth, government satellites are passing overhead with cameras going clickety-click at preset coordinates. That might not do any good for evidence on the Indiana bodies (who would take shots of the rows of corn in Putnam County?), but Calise had been found near Lake Forest and, the task force reasoned, Lake Forest is not that far from the Zion nuclear power plant.

The task force had visions of wrapping the case up in triumph. Suppose a sky-spy camera showed Eyler's truck at the scene or, better yet, the killer cutting off Herrera's hand or dumping Calise's body off the highway. The excitement accompanied Love and McPherson as they flew down to the naval intelligence headquarters in New Orleans, equipped with the detailed coordinates worked out by the Lake County engineering department.

A guard led them to a room in the large brick building where a naval officer had a stack of twenty-three black-and-white blowups. "You have to remember that these shots were taken thousands of miles up. You can still make out a semitrailer. Do you see that here?"

"It looks like a dot," McPherson said. "Hell, what can we make out of this?"

"I'm giving you what we can," the officer said. "Remember that you are just estimating the time and date."

Love thanked him and nudged his partner as a reminder not to let his disappointment show. The two men took the enlargements with them to Indianapolis, but a week of enlarging the photos still further and going over them with a magnifying glass failed to turn up anything incriminating.

The Illinois detectives had a good laugh over the satellite snooping. God, in a case like this, they needed a laugh.

One of the more elusive leads was Craig Townsend, a supposed Eyler victim left in a coma and severely dehydrated near Lowell, Indiana. He had slipped out of a hospital before he could be questioned. Speculation was that he was in Kentucky, but on October 26, Colin traced him to Chicago's North Side. On paper, at least, it seemed that Townsend would be the no-longer-missing link needed by the two jurisdictions. He had been taken from Uptown and assaulted in the vicinity where Eyler was seized with Darl Hayward.

The story he told was interesting enough, but Colin didn't know how much of it a jury would accept. For one thing, Townsend sought refuge from the world in a Hare Krishna temple on Lunt Avenue. Colin went into the former church and saw a large, bare auditorium and a shaven-headed monk sitting there in saffron robes. Townsend came over and had no trouble identifying Eyler from the six photos Colin showed him. Then he sat back and told the detective what he could remember about that night. Not much.

Townsend said that when he left work at a construction site on October 12 the year before, he had gone to Little Joe's and Big Red's, two gay bars, feeling a little tipsy. He had dinner at a small restaurant and saw Eyler in a red pickup truck. Eyler offered him some beer and asked if he wanted to take a drive. Before long, Townsend found himself in the truck headed for Indiana. Eyler gave him more beer and some black pills. "It's all right," Eyler said. "It's just speed." At the time, Townsend would have taken anything; he was feeling good. He took three pills, maybe more, that were offered one at a time.

Then everything became cloudy in Townsend's mind. He could recall fighting with Eyler, and when he regained consciousness he was in a Crown Point hospital, suffering from intoxication and exposure from being left out in a field. Townsend didn't know what had happened to him, but he didn't want to find out. He traded his hospital gown for his street clothes and walked out without anyone's noticing.

This did not interest anyone at the time but ten days

later, Steven Crockett was found dead less than ten miles away from where Townsend had been abandoned. Both had been rendered unconscious with ethchlorynol (Placidyl), an anti-insomnia drug. Why hadn't Townsend been stabbed? Maybe his fighting with Eyler broke the nightmare fantasy, or perhaps Townsend was only part of an experiment and was never meant to die.

But what jury would believe a Hare Krishna who had been so high on drugs and alcohol that he couldn't remember what Eyler might have said to him and who had fled a hospital in order to avoid talking to the police? At the bottom of the Townsend page of his running report, Colin typed, "Investigation to continue."

That afternoon Detective Roy Lamprich and Lake County sheriff's police Detective Curt Corsi drove to Cook County Hospital on Chicago's Near West Side, an aging facility that has the look of a last resort. All the officers had to go on was that Sally Dobrovolskis recalled that Eyler had been treated there some time in April. An administrator called up the suspect's name on the computer and found that he had been treated April 8. Lamprich immediately made the connection: that was the night Herrera was killed in Lake County, his hand severed. A rough diagram on one of the sheets showed that Eyler's hand had been cut between the thumb and forefinger, as if he had grabbed the blade of a hunting knife. What a struggle that must have been, the detectives said among themselves. Too bad Eyler won.

That afternoon, Lamprich made another of his daily phone checks on the FBI lab to see whether the technicians had learned anything of interest. There was nothing much to report. The blood at the haft of Eyler's hunting knife was A-positive, which was neither good nor bad for the investigation. Calise had A-positive, but perhaps Eyler did too. After all, he claimed he cut himself.

Four distinctive marks on the boots matched the impressions found near Calise's body, but this too was evidence-neutral. A cautious jury would not realize how uncommon it would be for one person to have the same type of boots with the same type of wear on them, along with the same types of tires from two manufacturers. The word *circumstantial* haunted the detectives because not one piece of evidence was decisive by itself.

Deputy Chief Investigator Smith was relaxing and thinking at the same time, as he was known to do. He was not in his office now but lounging in the room with separate desks for the detectives. Smitty could do more by relaxing without any show of expression than many policemen can do by running down leads.

"We still can't explain the three sets of footprints," Smitty said, by way of asking the detectives to start rethinking the case. There was one set of boot prints, presumably Eyler's; and there was one set of shoe prints, presumably Calise's; and there were the faint marks of someone walking in soft ground in his stockinged feet. "We won't get anywhere until we explain these. You know what the jury would say. Larry didn't do it because two men must have been involved, and we got no other guy."

"Larry had friends," Kurt Proschwitz put in.

"Do we really think two people killed Calise? I haven't seen anything like that. The body was thrown pretty far, but who knows how strong these killers are."

"Who goes walking in the woods in stocking feet after a rain?" Lamprich asked.

"All right, all right, let's figure this out," said Smitty, his quiet tone hardly more than a dawdle. "Let's talk about why someone would go out in boots and go out in stockinged feet either before or afterward."

One suggestion led to another, and what they came up with was a collaborative effort. Everything became clearer when they remembered that these were not just two men who stepped out of a truck. The killer had taken Calise there for sex, and those heavy boots were not made for comfort. The killer must have taken them off in the truck. Suppose the killer had stabbed Calise in the woods and decided to throw the body into a brush area rather than build a mound over him. The killer could not have done this in stockinged feet; he would have needed his lug boots for a better grip on the muddy ground. That would mean going back to the truck.

"Who's to say we're right?" Lamprich said to himself as well as to his colleagues. The Vietnam veteran tapped his corner-to-corner mustache, trying to visualize feet rather than faces in a murder. Then he said, "Let me make a call."

This was late in the normal working day, but he dialed the FBI lab again and asked if the technicians had found any traces of blood *inside* the boots they were preparing to ship back to Waukegan.

"How would we know that; we don't test the insides," the technician said.

"The only way to do that would be to cut the boot open," Lamprich said.

"We can't destroy property."

"Why not?"

"We've never done it," the technician said.

Lamprich let it go at that. It was just a passing thought.

Half an hour later the phone rang. "Lamprich," Roy answered.

"We had to use a saw," the technician said. "How did you know there was blood in there? It's all the way from the toe back to the heel."

It was one of those moments that make police work worthwhile.

In the Indiana task force headquarters, Cathy Berner was adding the information about the April 8 phone call from Cook County Hospital to Dr. Little's home to the elaborate calendar she was compiling on Eyler's where-abouts for each day since the murders had begun. Working with those credit card receipts, purchase records, and tele-phone bills gave her an eerie feeling, as if she were mak-ing a follow-the-dot outline for murder. If Eyler was not the killer, then he was following the killer's trail back and forth, day after day.

There could not be a complete outline because a number of the men killed had not been identified, so there was no way of knowing where they came from or when they disappeared. But with the identified victims, there often was a corresponding telephone call from near where the body was found to someone in the Terre Haute town house of Little or the Chicago home of John Dobrovolskis. Some calls did not correspond to a murder. Did that mean there were other bodies out there?

Lake County, Illinois, State's Attorney Fred Foreman— a giant of a man—still held out on placing charges. The trouble caused by the Lowell stop and later Ditkowsky's suit had made him cautious. He had placed the matter into the hands of his assistant Ray McKoski, who studied the police reports as they came in and was thoroughly familiar with what the police did and did not have. They were a long way from enough evidence to file charges.

On October 15 a Jasper County farmer near Rensselaer, Indiana, was disking his field when he felt his plow roll over something. He stopped, climbed down, and saw the skeletal remains of a young man. He left the plow were it was and called police. The field was near Interstate 65 and State Route I-14, a fifteen-minute drive from the barnyard where the four bodies were found. Investigators could tell from nicks on the bones that the Jasper victim had been stabbed to death, like the others. This brought the murder count to nineteen. The man remains unidentified.

Although no additional leads had come in, members of the task force drove up to Waukegan late in the afternoon of Thursday, October 27, to compare notes with the sheriff's police. The officers from the two jurisdictions convinced one another that they had enough to nail Eyler for the Calise murder, and they asked McKoski for a meeting.

There were too many people for the small corner room where McKoski usually worked, so they went to Sheriff Babcox's office on the first floor while he was away on business. Babcox might have told him to hang the bastard. Everyone was working down to raw nerves in this case.

The meeting began with the politeness of suppressed hostility and worked its way to a pitch that would never have been reached if Foreman were there. McKoski tried to explain in his almost adolescent tenor voice that a lot of probabilities aren't enough, but the officers weren't listening.

"We have the victim's blood on the knife, we have blood in the boot, tire impressions. We want a warrant for his arrest," Colin said from a desk across from McKoski. "The Calise case is probably the strongest we're ever going to get on this guy."

"The blood could be anybody's."

"Not Larry's; he was cut on the hand, not on the foot. What do you want, Ralph Calise's signature and driver's license?"

Almost at the same moment Smitty said, "Put him away, you asshole." His light-skinned face was red now. It was close to eight o'clock, and tempers were making discussion impossible. Then Babcox showed up and sat in, but for once he didn't say much.

"We'll take what we have to Foreman when he gets back," Colin said. "He's got to see it our way."

"I won't back you up," McKoski told him. That stopped him cold; there was no point in trying to tell McKoski what his job was.

"Your boss is out of town, and you just want to make a news release out of this," Smitty charged. "It's politics, that's all it is."

"Politics has nothing to do with it," McKoski answered.

"You don't have balls enough to do this without Fred's permission," Smitty added.

"Calm down," Babcox said. "If Ray didn't have the balls, do you think he'd say no to all of you? Jesus, maybe he's wrong but he's doing his job."

Smitty flung out his arms, wanting to hit McKoski in the mouth. "I tell you, if there's another murder you're going to be held personally responsible. Do you think you can live with that?"

A pause set in, then McKoski leaned over his hands, which were lying flat on the desk, and said, "I'll tell you what. I'll give you a warrant for hair and blood typing. Maybe you can do something with that."

This wasn't what the officers wanted, but it allowed them to settle back with the feeling that at least something was done. "When do we serve it?" Colin asked.

"Why not tomorrow?" McKoski said. The officers from

both states needed to be in federal court for a hearing on Ditkowsky's suit.

"I don't want any publicity," the sheriff said. In other words, he wanted to handle the publicity himself. "And for Christ's sake don't serve the warrant on federal property. They're two separate things, and keep them that way."

The next day, several television crews were trying to cover the lobby of the Dirksen Federal Building as if each entrance were a hockey goal. Reporter Mike Androvett of Indianapolis television station WISH asked Gera-Lind Kolarik to explain what was happening. WISH had supplied Kolarik with tapes and developments in the Indiana cases, and now she gave him some tapes from WLS and briefed him on whether anything important was likely to happen.

"All Larry needs is his pickup truck back," Kolarik said. "You see all these other crews? That's because they don't have any shots of him. Don't worry, this is just going to be a routine hearing." Predicting news in Chicago is as hazardous as forecasting the weather. In fact, the temperature had risen forty degrees since Tuesday's frost, and everyone was dressed for spring.

There was a crush of reporters at one of the revolving doors, and Eyler walked in wearing a black suit and looking almost handsome, even though his small mustache gave him the appearance of a Western gunfighter. The reporters hoped he would cover his face or snarl at them, but he walked past all the cameras with the indifference of someone who didn't know what all the commotion is about.

Seeing the WLS crew wrapping up, Androvett asked Kolarik, "That's it?"

"I told you it would be routine."

The other stations kept their crews there, as did the Indianapolis reporter. The WLS team had another story to cover, and Kolarik was sure that the police or the state's attorney's office would let her know if anything unexpected happened.

On the seventeenth floor, U.S. District Judge Paul E.

Plunkett filled in for Judge James Moran. Clearly the issues raised by the Lowell stop were a legal tangle, and he would just as soon let Moran worry about it on Monday. But Plunkett had this warning for Ditkowsky, an unlikely choice of a lawyer for a suspect in a serial murder case: "The law has been settled for a hundred years, that a federal court may not deal with property in control and possession of state officers."

Ditkowsky now attacked on another front. He asked the judge for the affidavit police used to request a search warrant for the truck, explaining that the document was sealed by order of State's Attorney Foreman.

"What is the reason?" the judge asked the lawyer representing the police in the litigation, Dan Field.

"Your honor," Field began. His tone was defensive. "It contains information that I think, if disclosed at this time, would be extremely detrimental to the continuing criminal investigation."

The question was put off since Field did not have a copy for the judge to examine, and Ditkowsky brought up another matter. He wanted to see the affidavit Indiana police had provided for the warrant to search Dr. Little's home in Terre Haute. The lawyer explained that he had never seen an inventory of the materials taken.

Attorney Louis Brydges, the senior law partner of the firm Field worked for, stepped toward the bench. He told the judge that Ditkowsky was improperly trying to obtain information in a criminal investigation rather than restricting himself to the civil rights issue at hand.

This animated Ditkowsky. "Your Honor," he said, "I had conversations with these police officers when I first got in on the case, and they told me they had absolutely no evidence concerning my client at all. In fact, hours before the complaint was actually filed, Smith told me he didn't have a scintilla of evidence against my client and he would have to return the truck."

Field handed Plunkett the affidavit, and the judge called a ten-minute recess to study the list of evidence the task force expected to find. He returned looking solemn, for he had seen more than a scintilla. He sat behind the bench and ruled, "The court finds that within the complaints are items which, if turned over, could jeopardize or interfere with a continuing investigation."

"I don't know why those should be secret," Ditkowsky grumbled.

"I have not ruled that you can't have them," the judge said. "I am ruling that you can't have them now."

Judge Plunkett ended the hearing, leaving Ditkowsky flustered. The Lake County officers rose from their seats and rushed out of the courtroom. Lamprich was carrying a warrant signed at 10:50 that morning by a Waukegan judge after reviewing these latest developments:

—FBI footprint specialist Bob Hallitt was so certain the tiny nicks that appeared in the plaster casts Smitty had made in August matched the wear on Eyler's boots that he was willing to fly in and testify;

—Dr. Helen Young of the coroner's office stated just yesterday that Calise's wounds could have been inflicted by the knife Indiana police had found in Eyler's truck;

—Lt. Mike Medler of the Indiana state police crime lab notified Colin on October 5 that the knife had human blood on it, type A-positive. On October 26, the FBI cut open Eyler's boot and found type A-positive blood. Eyler's blood type was unknown (further tests by the FBI proved that the enzymes found on the knife matched Calise's).

—Handcuffs seized from Eyler's home in Terre Haute were consistent with marks found on Calise's wrists.

—Robert Wilson, forensic scientist and tire expert for the Northern Illinois Crime Laboratory, affirmed that casts Smitty had made with dental plaster contained impressions matching the models and the positions of the tires on Eyler's truck: BF Goodrich Radial T/A P255/70 R15 on the front axle and BF Goodrich Radial All Terrain T/A 31×10, 50 LT M/S on the rear axle.

As Colin and Lamprich wished their elevator could go down faster, several Indiana task force officers were stationed like sentries around the exits, ready to report when Eyler passed through.

WISH reporter Mike Androvett sensed that something was happening. He didn't know Chicago well, but he had an advantage over the local reporters. He knew what the task force members looked like and the difference between when they were only standing around and when they were on a stakeout. Right now, Sgt. Billy Bob Newman was at a rear elevator speaking quietly into a walkie-talkie.

Androvett glanced at the cluster of other reporters, just biding their time. Why disturb them? There were, after all, limits to cooperation. He walked over to the detective and said, "Something's happening here, right?" Newman nodded. "Is it big?"

"We're going to take him in," Newman told him confidentially.

"Are you going to charge him?"

Newman answered with a smile, or perhaps just a neutral expression that Androvett mistook for a grin of affirmation.

Of course Androvett could have said to the other reporters, "Hey, guys, guess what!" Instead he walked nonchalantly to his cameraman and whispered for him to get ready. Then he noticed that Colin and Lamprich seemed to be waiting for something. Colin was of average size but looked short standing next to the six-foot former Marine. Androvett didn't know their names, but he could tell that police from both states were involved in what was about to happen.

The black elevator doors slid open, and Eyler stepped out with his attorney. Colin nodded to Newman, then he and Lamprich headed for one of the front doors. Newman went over to his commander, Lt. Jerry Campbell.

Sam McPherson positioned himself in the lobby close to where Eyler and Ditkowsky were talking to reporters about Plunkett's refusal to let them see the police affidavits. The crews filmed Ditkowsky and his client up to the east door of the glass and steel building, then forgot about them. Androvett leaned over to his cameraman and said, "Stay on him." He had no way of knowing how police would "take him," so he could not offer specific suggestions. The other cameras were turned toward the corridors as the television reporters tried to look imposing while delivering their favorite line: their name, their station, and "from the Dirksen Federal Building."

Androvett's cameraman went through the revolving door to Jackson Boulevard, then toward the subway entrance on the State Street Mall. Not many attorneys conduct their clients to important hearings by way of the Chicago Transit Authority. Eyler heard the WISH team walking behind him and turned around, but he paid no attention to the camera. He was unaware that the cameraman knew something that he didn't about the case, and not even Ditkowsky thought it odd that they should be trailing them.

Rather than arouse suspicion, Colin and Lamprich were following Androvett. Campbell and Newman went down the street to get the Lake County sheriff's police car ready for the Illinois officers.

The WMAQ-TV crew, putting their gear away, became suspicious. Too many people were walking toward State Street. So the WMAQ cameraman began following the WISH cameraman, who was following Eyler and Ditkowsky. Colin and Lamprich were still walking behind the cameras.

Ditkowsky and his client started down the steps of the subway. Colin and Lamprich sped up and reached the top of the stairs. Lamprich slid something from his pocket. "Mr. Ditkowsky," he announced, "we have a warrant signed by Judge Charles Scott this morning to take blood samples from Eyler."

The curly-haired lawyer halted on the step and twisted his compact frame to look at the officers standing in the bright sunlight. He turned to Eyler and said, "Forget that, we're going back to Judge Plunkett."

The Lake County detectives let them pass by, then followed for a few paces. Tired of the game, Lamprich said to Ditkowsky's back, "Are you interfering with the performance of my duties? Do you want us to read the search warrant to you inside or outside the building?"

Cameras to the left of him, cameras to the right of him, what else could Ditkowsky do but comply? "This is nothing but harassment," he complained.

With his pipe off to the side of his mouth, Colin quietly

said, "We are taking Mr. Eyler with us to the state toxicology lab; it's just three miles from here. They're going to draw blood and remove hair samples. There's no point in going back, Mr. Ditkowsky. Judge Plunkett has no jurisdiction; this is a criminal case."

The lawyer stopped with his hands at his sides; Colin and Newman took Eyler by the arm. "Here, take this," Eyler said, as he handed Ditkowsky a manila envelope of defense papers. "I have to go with them."

Colin and Lamprich took Eyler into their car as the task force men followed in their own auto.

Gera-Lind Kolarik knew nothing of this; she was working on several breaking stories in the WLS studios at the other end of the Loop. Over a scanner she heard WMAQ's two-way radio transmission: "We have b-roll of Eyler's arrest."

"Shit," her immediate boss muttered, "I knew we should have sent out two crews."

When a reporter misses a story, all stops are pulled to get hold of anyone who might confirm the information or provide a fresh angle; careers depend on it. Kolarik attacked a phone. Smitty wasn't available; neither was McKoski, Sheriff Babcox, nor State's Attorney Foreman. Her boss, Mort Meisner, kept running a one-way dialogue. "This is *our* story. We put the Eyler thing together. How could we blow it?"

Like the Seventh Cavalry at the end of a Western, the Indianapolis television reporter rushed into the Chicago newsroom with a tape in hand and shouted, "I got it all!"

Meisner and the news director moved people out of Androvett's way and cleared an editing room for him. Kolarik and the others gathered around a monitor to watch the silent tape. "It's a strange arrest," she said. "No Miranda rights, no handcuffs. Mort, believe me, it's not an arrest. They're taking him somewhere."

"For a one-way ride, let's hope," one of the editors remarked.

Androvett was not watching the monitor; he'd already seen the "arrest," although he was too far away to hear what the officers and Ditkowsky said to each other. He stood impatiently at the doorway of the small room and glanced at the wall clock for at least the third time before he said, "I have to go now. Can I have my tape back?"

"Yeah, but we're going to make a dub first," Meisner told him.

"I'm sorry, you can't." That stopped them all. "You're an ABC affiliate, and we're a CBS affiliate, and my news director has to OK it."

"We've been cooperating," Kolarik put in. "I lent him some background."

"Shit," Meisner said once more and turned to Kolarik. "You gave him *our* tape and *our* leads?" He sounded as if she had just confessed to treason.

"It's all right," veteran newsman Dan Allen said. "This is good stuff. We'll get permission."

The news director, Bill Applegate, gestured to Kolarik. When she walked past the tables and desk and the color-coded assignment map, Kolarik felt a strong pain in her stomach from her self-anger at missing the arrest. She grabbed her purse and went through her wallet for Valiums packed in a plastic bag for times like these. She washed one down with cold coffee. She picked up her beat books, took a deep breath, and walked in. "Close the door and tell me why we missed this," Applegate said. Meisner opened the door and stuck his head in. "Sheriff Babcox on the line for you, Ger." Meisner stayed inside to see what happened.

Kolarik excused herself and picked up Applegate's phone. "Mickey, this is Gera-Lind. What the hell happened today? I'm in hot water here. I've been with you guys from the start, you know that, and you don't tell me when you . . . It's just a search warrant?" She listened a moment longer and put the phone at elbow distance. "We don't have to worry," she told Meisner and Applegate. "It's routine. Blood and hair samples."

Meisner sauntered into the newsroom and announced, "We can all quiet down now; Larry Eyler's not arrested. Back to work, everybody."

The two police cars drove down the Taylor Street strip of Italian restaurants and narrow apartment buildings, then parked across from the slab gray, boxlike Illinois Department of Public Health laboratories building. The forensic toxicology unit was a small former storage room on the fourth floor and had had a temporary look for more than ten years. There was nothing here but some metal shelves for books and beakers, a few chairs, and a conference table made out of a three-foot-wide spool for telephone cables. Oh, and a few model airplanes that Dr. John Spikes had put here and there to make himself feel at home. A secretary was across the corridor, but Spikes had no other staff; whenever he wanted to run tests he had to go to one of the lab rooms down the cinder block aisles.

Dr. Spikes was a tall, stocky man with receding gray-white hair. He seemed grateful for something to do as he asked Eyler to roll up his sleeve. "This won't hurt," he said. The needle went in, and Spikes drew three samples of blood. Eyler hardly said a word and didn't even show curiosity. Each vial got a cap with a different color: gray, orange, and purple. "Have a seat, Mr. Eyler, please," Spikes said. "This will be just a few minutes."

Eyler sat next to Colin and Lamprich, fingering a small bandage over one of his punctures and then rolling down his sleeve and buttoning his cuff, looking at both detectives to make sure this was all right.

If the blood turned out to be A-positive, the same type the FBI found inside the boot, then there would be no way of disproving Eyler's claim that he cut himself. Police in two states still wouldn't have a case. The prosecution for as many as two dozen murders could be decided by a coin-flip of nature. Colin said nothing, and Lamprich cracked his knuckles. The Indiana officers kept their smalltalk to a murmur.

Sooner than the detectives expected, Spikes returned. Since he was not aware of the circumstances surrounding this court-ordered blood typing, his eyes gave nothing away and his tone was calm. "This man has type O-positive blood."

Colin smiled faintly as he nudged his partner. They had clinched their case at last, but there was more relief than excitement. "I have a call to make," Lamprich said, knowing that Smitty would be pleased.

Eyler, sitting obediently in his armless chair, had no understanding of the significance of his blood type, and Colin did not bother to tell him.

"Follow me, if you please," Spikes said and led Colin and Eyler a few yards west down the yellow-beige corridor. The office was small but private. Spikes removed a few strands of hair from Eyler's head, put them in a white envelope, and asked him to lower his pants. Eyler was embarrassed, and Colin looked away. The toxicologist put a few dark pubic hairs into another envelope.

"Is that it?" Colin asked.

"That's it," Spikes answered. The officers had entered the building at 2:05 P.M. and it was now only 2:49.

Eyler asked, "What now?"

"Now I guess we take you home," Colin replied. This wasn't the way the detective thought he would feel when the case was clinched; there was just a dull relaxing of that inner coil.

The phone lines were busy as the news traveled up the administrative ladder. As soon as Smitty received word from Lamprich about the blood type, he called prosecutor McKoski. He had to be formal, but everything in his tone seemed to say "We did it!" McKoski had the authority to approve charges, but he knew protocol. His boss, State's Attorney Foreman, had been gone for much of the day for a meeting in the city hall of Schaumburg, a northwest suburb of Chicago. McKoski dialed Foreman's beeper and caught the top prosecutor as he was driving back to the north shore city of Waukegan.

Foreman pulled in at a gas station and put in a call to McKoski. After hearing the report, Foreman said, "It's your case, Ray. What do you think?"

"I think we've got enough."

"All right. Get a charge and a bond. I'll get to my office in half an hour."

McKoski phoned Smitty, and Smitty called Colin's beeper. The pocket device went off like a robot canary as Colin and Lamprich were driving Eyler to his North Side home. Lamprich was at the wheel and headed for a phone even before his partner asked him to. Then Colin said, half to himself, "I think this is it."

"This is it?" said Eyler as a faint echo. He nervously rubbed a tuft of hair between his fingers.

Colin came back, and his expression was difficult to read. He put his folded arms against the opened window of the car and said, "Larry, you have just been charged with the murder of Ralph Calise. The state's attorney's office is asking for bond of one million dollars."

"One million dollars, Larry," Lamprich said dryly. "You don't happen to have it on you, do you?" His inflection was tired. The case had worn everybody out.

Sliding back into the car, Colin said, "Judge Plunkett wants to see us now, so let's turn around." He removed the handcuffs from around his belt and snapped them around Eyler's wrists.

The appearance before Plunkett was just a formality. Colin told the judge that a murder warrant had been signed and was being brought to the courthouse, and Plunkett told Eyler: "It looks like you're on your way to Lake County."

All the formalities had been observed, but everyone had forgotten Sheriff Babcox, and he was furious. The former mortician whose hobby was murder had never personally made a major arrest, and this was the most important case in his career. Usually he was convivial, but anger and determination now sent him out of his office. He wanted to hear about developments from his own staff, not reporters. "I told them to stay away from the press," he grumbled.

The sheriff staked out the intersection between the courthouse and the tiny morgue in downtown Waukegan, waiting for the car to appear. In his hand was a copy of the murder warrant. He carried it like a weapon.

The car drove down Washington Street and turned off into the jail entrance. As the officers took Eyler out, Babcox came up to them and formally read each word of the warrant to Eyler. Suddenly Babcox reached out and grabbed his arm. "Hey!" Lamprich called out instinctively. In his anger at the way things were handled, the sheriff threw Eyler against the green garage door leading to the jail.

Lamprich looked as if he were about to say something that could make the situation worse, and Colin spoke up. "We can handle him from here," he told Babcox diplomatically. The detectives opened the door and led Eyler inside, then turned him over to the guards.

When they came out, Lamprich asked Babcox, "What's wrong?"

"Nothing's wrong," the sheriff answered with the force of someone biting off the tip of a cigar and spitting it out.

That evening Father Ryan arrived from St. Alphonsus Church in Chicago. The jail was only twenty-two years old, yet it was so overcrowded that a new one was being planned. The priest was allowed to speak to Eyler only by telephone hookup past a transparent barrier. The priest had brought with him a consecrated host, but Communion was impossible. Eyler was angry that he had been denied the Sacrament. That meant he believed himself to be in a state of grace.

11

October 29, 1983
Waukegan, Illinois

The court doors opened and Eyler came out, appearing shaken for the first time. Two sheriff's deputies walked him past the crush of reporters and the glare of the television lights. Judge Alvin Singer on this Saturday morning had just refused to lower Eyler's million-dollar bond. For the defendant, it must have seemed as if he might never be free again.

As Eyler sat in Judge Singer's courtroom wearing a T-shirt with the stenciled letters for the Lake County Jail, Ditkowsky told of how his client had an unblemished record. Countering this, Assistant State's Attorney Ray McKoski portrayed Eyler as an unstable man who had trouble holding a job and who had more roots in Indiana than in Illinois. Colin told the judge that Eyler's record was unblemished only because stabbing victim Mark Henry had dropped charges after receiving money.

Although it wasn't yet apparent, Ditkowsky was trying an additional tactic. Besides keeping Eyler accessible to reporters, the lawyer persuaded him to overcome his reluctance to talk about his homosexuality. Jurors in the eventual trial must not feel that he's holding anything back.

Colin was waiting outside Singer's courtroom for John Dobrovolskis to pass by with the other spectators.

"Mr. Dobrovolskis, would you mind going with me to the sheriff's office?" the detective asked.

Dobrovolskis looked coldly at him and replied, "I have nothing to say."

Colin handed him a subpoena to appear before the grand jury on Tuesday. Dobrovolskis pushed the paper away and bolted down the corridor as Colin called out: "You have just been served."

"I have been served with nothing," Dobrovolskis said and hastened down the corridor.

Reporters had just enough time to finish their notes, pack up their tape recorders, and pick up their cables to cross the way and set up shop inside the sheriff's office for a news conference. Fred Foreman was there to lend authority but had no idea what Babcox had written up for himself to say.

The sheriff preferred one-on-one interviews with reporters, but a news conference would look good to the voters as he prepared for reelection next year. "This type of sordid crime can be compared with the sadistic gratification that John Wayne Gacy must have enjoyed in his vicious crimes," said Babcox, reading from a paper. The sheriff added that Eyler matched the FBI profile worked out from the Indiana crimes, although Eyler was charged with just the Calise murder. "He is a macho-image, beer-drinking homosexual with a hate for himself because he is homosexual."

Foreman remained silent as he stared at the spectacle of a sheriff enjoying his fifteen minutes of fame. Babcox became carried away and departed from the paper. As Detective Kurt Proschwitz said of him, "That was one of Mickey's things: if you don't know, make it up." Babcox mistakenly told reporters that hair samples from Eyler matched hair found at the Calise scene. No hair had been found.

As the news conference was being held, deputy sheriffs were serving grand jury subpoenas on Sally Dobrovolskis in Chicago and James Williams in Indiana. In his jail cell, Eyler found himself swept over by waves of helplessness. He became easily upset at anything that deprived him of feelings of security, such as a rosary or a Catholic version of the Bible. He may have felt better when Williams assured him by phone that he was not the one who had turned his name in to police.

Most of his calls were to his mother in Richmond, İndiana, near the Ohio border.

"Mother, I didn't do it," he would say.

"Why didn't you call? Didn't you think I loved you enough to suffer through anything?"

"I know you love me enough, but I didn't want to make things bad for you. I wanted to be able to call you and say that it was all over and had been a bad mistake."

The subject was always the same: love and innocence.

After testifying in Judge Singer's court that Saturday, detectives notified the Illinois Department of Children and Family Services about the unusual household of John, Sally, and Larry. All three of them seemed to love children, but there was no way of being sure that those boys and the girl would have a normal upbringing if conditions continued. Detective work is more than solving crimes; sometimes it's helping to pick up the pieces.

Now that the jurisdictions were working together, the investigation had taken on a life of its own. No individual was leading, and anything learned about one victim might help understand the killing of another. Hunches came easier, and police were starting to comprehend the lines of thought in the nightworld.

One thing troubling the Illinois investigators was the disappearance of wallets and T-shirts in most of the cases. Perhaps there was a "trophy case" somewhere. After all, there was as much love as hate in serial murders, and several killers were known to keep reminders of their victims near them, from religious medals to their wallets.

This was what Colin was thinking about as he was off that Sunday. Children in his suburb of Round Lake were celebrating Halloween a day early in their clown costumes and witch's hats. The mild day was clouding over as a cool wind blew in. He decided to make a call to Indiana.

McPherson and Sergeant Love were already planning a second search of Dr. Little's home. Colin told them it was imperative they specify in the affidavit for the warrant anything of the sort a serial killer might have, including identification cards or photos of the victims, body parts, and shovels. A judge signed the warrant at 5:55 P.M. October 31, and police were ready to go trick-or-treating at the attractive two-story town house on Keane Lane.

At 8 A.M. Tuesday, November 1, they flashed the warrant and went through the kitchen, living room, bathroom, and three bedrooms, as well as the garage that fronts the street and overlooks Terre Haute's major park.

The officers did not find anything that would make them say "Ah-hah!" but they carried out nine boxes of belongings to be studied, including T-shirts with logos, work gloves, six baseball caps, and eighty-eight pairs of socks. (None belonged to a victim.)

The college teacher stood by while ten detectives scoured his home and grounds. The home fronts a small rise in the land, more of a wrinkle than a hillock, and a few yards to the left is a woods. There were no signs of fresh digging, and policemen waded in freezing water in a nearby creek to look for awls or knives.

The officers in the house could not be sure what to take, so they dropped into their boxes anything that looked suspicious, including some of Little's books such as *Criminal Law and Procedure*. The officers carted out whole dresser drawers and took with them fourteen bottles of prescription drugs. Many of them were tranquilizers or sleeping pills. The closest the task force men came to anything incriminating were an ice pick (later discounted as a weapon) and a bondage item: a black leather collar with studs.

One box was heavy with fifty-three bottles of liquor ranging from grain alcohol to Korbel champagne. These were considered necessary for fingerprint comparisons. But the box was so heavy—the officers didn't think of getting a second container—that it dropped as they were unloading it in the parking lot of the former school building in Indianapolis. Being professionals, they did the best they could under the circumstances to preserve the evidence. They took pictures of the broken bottles.

The officers dumped the other items on long tables set up in their headquarters. Detective Henry picked up the prescription bottles one by one and studied what their labels could tell him. One was authorized by Eyler's friend, Dr. Smith, on June 18, 1981. It was for Placidyl. Other prescriptions issued by Smith were from October 14, 1980 to September 11, 1982. For what it was worth, the final one was nearly six months after the bodies started turning up. Possibly more interesting was that the dates on the bottles showed that Smith was seeing Eyler at least in a professional capacity a year before the time he gave the police, and the last prescription was written eight months after the time the methodical physician said he broke up with him.

As the task force was hauling away the 221 items of possible evidence from the town house, Assistant State's Attorney Ray McKoski was addressing the Lake County grand jury in Waukegan. The first witness was Colin. He testified that Calise was not only stabbed seventeen times, he was eviscerated as if he had been some wild animal killed for sport. A portion of the intestine had been removed and placed outside for reasons known only to the killer.

Sally Dobrovolskis was called next. She told how Eyler lived as a friend and fellow tenant with her, her husband, their two sons, and their three foster children. Her natural sons were ten and four, and of the foster children the girl was five and the twin boys were four. She testified that she had quit her job at an insurance company to care for them and that they were being raised with love and discipline.

As she spoke a social worker came to the home and told the babysitter that she was there to remove the three foster children. There was no warning and no explanation. Adam, the son of John and Sally, cried along with Sally's son from her previous marriage as their "brothers" and "sister" were taken from them. They already had been told that Daddy's friend Larry was in the hospital rather than being told the truth about his arrest. The family—their only world—seemed to be coming apart.

In her grand jury testimony, Sally unintentionally presented herself as a servant in her own home rather than as a wife. She was an adaptable young woman married to a headstrong man, and she could only be an outsider to his milieu. Once when asked to describe herself, she replied, "Someone no one pays attention to."

Her testimony and the account of the following witness, James Williams, made it possible for the grand jury to envision the circumstances of Eyler's life for the hours before Calise disappeared in Chicago.

Williams and Dobrovolskis went out together the night of August 30 after tiring of waiting for Eyler to show up. Eyler had said he needed to go to the Male Hide leather store for a pants fitting, but that had been four and a half hours before. This was an uncomfortably humid Tuesday night, and for some reason Eyler had wanted to be by himself. The two men told Sally they would be going to the Loading Dock, a gay bar, and if there was a good crowd they would stay; if not, they would go to some of the other places. They left the converted coach house on Greenview Avenue at 11 P.M. and noticed Eyler's truck parked outside.

Eyler returned a few minutes later. Neither Sally nor Williams gave an explanation, but the timing was suspicious. Eyler sometimes laid traps for Dobrovolskis, testing his loyalty. His spending five hours at a fitting might suggest that he had just been waiting to see whether his lover would go out with someone else. Whatever the reason, Eyler decided to go out on his own. He showered and shaved, threw his jeans in the dryer, and "fiddled with his hair." He left home around 12:30 A.M., August 31. Sally assumed Eyler would try to meet up with his friends by checking the bars along Halsted and Clark streets, but apparently that's not where he went.

Dobrovolskis and Williams returned from the bars and a restaurant at 3:30 A.M. or so, and Eyler had only recently returned. He was in a T-shirt and jeans and seemed to be waiting for them this muggy night. "Did you have a good time?" Eyler asked. "I'm sorry I missed you." The two men, who had been drinking for a few hours, laughed at that. At this moment Ralph Calise, who had disappeared at around midnight a few miles away, lay dead in Lake Forest.

Eyler turned his back to the men and went to his room upstairs. Dobrovolskis and Williams, his houseguest for the week, sat in the living room listening to music until nearly dawn.

One item of interest to the jury was Williams' reference to a two-inch key Eyler kept on his key chain ready for use. It looked like a miniature skeleton key, but Williams said he assumed it was for handcuffs. No, he didn't think it was strange.

After the grand jury deliberated just five minutes, the forelady announced the indictment. The case was open and shut. No one had ever heard of a serial killer who was freed after a grand jury took action.

The next day, Eyler stood in a white T-shirt and blue jeans before Lake County Circuit Court Judge William Block for a hearing on defense motions. Block was a friendly man with a youthful face and contrasting salt-and-pepper hair. He enjoyed a touch of levity when appropriate and would lean forward at his bench with almost an eavesdropper's curiosity.

As usual, Ditkowsky made allegations about everybody, citing violations of the First, Third, Fourth, Sixth, and Fourteenth amendments to the U.S. Constitution and asking for permission for Eyler to be interviewed by the news media. McKoski showed bewilderment as he stood up with his knuckles on the prosecutor's table. Usually lawyers keep their clients away from reporters to avoid pre-trial publicity, but Ditkowsky had a different strategy.

"I would like to conform to the wishes of certain members of the press to interview my client," Ditkowsky explained, "so they can determine he is not a monster." Reporters were heard whispering to one another, and some left to call their city editors.

Eyler said he understood that he could be jeopardizing his defense, and the judge approved the request. Then came the matter that a rosary was denied Eyler. Ditkowski said that only the King James version of the Bible was available on the jail library cart that went from cell to cell.

"I don't have any problem with the Bible," McKoski said, "but I'm not so sure that I'm familiar with the rosary.'' The prosecutor sounded as if he were speaking of a secret weapon.

Judge Block felt the courtroom was an awkward place to discuss theology and said self-consciously, ''They all basically have the same number of beads, but they come in all shapes and sizes. I imagine there would be some—''

''Big enough?'' McKoski asked, imagining how one might be used to attack a guard.

''There would be some that weren't big enough to pose potential harm to other persons or the defendant,'' the judge continued. He said he would not object to supplying Eyler with a rosary consistent with security.

As to the complaint that Father Ryan could not give Eyler Communion, Judge Block told Ditkowsky, ''The jail isn't a hotel, and we don't have room service.''

Maintaining judicial neutrality when the defense attorney was trying to convert this into a federal civil rights case wasn't easy. Then Ditkowsky overdid it by charging that Sheriff Babcox's remarks the day before had created ''a lynch mob attitude.''

''I don't know what that has to do with the nature of the offense, the nature of the proofs, the background of the defendant, and whether he's going to appear in court should he be released on bond,'' Block said.

The judge admitted privately later that he was hoping Eyler would find a lawyer with more experience in criminal law, and that Ditkowsky seemed to have the same feelings.

The hearing ended, and the sheriff's police prepared Babcox's office for the news conference. Standing in the back of the room, Babcox muttered to Colin, ''This is the nuttiest thing I have ever seen.''

As the judge had warned, anything Eyler might say could be used against him. No camera crews or photographers were allowed, but sheriff's deputies laid out several microphones along the conference table.

Another deputy led Eyler into the room. He was not handcuffed but looked ill at ease. At least in Ditkowsky's theory, anything Eyler said would prove his innocence. The lawyer was so sure of his strategy that he had not worked out what Eyler would discuss or even asked him whether he could conduct a news conference. Not many people can.

The suspect waited until everyone was ready, then waited a little more. At last he began. "I'm not guilty; I just want you to know that," he said, facing twenty reporters.

"Then how come police state that you may be responsible for as many as nineteen murders?" one newsman shot off. The sentence wasn't a question; it was a veritable poke in the ribs to see how Eyler would respond.

Before Eyler could think of a reply, another reporter asked, "Then how come your boot prints match the prints at the scene?"

Flustered, Eyler turned to his lawyer and shook his head in helplessness. He felt skewered and mentally slithered into his submissive mode. "I'm sorry," he said to Ditkowsky in his soft-as-cotton voice. "I don't think I can do it. I just want to go."

Eyler lowered his head to avoid the glare of reporters from Waukegan, Chicago, Hammond, Gary, Terre Haute, and Indianapolis. Moving closer to the microphones, Ditkowsky said, "I wanted this news conference to tell our side. Let's stay away from the crime. He's very upset."

Easing up a little now that he felt he wouldn't be asked about the killings or his homosexuality, Eyler told the reporters that he had been treated fairly in jail, made some friends, and had talked by telephone to a priest, his lawyer, and his mother. For the most part pens stayed above paper: there wasn't much to quote. At least Ditkowsky had succeeded in showing that Eyler was no monster; he was as vulnerable and pathetic as any other person would be.

"I took Larry Eyler's case because of the horrendous violations of my client's civil rights," Ditkowsky said. "They have an innocent man who's being railroaded. Thank you." He motioned to the deputies that they could lead the defendant away. The reporters were saying among themselves "Is this all?" Babcox grumbled from the back of the room, "I can't believe this."

* * *

The police wondered how many other men were out there who might know more about Eyler's secret life or who could link Eyler to a victim. On Thursday, November 10, Colin had a talk with Smitty. He wanted a saturation of the Chicago gay neighborhood: every detective available showing every photo they had from the Illinois victims. At the start of the investigation, Smitty had to fight for all the overtime Colin and Lamprich were putting on this case, but now they had the go-ahead from Babcox for whatever they felt was necessary.

At eight o'clock that night Colin, Lamprich, Curt Corsi, and James Rowley piled out of a sheriff's police car on North Halsted Street and started making the bar scene in pairs. Winds of forty-five miles an hour swept in from the lake, making people run across streets and down sidewalks. Signs wobbled and street debris swirled past second-story windows.

Once they were inside Touché, a two-and-a-half-foot outline of a phallus in neon lights reminded the detectives what kind of place they were in. The bartender wore a leather vest over a sleeveless shirt and had a pewter anchor dangling from one ear. He looked as if he would be happier on a pirate ship than washing glasses and pulling down the taps; but, as the patrons knew, it was all just fantasy. He gave a quick glance at the men coming in and probably spotted them as cops as soon as they passed the threshold.

The dimness and odd dimensions of the place resulted from the tavern being built into what had been a first-floor home. The only other person at the bar was an old man with a Santa Claus beard and belly, and he was just reading a newspaper.

The pirate had time to talk, but he didn't have much to say. He studied the pictures of Steve Crockett, Ralph Calise, Jimmy Roberts, John Johnson, Gustavo Herrera, Craig Townsend, Larry Eyler, and John Dobrovolskis. "These other guys, maybe they came in here and maybe not. You see a lot of faces around here. But this one"—he held onto Eyler's photo—"I've seen this one before. Couple of times. One of the bodybuilders. He's probably a regular at the other places, too. What's his name?''

"Larry.''

"Larry, that's it. He drinks beer; that's all I can tell you.''

Lamprich and another detective went to the bars along Clark and Illinois streets, close to downtown, which served generally older, rougher men. Lamprich, the six-foot ex-Marine who had lost a finger to a land mine in Vietnam, was uneasy about going into Redoubt. The bartender told the detectives that most of the men were downstairs. Lamprich put his hand on the bannister and quickly pulled it away when he realized what the post was carved to resemble.

The detectives still hadn't gotten over seeing a barfly at one of the other places kissing man after man for drinks. Now they were in a sadomasochism basement of whips, leashes, and harnesses.

Inside "the pit" in the basement of the next door Gold Coast leather bar were several private rooms. A tunnel led to the Male Hide leather store where Eyler bought his pants. For some time, Lamprich had been thinking of leaving the police business, and now he was sure he should quit.

Chicago police did not routinely harass the gay community, and the bar clients did not try to stonewall them. But no one could tell them anything about Eyler or the others. As the men were leaving, one of the patrons gave Lamprich a pat, probably as a joke because of the let's-get-out-of-here expression on his face. The other detectives laughed over that as they headed back for Lake County, but Lamprich wasn't amused.

The saturation night was a good idea that didn't work out. For Colin it seemed the end of the Calise investigation. The case would have to stand or fall on the basis of the evidence untimely seized in Indiana.

From now on he would have to concentrate on the teenage boy who was found hacked to death and covered with paneling and brush in the woods near Lake Forest on April 15, four months before Calise was killed. Colin didn't look forward to the work. How far can you get without a name, a motive, or a clue?

This was the murder that helped mislead Colin into thinking that satanism was involved, because the body was put on top of a dog that had been stabbed to death as well. Dr. Helen Young of the coroner's office, who had performed the autopsy on Calise, reported that the teenage boy had eight or nine stab wounds in the upper right portion of his back. At least two were so hard the knife had gone through the bone and probably pierced the lungs. Young couldn't be sure because the organs apparently had been eaten by wildlife in the three to four months the body had lain there.

In addition, there was a skull fracture on the left side of the head, and the throat had been stabbed. The boy did not match anyone in the missing persons reports for Lake County, meaning he was probably a runaway from some other part of the Midwest.

To a pathologist we are all jigsaw puzzles to be disassembled for study. Young removed the jaws to help chart the dental work, then she removed the boy's hands and sent them to the FBI laboratory in a cardboard box. None of this led to anything, and the case remained just an open file.

Lamprich, doing the initial work, had confined his investigation to the northern suburbs. But that was before all the other murders were known. Taking over the investigation, Colin decided to see if the boy came from Uptown.

When he and Lamprich drove to Chicago he didn't take along a photo of the facial reconstruction, and that was an advantage. Sheriff Babcox and Coroner Barbara Richardson had asked retired high school art teacher Jane Craner to make a mask of clay over the skull to give a general suggestion of what the victim may have looked like. A police sketch released in September was that of a boy of fifteen or sixteen, but the Indiana cases made the pathologist and sheriff believe the victim was older.

Usually reconstructions are done by anthropologists. Craner had learned the technique at Colorado State University but lacked the training to determine age from a skull.

She used Vaseline and a mixture of plastic and modeling clay, then topped it with a dark wig. Out of necessity, the face that appeared under her fingers lacked the detail that would have given it character. The head was made to resemble someone in his twenties. Instead of aiding the investigation, the "likeness" became just one more false lead.

In Area 6 headquarters on Chicago's North Side, Colin and Lamprich sat in an upstairs room going over reports of runaways and children who probably went off with a parent after a custody battle. They were looking for anything about a teenager last seen in a football jersey with number thirty-two on the back.

"We got one," Lamprich said and pulled out Chicago police report EO56949: Ervin D. Gibson; white male; date of birth, May 8, 1966. That would have made him sixteen at the time he was killed, nearly ten years younger than the facial reconstruction would suggest. Gibson's address: 4509 North Magnolia Avenue, right in the heart of Uptown.

The next day, Wednesday, Lamprich and Colin gave Detective Corsi a dental chart with X rays of the Gibson boy that they had picked up from a Chicago dentist. Four and a half hours later, Dr. Carl Hagstrom, a forensic odontologist who had assisted in the autopsy, arrived at the sheriff's office with records from his office in north suburban Fox Lake. The detectives watched as he put his charts and those of the Chicago dentist side by side.

"There are discrepancies," Hagstrom said, "but in my opinion, this is the same body."

Afterward, Colin and Lamprich sat around not saying much and gearing themselves for notifying one more family that their son had been murdered. At least there probably wouldn't be the painful moment of informing the relatives that the boy may have died after hustling a homosexual. Since the mother had waited almost a month before reporting Ervin missing, she may have been used to her son going off by himself for long periods.

Since Lamprich had been involved in the early part of this investigation, he was the one who drove up to the mother's home just after noon on another cold, overcast, very windy day. Naked tree branches shook threateningly, and window frames rattled.

Sylvia Gibson had prepared herself for the news that her son was dead, and the appearance of the detectives at her doorway spoke for itself. She sat down with them and was as open as they could expect.

Mrs. Gibson knew her son hustled on the street. He had been like that ever since his last year in grammar school. Ervin never attended high school. He spent his adolescence at the correctional facility at St. Charles, Illinois, where he was released in August 1982. Just five months later, on January 24, he walked a twelve-year-old friend to the boy's apartment in a transient hotel on Wilson Avenue. Ervin never came home. His mother thought that perhaps he had gone to another state or taken up with some man. She didn't notify police until February 12.

The woman told Lamprich and Colin that she was doing the best she could to raise two sons and two daughters without a husband or a job. The detectives understood. It was the Uptown story.

After the task force in Indianapolis completed an inventory of belongings seized from Dr. Little's home, they notified the news media that the clothing would be available in the former schoolhouse for public viewing. Police were hoping that the family of some of the unidentified victims might recognize something. Several parents, brothers, and sisters came by over the next few days and slowly, sadly, looked over the T-shirts and other pieces, but no one recognized anything.

This meant that the only solid physical evidence in any of the cases remained in what was seized at the Lowell stop in Indiana and the truck tires removed in Illinois, and all of it pertaining only to the Calise murder. No matter what Sheriff Babcox said, everything else was speculation.

12

Saturday, November 12, 1983

Two deputy sheriffs led Eyler to the basement of the over-crowded jail so that he might meet the man recommended by Ditkowsky as his new lawyer. David Schippers had already been approved by Dr. Little and Eyler's parents. He wore his silvery hair long and went about in a trench-coat and gray porkpie cap, as if embarrassed at being successful.

In his prosecutor days, Schippers had earned respect across the board as the man who jailed top Chicago mobster Sam Giancana. Giancana's biographer, William Brashler, said, "At few times in the history of the govern-ment's effort against organized crime had one prosecutor had so much information against one man."

Schippers always enjoyed going on the attack, but he hated playing politics and had seen the Giancana case frit-tered away by his politically ambitious boss, Edward Han-rahan. When Schippers became a defense attorney, he stopped trying to look like a team player. He let his crew cut grow out and adopted eccentricities such as jogging in the Loop and having a vintage gumball machine near his desk.

With him at the initial meeting in the jail was Linda Holmes, his paralegal. The woman, who was in her early thirties, did more than just take notes, do research, and help prepare his trial strategy. She tightened his cases by trying to find fault with every tactic he suggested.

It was mid-November, but the heating pipes made the

basement seem like a waiting room in Hades. Schippers already had his tie loosened and suit coat on the back of his chair when Eyler was brought in. The boiler heat made Linda's blouse stick to her back and arms.

Eyler sat down with a guard just a few inches away and seemed uncomfortable at Holmes' presence. The lawyer knew why. "Anything you tell us won't bother us, Larry, and it stays with us," Schippers said. "We're here so you can try us out, see if you want us to represent you." To encourage him to lighten up when talking about sex, Schippers even made up lurid fictions about his staff. Within an hour, Eyler said he felt he would like them to take over his case.

Schippers immediately told Eyler he had decided to reverse Ditkowsky's strategy. During his prosecutor days he was not above trying to create a favorable atmosphere for a grand jury by feeding newspapers information, but he knew that any publicity now would prejudice a jury in the Calise case and ripple down to any other murders he might later be charged with.

Also Ditkowsky had encouraged Eyler to admit his homosexuality in talking to reporters. Schippers knew that some jurors might fall into a false syllogism: Calise was murdered by a homosexual, Eyler is gay, therefore he is probably guilty.

"No more interviews with anyone from the media," Schippers told Eyler, "and you only give facts to me."

For hours Schippers, sitting in the overheated jail basement, kept asking Eyler to recall specific points from the Lowell traffic stop, to re-create everything that he saw and heard from 7 A.M. to 7 P.M., each time in more detail. Eyler couldn't grasp why such minor things were relevant; he was on trial for murder, not for a traffic offense.

The next day Schippers called Lake County prosecutor Ray McKoski and introduced himself to head off the hostility that many defense lawyers automatically feel for the other side. Rather than prolong the case by waiting for a discovery motion to be filed, McKoski agreed to send him all the documents that had already been submitted in court. That allowed the defense to build its case at once.

A wintry wind blew curled-up leaves across the police academy parking lot that week as Colin and Lamprich headed for the task force headquarters in Indiana. The purpose was to go over all the details of each murder and establish the common links.

Cathy Berner was ready for them with print-outs of evidence and other information pertaining to each victim. That included Steven Agan. His body apparently had been hung upside down and savaged in a way that none of the others had been, but there were enough similarities to consider him a victim of the highway killer.

"A key," Colin said, going over the evidence sheet. "Did anyone find out anything about this key?"

"We don't know what it's for," Love remarked. "There's nothing we can do but go around trying to open a few million doors."

"Not a few million," Colin said with a touch of irritation. "We're all agreed that Larry is the killer, right? Then there's a pretty good chance this key opens a door that Larry used regularly." From their expressions he knew that the Indiana officers were not enthusiastic about the suggestion, and he let it drop. After all, Agan was their case.

The Illinois officers went home with a lot of data showing where Eyler and the victims were on various days, but nothing put them together. The Indiana officers went home with the suspicion that Colin might be right about the key.

The next day Love, McPherson, and Newman drove to the old brick building that once housed the county office where Eyler worked. They brought with them two keys: one found under Agan's body and one that had been seized from Little's home November 1. To them, the keys looked alike.

The officers stood at the front door, and Love tried the one they knew was Eyler's. The key fit, but Love couldn't turn the knob. He tried again, and again the door stayed locked. Then he slid into the lock the key that had been found under Agan. This time it lifted the tumblers.

"That proves it," McPherson said. Only, it didn't. Defense attorneys could point out that anyone who worked in the building could have lost the key and that if Eyler had lost it, then someone might have picked it up and carried it with him to the scene.

The officers went to the locksmith who made the duplicate, but he couldn't identify Eyler from the photographs. That meant the police had one of the strongest pieces of evidence yet against Eyler—the strongest evidence for any Indiana case—but they couldn't use the key by itself for an indictment. A prosecutor couldn't say to the grand jury "Why else would Larry Eyler carry a key around with him that didn't work, keeping it even long after the office was closed, unless it was to pretend he never lost the key that did work?"

That same Thursday, Schippers put his coat over a chair in a Lake County courtroom and introduced himself to Judge Block. The judge slid off his glasses and said with a smile, "Mr. Ditkowsky made some strong references to his lack of experience in criminal proceedings, Mr. Schippers, and the court, frankly, for the record, is happy to see you."

Schippers thanked Block and immediately requested that no further interviews be granted for Eyler. "There has been some unbelievable publicity from both sides of this case," he said. "I am thinking that—I talked to the counsel for the state, and we're both in agreement—that this case should be tried in court, where it's supposed to be."

At the request of both sides, Block agreed that all evidence and documents in the case be sealed and kept in the circuit court clerk's office. Block added that this was not a gag order, but reporters knew the ruling came close.

Schippers was taking over the case in midstream and knew he would have to make the stream go in another direction. Ditkowsky, in insisting that this was a civil rights case, had failed to concentrate on briefs that addressed the most vulnerable point in the investigation—possible violations by Indiana police of search-and-seizure protections in the Fourth Amendment.

Like Ditkowsky, Schippers was sure police had the wrong man. There wasn't a moment Eyler hadn't been personable and grateful for everything that was done for him. Eyler's soft voice and submissive ways naturally drew protectiveness from older people. Schippers almost hoped that there would be another highway murder while Eyler was in jail, just to show everyone that he was innocent. The defense attorney, with his ten sons and daughters, had a strong paternal feeling anyway.

Schippers began looking for gaps in the prosecution's case. For one thing, although Eyler lifted weights it seemed unlikely that he could hurl Calise's body eight to twelve feet. And another thing—those boot prints. Schippers and his paralegal had a laugh about them, because one of his own sons had boots pretty much like those. The validity of the evidence didn't matter; he was determined to make police start from scratch. If they had the right man, that shouldn't be too difficult.

Schippers would sit for long periods in his office overlooking Monroe Street in the heart of the Loop and adjust his concentration as if focusing a microscope: he'd consider a line of reasoning, pull back, then go deeper.

Linda was usually a cynic about clients but was completely won over by Eyler. Despite his intelligence and muscular build, he seemed to have the maturity of a twelve-year-old and could be almost endearing. But now she had to play the devil's advocate, as if she were sure he committed not only the Calise murder but all the others.

"There's got to be an Achilles' heel," the lawyer told her when things were getting too easy for him in their back-and-forth exchanges. "Come on, let's keep going. Show me I'm an idiot."

Sometimes they became lost in their role playing. The voice of the paralegal would harden, and they came close to shouting; but the two of them had done this so often for other cases that no apologies were needed.

During a break, Schippers would go back to thinking the issues through and Holmes would read the reports again. She and Schippers' legal secretary had gone over every word and remarked at how refreshing it was to work on a case where the police and the defendant said exactly the same things. This meant that Eyler was being completely truthful about the events surrounding the Lowell stop, and so were the police. Schippers had known this all along, but now it hit him with the force of a revelation. "Jesus Christ," he said, "we've got a shot!"

"What, that they're telling the truth?" Holmes asked from her chair at the conference table.

"That they'll say on the stand just what they say in these reports. If we can pick the reports apart, we'll be able to pick them apart." There would be no cover-ups, no after-the-fact justifications to contend with. The Indiana police believed everything they did was right and probably still did.

Schippers slipped his hands under his belt, behind his back pockets, and started a slow pacing. "I get the feeling that this is going to be a long one," he said of the night.

He was not one of those attorneys who could deliver a stirring defense and not believe a word of it. Schippers, a devout Roman Catholic, needed a sense of moral obligation to take on a major case. Now all he had to do was to convey this sense that a moral wrong had been committed by well-meaning officers. If Schippers could carry off his plan of attack, this seemingly open-and-shut case would never reach a jury.

When Schippers needed to throw some fresh air on his mind he would take off his street shoes and put on sneakers he kept tucked away in his office. He would take an elevator at perhaps one in the morning and jog down the empty downtown streets. Then he would come back to his office with its peeling paint ready to start fresh.

Out of a few days of thinking in his chair, jogging along empty streets, and bickering legal points with Holmes came a decision to file so many motions he would wear down the Lake County state's attorney's office and buy some time.

The Indiana task force received a tip on its hotline that Eyler had a suitcase in Terre Haute that he didn't want anyone to know about. Sam McPherson and Frank Love felt like slapping their foreheads. They remembered seeing a trunk in Dr. Little's garage during the November 1 "raid." So at 5:12 P.M. on November 22 they obtained a search warrant and once more went through the town house on Keane Lane, with its model-home tidiness. The footlocker was gone, but the police took with them anything else they thought might be of interest.

But what they got was a lot of nothing, even after three separate sweeps. No one in the task force could remember any case where so much was confiscated without finding anything that could be tied to a victim or entered into evidence. Even the Agan case was slipping away from them. The officers had the key from near where the body was found and a credit card receipt showing that Eyler was at a nearby Shell station around the time of the murder, but there was still no clincher.

There were all sorts of rumors. One was that Agan was seen buying beer and that he might have been at a wild Christmas party with underage drinking when or just before he was killed. Several cans of beer of the same brand were found near where the body had been dragged to. But no one could confirm that there was a party, and the autopsy had not established the time of death.

The Vermillion County prosecutor compiled a list of witnesses to call before a grand jury but then decided not to seek an indictment. After all, there would be the added cost and paperwork of extradition and trial. Besides, Illinois authorities had a solid case against Eyler in the Calise murder—didn't they?

Just when the task force officers felt they had come to know Eyler, something would come along to show them how complex he was. Cathy Berner, for example, traced two mysterious calls. They were made a few days after the John Roach murder in December 1982 and the Danny McNeive killing the following May. But the calls weren't to any of Eyler's known friends. Phone records show that both times he called St. Mary of the Woods Convent southwest of Terre Haute. "I guess we've got to go there," Love said with a tone suggesting that Illinois police had it easy; they just had to interview people in gay bars.

With McPherson standing beside him, Love rang the buzzer and showed his police identification to a two-way mirror. Then they were buzzed into an alcove. But no one was there.

"Good afternoon," came a voice from behind a door. "I am Sister Theresa."

So that was how it was going to be. The officers sat in chairs and faced the door.

"Sister, did you ever answer any calls from Larry Eyler, and what did he talk about?"

She told them that he spoke about possibly being an alcoholic and about being abused as a child.

"Sister," Love put in uneasily, not certain of the rules of the religious orders, "did he ever talk to you about the murders or hurting people? Can you talk to me about this, or is that a confession?"

"He never talked about murders. I have another sister here that knew Larry very well. She went to school with him and dated him."

McPherson shook his head and muttered, "Larry Eyler dated a nun . . ."

"No," came the voice, "she is a novice now. She is new to our order. Would you like to speak to her?"

"Please, Sister," Love answered.

In a few minutes there was a new voice from behind the door. The young woman said she had met Eyler at Indiana State University in Terre Haute, and they could tell from her answers that their relationship had been more than just casual dating.

Love was a big, tough man, but his embarrassment showed as he realized he couldn't ease into the next question. "Sister, could you tell me if he was homosexual . . . you know . . ."

"Oh, no," the novice replied as if surprised the thought should come up, "not Larry Eyler."

The young nun knew Eyler as kind, caring, even sentimental. He was intelligent and had great potential. McPherson stopped writing notes because he felt the sister saw only the side of Eyler that he wanted people to see.

Thanksgiving was just two days away, and the approach of winter was adding a sense of urgency to the investigation. Bare trees would make it easier to notice any more mounds the killer might have left behind. But before long everything would be covered with snow until spring.

State police pilots warmed up the motor of the small plane in their hangar at the Indianapolis Airport and took turns crossing the northwestern quarter of the state for disturbances on the ground near crossroads.

The holiday season increased the anguish for dozens of families whose sons had disappeared in the last three years. One call to the task force came from New Mexico. A man now living in Albuquerque had separated from his wife when their son was twelve, and the boy went with her. Then the boy left to live on his own and disappeared. The father sent copies of the boy's dental charts to see if they matched any of the unidentified victims, but the charts were too old to be of any use. Maybe the mother would have more recent ones.

Some of the officers couldn't get over how often divorce was a factor in the disappearances of these boys, most of whom were probably just thumbing rides or working at construction jobs or in transient trades. And some, no doubt, were hustling.

A man in tears called the unit and said his son was coming from out of town for a holiday visit but hadn't shown up. Usually boys like that just want to stay out of touch with their parents. It's a painful revenge.

One girl who called was afraid her brother might be one of the victims, but "my mother still thinks he's out there." The dental records the girl sent did not match any of the victims.

State police Sgt. Ted Knorr, one of the men who led the investigation into the four bodies found in a barnyard in Newton County, couldn't help but feel that if these were daughters killed instead of sons, there would be considerably more cooperation by the families. Knorr also said that, in a way, police were relieved that the killings may have stopped after the Calise attack in Illinois on August 31. The bodies being found now were barely more than skeletons. That work might seem more grisly, but there was less of a human element to deal with. "It's impersonal," he said. "Just bones and clothes."

John Pless, the Marion County pathologist who was the first official to realize that there was a serial killer stalking the highways, was putting much of his spare time into studying the bodies for clues. So was the Newton County coroner, David Dennis, who maintained a private dental practice. Now he was being flooded with requests from state police to match dental charts.

The most pressing work involved the four men found in the barnyard. One was wearing a parka, and the others were dressed for warmer weather, suggesting that all were killed separately. Police were unable to determine if they were murdered in the barn or if their bodies were brought to the scene in a vehicle for burial.

Until more leads turned up, these victims were just pins on the eight-foot map of Indiana that Berner was keeping up-to-date in the task force headquarters. A blue dot represented a body, a green one showed where a collect call was made to one of the homes where Eyler lived, and a yellow dot marked where Eyler used a credit card. With an average suspect there might be no correlation, but in this case, nearly every blue dot was near a green or yellow one or both.

On the Monday after Thanksgiving, Dr. Dennis identified one of the four bodies as that of Michael Bauer, a pizza delivery man from Chicago's Northwest Side. Sergeant Knorr of Indiana state police telephoned Michael's father, Edgar, and said: "The media may be contacting you soon." Bauer didn't know what the officer was talking about. "Haven't you heard yet? The dental records you sent us matched positively to our second victim in Newton County."

It was better than learning of his son's death the same way he recognized Michael's hooded coat, by a television newscast—but not much better. All the grief that Bauer had been holding back hit the man and he couldn't speak.

Another kind of nightmare began. From that late afternoon, Edgar Bauer became withdrawn and his wife, Harriet, seldom went outside. They buried a part of themselves with their son.

The other bodies would not be so easy to identify. As

with some of Gacy's victims, they evidently were young men who had severed all roots with their families, to lie unmourned.

The task force on November 29 threw open whatever it had to police of any jurisdiction with a case involving the stabbing of a young man. In the academy room were large charts tracking Eyler's whereabouts as well as the phone records and credit card receipts themselves. One of the officers perusing the material was Mark Baldwin of the Cook County sheriff's police. For more than six months he had been investigating the murder of Jimmy Roberts, who had lived in Chicago's high-rise ghetto neighborhood on South Federal Street and was found in Thorn Creek south of the city on May 9. One doesn't brush aside thirty-seven stab wounds as just another unsolved homicide.

Baldwin stared at the whereabouts chart for a few minutes, trying to make sense of it all. Eyler had bought gas in Indiana near the Illinois border on May 7, and he had bought gas on Chicago's North Side on May 13. To Baldwin, that placed him in the city that Mother's Day weekend. Of course he was frequently traveling between the states, but on May 9 the Park West night spot at Clark Street and Armitage Avenue had held a "Mr. Leather" show, where men were dressed in cowhide and S & M harnesses. Baldwin was sure Eyler would have attended.

But there was still no way of tracing Eyler to Roberts. The officer knew that Roberts had turned tricks for money, and on that cold, windy weekend he was in the North Side visiting friends on Sheridan Road. He left them around midnight and perhaps looked for a little cash or just a lift back to the South Side. Could it be that Eyler's truck pulled over for him?

On December 5, a trapper looking for beavers along a creek passing under Interstate 70, five miles west of Effingham, Illinois, found the nineteenth body. The tall, thin young man had been thrown from the bridge apparently some time that summer and remained undetected between some trees. He had been stabbed a number of times in the chest and abdomen. There was no shirt, his pants were pulled down, and, as with several of the others, he was wearing white socks. The body was never identified.

Schippers was preparing the criminal defense, but attorney Kenneth Ditkowsky continued his federal suit against the Illinois and Indiana state police. He called information they gave out before Eyler's arrest a "psychological battle" of questionable legality. He wrote letters to the governor of Indiana, senators, and the U.S. Attorney General but got nowhere.

Funds were running out for Eyler's defense. Schippers had accepted the offer of a ten-thousand dollar retainer, and Ditkowsky was still waiting for his own payment of nearly that much. By the end of November Eyler's parents, John Dobrovolskis, and Dr. Little had themselves incorporated as the Society for the Defense of Constitutional Liberty, Inc. Its purpose was "to promote understanding of the basic civil liberties protected by the Federal and State Constitutions and in particular to provide assistance including, but not limited to, grants for legal expenses to persons who are falsely accused of crimes, victims of unreasonable searches or seizures, or who are victims of government persecution"—in other words, to pay off Ditkowsky. The paper organization soon faded out of existence.

In Illinois detectives found themselves drawn into an ever-narrowing circle of circumstances proving that Eyler moved about in areas frequented by the victims, but no one had seen them together.

A victim who was found dumped in a Kankakee County cornfield in October 1982, Steven Crockett, had lived in the Sovereign Hotel on West Granville Avenue. The landlady not only recognized his photo but those of Eyler and his lover, Dobrovolskis. Apparently since it would be improper to carry out their affair in the same house with Sally and the children, Dobrovolskis rented an apartment there on June 1, 1982. That lasted until August 31 the following year. Colin wondered whether there was a lovers' quarrel, or if it was coincidence that the love nest ended the day Ralph Calise was killed. The landlady could not be mistaken about the men, she told Colin; they still owed her $913 for rent.

Also that drizzly, cool day, Colin went to the apartment building next door to see whether anyone could recognize the men in the photos. Colin learned about Marie Sullivan, who knew Calise, Jolene Red Cloud, and, even more promising, young Wayne Jewels. He was the twelve-year-old boy who was the last person known to have seen Ervin Gibson, the sixteen-year-old boy whose body had been found near Lake Forest in April. Wayne's family had moved away, and not even the word-of-mouth network of bag ladies, drifters, recluses, and bar people in Uptown could learn where they were. Now police had a chance of finding the boy.

On Wednesday, December 7, Red Cloud accompanied Sullivan to the corner of Winthrop and Bryn Mawr on Chicago's North Side to give her support as she spoke to police. Sullivan couldn't give any information about Eyler, but she shyly told Colin and Lamprich that the Jewels boy had returned from West Virginia and was staying with his grandmother on North Malden.

The officers drove a few blocks to the home Sullivan had described, and there Wayne pointed out three photos: his friend, Ervin Gibson; another murder victim, Steve Crockett; and Larry Eyler.

"This is important, Wayne," Lamprich said. "Are you sure you've seen this man? Maybe it was someone else."

"I seen him by Butera's," the boy answered. He referred to a supermarket on Clark Street near Montrose Avenue. It was a normal area, with some welfare recipients living near middle-class families, but it was also a hangout for boys anywhere from ten to sixteen when they wanted to start hustling for easy money. People living in the area hardly noticed them.

"Was this man in a car?" Colin asked Wayne. Eyler drove only pickup trucks, but the detective didn't want to lead the boy into a false memory.

"Uh-uh," Wayne answered. "It was a Ford pickup truck, kinda bluish. With a dent on the right side, I think.'' Colin didn't remember a dent, but a silvery gray might appear ''bluish.''

''What were you doing—were you buying something from the store?''

''I was just going by on a bicycle, and he was coming out,'' the boy said.

Colin wasn't convinced. A boy just glancing at a car pulling out of a parking lot doesn't remember all that detail. Maybe the boy had reason to walk up to the truck, and maybe something had happened for him to remember it; but if so he wouldn't admit it.

''All right,'' Colin said. ''You've been a real help.'' What else could he tell the boy? ''If you remember anything more, call me. Promise?''

Colin left the card with Wayne's grandmother as he had done with probably hundreds of people, yet few ever called back.

Snow was starting to fall that late afternoon in northern Indiana. Billy Bob Newman was answering a call in the task force office as Sergeant Love went over the printouts on what little police could learn about the multiple burying ground in Newton County.

''They found another body!'' Newman shouted, holding the plastic mouthpiece just a few inches from his face. Cathy Berner and the officers gathered around Newman as he said a few words to the trooper, then he repeated the responses to them.

''U.S. 40 again,'' he said. ''A hunter found a . . .'' Newman turned away from them and concentrated on what the trooper was saying. The others didn't hear the words but could feel an almost magnetic pull between them and the call.

Newman said ''Hold it, will you?'' to the officer and turned to the task force members around him. ''Two bodies, so far as they know. Out by Belleville.''

''Tell them not to touch anything,'' Love said.

''They know that.''

''Tell them! We're going right out.''

There was no need to direct the officers; they knew

exactly what to do by now. Newman hung up and went to the little box of colored pins. "The bodies are in a field by an access road—"

"And lovers' lane, right? 'Bout a quarter mile east of Cox's plant farm and Clayton-Hazelwood Road," Love said and pushed the pin into the map for him. "Hell, I know that area. It's two miles from my home; I pass it every day."

"So does Larry," McPherson said. As the task force men were trailing Eyler early in the investigation, he had passed by that spot at least three times.

The task force officers pulled up at the field and flashed their badges to the Hendricks County officers and the state policemen standing around each side of the evidence tape stretched between sticks pounded into the earth. In the gray twilight Love, with his hands in the pockets of his parka, stepped over to the nearly skeletal remains partly under a mound of dirt and dried leaves. A few feet away a less decomposed body was glimpsed here and there in the tangled remains of an old mobile home that had been burned.

Coroner Steve Matthews came out of his station wagon and told him, "We don't know age or sex yet."

"Yes you do. Men eighteen to twenty-six. Probably had mustaches."

The jogging pants of the victim partly covered by dirt had been pulled down. McPherson crouched and said to Love beside him, "Look, you can see a nick where the knife hit the bones." The body also had white tube socks, another trademark of the highway killer.

McPherson didn't say anything when he looked over what he could of the body under the metal remains of the trailer home. But as he and Love were talking over what they had, he said, "Hell, I think we could have a lot more than just two bodies here. Isn't this only about five miles from where McNeive was killed?"

Love looked at the coroner, who was waiting to supervise the removal of the bodies, and turned to one of the troopers. "Seal off this area, and put someone here all night. I want this area dug up right, by professionals."

Not even McPherson knew what he meant, so Love added, "I want to bring in some people from Indiana University and do this crime scene like a scientific dig."

McPherson shrugged and said, "Heck, what do we have to lose?"

The next morning, a team of eight men from the archeology department walked across the soggy ground with picks, shovels, and brushes. The sun was melting the half-inch of snow, and everyone was stomping around with shoes and boots heavy with mud. Police went over the ground with metal detectors as the archeologists treated the murder victims as if they were Mayan artifacts. They logged how many centimeters of dirt the bones were found in and sifted the nearby soil. For all that, they found no clues and no other bodies in the cordoned-off quarter acre.

As Love waited, he bent down with a creak of his knees and put two fingers into the pants pocket of the man partly covered by dirt and pulled out a bus ticket. Weather had worn away some of the letters, but he could read "P IER".

"Well, Sam, we've got another who hung around bus stations."

The victim under the metal appeared to have been a black in his late twenties. Neither of them had jewelry or a wallet to help identify him.

During the long wait, Love sat in the car and from time to time looked at the ticket. P IER. He took out a map of Indiana and went over the name of every town that had those letters but couldn't come up with anything. McPherson was still walking aimlessly in the cold, kicking up the mud.

The bus ticket remained a mystery for less than twenty-four hours. Love came to work early on Friday morning and asked Berner to make a index of the towns reporting anyone missing. Next he called state police posts to check on missing young men. Berner saw him jump up and shout "The *L* is missing, the *L* is missing!"

The victim was seventeen-year-old Richard Wayne, who disappeared March 20 after phoning his mother in Montpelier, Indiana, from the Indianapolis Greyhound station to say that he had arrived safely from California.

For Richard's mother, Jackie, the agonizing wait was over. For nine months she would jump whenever the phone rang, expecting police to be on the other end. She suffered from multiple sclerosis, and sometimes it seemed that her son was her whole life. The boy had dropped out of school and wouldn't stay in a job. His father wasn't living with the family, and the boy couldn't accept obligations.

Mrs. Wayne sent him to relatives in California to see if he might find himself. He said he did. Richard was coming home when he called her from the Greyhound station between buses. "Mom, I have it all together now," he said over the phone. "I'm going to finish school and get a job and build a big house for you."

She told him not to trust strangers, even though she was sure he knew that, and her last words were, "I love you, Richard."

She was watching the news that December day when she saw police remove the skeleton of a young man. The reporter described him as six feet tall and blond. Mrs. Wayne called the state police, and they gave her the number of the task force. The next day she had a messenger deliver Richard's dental records. They matched.

As for the black man, he remains unidentified.

On the morning that archeologists were carefully lifting the bones from the snow and mud in Indiana, lawyers in the Eyler case returned to the courthouse in downtown Waukegan for pretrial matters. Defense attorney David Schippers introduced motion after motion to Judge Block as Assistant State's Attorney McKoski stared in dismay.

"I'm not trying to be cute in filing all these separate motions to suppress," Schippers told the judge.

McKoski felt like saying "The hell you aren't!"

"If I may, your honor, I think that the key to all my motions is the initial search and seizure on September thirtieth, which was done without a warrant by the Indiana state police. Everything flows from that. If that, in fact, was a bad search and that evidence is suppressed, then probably 90 percent of the material used for the affidavit for the [subsequent] search warrant falls. It would be a domino effect.''

"Do you agree?'' the judge asked the prosecutor.

McKoski was caught off guard. "No,'' he answered. "I think a lot of the searches and seizures could stand independent of the other ones.''

When Block set December 19 for a tentative hearing, McKoski expressed surprise. That was rather soon for all the motions that had been filed. "I know you got a pile of them,'' the judge remarked wryly, and he agreed to make December 19 just a status hearing in which attorneys for each side would say they were ready for trial or explain why they needed more time.

McKoski went through the double doors of the court with the Eyler papers under his arm. At first the impact of the new defense strategy didn't hit him; he was just thinking about how much work Schippers was making him do. But as he was walking down the corridor and into the elevator he began to realize that "a domino effect'' was not empty rhetoric.

13

Thursday, December 13, 1983
Waukegan, Illinois

The conference room in the warren of Lake County state's attorney offices that evening resembled a college dormitory the night before a major exam. Stacks of books from the courthouse library were heaped on the long table in the windowless room. Two relatively young prosecutors had the room to themselves, leaving six chairs empty. In the far corner was a locker, and next to it was a television set with a telephone on top.

Ray McKoski was taking a break and chain-drinking Diet Cokes. He was a trim man with a broad mustache over his thin upper lip to offset his youth.

With him was his friend and coprosecutor Peter Trobe. Trobe's hair was dark brown, his forehead was growing by the year, and he didn't mind it when some people thought he lacked the dignity of his profession. For McKoski the law was a challenge; for Trobe the law was fun.

The men were a team as only opposites can be. The usually serious McKoski would make jokes only once Trobe was in the room; McKoski was the moon to Trobe's sun. Now Trobe was sitting back in his chair, scratching notations on one of the yellow legal pads that kept getting switched from here to there as the men tried to find a more comfortable spot in the small room. From time to time he would say funny things about what they should do to Schippers for all the responses he was demanding from them.

First grade class of St. Joseph's Catholic school, Lebanon,
Indiana, 1960. Larry Eyler is in the back row, first child on
the left.

July, 1983. Larry Eyler outside Andy's Liquor Store in
Greencastle, Indiana, photographed by an undercover
officer of the Indiana task force.

July, 1983. Eyler at a gas station next to Andy's Liquor Store, photographed by undercover task force members.

September, 1983. Police photo of Eyler taken at the Indiana State Police post in Lowell soon after he was stopped for a traffic violation.

October 19, 1983. Indiana State Police investigators at the barn where four bodies were found in Newton County, Indiana. Only two victims were ever identified.

(Top photo by John Mitchell, courtesy of *The Post-Tribune*; bottom photo by Dave Fryer, courtesy of *The Post-Tribune*)

October 29, 1983. Lake County Sheriff Robert "Mickey" Babcox conducts a news conference in his office the day Eyler is charged with the murder of Ralph E. Calise.

(Photo by *Gaylife*, courtesy of *Gay Chicago Magazine*)

The evidence against Eyler: the boot soaked with blood matching the type of Ralph E. Calise, the knife with blood stains under the handle, and Eyler's truck tire and its matching cast print.

(Photo by Charles Eshelman)

February 6, 1984. Larry Eyler walks away from the Lake County jail with his mother Shirley DeKoff, freed on $10,000 bail.

(Photo by *Gaylife*, courtesy of *Gay Chicago Magazine*)

Dan Colin, investigator for the Lake County,
Illinois, sheriff's office, in 1990.

(Photo by Charles Eshelman)

David P. Shippers, the Chicago criminal defense
lawyer who defended Larry Eyler during the
Calise murder charges, the suppression hearing,
and the murder trial of Danny Bridges.

(Photo by Charles Eshelman)

Ray McKoski (left) and Peter Trobe, the Lake County state's attorney team that headed up the Calise murder charges and the suppression hearing.

(Photo by Charles Eshelman)

Sam McPherson and Frank Love outside the Indiana State Capitol in 1991.

Wilma McNeive and her daughter Missy, in front of a portrait of their slain son and brother Daniel Scott McNeive in 1991.

Crime lab technician Marion Caporusso in March, 1991. It was her idea to test Eyler's Chicago apartment with luminal, a chemical which highlights bloodstains in darkened rooms with a luminescent green glow.

The Dobrovolskis family: Sarah (left), John (seated, right), and their two sons Adam and Matthew.
(Courtesy of *The Daily Herald*, Arlington Heights, Illinois)

August 21, 1984. Police and sanitation workers search for more evidence after parts of Danny Bridges' dismembered body were found behind Larry Eyler's residence at 1628 W. Sherwin, Chicago.   (Photo by Howard Greenblatt)

Chicago Police team. Left to right: Paul Caroll, Commander Edward Wodnicki, and Brian Kalacki.

July, 1990. The author walking with investigators in "Blood Alley" at Broadway and Wilson in Uptown. Left to right: Kurt Proschwitz of the Lake County Sheriff Police, the author, Dan Colin, and Undersheriff Willie Smith.

(Photo by Charles Eshelman)

Danny Bridges as he was interviewed in Chicago by NBC correspondent Mark Nykanen and producer Chuck Collins for the documentary "Silent Shame."

(Photo by Robyn Ross, courtesy of WMAQ)

Carmen Pauli looks at a photo
album commemorating her son,
Ralph E. Calise.

(Photo by Charles Eshelman)

March, 1991. Law clerk Daniel DeLay and legal
secretary Kathryn Gasser work with Kathleen Zellner
(center) in an effort to get a new trial for Eyler on the
Bridges conviction. (Photo by Sharon White)

Daniel Scott McNeive's body was found near Indianapolis on May 9, 1983. He was 21 years old.

July 2, 1983. An artist's facial reconstruction of an unidentified Hispanic male in his early 20's who was found stabbed to death in a field in Ford County, Illinois.

The skeletal remains—showing signs of a stabbing death—of John Bartlett, 19, were found on October 19, 1983. He had been missing since March 3, and was one of four men found buried around a barn in Newton County, Indiana.

Ralph E. Calise, 28, was found stabbed to death in a farmer's field east of the Tri-State Tollway in Lake County, Illinois, on August 31, 1983.

Steve Agan, 23, of Terre Haute, Indiana, was found stabbed to death near Newport, Indiana, on December 28, 1982.

January, 1991. Indiana State University Professor Robert David Little arrives at the Vermillion County Courthouse to plead innocent to charges against him for the murder of Steve Agan.

At the time of the events covered in *Freed to Kill*, crime journalist Gera-Lind Kolarik worked for the ABC News affiliate in Chicago. From that news desk she was the first person to recognize a serial murder pattern that crossed state lines. She won an Emmy for Best Spot News Coverage in 1984.　　　(Photo by Charles Eshelman)

There were motions to suppress evidence taken at the Lowell state police post on September 30; to quash the search warrant and suppress the evidence seized during the search of Little's home on October 1; to suppress evidence taken from Eyler on October 3, meaning his truck; to suppress statements he made in Chicago and Waukegan October 3 to 4; motions to quash the search warrant and suppress the evidence seized in the Lake County search of the truck on October 6; to nullify the search warrant and suppress the evidence seized during the subsequent raid on Little's home November 1; to quash and suppress for the third search on Little's home on November 22; to divulge electronic surveillance if any (there was none); a motion for an order requiring the state to give notice of any intention to use other crimes alleged against Eyler in preparation for the Calise trial; a notice of alibi defense . . .

Trobe jumped up, waving his free hand while holding the note pad in the other. "A warrant is sufficiently descriptive if it enables police with reasonable effort to identify the place intended. *People v. Fragoso.*"

Suddenly drawn from his own research, McKoski had no idea what his friend was talking about. "*Which* motion?"

"The October first search warrant, what did you think? This supports the theory that the premises to be searched are sufficiently described in the warrant and the affidavit, then I go to *People versus Bauer* and then *People v. Fragoso*. Then I state the place to be searched in the instant case, defendant's residence, was described as follows and I give the details: two-story frame . . ." Trobe waited for a reaction after his voice trailed off. "Well, what do you think?"

"Pete," McKoski said in a tired tone, "I think that is a hell of an argument." He stood up and snapped open another can of Diet Coke. McKoski's mind was elsewhere.

"Then I footnote at the bottom of the page—"

"Good. Judges just love footnotes."

"—that courts have concluded it is reasonable to assume the evidence of violent crimes will be found in the defendant's home. In the matter of a search warrant, *supra* at 1076; *People v. Hammers*, 35 . . .''

McKoski wasn't hearing any of this. It was now past 1 A.M., and his attention span was shortening. He saw Trobe hold up a book, no doubt one containing *Gates v. Illinois*, but he said, ''I'm too tired to look, Pete. You look for both of us.''

''Say, Ray, is everything all right?''

''Do you know that Christmas is thirteen days away? No, twelve or whatever.''

''And Judge Block is six days away,'' Trobe said from the table. ''Are you thinking about your wife? Why? There's plenty of time to get her a gift.''

''Sure, it only takes half an hour. . . . It's the time I haven't spent with her. That time is just lost.'' McKoski leaned against the wall, his arms crossed except for the hand holding the Diet Coke. ''It just seems like we're never going to see the end of this case.''

''Come on, all we have to do is dig a little more,'' he told McKoski. ''Common sense tells you the search was justified.''

That was no help. All those hundreds of books on shelves just outside the door proved that common sense had nothing to do with the law. He dragged himself home without any idea of how this case was going to turn out.

The law library was fairly large for the size of Lake County, but the prosecutors felt there had to be more. When the day came for them to drive down to Indiana with Detective Colin to interview the policemen involved in the Lowell stop, McKoski and Trobe asked to make a side trip to the law library of the Daley Center of county offices in Chicago. They hardly paid attention to the eighty-foot Christmas tree as they crossed the plaza.

The prosecutors didn't know what they were looking for in their hurried page turning through a few books, and they didn't find it. They came away with the feeling that there might not be some golden precedent to justify the searches and confiscations.

They probably would have to settle for a preponderance

of well-established cases to whittle away at one detail after another.

McKoski caught some rest by closing his eyes in the back seat of the sheriff's police car as they headed south for Lowell. Every now and then he would refresh his memory with the police reports of the stop and initial search of the pickup truck. Snow clouds with iron-gray bottoms filled the sky, and fresh snow covered the fields.

When they reached the small boxlike police station, the detectives and prosecutors introduced themselves to the post commander and asked for an assembly of all the officers who took part in the stop and Eyler's questioning. They explained that this had nothing to do with the federal lawsuit, just the criminal case. The prosecutors wanted to interview the officers chronologically, starting with Trooper Kenneth Buehrle.

"Ken," McKoski, began as they sat in the interrogation room, "just why did you stop that pickup truck? Don't read off your report, we know what that says. You'll have to re-create from memory in court."

Buehrle was virtually the only one whose actions weren't being challenged by the defense. The young officer, with his crew cut and blue uniform, answered each question firmly in paramilitary style and rattled off a procedural reason for everything he had done that day. He would sound good to a jury.

Then came Sergeant Popplewell, dispatcher Max Hunter, and . . . where was Sergeant Cothran? This was his day off, and someone forgot to tell him that he was needed down at the post. The Lake County people were told he was selling some of his goats. Goats! "Hicks," Colin muttered.

Time could be told by the way paper coffee cups and empty soda pop cans were piling up in the trash.

Eventually Cothran arrived and told how he had reached into the truck and looked inside a suspicious bag. The tall slender man explained that this was how the officers knew that Eyler might have murder in mind, because he found ropes and tape.

Next came Sergeant John Pavlakovic, who was starting

to feel that for the rest of his life he would be hearing questions about why he changed the course of an investigation with the words "Have them brought into the post." He could read in the faces of these outsiders that they expected him to be ashamed of his order. Pavlakovic reached halfway into his folder and said, "You read the statements we got from Darl Hayward and Eyler, didn't you? I have copies here if you don't."

McKoski said thank you, but it wouldn't be necessary. He and Trobe were familiar with the case; they just wanted to form an idea of how the officers would sound to a jury.

"What do you do, say 'Howdie' and just let Larry drive away with a kid in his van?" Pavlakovic asked. "Hell, we got him with a kid, with ropes. We got a knife with blood and the boots, and you people found out there was blood in the boots. We didn't take all that stuff; we *asked* to search and he signed a waiver. I got a copy of it here, his signature. He had the run of the place. We bent backwards for the bastard, and you're saying it was illegal?"

"Unfortunately, John," McKoski said, "the law does not take into account that the guy cooperated. The judge has to consider his state of mind."

"I did what was right!" the longtime sergeant insisted. Then he lit a cigarette to help his composure and sat back.

"We're not blaming you or your men," McKoski said. "We just have to establish probable cause for the search." The old-time cop greeted that with an "oh yeah?" expression.

"What can I tell you," Trobe remarked. "This is the 1980s."

The prosecutors had done all their homework and backed up the case with every precedent that could be found. But they knew Schippers could find just as many rulings for his side. The issue had become a lot more than whether rural police had made the right decision in detaining a suspect. Even so, they were as ready as they would ever be.

Rather than appear stern or disinterested as some judges do, William Block normally seemed as if he were watching an entertaining show. Now he looked surprised when he saw that McKoski and Trobe did have rebuttals prepared for all the defense motions. They even brought a few law books with them, ranging from new ones to volumes from the 1920s. McKoski glanced at Schippers with a gloat of triumph and announced, "We are prepared for any kind of argument that is necessary on those motions today."

Taking them at their word, Judge Block lowered his glasses down his nose and said, "The motions to suppress."

"The motions to suppress!" Trobe let out. So much for being prepared for any kind of argument. Actually what set him back was the thought that all the separate searches might be considered together. That could lead to a legal labyrinth. Trobe instinctively looked at McKoski and faced Block again. "Judge, the motions to suppress that we think require a hearing are the motions to suppress evidence taken on September thirtieth."

"The original stop, you mean," the judge interposed.

Defense attorney Schippers spoke up. "I think those first two stops, October third *and* September thirtieth." Those were the confiscation of evidence from the truck at the Lowell police post and the seizure of the truck by Lake County police who had gone to Eyler's home in Chicago.

Block pushed back his glasses. "And I take it," he said with a nod to Schippers, "it's a question of the poison tree, et cetera." Evidence taken by police who came across it without probable cause or a warrant has long been known as "the fruit of the poisoned tree."

"That's true," McKoski conceded in an undertone. "Those are the stops and statements and seizure of physical evidence that were not accompanied by a search warrant."

"I have one problem, though," Schippers told the judge. "Nobody seems to be able to find a search warrant that was issued on October first." That was the first evidence sweep of Little's home, yielding critical credit card and telephone records.

McKoski lowered his head in agreement.

With his well-practiced, offhand way, Schippers raised another request: to see all information pertaining to any surveillance that might have been conducted the night of the Calise murder. Not that Schippers believed that there were such reports; he was just trying to create an atmosphere favorable to the defense.

Such questions could be settled at the next hearing, the judge said. He looked through his calendar of cases for a period when he would have three days free after the Christmas backlog. He set the date for January 23.

Schippers walked to the table where Eyler sat but turned and looked back at the bench. "There is one more point, Judge," he said. "I am more or less certain that the state intends to go into the other crimes' evidence, so perhaps you would prefer to do that at the same time."

My God, McKoski thought, he wants to sweep everything off the table at once. "That's fine," the prosecutor said. What else could he say?

The temperature outside was well below zero as northern Illinois settled into what would be its coldest December on record. Inside the sheriff's offices was another kind of chill. All the leads in the highways murder case seemed fairly played out. If the judge restricted the evidence from the Lowell stop, they would have nothing to fall back on.

At such times you put the case from your mind and keep up with your other work. Instead of thinking about the unsettled investigation, you look at the ceiling or out the window now and again. Day after day of bright sunshine and bitter cold seemed to fit the mood.

Deputy Chief Investigator Willie Smith was thinking over a tip that had come the week before from police in Sarasota, Florida. A man arrested for burglary and home invasion down there was claiming numerous murders in Illinois and Indiana, and while living in a Chicago suburb a few weeks ago he said he knew Eyler was innocent. To Smitty it seemed that the man was a crackpot, but he felt he should send two officers down there.

Of course one would be Colin because he was in charge of the Illinois murders. Lamprich would have been a natural choice for the other detective, but the man with the amazing memory had left police work for an insurance job in New Jersey. The other officer sent to Florida need not have a great deal of experience, but Smitty thought about the weather and decided to send himself. Two minutes after Smitty made the suggestion, Babcox was making plans to go.

Pam Colin was about to receive the phone call she had been dreading. Ever since November when the investigation began to stall, she kept thinking, What if Dan isn't home for Christmas? As a modern woman and an old-fashioned woman, as a policeman's wife and as a mother, she led a fragmented life, but all the pieces would come together at their shared times. The short, attractive woman was working at the K-Mart in Round Lake Beach when she received the call. "We have to go to Florida for Eyler," Colin said. "Don't worry, I'll be back for Christmas. Would you pack my bags?" There was more feeling than just the words let on, she knew that. You get used to it.

"That's all right, isn't it?" Colin asked.

"That's fine," she told him.

The Eyler case already was frazzling Pam, especially since all the work Colin was putting in was in addition to the other crimes he was working on. A few times since the fall she found herself buying clothes the family didn't need and decorations for the house. Nothing expensive, just things she never would have bought if she had not been upset at the dwindling times they had together.

Their son Danny was the one who let his resentment show. He wanted his dad to cheer him on at the nighttime softball games and to be applauding when he sang in the school chorus. Once the boy said, "Daddy works too much too late."

Just the other night, Colin couldn't make it to his daughter's graduation from kindergarten. The little girl, with hair as bright yellow as a dandelion, cried inside the basement of St. Joseph's Church. Pam had to assure her that her father still loved her and that life wouldn't always be like this.

So Pam packed her husband's bags for Florida with a discontent she tried not to show, and that morning she kissed him goodbye. In the evening, rather than sleep in their bed without him, she watched television until she could doze off in her chair.

Colin, Smitty, and Babcox arrived in Fort Myers when the sky was a gray blanket, and there were off-and-on showers. The big local scandal of the day was that the Sarasota County sheriff had been indicted for taking a county plane to the Orange Bowl. Babcox, who was planning on some deep sea fishing, pretended to be shocked that a law official would use public funds for a pleasure trip.

The man Lake County officers wanted to see was Eddie Daniels, who was in the county jail, but Colin wanted to speak to his family before talking to him. A bartender in Calumet City, a south suburb of Chicago, had told Colin that a week before Thanksgiving Daniels had come into the tavern and said life was not worth living and that he was going to turn himself in for all the killings he had committed. Confessing to crimes one didn't commit is common for a person in depression, but police couldn't rule him out. The next day the man returned to Florida, but apparently the depression followed him. He kept making a nuisance of himself until he was thrown in jail, where he no doubt wanted to be all along.

The Sarasota County police took the officers to North Fort Myers, where a cousin of Daniels said she would tell them whatever they wanted to know. But the woman became defensive when they asked whether Daniels was homosexual. Such questions were necessary because it would be incomprehensible if a heterosexual left a trail of young men as his victims.

Not far away, the officers tracked down Daniels' half sister. They heard the usual story in cases like this of divorce and the son being raised with his mother and sisters. They had accepted his homosexuality ever since he was a teenager, but his father hated him for it. Daniels had his problems, she said, but he was never violent.

At 10:30 that night the Illinois detectives arrived at the county jail in Sarasota to speak to Daniels. They were facing not a killer but a rather pathetic man. Each time he mentioned Eyler, there was love in his voice—no matter what Eyler may have done and the way Eyler had led him on only to be cold to him.

They had met in a Fort Myers bar, the Blarney Stone, around 1979 while Eyler was living with two men. He was staying in Florida to be near his sister. When Daniels got off work they would meet behind the tavern and spend the night together. That happened every night for a month, except two or three times, yet they never had sex, Daniels said.

"Why not?" Smitty asked.

"Larry was—Larry was very closed-mouth about it."

"Well, what did he say? Anything about bondage?"

"He didn't say anything. He wouldn't discuss it, I told you."

Larry Eyler, the would-be priest. Maybe he was struggling with his nature, Colin thought. Maybe bondage for him wasn't the fantasy acting-out it is for some other men. His urges could have been leading him to violence all along, and bondage might have been a way of telling himself that he could control them; it was a lie he could live with.

Daniels told the detectives that Eyler had returned to Terre Haute for a while but came back to Florida. Daniels wanted to join him but Eyler said no, he had other friends now. Eyler let it be known that he didn't want to see or hear from him again. Daniels sent him some letters but eventually stopped writing. In time, Eyler returned to Terre Haute to stay, and Daniels had moved into Calumet City. Eyler agreed to come over for dinner once but never showed up.

"Your family says you were upset around Thanksgiving," Smitty said.

"I was pretty drunk that week, then some Quaaludes. I wound up putting my arm through a storm door. Maybe it was Larry's arrest."

"Is that why you said you killed those men?"

"I just couldn't believe that Larry did it. I still can't."

What Daniels told them helped them understand Eyler a little better, but it didn't mean anything to the case; neither did long hours of talking to Daniels' other relatives the next day. Babcox stayed the whole time looking at the drizzle from his room in the Holiday Inn. The men gave themselves a little vacation the third day, fishing off Key Largo and talking about the weather back home—eighteen degrees below zero and a windchill of sixty-two below.

In a way, Colin was glad that this Florida trip was wasted. That meant he would be home for Christmas.

Gallows humor was settling in at the task force now that everyone was sure the case was wrapping up. Cathy Berner decided to have a cake and ice cream party to celebrate Eyler's thirty-first birthday on December 21. Detective Don Henry brought a small chocolate cake from a local bakery, and Cathy brought the candles, half gallon of ice cream, and paper plates. She made a banner reading "Happy Birthday Larry Eyler" on computer paper and strung it across the bulletin board. When the treats were just a few crumbs on soggy paper plates, it was back to work as usual because there were a lot of loose ends to tie up. Technically, there were twenty-one murders yet to solve.

Just two days later members of the task force gathered at the academy for their modest Christmas party. They all brought in something to fill the table and take their minds off the highway map with all those blue dots and the boxes of subpoenaed records and confiscated belongings. Billy Bob Newman supplied the radio for Christmas music. The party became official shortly after noon, when Cathy turned off her computer. Frank Love snapped back the top of a soda can and proposed a toast. "Everyone has worked very hard together and it has paid off, but now it is really up to the guys in Illinois to help us," he said in his fatherly way. "This may be our first and last Christmas together, we hope."

They all laughed.

Two hours later, Gera-Lind Kolarik was playing Santa's helper to thank police in Lake County, Illinois. Every year the news director at WLS-TV paid close to four hundred dollars for bottles of Seagram Seven or J & B scotch to be delivered by courier to one hundred thirty news sources that helped throughout the year. But Kolarik was so involved in the Eyler investigation that in 1983 she wanted to deliver the bottles personally. Her first reaction when she saw tanned Sheriff Babcox in his office in Waukegan was "Have you been under a sun lamp?"

"I took the guys to the keys to do some ocean fishing. We deserve it."

The stocky man with a face like a rumpled rug took her by the arm and invited her to a late lunch at Mathon's, a restaurant two blocks away. One glance at Babcox with pearl-handled revolvers strapped to his sides and the maitre d' gave them immediate seating. In the subdued lighting of the Greek-styled restaurant, the sheriff tried to be his usual jovial self but Kolarik knew he was worried. For one thing, he was chain-smoking. For another, he hardly said a word except to order; when he did speak, his words had a darker tone.

"Is there a problem, Mickey?" she asked.

He squeezed her hand and moved closer to her. "Yeah, Gera-Lind. The cops in Indiana fucked up. The only thing that wasn't screwed up was when we seized his tires."

"So what," she said. "All the evidence points to Larry. Even if it didn't, this is Lake County and you're the head of the Republican Party out here. There's no judge that would ever rule in his behalf. You're the good old boys."

Babcox lit another cigarette and said, "Don't be so sure."

"Mickey, suppression hearings are routine. So a lawyer finds one or two mistakes by the cops; that always happens. The evidence is never suppressed unless they beat the prisoner or hold a gun to his head. Mickey, this case is sewn up. He murdered twenty-one boys. You have three strong pieces of evidence: the knife, the boots, the tracks. Mickey, a judge takes all this into account."

"Gera-Lind . . ." he said tentatively and paused. "There is a fine line in this case."

The next day, the slightest movement of wind made flesh feel like glass. Whoever heard of a windchill of eighty-two degrees below zero on Christmas Eve? The weather matched the mood of police and prosecutors as the Eyler case dragged on without a fresh break. Assistant State's Attorney Ray McKoski had told Peter Trobe that when the case was over he wanted to move to the other side of the bench. "At least I know the hell and the time it takes to make a case."

Lamprich had already quit, and Colin heard that Sam McPherson was thinking of giving up police work and becoming a farmer or a store owner. Colin himself was feeling down. Ralph Calise's mother, Carmen Pauli, called him frequently to learn developments. She sensed the mood and became the den mother of the investigation. "I'm sure everything will work out," she said.

Colin would mail her clippings about the case from the Waukegan paper. She added them to her scrapbook to chart the progress and to make her son seem a little closer to her. Whenever Colin notified her of something, she would videotape the newscasts. Since police had all that evidence and bodies kept being found, she couldn't understand why the investigators seemed downcast. Besides, she was sure the case was too big for any judge to let Eyler back on the highways.

On a bitter cold Thursday, December 29, authorities in Indiana identified one of the four barnyard bodies of Newton County as nineteen-year-old John Bartlett. He had come from Uniontown, Pennsylvania, but was living with his sister on Chicago's North Side after his Army discharge.

The sister had to tell police several times that Bartlett had vanished March 2, 1983. They needed to make sure of the date because the task force had worked out a chronology for Eyler that was so tight they could now begin filling in the spaces. The day after Bartlett disappeared, someone made a call to Little's town house in Terre Haute from the YMCA in Niles, a small community of tiny brick bungalows just north of Chicago. The information was relayed to Lake County police, and Colin went with Detective Corsi to see if there might be a connection between this haven from crime and one of the worst string of murders in American history.

The detectives were taken from the lobby of the YMCA to the administrative office. The staff verified that Eyler had been a member there since September 20, 1982, which was while he and Dobrovolskis kept an apartment at the Sovereign Hotel. Eyler would come in sometimes to lift weights, but there was no record of Bartlett.

Colin wasn't ready to dismiss this as another dead-end lead. The tight paper trail the officers in two states had been able to create suggested that Eyler didn't call his Terre Haute home because he felt lonely or thought he had left meat on the stove; he appeared to call after each murder. To tell someone? Or perhaps just for emotional release without letting on? Either way, he called, as though he had built-up energy like a storm that needs to discharge into the earth.

The detectives were buttoning their winter coats to leave when a man who had been working in another part of the Y opened the door of the office and poked his head in. This was John Loergan, who had been asked to talk to the officers because of his memory for faces.

Loergan looked at the photos one at a time and said, "Yeah, this guy would come in here." He meant Eyler. "This one, too." Loergan's finger touched the photo of Bartlett.

"Did you ever see them together?"

"No, why?"

Why? Because unless someone saw Eyler with a victim, defense attorney Schippers could say that all police had were coincidences. Dozens of them.

There wasn't much for Colin to celebrate on New Year's Eve, with the most important case of his career slipping through his fingers. He didn't take the setbacks as much to heart as he might have a couple of years ago. The man was mellowing. He was more social and less tense, or as his friend Kurt Proschwitz might say, more human and less fish.

When Colin returned to work after the holiday he saw a message from twelve-year-old Wayne Jewels, the friend of murder victim Ervin Gibson. Colin had to work on other cases and put off the meeting until later in the week.

In a spare moment he dropped by the state's attorney's offices in the courthouse across the way from the sheriff's offices. He found McKoski and Trobe in a playful mood and knew they were onto something. "Do you want to hear how we took apart the exclusionary rule and made it into the 'inevitable discovery exception'?" McKoski asked.

"OK, Ray," Colin said, sitting back and already smiling.

McKoski cleared his throat. "Drum roll, please." Trobe batted his palms on the table.

"This exception allows admission or use of evidence in fact from an illegal search or interrogation, but that would have been discovered without the illegal police action."

"What are we talking about now?"

"Sergeant Cothran examining the bag inside Eyler's truck without asking permission; and finding bills and leads in Dr. Little's house October first," Trobe said with his deep voice.

"State police say they had a warrant."

"Nobody can find it, but we say records would have been seized anyway in the later search."

"Please, let's not get ahead of ourselves," said McKoski. "The exclusionary rule does not come into play merely because the proffered evidence is in fact the product of an illegal act. If the illegal act merely contributed to the discovery of the allegedly tainted information and such information would have been acquired lawfully if the illegal act had never transpired, the presumptive taint is removed."

"You're making this up," Colin said.

"The hell we are," McKoski answered. "Look at this; it's in an article by Maguire on 'How to Unpoison Fruit' in *Criminology and Police Science*."

"So what you've got isn't something new?"

"Not exactly," Trobe replied. "That'd be like suddenly discovering *Miranda v. Arizona*, but it's already stood up in the Seventh Court of Appeal and the Illinois Appellate Court."

"That doesn't mean that Judge Block has to rule that way."

"No," McKoski told him, "but it means we've got a chance."

* * *

On Friday, January 6, Colin picked up Wayne Jewels after school on Chicago's North Side. "Well, Wayne, what do you have for us?" the detective asked.

"I remember some more," the boy said.

He recalled that two weeks *after* Ervin Gibson had disappeared, he saw his friend again, but only for a moment. It was at Leland and Clark, not far from Montrose and Clark where early teens pick up a few dollars hustling drivers. Jewels didn't remember the date but said it had been around 10 P.M. He saw his friend get into a truck.

"What kind of a truck, Eddie? A semitrailer or—"

"A pickup truck," the boy said.

"Ten o'clock is pretty late; what were you doing out?"

"My dad's the lead guitarist in a band; I was waiting for him to finish. Ma wanted me to pick up the check."

"Child support?" Colin asked.

The boy nodded.

"Did you see the driver of the truck?" The boy half nodded and half shrugged. "Can you describe him? I mean, was he tall or short? Was he fat? Did he have white hair?" The boy didn't know how to start. "I'll show you a few pictures, Eddie. Tell me if any of these men look like the driver you saw."

The boy picked out one: a muscular young man with a baby face and a small mustache.

"Then the truck drove away, and you never saw Ervin again?" Colin asked.

The boy shook his head.

Colin at last had his first link to Eyler, something that couldn't be dismissed as coincidence, but he knew it wouldn't hold up. If only the boy were older, if only he had remembered the incident right away rather than weeks after the initial questioning, if only he had seen Ervin in the daylight instead of the night, and if only he had identified Eyler's photo before Eyler was on television and his picture was in the newspapers.

"Thanks, Wayne," Colin said, "you've been a big help."

14

Saturday, January 21, 1984
Waukegan, Illinois

So that the Indiana officers might be refreshed when they appeared at the suppression hearing in Waukegan, the Lake County state's attorney's office put them up in the Holiday Inn at the Illinois Beach State Park. Lake Michigan can be pretty in winter, but no one wants to walk along the sand in January. The officers had the place much to themselves for the Super Bowl weekend.

McKoski told the men he was sorry to ask them to repeat their accounts of the Lowell stop, but he wanted to make sure they remembered enough details so that Judge Block would not think that what they did was arbitrary. A little into the questioning, Sheriff's Detective Kurt Proschwitz touched McKoski's arm and said, "Ray, we have a problem here."

Although Proschwitz never looked serious, he had special training in administration and could sometimes see the broader aspects of an investigation. Until now the Illinois police had not known that Eyler was handcuffed and kept in a cell for a few hours. They were told he had the run of the place, which was true for only the last few hours of his stay.

The Illinois sheriff's policemen and prosecutors didn't press the point. Instead they found an excuse to leave, then regrouped in one of the other rooms.

Proschwitz looked at McKoski and Trobe with his hands out for an explanation. "Well? You guys are the experts. The handcuffs and that—is that going to hurt us?"

"It depends on the judge," Trobe answered.

"Because if the Indiana cops blow it, *we* lose the knife, the boots, everything."

McKoski ran his fingers through his hair, as he sometimes did when things weren't going well. "You're right," he said. "It's a crapshoot."

"Twenty-one murders at least, and that's the best you can say?"

"What can I tell you," McKoski said to Proschwitz. "You go into court with what you've got; that's all anybody can do. Pete and I have been working as hard as you guys, and we think we've put together a pretty good argument. What do you want, a guarantee?"

The contingent broke up, and the men returned to the room with the Indiana officers. There was a sudden coldness between them, and the conversations for the rest of the weekend were bleak. Outside their hotel windows, the cold wind kept crashing the lake against the white sand.

Usually pretrial hearings are routine, but word was out that this one could be crucial to the case. And news crews made a gantlet for attorneys walking along the narrow corridor to the last room on the floor.

Oak paneling gave the courtroom a comfortable, subdued look. The judge's bench was at an angle toward the left end of the courtroom. Although this was one of the larger rooms in the modern building, plastic chairs had to be lined up against the back wall to accommodate all the spectators.

Down the corridor the door of the women's washroom opened, and a television artist walked out with a jar of water to dab onto her splats of color. A moment later, all rose as Judge Block entered from a door hidden by the paneling.

Eyler wasn't on trial now; the evidence was. Block had no way of knowing whether the seizures in dispute were fundamental to the case or whether the prosecution might be using the evidence in the Calise case as a forum to test its strength for other murders Eyler might subsequently be charged with. Block also had only the vaguest understanding of what led to the Indiana detention, since justice must work in a vacuum.

Trooper Buehrle told of driving on I-65 at 6:50 A.M. on September 30 and observing two men walk toward a pickup truck.

As Schippers saw it, everything the police did that day would be proper under some circumstances—but not in Eyler's case. He felt that he needed to clarify for the judge that his client had done nothing to justify the actions.

"Correct me if I'm wrong," Schippers told Buehrle. "When you first put Mr. Eyler in your car, you began writing a warning ticket, isn't that right?"

"Yes, sir."

"At that point, Mr. Eyler had done nothing but park alongside the road in violation of Indiana law; isn't that right?"

"Yes, sir," the trooper said.

Next Sergeant Popplewell testified about the statement that hitchhiker Darl Hayward gave police concerning the conversation he had with Eyler near the ditch. Prosecutor McKoski asked, "During that conversation, was there any mention of clothing or removal of clothing?"

"OK, Hayward told me that while they were down there that Eyler had asked him to raise his shirt, which he did. And he stated that Eyler saw his bare chest and abdomen, and then told him that it looked great."

McKoski finished his questioning of the witness by asking about the "flyer" Sergeant Love of the task force had called into the state police post, asking to be notified if the truck were seen.

Schippers rose from his chair and thumbed his silver-streaked beard. Then he said, "There was no information for a warrant outstanding for his arrest, was there, Sergeant?"

"I had no knowledge of any warrant," Popplewell answered.

Referring to the frisking Eyler had undergone, Schippers asked, "By the way, there were no weapons found, were there?"

"Not to my knowledge."

"You told him [Buehrle] to handcuff him at that point, did you not?"

"That's standard procedure when we're going to take a subject in a vehicle like that."

Schippers turned so that he could look at Popplewell yet address his meaning to Judge Block. "Is it standard procedure to handcuff an individual who's going to be written a warning for parking alongside the road?"

"Is it standard procedure?" Popplewell echoed. "Only if he's going to be transported into the post in a police car."

"What percentage of the individuals arrested in northern Indiana—or not arrested but given warnings for parking alongside the road—are handcuffed and transported into the Lowell post that you know of, Sergeant?"

Popplewell knew only too well how bad the decision seemed out of context, but he said there had been other cases.

Easing toward a file at the defense table, Schippers asked him about how he came to question Hayward about Eyler's propositioning him. Then he asked, "Is there one word in that report that you ever talked to Mr. Hayward?"

"Pardon me?"

Holding the paper up before the witness, Schippers asked, "Is there one word in this report that you took a statement from Mr. Hayward? Do you want to look at it again? Is there one word in your report that mentions that you interrogated a hitchhiker, yes or no?"

"No, sir," Popplewell answered with a hint of the hostility he felt for anyone trying to use his actions against him. "There's nothing in the report that I took any kind of statements from Hayward."

Sergeant John Pavlakovic waited out the lunch period by smoking a cigarette and looking out one of the parallel slots for windows on the outside wall of the softly lighted corridor. The temperature this morning was thirteen below zero, and he was looking at a city tied down by arctic cold.

"OK, John, you're next," Ray McKoski said. "Remember what questions I told you I was going to ask.

Relax. Take it easy. Schippers is going quickly over every detail he can. He's trying to make routine procedures look out of line. Don't let him rattle you; what you did was all right.''

Eyler was brought back into the courtroom and took his place behind his attorney. His mother sat on a spectator bench directly behind him, looking frail under a puff of pale yellow hair.

McKoski led Pavlakovic through the disputed morning, and his order to "bring them both in," and his refusal to give Eyler the aspirins. Schippers leaned forward as Eyler whispered to him and McKoski finished questioning.

The defense attorney then rose to his feet and walked to the officer on the stand. Schippers questioned why no one thought of having a judge sign a warrant to seize possible evidence in the truck at the Lowell station. "Was it your intention to hold Mr. Eyler until such time as you either got a consent or charged him?"

Pavlakovic fidgeted in his chair. "To hold him until I got a consent or charged him? No."

Raising his voice, Schippers asked, "How long did you intend to hold Mr. Eyler?" The attorney turned around and walked toward his client, then faced the sergeant for an answer.

"Until he protested or we had—"

"In other words, you would have held him for over twenty-four hours unless he protested and asked to be released; isn't that right?"

"I would not have held him for twenty-four hours."

"You would have held him until he either protested or gave you consent; you just said that, didn't you?"

The sergeant leaned over and looked at McKoski, sitting at the prosecution table, but McKoski couldn't help him. "No, that is not what I said," Pavlakovic responded calmly.

Grinning as he spoke, Schippers asked, "What *did* you say?"

"I said, 'or would have charged him' probably with it." He meant soliciting for prostitution.

"Now, you held him for twelve hours, didn't you, Sergeant?"

"He was in custody, yes."

With a lowered voice, Schippers asked: "He was under arrest, wasn't he?"

"No, sir."

"Well, do you put people in holding cells who have not been arrested?"

"That's a technical term," Pavlakovic replied. "He was in custody, he was not under arrest."

Schippers picked up a legal pad that his paralegal Linda had been using, then he turned toward the sergeant. "When is a person arrested, in your opinion?"

"When he is physically charged with a crime."

"In other words, you just handcuff somebody, hold them on some status, search him, put him in a holding cell, keep him in a room, keep him for twelve hours, and—unless you charge him—he's not arrested. Is that what you're saying?"

"In an unusual situation, yes, sir."

"You never did charge Mr. Eyler with soliciting a prostitute, did you?"

"No, sir, I didn't."

Schippers didn't pursue the matter. He worked for an impression, then moved on.

When Schippers was through with him, McKoski went up to Pavlakovic for redirect questioning. "Sergeant," he said, "your purpose in holding Mr. Eyler at the Lowell post was to wait for the task force to arrive, is that right?"

"That's correct."

"Did you ever intend to hold him indefinitely?"

"No, sir."

"Nothing else, Judge."

When Sergeant Pavlakovic stepped down from the stand, he stared at Eyler as if to penetrate his dark recesses. Then in the hallway, under the television lights, the sergeant lit another Lucky Strike and shook his head in anger.

On Tuesday prosecutor Pete Trobe played in court a twenty-eight-minute tape of Eyler's statements to Indiana police after he was brought out of the holding cell. Schippers had seen the transcript as People's Exhibit #11 but had never heard the cassette. He sat with a knuckle pressed against his lips and didn't let his reaction show.

When testimony resumed, Sergeant Love of the task force told about the hours he saw the suspect at the Lowell station. A few minutes later, Schippers said in his offhand way of leading to a major point, "Sergeant, as I recall, you had been watching Larry Eyler's home on Keane Street, is that right, from time to time, driving past there?"

"Yes, sir, we'd drive past; but we didn't set up a formal surveillance on it yet."

"Had you found Larry Eyler's truck there, would you have stopped in and arrested him?"

"No, sir."

"You didn't have probable cause to arrest him, did you?"

Trobe stood up and Judge Block sustained the objection. Schippers rephrased the question.

"You did not have enough on Larry Eyler in your mind, the mind of the task force, when you got off that helicopter—you didn't have enough on Larry Eyler to arrest him, isn't that right?"

"I personally didn't think we did, but most of the other guys did."

"After you had your conversation with Larry Eyler, did you arrest him?"

"No."

"After you caused his truck to be searched, and saw all the information that had been taken out of there, did you arrest Larry Eyler?"

"No, sir."

"As a matter of fact, as you sit there today, Larry Eyler has never been arrested by the Indiana police or by the task force for any of these events down there, has he?"

"That's true."

"Nobody told him that he was free to leave before he signed the consent, did they?"

"That's right."

"Nobody asked him if he was aware of his rights to leave, did they?"

"No, sir."

"And nobody said to him, 'Larry, you know you have a perfect right not to sign this consent to search, and we'd have to let you go,' isn't that right? Did you tell him that?"

"No, sir."

"Well, did you say, 'My God, what are you putting him in a holding cell for if he's not under arrest, we're not allowed to do that'?"

Love responded that he did not use words such as those but conceded, "I was rather concerned about it."

"What were you concerned about?"

"The detention."

"That he had been detained without being charged for an improper length of time, and improperly. Right?"

"Yes."

"Without probable cause, right?"

Love, showing regret over what had been done, nodded rather than spoke.

"Thank you, Sergeant, I have no further questions."

But McKoski did. He needed to correct any misunderstanding the defense attorney might have produced. McKoski obtained from Love a statement that he believed police did have enough evidence to charge Eyler with a crime—soliciting.

Then McKoski asked, "Was there any doubt in you mind that Larry Eyler understood his constitutional rights?" In other words, even though no one told him he could call a lawyer and no one told him that he was not formally under arrest and therefore could leave the police station, did he know that such options were open to him?

"Objection," Schippers said. "It calls for a conclusion."

When Judge Block said he would allow it, Schippers asked with a touch of disbelief, "My objection is being overruled, Your Honor?"

"Overruled," the judge answered.

Love then answered that he felt Eyler did understand his rights.

The next witness was that tough-looking, old-fashioned Indiana police officer, Sam McPherson. With his rural drawl he told of a conversation he had with the suspect in the interrogation room when the tape was turned off and Love and Newman were away. "I looked at Mr. Eyler, and I told him that I thought he was involved in the murders that we were investigating, and we were going to do everything we could to prove it, and he said he was shocked that I would say that."

When McKoski asked the officer what he noticed on the sole and heel of the boots that Pavlakovic had brought in, Schippers called for a sidebar conference. The judge and the attorneys agreed that it would be fair to ask whether the patterns on the boots were "similar" rather than "identical" to the plaster casts the Illinois police had made at the scene of the Calise murder.

When the testimony resumed, McPherson said he had examined several hundred shoes in his career and studied ten to fifteen "footwear impressions," then added, "I felt in my own mind they were close enough, to memory, with what I had recalled of the September eighth meeting, to warrant a further investigation."

When Schippers took over, he questioned McPherson at length about how the boots had been removed hours before the task force men arrived and how they were regarded as evidence the moment that McPherson remarked that they resembled the boot print casts in Illinois. "Larry didn't say, 'Well, how am I going to walk out of here without any shoes,' did he? He just said, 'OK'? He'd been giving you everything else, he might as well give you the shoes, right?"

"I don't believe that, sir."

Schippers turned mocking when he referred to evidence that was so "significant" that the Indiana police had let Eyler go without charges. "You decided you'd held him long enough, is that correct?"

"That's correct," McPherson answered firmly.

Shortly after lunch, Eyler was sworn in and took the stand as the television artists swiftly sketched in his outlines, to be filled in with watercolors during mundane testimony. Eyler sat facing his accusers with an uncommon ordinariness.

The young man, looking a little heavy now that he was no longer pumping iron at gymnasiums, told of his college years and how he had worked at a social service agency in Terre Haute for a year. He said he had been arrested twice: once for assault and battery, but the charges were dropped (the Mark Henry attack, in which Henry accepted a check rather than testify) and once for "promoting drugs." That was when he gave pills to young Fred Harte, only to have the charge dropped again.

Eyler explained that he signed the consent to search "because I figured I was gonna be there until I did it. I had been in a cell. I couldn't get aspirin. I just didn't think I could go."

Unconsciously twisting small strands of his hair, Eyler said that when they were alone, McPherson told him "I think you're a cold-blooded murderer, and we're going to do everything to prove that you did this."

Under questioning by McKoski, Eyler—who had been so reluctant to talk about homosexuality, even with a forlorn lover—admitted that the rope in the thin plastic bag was for an agreed sex act.

He made a credible witness, answering all questions openly and without hesitation. The officers watching him knew he must have gone through some painful coaching. He even admitted lying to the officers in saying that he had pulled over to the ditch to relieve himself, that the real reason was to have sex with Hayward.

Eyler said that he had been scared and confused by the arrest. About his not eating anything, he admitted that he hadn't been terribly hungry. "Hunger was not the most important thing on my mind." As to why he agreed to let the police take his boots and other possible evidence, he quietly said, "I told them they could do anything they wanted; I wanted to get out of there. I was willing to waive my rights for everything."

McKoski hammered away as if trying to fluster Eyler, and it was beginning to have an unsettling effect. The prosecutor asked, "As part of that cooperation, whether you expressed it or not, were you willing to give your boots to take tests on? Were you willing to do that?"

"If they would have asked me, I would have. I know they didn't ask me, 'Can we take your boots?' I do remember them saying they were going to keep them because at the time I didn't have any shoes on."

Eyler said that of course he had understood the Miranda rights that were read to him, "but in my mind at the time I wasn't thinking 'I have got a right to do this.' I was thinking 'I am scared, and I want to get out of here.' " He went back to the nervous habit of twisting his hair.

When McKoski asked him the reason he had signed the form, Eyler replied, "It was my concern I was cleared, but I wasn't thinking 'Gee, I hope they search my truck to find out that there is nothing in there.' "

Judge Block sustained objections whenever either lawyer tried to use Eyler for a pretext for summing up the body of his case, such as when Schippers in redirect questioning picked up a chance remark by McKoski that Eyler's memory of the Lowell stop was good. Schippers said, "How many times have you been stopped on the highway and arrested, searched, handcuffed, and thrown into a holding cell for five hours and not told what you were in there for?"

"Never."

"That tends to make your memory pretty sharp, doesn't it?"

"Objection," McKoski called out.

"Sustained," Block replied.

McKoski came back for a few more questions, including why Eyler had refused to talk about his going to gay bars while he was in the interrogation room of the Indiana state police station. "I didn't know exactly what they would do," the defendant answered. "I didn't want to listen to ridicule. I didn't know whether they would say 'Hey, faggot' or something like that. I simply tried to avoid that."

Questioning him further along this line would be self-defeating since the presumed motive behind these killings was an inability to deal with homosexuality, and the Larry Eyler on the stand seemed at ease with himself.

Next Dan Colin was sworn in. Eyler's eyes met his in a cold stare. Neither blinked. Many officers took part in the case, but it was Colin who was personally involved and who developed the most links to the other murders.

After preliminary testimony, Colin was questioned at length about how he and Chicago police confiscated the truck in front of Dobrovolskis' home.

Schippers paced back to his desk, then eased into a tone that was just a little louder, as if he were pressing gently on an accelerator. "Now, when you talked to Willie Smith a little earlier when he said 'I am sending a truck down,' did you say to him 'Why don't you wait until we get consent?' "

"No."

"Did Willie Smith say 'We are sending a truck. You get the car, I don't care how you do it'?"

Colin emphatically said, "No."

Schippers smiled and turned to Block, then asked, "Do you want to quit now, Judge?"

The suppression hearing was continued until the next morning, but that didn't mean Block could dismiss it from his mind as if the law were an assembly line. The judge retreated to his chambers and went over his careful notes. He also spent a few hours more in the courthouse law library. Block was hoping for precedent first, then wisdom. Both sides had done an extraordinary amount of research on whether the evidence should be allowed to stand. From his nine years on the bench and from the briefs filed by each side, Block felt that he had as much information on the question of search and seizure as any judge in the country. That did not make consideration of the testimony any easier.

Colin returned to the stand on January 25, the third day of the hearing. Even more spectators were sitting in the chairs along the walls than at the start because of interest generated by newspaper articles.

Schippers immediately asked Colin about the homosexual nature of previous murders, which had not been mentioned until now. "A lot of them were hustlers, male hustlers, and hitchhikers?" the defense attorney asked.

"Correct."

"Now, Ralph Calise was not a homosexual, was he?"

McKoski jumped in with an objection, saying, "I don't see the relevancy to the suppression."

Judge Block overruled the objection, contending that in the course of an investigation there might be a number of factors that could contribute to probable cause. That could include a victim's sexual nature.

Colin testified that as far as the police knew, Calise was not homosexual. He added that there was no sign of homosexual assault in the murder. Again, McKoski questioned the relevancy.

Schippers explained to the judge that the evidence found at the Calise murder scene pointed away "from the same type of murders that have been going on in Indiana." His use of the present tense and omission of the other Illinois victims seemed to suggest that they had nothing to do with Eyler.

McKoski and Trobe were playing the game too. They kept waiting for a "hole" to open up for them to introduce what they had on the other murders. But Schippers was careful and made sure that the testimony pertained only to the specific evidence seized, without regard to their meaning in any crime.

When the afternoon session began at 1:30, a number of the spectators were courthouse workers who were sitting in during their lunch breaks. They were expecting drama, not a ripple of laughter.

McKoski had asked to call a witness out of order, concerning Eyler's motion to quash the search warrant for the October 1 search of Little's home in Terre Haute.

"I have no objection," Schippers said. "I know who the witness is, and I know what it's about, and I have no objection whatever. The word is 'Eureka!' "

Judge Block smiled and said, "I take it you found the search warrant?"

"That's true, Your Honor," Trobe answered, and he called Indiana state police Cpl. David Hawkins, a shift commander. He told how the warrant was brought to the station by a judge from Terre Haute after someone left it in the courthouse overnight. McKoski then introduced the document as Exhibit #14. The warrant had been lost in a file until Hawkins made a search Tuesday night. Instead of being filed under Eyler's name, the warrant had been put in the "open investigations" file for Steven Agan, one of the victims. Both sides seemed relieved that the Indiana police were vindicated.

But the mood deepened as Schippers cross-examined former Lake County detective Roy Lamprich. Referring to the questioning Eyler underwent in Waukegan after Illinois police seized his truck, the defense attorney asked, "Did you ever see Officer Colin poke Larry and say to him, 'How does it feel when the knife went in here?' "

"Judge, I object, if this is impeachment," McKoski said.

"Overruled," Block responded.

To Schippers' continued questioning about the poking incident, Lamprich answered, "I don't recall any type of atmosphere like that." Indeed, he had been out of the room at the time.

During the cross-examination, John and Sally Dobrovolskis sat in one of several chairs along the inner wall of the corridor. Dobrovolskis was a man of style. One would never guess that he was unemployed, that his phone service had been cut off for back bills, and that he and his wife lived on money they had been receiving for three foster children until the state took them away. Now they were selling their furniture and facing eviction. Dobrovolskis' sandy hair was styled back, and he wore a tweed sports jacket with a plaid sweater over his tie. He even puffed on his cigarette with style, as if waiting for someone to snap a candid photograph.

When Sally was called to the stand, she said her husband had insisted that the Lake County and Chicago officers not come into their house on October 3 but that Colin told them, "We can be back in ten minutes with a warrant and just make things more difficult."

Schippers asked, "What did the police officers do when you and your husband walked into the house?"

"They followed us in the house. My mom, she was

sitting in the living room, she asked me 'What's going on? Do they have a warrant?' and I said 'I guess they don't need one.' ''

She also told how the officers had tried to take Eyler's truck without damaging it. One of them said "If you don't give us the keys, we're just going to take it anyway. It is going, definitely."

When Assistant State's Attorney Peter Trobe faced Sally, it was with Exhibit #16 in his hand, a copy of an affidavit for Ditkowsky's federal suit filed against eleven police officers. "Directing your attention to paragraph three, would you take a look at that? Doesn't it state, under oath, that you observed Lamprich, Colin, and others attempting to break into Larry's vehicle?"

"Yes."

Trobe let the matter drop there, after creating suspicion that Sally might be making accusations against police in furtherance of the suit.

Mrs. Dobrovolskis was followed by her husband.

"What is your relationship to Mr. Eyler?" Schippers asked.

"He is my lover," Dobrovolskis said.

"You are a homosexual, are you, sir?"

"Yes."

And so the defense attorney was able to suggest that Eyler was not a man warring with himself, that there was nothing to hide in his relationships.

Then he moved on to the evening when Illinois police seized Eyler's truck in front of the Dobrovolskis home. "I asked Larry what was going on, and if he wanted me to call an attorney. Officer Lamprich stepped in front of him and said, 'You should not call an attorney, he has not been arrested, we just want to talk to him.' I asked if I could go with, and they said, 'No.' ''

McKoski briefly rattled Dobrovolskis with questions about discrepancies between his testimony and the affidavit he signed for Ditkowsky's suit, but none of it pertained to the evidence, and he was able to smile as he stepped down from the stand.

As Dobrovolskis walked out of the courtroom, Schippers whispered something to his client. Eyler was then called back to the witness chair.

"Did you at any time voluntarily consent to have your truck taken to Waukegan?" Schippers asked.

"Never."

"Were you warned of your rights while you were on the street?"

"No, I wasn't," Eyler answered, but he said he signed a Miranda waiver after he was taken to Waukegan.

During the cross-examination, Trobe seemed to badger Eyler about the Waukegan questioning. He then steered Eyler toward the federal suit Ditkowsky had filed, as McKoski had done with Sally and John—as if to imply that seeking damages from police officers diminished them as credible witnesses. He repeatedly questioned the suspect about what was going on in his mind after he was released from Waukegan. Sarcastically, Trobe asked, "You couldn't believe it was happening, because this is America and you've got rights, is that right?"

"I couldn't believe that this whole thing was happening, no. I couldn't believe the whole thing was happening to me. America and my rights were not on my mind at that time."

The defense had no more witnesses, and McKoski called Colin the next day to go over the questioning in Waukegan once more. By then northern Illinois had at last pulled out of its midwinter deep freeze, and the temperatures were in the forties.

Schippers brought up almost as an afterthought at the end of nearly a week of testimony that while Eyler was being questioned in the Area 6 station in Chicago, Lake County police never went down a hall to obtain a search warrant from one of the judges.

That was how the crucial hearing ended, without a major disclosure to make the issues clear. Reporters who may have been hoping for dramatic disclosures were disappointed. With attorneys from each side at his bench, Block said two issues were foremost in his mind and he would welcome their thoughts and additional legal arguments to clear them up.

One issue concerned the seizure of boots by state troopers as soon as Eyler was taken in handcuffs to the Lowell station. That may have been routine, but the boots were never returned to him. Officers had decided among themselves to hold them because the heel and sole resembled the photos of the casts. Illinois police then came into possession of them through a subpoena, but the boots were never formally seized by Indiana authorities.

The other question concerned whether there was probable cause to confiscate the truck or the tires. In all four days of testimony, the tires had hardly been mentioned, but they disturbed the judge since they perhaps provided the strongest evidence police had in the Calise murder.

The judge sat back, obviously not happy about the loose ends, and he continued the case to the following Wednesday. He also indicated that he was bothered by some other circumstances, including the bag of ropes that had been cited as a main reason for hauling Eyler into the Lowell station even though the bag had not been in plain view, and McPherson's threatening conversation with Eyler after the tape recorder was turned off. He dismissed the court with a troubled mind.

As Eyler stood up he averted Colin's threatening glower and seemed almost relieved when a deputy led him out one of the doors in the oak paneling.

15

Judge Block had told both sides what disturbed him most about the testimony, hoping that the lawyers might help him make his decision. He had considered the issues often in the last week, and perhaps just as often he put off thinking them through to await the summations. None of his conflicting feelings showed as he sat back motionlessly as the lawyers from each side tried to sway him.

Defense attorney Schippers was sure that precedents alone would not convince the judge. There needed to be an overriding thought to put all the details in perspective. He sat alert, waiting for a hook to hang his argument on.

"The operable fact," said Assistant State's Attorney McKoski, "is whether there is probable cause to seize the man or hold the man, not whether he's subsequently charged with the same crime or a different crime—or not charged at all."

"May I comment up to this point, Your Honor?" asked Schippers. "First of all, the arrest of Mr. Eyler is clearly illegal. There was no probable cause to put him in handcuffs and take him to the Lowell police station. The fact is, if the state's attorney's theory is adopted, the police may grab anybody they will on any type of pretext whatsoever. And if they luck out and during the course of their investigation, no matter how long it takes, they come up with the same probable cause for some kind of arrest, then that will 'legitimize' the original detention."

Schippers had succeeded: he laid before the judge a

moral obligation that went beyond a legal consideration. The judge still showed no hint of which way his mind was running.

To clarify his interpretation of the circumstances, Block proposed now that the original stop and everything Trooper Buehrle did was lawful, but the question was whether Eyler should have been detained at the station.

The state's case was based on the "good faith" issue raised in *United States v. Williams* just three years before. The Fifth Circuit Court of Appeals had defined the exception this way: "Evidence is not to be suppressed under the exclusionary rule where it is taken in good faith and in reasonable—though mistaken—belief that they are authorized."

The Indiana police had not been out to get Eyler. Everything started out going wrong when they misread the flyer asking that police notify the task force if Eyler or his truck were seen. But to Block it seemed they should have known better.

The *Williams* case created an exception to the Fourth Amendment protection against unlawful seizures. "The exclusionary rule exists to deter willful or flagrant action by police, not reasonable, good faith ones," the appeals court had ruled. "The costs to society of applying the rules beyond the purpose it exists to serve are simply too high . . . with few or no offsetting benefits."

After hearing several hours of arguments, Block adjourned the hearing until Friday and had no idea how he would rule.

When he was just starting on the bench he felt cushioned by the appellate court, but he soon realized that an error would need to be flagrant for a decision to be reversed. The preparations for the hearing had made it clear that there were sufficient precedents for admitting the evidence and also for suppressing it, and Block felt that the appellate court would uphold his ruling either way.

In his paneled chambers, Block removed his robe and placed it on a wire hanger on a hook near his door. In the silence of contemplation he looked out his window at the snowy streets. Around him were bound copies of Illinois Supreme Court cases, but they didn't help him now.

From a small refrigerator he pulled out a can of 7-Up. Was Eyler guilty? That wasn't the question Block's ruling would have to answer. He wished he could think in terms of justice. That is the ideal world where the guilty are punished and the innocent go free. Instead, judges live in a system of laws, and that is something else again.

Lots of thoughts crossed through his mind, including "Why me?"

One hand on hip, Block drank from the soft drink can. Over his shoulder was a painting he had done years ago of a snowscape at a pond. Painting was comforting. That pond was his secret hideaway. When he was alone with nature, the issues became clearer.

He put some law books into a two-foot-square box but sat in his black leather chair for a while to go over once more the motions and his notes from three days of testimony, each day's legal pad in a different folder. Ever since January 23 he was hoping the state would come up with something that would justify the Lowell seizure, but the prosecutors never did.

The judge piled the notes into a bag and put on his overcoat. He went to his car and drove to his home in a rural area of woods and low hills near Prairie View.

His wife was cooking dinner when he came in with the bag of notes and box of law books. She understood a little of what he was going through, being a judge's wife and working for a state representative. She knew how the law can be elusive and frustrating.

Her husband didn't say much, and she tried to take his mind off the case by talking about her day. Their fifteen- and twelve-year-old daughters came into the kitchen and soon were bickering over something about school. As with any other father, they asked the judge to settle the spat. He shook his head and stood up. "Just leave me alone," he snapped.

"Bill!" said his wife.

He grabbed a coat from a hall closet. The night was cold but had the breath of warmth in it as he sauntered out. His neighbors thought he was crazy whenever they saw him walking along his land for what seemed no particular reason. Sometimes the give-and-take arena of the law only made sense as he strolled aimlessly.

Oh, he knew one kind of decision he could make: rule with the prosecution and you're generally on the side of the heroes. If he ever ran for appellate court, he could boast that he sent Eyler to prison. He would be a speaker at Republican fundraisers for the sheriff and state's attorney.

But the behavior of the Indiana police disturbed him. It was more laziness than anything, an assumption that police in a major case could do pretty much what they wanted as long as they didn't beat anyone. He recalled Schippers' words: "The police may grab anybody they will on any pretext whatever." They were a half a century behind the times. He wished he had the authority to impose some penalty on them for cutting corners, but all he could do would be to throw out all the evidence Indiana police seized, even though it was the basis of the Illinois case. If another judge ruled the opposite way, Block knew he wouldn't think less of him.

He was walking along the cattails of his pond a few hundred feet from his home. What he could do was suppress some of the evidence but not the rest, Block told himself.

There were icy stretches from Sunday's snowstorm and a few patches of spongy bare earth as he circled the pond, just trying to sort everything out.

True, the U.S. Supreme Court in the 1980s had been getting away from what Block called the "bottom-line decisions" of individual rights, but he hadn't seen anything showing that the high court let the exclusionary rule fade away.

Locking Eyler up without a charge . . . taking the boots without a waiver . . . going through Dr. Little's house waving a piece of paper they claimed to be a warrant, and the warrant mysteriously not showing up until months later . . . Block supposed it took only a few soft decisions now and then across the country to create a police state.

Besides, not only the Calise case was involved. There was the possibility of tainting jurors in the Eyler murder trials yet to come.

He returned to his home and sat down at the kitchen table. He could seem more like himself now when his children told him of all the petty things of school and going places in the flush of adolescence. He hadn't fully made up his mind yet, but the pressure had lifted. Block ate little and walked to his den, taking his notes and law books with him.

It was around 9 P.M. when Mrs. Block came in with coffee for him. He sat back and looked at his wife and said quietly, "You know, I may have to let that bastard go."

He didn't expect her to understand his reasons. But her expression said "Whatever decision you make, I'll stand by you."

Block went to bed at 11 P.M. but awoke around 2 A.M. Then he went downstairs and reread the motions and his notes, hoping to find some line of reasoning he had overlooked.

On Thursday he finished writing out in longhand his response to all the motions, not trying to put them in cogent order.

He appeared in court the next day showing none of the strain. There was still a way out for what he was about to do, if the prosecution could turn up some additional evidence. He apologized to Schippers and the assistant state's attorneys for what he was about to say in a disjointed fashion and without having a copy typed up for their reference.

Block ruled that there was no justification for taking Eyler into custody under the *Terry* stop ruling or any other decision or for impounding his truck. Nor were police allowed to remove a bag of ropes from under the seat and look into it. "Every act that followed was a direct consequence of the illegal arrest and detention for those investigative purposes," he held. Block also ruled that there were not sufficient facts in the police affidavit to obtain a search warrant the next day to search Little's home.

Schippers turned to Eyler and whispered, "We won."

Concerning the seizure of Eyler's truck by Detective Colin, Block concluded that he had "some credibility problem with some of the defense witnesses." The decision to take the truck to Waukegan was based on Eyler's cooperation. Although "tainted," the police actions were legal, Block ruled, and the tires seized were "therefore admissible."

He also decided there was insufficient probable cause for the October 31 search warrant of Little's home, but he denied Schippers' request to quash the search warrant for hair and blood samples that had been taken from Eyler as soon as he left the federal court building.

That left the prosecution with tires, which wouldn't be enough for a conviction; hair samples, which also would not be sufficient; and a blood type verification that was meaningless because the boots containing blood matching Calise's type would not be allowed into evidence.

The assistant state's attorneys were speechless.

Schippers said, "Thank you, Your Honor" and then approached the bench with a request for bond.

This led the judge to ask the prosecutors how they planned to proceed now that their most damning pieces of evidence were taken away from them. Frankly, the men didn't know. With the dry throat of defeat, McKoski asked the judge to continue the hearing to Monday because there would likely be an appeal.

No appeal was filed, and Block walked into the Waukegan courthouse Monday still hoping the prosecutors would pull something out of a hat. A new witness, a new link, just anything to justify keeping Eyler in jail on one million dollars' bond. Block stepped up to the bench, saw the faces of the prosecutors, and knew they couldn't.

Eyler, who had been in the overcrowded jail for sixteen weeks, stood before the judge in a blue suit. He kept his eyes lowered as prosecutor McKoski asked that the high bond remain and that Block consider evidence. But there was no real evidence to consider. The judge had to push from his mind the knife, the boots, the blood, and everything else he had ordered suppressed.

Sitting in the front spectator bench, Colin saw the investigations and the hopes of all the families crumble. Schippers seemed happy as he asked for a new low bond. My God—the thought just occurred to Colin—perhaps Schippers really believed his client was innocent.

"Larry has no intention of leaving the state or going back to Indiana," Schippers said. "That's one state I know he'll never go back to. He'd be crazy to go back to Indiana."

The allusion to the state police was not lost on Block, who had been so upset by their cavalier approach that for a while he had even considered releasing Eyler outright. The judge felt that if he lowered the bond to something Eyler's family could meet, it might hold his impulses in check and yet warn police to be careful in all their investigations of multiple crimes.

"Bond is set at ten thousand dollars," Judge Block ordered.

McKoski was so shocked he unconsciously took a step backward. Eyler's mother showed emotion for the first time in all the hearings. She gasped in joy and grabbed Sally's hand. All the family had to post was 10 percent of the appeal bond, a thousand dollars.

Eyler hugged Schippers and Linda Holmes. "You go downstairs and change into whatever you want," Schippers told him. "In an hour or so we can leave."

The deputy leading Eyler away paused long enough for the Dobrovolskises to embrace him. Schippers left his coat and hat behind to talk to reporters in the corridor. Colin stayed where he was as the courtroom emptied, then walked over to McKoski. "Hey, Ray, do you have any objections if I show Schippers what we have? He really thinks Eyler is innocent."

Ray shrugged and said, "I don't care." Reporters asked Schippers if he was surprised at the appeal. "Without the evidence, they have no choice. I don't think the state had a strong case even with the evidence."

When the reporters were satisfied, Schippers went back for his coat. "Dave," Colin said.

"Oh, hi, Dan."

Colin's eyes darted to Holmes, then to the bearded attorney. "I want to show you something," he said quietly. Schippers caught the tone and stopped putting on his coat.

"You were brought in late on this, and I just thought you might want to know who you're representing."

"What's the matter?"

"Did you know the FBI was so sure of those boots that they were going to send an expert here to testify that they were without a doubt the same boots that made the prints by Calise?"

"It's just a boot."

"Once you wear a boot a while it gets almost as many identifying marks as fingerprints," Colin said. "Do you know the blood inside wasn't Larry's; it matched Calise's?"

Schippers paused. Those were the boots he and Holmes had been laughing about because they seemed so trivial a clue. "You've developed a lot of evidence?" he asked. Colin nodded. "Sure, we'll go with you."

Colin waited for Schippers to clear all of his papers at the defense table in the empty courtroom, then led them into the cold sunlight of the courtyard. The detective took them through the front entrance of the sheriff's office, past the secretaries and the waist-high brown door.

Colin pulled out a drawer of his desk and laid out the "calendar" that everyone had been working on. It was a large sheet of white paper with small notations in lines of boxes.

"Go ahead, sit down," he said.

Schippers took the detective's seat, and Holmes stood beside him. Colin pointed to the sheet and said, "The Indiana task force and we were able, working together, to trace Larry's movements for an entire year. There are twenty-one murders that we know of. Through receipts and bills and what have you, we were able to place him at nine of the scenes."

His fingertip moved down from one small box of notations to another. "Here is the date Steve Crockett disappeared, here is when he was found, and here is when Larry bought gas nearby. Over here is a collect call made from the gym where Larry and John Bartlett worked out. Here is when Bartlett disappeared, and here is a gas receipt from practically where Bartlett was found."

Then came links to Michael Bauer, the amateur hockey player; young Ervin Gibson; and nearly half a dozen others.

"So . . . what are you saying?" Schippers asked.

"I'm saying he's going to do it again."

"This could fit a lot of people," Holmes said.

"Don't you see the pattern? He kills, and then he makes a call." Colin's finger thumped on the paper. "He killed," he said and thumped again, "and he called. He killed and he called." His finger moved from date to date. "It's his pattern. We've all been working on it; we all know it. Now that you got him off, you better damn well better hope there aren't any more long-distance calls to Terre Haute."

Schippers let it all sink in for a moment, then stood up, complimented Colin on the exhaustive work he and the others had done, and gave him a professional handshake of farewell. He took Holmes' arm and turned toward the door, revealing nothing that was on his mind. But later Schippers would admit, "What he gave me was some information he had showing a pattern that shocked me out of my shoes and scared the hell out of me."

The attorney didn't know what to think as he walked downstairs to the lockup. He couldn't question the police work, yet he had never been more convinced of a client's innocence. Perhaps there were other explanations. Colin and the task force never made a "calendar" for Little, Williams, or other friends of Eyler.

Newspaper cameras flashed as Eyler walked free, wearing jeans, a flannel shirt, and a fleece-lined jacket. He was never comfortable in a suit. Someone opened the heavy door for him, and the real meaning of freedom must have hit him. A television cameraman walked backward to capture the faces of Eyler, his mother, and his attorney as they walked toward a black car that had pulled up at the ramp.

Balding sheriff Mickey Babcox watched the car drive off toward Chicago. He flicked a cigarette to the ground and stamped it out as if he wished he could do the same thing to Judge Block. This was a side of the congenial former coroner that reporters had never seen before.

"He's freed to kill," Babcox spat out. "Hell, it's only a matter of time."

The reporters closed in on him, but this aging man who loved to talk to journalists growled, "Not now, fellows." He had too much he wanted to say to speak. He would have to cool down first.

Everyone celebrated at the Italian Village restaurant next to Schippers' Loop office. In the atmospheric third-floor dimness, as waiters carried large trays of pasta, Schippers explained that he had set up a hotel room for Eyler so he could clean up and relax without the media bothering him. He and Dobrovolskis could sneak out the back way of the restaurant.

There were a lot of things to be done, since Eyler would have to find an apartment somewhere. John and Sally wanted their foster children returned and couldn't have them if Eyler moved back in. Eyler also would have to find work, even though he had no marketable skills.

"Another thing," Schippers said at the small table. "The cops are out there for you, and you can bet that they will try to pin any murder they can on you. You are going to be watched. Larry, believe me. You aren't really free. You must have someone with you at all times, or someone has to know where you are."

"Aw, come on," Eyler said with a shake of his head.

"I mean it, Larry. You are to call me or Linda daily, and we'll log where you go. Look, the cops have their own log on you, did you know that?" The lawyer leaned over, looking directly at Eyler but speaking to his assistant. "Now, if a cop stops you—Linda, what does he say?"

The angular, dark-haired woman recited "I will not talk

without my attorney present; my attorney is David Schippers, please call him.''

"Remember, tell them nothing. Nothing. And always have someone with you.''

"How am I going to work?''

"I told you, we will help you get started, Linda and I. This is going to be a fresh start, Larry. Now, do you believe me or not?''

There was a weak smile on Eyler's face.

Schippers blotted his mouth with a napkin and shook Eyler's hand. "OK, now. You two sneak out.''

Holmes said, "Don't worry, Dave, he'll check in,'' and she led the two men toward the kitchen exit of the restaurant. Schippers left to distract the reporters.

III

THE TWENTY-THIRD VICTIM

16

Chicago

Nothing is real inside the Galaxy game room; it is a house of pretend power. The aisle between the machines is illuminated dimly by thin snakes of tiny yellow lights. From the token machine just inside the entrance to the pool room, two dozen electronic games offer opportunities to assault and massacre the enemy; to be a ninja, escaped POW, vindicator, wrestler, or spy hunter. More of the same and five pinball machines line the other side of the single aisle.

Just outside the front door of the Galaxy are the curving overhead Chicago Transit Authority tracks, keeping Broadway and Wilson Avenue in yearlong darkness as if to cut off the neighborhood from the rest of the world. When an evangelical street minister does his rounds to help young drug addicts and runaways, he usually makes the game room his first stop. Then he zigzags along Leland, Malden, and Magnolia.

Uptown is a way station for families moving up from West Virginia, Tennessee, and Arkansas. Unlike the middle-class neighborhoods west of the river or the poor neighborhoods of the South and West sides, in Uptown the streets are an extension of the homes.

People don't talk about politics or community improvement. The older folks think back to the mountains and the country roads and of going back after they've made a little money.

There is tension here—lovers who get revenge with

arson, street-gang members, and freewheeling neofascists roam the streets—otherwise the neighborhood is friendly for insiders. Younger children sit on cars and talk if the weather isn't too bad. Older children might be looking for glue to sniff or hanging out where they can hustle. A family with four children might have one daughter and two sons in prostitution.

At the neighborhood Butera supermarket kids nine to eleven hang around the exit doors and ask men carrying packages if they can help them to their car. Sometimes they get a quarter tip and that's it, but the boys or girls feel that if they're lucky the men will offer them a ride and they will get twenty-five or fifty dollars out of it. Then the children go back to their friends and brag about how smart they are.

One of the boys who frequented the hangouts was Danny Bridges. He would bend over the pinball machines in the game room while some other boys introduced themselves to men by asking for quarters and hoping to strike up a conversation that could lead to a few dollars. The machines in the game room pinged and powed away in a wartime din.

Sometimes Danny would put his hands in his jacket and lean against the old brown bricks of Blood Alley and talk to the girls or boys waiting to be picked up for an hour. The odd, curving alley runs for only a block between businesses and opens onto Wilson Avenue by the elevated tracks. It's just a few yards away from the game room.

Danny was not handsome, but he had a friendly, open face, and his blond hair was usually tussled from unconcern. He would have fit in well as a companion to Tom Sawyer and Huckleberry Finn. The boy knew in grammar school that his looks could bring him a lot of money if he wanted to go on the streets, as some of his friends were doing. To them it wasn't exactly prostitution. Sometimes the men gave them drugs and just took pictures. One man who picked up kids in Blood Alley would pay them twenty-five dollars just to watch as they masturbated.

The boy was the last of thirteen children from an Alabama family, and his mother and father were old enough to be grandparents. All he knew were overcrowded apartments and quarrels over money. Charles, his father, was a friendly-looking man but very quiet. He was a punch press operator and mover who had lost much of his hearing. The boy's mother, Augustine, originally from Missouri, was in charge of the family. With thirteen children, she couldn't give them all the attention she supposed she should have. Danny's sister Sharon acted as an additional mother and tried to interest him in religion. The two of them could be mistaken for twins despite their age difference with their slender builds, full lips, brown eyes, and wavy dishwater blond hair. They had the same serious attitude enlivened by occasional impishness.

When Danny was nine a neighbor invited him to his Uptown apartment and molested him. There was more to what happened than a physical assault. All Danny would say about it was "It happened so fast. I was almost raped." His innocence had been betrayed, and no one seemed to care. With the desperate illogic of a child, Danny mistook the abuse for love. He never fully rid himself of this confusion.

We don't know much of what happened in later years. His family knows a little, but just a little. One of the unwritten rules of the child prostitutes who grow up in Uptown is that you don't talk about yourself, and Danny was quieter than most.

The boy ran away from home to live with a friendly couple for a while, as if a child could swap families at will, but he returned home and spent more time on the streets than in his apartment. He was passing his subjects in grammar school but had no interest in learning. He had a career. By the time Danny was twelve, he was a "chickie." Sometimes he brought the money home; sometimes he spent it on sodas and pinball and outings with friends. One of them was Sammy, whose older sister was already a prostitute. Sammy remains a birdlike man waiting to be bought. At least he always knows what he is getting into. Danny was different. "He had a sort of innocence about him," says Sammy. At fourteen, Danny still had the wonder and bottomless trust of a six-year-old.

People in the business of helping troubled teenagers call it "learned helplessness." For prostitutes, male and female, that's always dangerous. They "seem to send out vibes that offenders pick up," said Dr. Richard Seeley, an expert on sexual aggressiveness. "It's like radar."

Such was Danny Bridges, who died at the age of fifteen. He was the twenty-third victim on the list attributed to Larry Eyler. Yes, he had heard of Larry Eyler and even met him on the streets. Eyler was known around Uptown as someone who paid well. Besides, the Calise murder charge against him had been dropped or thrown out or something because of insufficient evidence, the boy thought.

State's Attorney Fred Foreman immediately filed an appeal to Eyler's release and angrily pointed out that people charged with marijuana possession were being held on higher bonds than ten thousand dollars.

There were no fiery editorials; the story of Eyler's release was handled in a few perfunctory paragraphs in the newspapers and did not make national news. No one except those intimately involved in the case realized what repercussions Judge Block's decision were likely to have.

The appeal was expected to take sixteen to eighteen months, putting Eyler in a long limbo. He was legally free to go anywhere in Illinois, but his truck was still impounded, he had no car, and he had been warned by Schippers that wherever he went police would be watching him.

Virtually tossed into the role of a celebrity for at least a few days, Larry lost his secret world. In Little Jim's, the Gold Coast, and other gay bars people shook his hand and offered him free drinks because he had been brave enough to stand up to police harassment. Some people believed that the murder charge was just the police department's way of getting even for Ditkowsky's federal suit.

No one supported Eyler more than his own attorney. Schippers had rechecked the telephone calls and credit card data that supposedly linked his client to other murders and came away convinced that police were trying to build a case against an innocent man. That's what Schippers told Colin after a routine hearing in Waukegan in mid-February. Colin answered with a cold stare, followed by "Maybe you just want to believe."

Schippers indeed had grown fond of the young man, who seemed like a son to him. Later Schippers would say, "I was totally, completely, unutterably convinced that Larry Eyler was innocent."

On Wednesday, February 29—leap year day—Dr. Little came to Chicago and signed a rent application for an unfurnished apartment for Eyler in a well-kept building at 1628 West Sherwin Avenue, in a quiet part of the North Side. Most of Eyler's neighbors were elderly. At thirty-one, Eyler hardly seemed to belong there. People lived out Norman Rockwell lives, discussed doctors and grand-children, and the only noise came from the 6 A.M. clatter of janitors down the block hauling garbage from the day before.

In a way Eyler seemed happy. The small apartment was the first place he had ever had of his own. He didn't know how long he would be able to keep up the rent, but Schippers told him not to worry; there would be one kind of work or another for him at least for as long as the appeal lasted.

Little bought him a bed, lamps, and a television set. Schippers' paralegal Linda dropped by and thought the place too bare, so she helped him buy second-hand chairs and bring in an old sofa.

With the apartment at last beginning to take shape, Eyler was less at a loss for what to do with himself, as if his impending trial meant nothing. He applied for admission to two colleges at opposite ends of the country, City University of New York and California State University in Long Beach, but Judge Block refused to let him leave the state. Local colleges didn't interest Eyler; he wanted to go somewhere that had never heard of him.

With his fantasy of being a perennial student cut short, he would often drop by at Schippers' office downtown. The lawyer's room was dominated by a desk shaped something like the head of a bishop's staff, wrapping around the big chair and serving as cabinets against the wide window. On the cabinet portion were a brass scales of justice and a small dispenser for nuts. Elsewhere around the room were a miniature chess set and a statue of Don Quixote.

Speaking to Schippers as if he were talking to an uncle instead of his attorney, Eyler sat down and told him of his problems finding work. He might have felt that a reason was the charge against him, but it was his inability to assert himself that was holding him back. The public mind forgets easily, and his name probably meant nothing to prospective employers.

"I tell you what," Schippers said from behind his wraparound desk. "This place needs a new coat of paint. You're a painter; do you think you can do it?"

"Sure," Eyler said with a shrug.

Eyler showed up the next day with white coveralls and a ladder in the fourth-floor offices of Schippers and Associates on Monroe Street. The lawyer had a collection of opera and Frank Sinatra records, but Eyler preferred country and western tunes as he scraped away peeling paint and cracked plaster. He filled in the gaps with plaster of Paris and carefully spread a coat of beige on the walls. He worked with the deliberation of someone not used to labor.

Secretaries quickly came to like Eyler, as if he were only distantly related to the man suspected of all those murders. He was considerate, and he amused them as he joked about himself and their world.

Eyler shouldn't even have been seeing Dobrovolskis, but his lover insisted on resuming the volatile relationship as if unaware of the possible consequences. Eyler had refused to give him his address, at Schippers' request, but told Dobrovolskis by phone that he was buying a bed from the North Side branch of Sears. Dobrovolskis called the store, gave his name as Larry Eyler, and said, "I want to make sure you've got the right address." The clerk read it back to him. From then on, there was no stopping him.

Eyler often would call Dobrovolskis during the day for long, rambling conversations. Sometimes he would abruptly turn angry, incapable of getting off his roller coaster ride of jealousy and reconciliations.

Eyler did good work, and Linda was glad to hire him to redecorate her ranch-style home on the far Northwest Side. He brought one or two of his friends along each day, including an exceptionally nice young man named Bob. One night she tried to call her home to ask if the men wanted her to pick up anything on her way back, but she couldn't get through in several attempts. When she arrived she found Bob alone working in the bathroom and Eyler downstairs on the phone, talking to Dobrovolskis.

"I have to hang up now, Linda's angry with me," Eyler said.

"You're damn right I am," she said and pushed the receiver button down. "If you can't do the work, get out!"

In a moment he was in tears—a muscular, nearly six-foot weight lifter was weeping in apology.

Separately she liked most of Eyler's friends, but when they were together they formed their own world. Once Bob and Eyler pulled up in front of the home of Schippers' secretary to do some work for her. The men quarreled for a couple of hours before driving away, without ever stepping out of the car.

From the several quarrels that Linda heard, she saw that the men quickly went for the throat. They didn't seem to concern themselves with the truth; they said anything just to hurt. You're not so hot; you don't know the other men I was with; you thought I was home, but I was out with four other guys . . .

One day in March, Cathy Berner came to work at the task force office and found that her computer was gone. So were all the boxes of evidence. She called her supervisors at the state police headquarters and was told that she had been reassigned. Now that Eyler was confined to Illinois, the task force was being phased down to the minimum needed for taking down tips and keeping in touch with other jurisdictions.

She sat down and felt like crying as she looked at the empty space on the desk. When she began work on the task force, she had hoped to find that hypothetical 1 percent of the evidence seized that might link Eyler to some of the victims. Now she never would.

That early spring, Eyler was becoming careless and irritable now that the newness of his freedom was wearing off. He seemed to have the ability to dismiss from the surface of his mind the reality of the situation. During those weeks he was scaling down the world to just himself and Dobrovolskis. They became two highly charged people exploding at each other.

In early April, Linda was coming down the stairs of her house when she saw a chance remark from Dobrovolskis send Eyler into a rage. Eyler acted like one possessed, and Dobrovolskis tried to hit him. Eyler ducked and pulled all his muscles taut to avoid hitting back. Linda didn't see love between these men; what she saw was obsession.

A little while after that quarrel, a street person was going through the trash filling a dumpster in the alley behind Eyler's home. The ragged man shivered when he found a pale human hand. He went to a phone and called the 911 emergency number, but police were never sent. The dispatcher felt that all you can do with such people is humor them. Who knows what he saw, the dispatcher must have thought. Perhaps it was a prank, something a medical student might have brought home to scare a roommate.

To this day, no one knows whose hand that was, but police investigating the murder series have no doubt. Around this time a teenage drifter called Cowboy disappeared from the streets of Uptown. Officially, he exists only as a missing person's report. The garbage from the alley was hauled away and buried in a sanitation landfill in southwest suburban Hillside. The hand remains there to this day, along with whatever else may have been in those large plastic bags. The victim never made the list, which stood at twenty-two deaths.

Dr. Little or Eyler's former lover James Williams would drive up from Indiana on weekends to be with Eyler, since he couldn't cross the state line. Williams would go with him to the gay bars until the early morning.

On May 7, a farmer was plowing a field on Crawford Road south of Route 173 in Lake County, Illinois, around Zion, when he stopped his tractor at what appeared to be a body or skeleton by a grove. When Deputy Chief Willie Smith heard about this he immediately thought of Eyler. Detective Chester Iwan walked past a windbreak of bushes and headed for an elm tree. There, close to a barbed wire fence, lay the human rubbish that had once been a man. The head was gone but was found nearby, probably where it had been carried by wildlife. There wasn't much left of the body to tell what happened, but the greenish-blue plaid shirt was bloodstained and ripped repeatedly by knife slashes.

This time police did not have to wait long for an identification. The twenty-two-year-old victim was David Block, a Yale student who returned to his family's home in affluent Highland Park for the Christmas holiday in 1982. He disappeared after saying that he was going to meet a friend in small north suburban Highwood, but perhaps he went to the North Side bars in Chicago instead. "Which one is this?" Iwan asked as the detectives talked about the case in their office in Waukegan.

"Who knows," Smitty said. "I don't think we're ever going to find them all."

"Well?" Iwan asked.

"Well, what?"

"Do we call Eyler and ask him where he was December twenty-ninth?"

"We can't, that would be harassment. We have to get evidence that points to him first, and after a year and a half what do we have—a shirt. He's going to get off on this one, too. Isn't the law wonderful?"

In Chicago, Danny Bridges was at perhaps the high point of his life. He had been raised in a family that could barely make ends meet, but now he was living with a man on North Lake Shore Drive, one of the glories of the city. This was in mid-May, and the crab apple trees behind the building were showing their whitish pink buds.

The boy wore Mark Shale pants and polo shirts. He ate well and stayed in a condominium with satin chairs, silver bowls, and crystal vases. The owner was a doctor in his late fifties who found that keeping a teenage boy made him feel younger. Danny found love and comfort, and it seemed the easy life would never end. But what he did not have was the independence to be himself. Danny did not have much spending money and he was not free to come and go as he pleased.

The boy asked if he could go home for Mother's Day. The doctor saw nothing strange in that. But after Danny left, the man discovered that a silver pitcher was missing. When Danny returned to the condo he admitted stealing the pitcher and said he had wanted a present for his mother. The relationship with the doctor was over. The man took back the clothing and the token gifts of jewelry he had given Danny over the last few weeks. Then he drove the boy back to Uptown. When the man returned, he told his doorman never to let Danny back into the building.

The standoff continued. The task force dwindled to two officers and then just Sergeant Love, who was finally returned to his normal assignment in the summer. Ditkowsky's federal suit against the Illinois and Indiana officers was withdrawn in March. Officially the Lake County state's attorney's office was preparing to try Eyler for the Ralph Calise murder, but they had no case. There was nothing to do but wait. At least his truck was still impounded.

Judge Block lived in social isolation long after the decision to free Eyler, which he knew would cripple his career. Sheriff Babcox, the behind-the-scenes power of the powerful Republican Party in Lake County, generally stayed away from him, but the two men were drawn together on a sweltering evening in late June 1984, when former prosecutor Tom Briscoe opened a law office across the street from the courthouse. As usual, more liquor was used to inaugurate a law office than to launch a ship.

Gera-Lind Kolarik was pouring Jack Daniels into glasses for attorneys, reporters, and some off-duty policemen. Block was sitting with his wife at the same large table as the sheriff. Kolarik misjudged the moment and thought this would be a good time to ask a question that had been troubling her for months.

She sat next to the round-faced judge and said, "Hey, you know, I want to ask you about why you ruled the way you did with Eyler. Couldn't it have gone either way?"

Babcox looked up, turning florid. "Hell, he could have," the sheriff boomed. "There was only one way he should have ruled, and that was not to free the guy."

"I ruled the way I did because the law demanded it," Block said.

Babcox pushed his chair back and grabbed a can of beer on the table. "Bullshit you did! You freed that son of a bitch; you freed him to kill. You had the evidence to stop him, and you knew it!"

Kolarik and the others scrambled to their feet, afraid that Babcox was about to throw something at the judge. One of the lawyers attending the party grabbed the sheriff's muscular hand as it seemed about to hurl the beer can at Block. Babcox pushed the attorney's arm away and slammed the can down so hard that beer shot up and foam ran over his knuckles. He started walking away, after muttering, "You son of a bitch!"

There was a silence as Judge Block sat unmoved in his chair. He looked up at Kolarik, but she turned away from him and tried to apologize at the same time. Here was a man with nothing but his integrity left. The tenseness eased only when Block's wife said, "It's time to go, Bill. It's getting late."

In July Schippers was able to force Smitty to release the pickup. That day the lawyer received a call from Dan Colin. "I hear Larry got his truck back," the detective said angrily.

"How do you know?"

"I just know. Let's give him another month. This is the fifteenth? Let's give him thirty days and see if we find a body. I'll keep in touch." He hung up.

Linda asked what that was all about.

"Dan thinks there's going to be another victim in a

month.'' That would be by August 15. There was silence in the office.

"The truck is part of his problem," Linda said.

"Well, we can't babysit him forever," Schippers remarked uneasily.

Dr. Little paid for extensive repairs and new tires for the truck. It wasn't until late July that it was towed to Chicago. Eyler signed a receipt and was like a child when a lost toy is found. His joy was cut short because there was nowhere to go. He couldn't cross the state line and felt that police would be making a note whenever they saw the truck. He stayed off the highways and confined his driving to just a few miles on Chicago's North Side.

That summer, Schippers paid Eyler to paint the inside of his house and do woodwork stripping with his friends and then plaster the bathroom. The attorney watched him doing the work. What was he worried about?

Taboos last only until someone approaches them honestly and with skill. Ever since September 1982, local NBC television producer Chuck Collins had been working with reporter Mark Nykanen in putting together a network special on child pornography and prostitution. The story took them to several parts of the country and Denmark, but much of the footage was filmed in Chicago. The city does not have a notorious district such as Sunset Strip, but in the 1970s it had a computerized ring that sold boys to customers in other states. The operation was called the "Chicken Delight Escort Service." One druggist on the North Side always used boys to "deliver medicine" to plush high rises on North Lake Shore Drive, the address of respected doctors and lawyers.

The NBC project was not one of those rush-in, rush-out jobs that local stations would do in advance of a ratings survey. Night after night the crew spent hours on stakeouts and following the police on raids, even though most of the work would be edited out.

Collins was a husky man with a flowing black beard; he looked more like a quarterback than the winner of a Peabody Award and six local Emmys. He was regarded as one of the best investigative reporters in the competitive field of Chicago television news.

Collins didn't want safe coverage; he intended to be the first producer to give a close look at "the rough trade," a catch phrase for juvenile male prostitution. Many of these children came from Uptown, where half of the boys making the rounds of the game room, street corners, and the Leland Avenue vacant lot are believed to be runaway wards of the state. People who work with child prostitutes say there is nothing to be done except help them where they are, since most of them are untrainable for jobs and anything beyond the casual relationships of the streets is beyond them.

In addition to work with his camera crew, Collins went to gay bars—a patron kicked over the NBC audio box in contempt—and also conducted several background interviews with boys on the streets. One of them was Mikey, who had just turned fourteen.

The boy, sniffling from a cold, said he and a friend were gathering pop bottles for the deposit when a man invited them to his home and told them how they could make some money. Mikey was nine or ten at the time. "It made me feel bad," he said of oral sex, "but I needed the money."

"When money's involved, they got no choice," he added in his piping voice, speaking of the other boys he knew on the street. "People make them think money's the most important thing. Somebody waves money in their face; they gotta have it. They'll do anything for it."

Mikey said the man "waved fifty dollars, a hundred dollars—handed me his wallet. A couple of times I just threw the wallet on the table and walked away."

The boys played it smart, Mikey told Collins and Nykanen. He always brought along someone else to stand near the door in case there was trouble, and he never let the man take him into the bedroom. But Mikey's seven-year-old brother wasn't so streetwise. Mikey turned on the man when he learned that his brother was "touched . . . hurt" while trying to get money to go to a street carnival.

"I hate them—these people who hurt little kids who

don't know what's going on in this world," Mikey said. "What scares me is they can offer these kids five dollars and then kill them."

The camera crew was closely working with Youth Officers Brian Killacky and Sam Christian in the late winter and early spring as they traced chicken hawks looking for boys around LaSalle and Hubbard streets, just a short walk from the Loop. Killacky belonged to the night world, with his orange hair kept long and his beard untrimmed.

The undercover officer was one of three who had been recruited for the "proactive" investigation, after a Catholic nun suggested that more be done to stop the exploitation. A few hours after helping the NBC team film the arrest of a man who had picked up a fourteen-year-old, Killacky led them to the Northwest Side for a raid. Wearing a flannel shirt, blue jeans, and cowboy boots, he went in to mix with the others at a small party. Christian stayed in the police car, occasionally looking at his watch. Collins sipped coffee from a thermos the television crew brought with them. Then Christian took the walkie-talkie off the dashboard, glanced behind him to the crew installing the battery belt in the camera, and said "Now."

He ran across the street with the crew, and Collins hopped over ice patches on lawns in the neighborhood of bungalows and small apartment buildings. They went up in the elevator, and Christian knocked on the door.

Killacky, pretending to be part of the sex party, said, "Yeah, man, we got reefers" and let him in.

Christian looked as scruffy as he could, wearing a full beard and leaving his shaggy blond hair grow past his shoulders. Once he was inside, Christian joined Killacky and told the others in the room, "You're under arrrest. Put your hands up against the wall." The officers charged a man and a neatly dressed Hispanic boy who had just a shadow of a mustache over his lip.

During one of the long waits for something to happen, Killacky approached Collins with an idea to humanize the documentary by concentrating on a single teenager. "He's a kid who I know is willing to talk about his life on the streets. Trouble is, we lost track of him. Who knows where he is, but if he shows up you'll really have something. He's quiet, but a real nice kid.''

When he was fourteen, Danny was living with a man above a strip joint in Lyons, near a wide-open west suburban unincorporated area that encouraged trade by motorcycle gangs. Whenever Danny went back to Chicago he would hang out in Joe's Juice Bar, and he was arrested there when a friend, Sammy, propositioned an undercover policeman.

Killacky felt that he was onto something. Danny and his friend not only answered all the questions, they said they would be willing to go to court. But where could he put them where they were safe? He decided to bring them to Cathy Ryan and kick some ideas around.

Ryan, a nun of the Sisters of St. Francis, was in charge of the juvenile division of circuit court. On this late afternoon of Holy Thursday, 1982, she was preparing for a long Easter holiday.

The detective introduced the boys to her in her West Side office, had them sit down, and outlined the problem. ''You've got to protect them,'' he said. ''If you don't keep them somewhere safe this weekend, we might never get them back.''

Not only were their lives possibly in danger, the boys might drift back to their old ways if returned to the street or might decide against testifying if kept in the juvenile detention home. Ryan understood that, but there was no precedent for protecting juveniles. None had ever come forward before.

''Look, no one told me to do this,'' Killacky told her. ''I'm supposed to lock them up, but I'm not going to do that.'' She understood what he was hinting at: he was willing to put his career on the line.

Ryan was the shortest person in the room. She looked at each boy and asked, ''Are you two aware of what might happen?''

Sammy looked a little scared, but Danny shrugged as if to say that it's something that has to be done. She told them she would see what she could do. Next she called her boss, State's Attorney Richard M. Daley, the son of the late famous mayor, Richard J. Daley.

When Daley heard the situation he immediately said, "Let's do it. I'll back you one hundred percent."

There were no shelters for street teens in the city at that time. The only place she could think of was Maryville Academy in north suburban Des Plaines, a former orphanage that lately had been concentrating on sexually abused children. She called the executive director, the Reverend John Smyth, and he said, "Sure, bring them out here. We'll make sure they're safe."

Danny looked around in his chair, confused. He thought that Killacky was going to take him to a school. Ryan explained that it was more of a huge home. "You'll have to do chores and abide by the rules, Danny, but you might like it," she said. "Is that all right?"

The blond boy shrugged again and smiled faintly.

The academy was intended to be a Great Lakes version of Boys Town. Father Smyth was a powerhouse former basketball star at Notre Dame. The primary concern of the academy was caring for girls and boys who had been sexually abused by strangers or relatives, sometimes over years. The friendly discipline of the school and dorms was intended to provide the normalcy they had needed in their lives before they began to die inside.

The street kids who wound up there were harder to reach because they thought they knew it all. The feeling of these teen prostitutes seemed to be that they wouldn't get into anything they couldn't get out of, and yet they never thought they were going to see their twenty-second birthdays.

When Smyth saw thirteen-year-old Danny, with his hair dyed bright yellow, he felt that here was a kid "dripping with the street influence." The priest knew at one glance that Danny had been hustling.

The boy was shy but enjoyed company, and he appeared less naive about others than he was about himself. As with every new arrival, Smyth and his assistants let Danny relax and talk about life for three to five hours that Thursday, if only to let him realize that he could speak openly and no one would make moral judgments about his behavior. Smyth came away from the session convinced that despite what the boy did, Danny was not homosexual and that "the pure business with him was survival."

Unlike a lot of child prostitutes, there was no crust around his feelings. Danny proudly carried pictures of his nieces and nephews in his blue jeans and would show them to the priests and others at the academy. He and Sammy stayed over the long weekend and then ran away, just to be found again by Killacky. He brought them back for their own safety.

After finishing his court appearances about the juice bar owner, Danny wanted to go home. He didn't need protection any more, he said, and he missed the unstructured life of his family.

Everyone liked Danny, but Smyth had another reason for wishing Danny would change his mind. The priest always tried to be upbeat but he thought that Danny's going back wouldn't work out, that no matter what the boy said he would drift back to the streets. But there was nothing Smyth could do.

So the Bridges family, which had moved from Uptown and taken an apartment on the Northwest Side, was counseled on how to cope with the boy's problems before he returned home.

Augustine and Charles Bridges were told to accept the boy for what he was and not to make him live by high standards. They should expect some absenteeism at school, perhaps some returns to the street, the counselor said, but Danny gave every indication of being able to work out his problems in the long run.

The boy felt his parents had little to do with his life, but he was happy to be back with his sister Sharon. She was only six years older than her brother, but her relationship with him ranged from friend to substitute mother. When she was twelve she would wake six-year-old Danny and her seven-year-old brother to bathe them, give them breakfast, and walk them to school as their parents slept off last night's drinking.

Sometimes while Danny was still in grammar school

they would take a bus to Lincoln Park a few miles from their home to search the garbage for pop bottles they could bring to a store for money. Once Danny found a porcelain jewelry box with blue flowers painted on it, and they made up a fantasy that it came all the way from China. Another fantasy was that they would run away to California and live by themselves.

They sometimes walked down the cobblestone alleys of the North Side and imagined living in one of the Gothic houses lining Deming Place. They would have chandeliers and servants and let accountants worry about their taxes.

But when Sharon was fifteen and Danny's life had just begun to be troubled, she became pregnant. Two days after delivering the baby, she gave it to her older sister Connie. But Danny was starting to feel cut off from her. She was now virtually a woman and living her own life. Sharon became pregnant again three years later and kept the baby. She named the boy Danny.

But Sharon and Danny, her youngest brother, were still the best of friends. One hot summer afternoon they sat in the kitchen with a bottle of India ink and a needle. They tattooed their left hands with three mysterious dots, just as they did a lot of crazy things together. But his sister couldn't give him all the attention he wanted, and he would stay away for weeks on end. She knew he was living with men. Every now and then he would call to say he was all right.

Danny was still a police informer on the street. His steady contact was Norma Reyes, a pretty Hispanic woman who worked out of the juvenile court building on the West Side. He would sip a Coke and share a joke with her in her office and never seemed afraid that something might happen to him.

Danny was a lean boy, five feet nine and weighing a hundred forty-five pounds. That added to his helpless look, which seemed to draw pedophiles to him. His boyishness also made him endearing to the police officers and state's attorney's office administrators who worked with him.

He responded immediately to any kind of encouragement, and in his months of appearing on the stand in

unpublicized court cases against child molesters he had a
96 percent conviction rate. Judges and juries always
sensed that here was a kid who was messed up but told
the truth about the subworld of Uptown.

In that summer of 1982 Sharon's cousin was dating a
good-looking young man named Steve Crockett. He disappeared in October, and she was shocked to learn that he
had been stabbed to death in Kankakee County. Later the
newspapers and television stations said Larry Eyler was
the suspect.

When Danny returned home he was fun to have around.
He would hum made-up songs to Sharon's little daughter
and jiggle her on his knees. But the boy could never stay
long; there was a restlessness in him, a need to be dominated by some man.

He might have thought that he was in prostitution for
the money, but there was no goal for the money other
than to have it awhile. Journalist Jon-Henri Damski, who
is familiar with the undercurrents of Uptown, notes that
when "male whores" make a score with enough money
to pay the rent and food for three days they feel "higher
than God." Danny said that he would come back from the
doctor's apartment on North Lake Shore Drive with three
hundred dollars.

Like his lifelong friend Sammy, Danny graduated from
the Montrose Avenue chickie district to the rougher areas
around Clark and Diversey, about a mile closer to the
Loop. Yet Danny never learned the first lesson of street
hustling. You're supposed to look like an easy mark but
be tough enough to handle the deceptions and sometimes
the beatings. With his soft way of speaking and his loose
way of walking, Danny seemed to proclaim "Whatever
you do to me, I'm helpless."

Danny drifted through bouts with alcohol and drugs. He
wandered around pickup corners in Uptown and the Lake
View neighborhood, losing a sense of who he might be.
A middle-aged man, Greg Lang, took the boy under his
care. Whatever the man promised, that's not what happened. Lang wanted a sex slave and kept Danny in a filthy
basement apartment on North Leavitt Street. "I saw the

handcuff marks," Sammy said. "Danny was afraid. Really afraid."

That was when he disappeared, in May 1983. In October when the mass graves were discovered in Indiana, Officer Killacky feared that Danny might have been one of the victims. From his personal concern, he sent the boy's dental records to the task force in Indianapolis. He was relieved when there was no matchup, but police still had no idea where Danny was.

The detective showed Chuck Collins the Leavitt Street apartment where the boy had been kept in dread of the insects, mice, and cobwebs. Near the filthy bed was a drawing Greg Lang had made. It was a heart and in it were the words "Greg loves Danny."

The boy felt he couldn't go back home; his mother was still drinking. He couldn't stay on the street, or he would be trapped forever in the slave world that most people are unaware exists. And no shelter in Chicago at that time would admit a male prostitute. When Sammy suggested they go to North Carolina, it seemed as if he were being offered a second chance. "I thought there was more freedom there," Danny said later.

On a raw, drizzly day—Saturday, February 18, 1984—Killacky and Collins got lucky. Somewhere on the street Killacky ran into a hooker and drug addict. He suggested that he wouldn't bring her in for soliciting if she could tell him where Danny had gone. The woman was in need of a fix and begged for money. As a policeman, Killacky couldn't do it, but Collins told the burned-out woman that she could have the hundred dollars he was carrying if she would tell him where the boy might be.

The streetwalker gave them the phone number of a woman in High Point, North Carolina, who had helped Danny become involved with a prostitution ring with a friend of his from Chicago. Collins followed the undercover officer to the car and watched him dial a number from a mobile phone. Killacky handed the receiver to the woman, and she asked to speak to Danny. From her expression, the men knew that she had reached him. She gave the phone back to the detective, and the television producer handed her the money.

"Danny? This is Brian Killacky, the Chicago police. Don't get scared; you're not in any trouble. You've helped the police before, and we'd like to know if you wouldn't mind talking to some TV people. We'd like to bring you back to Chicago—pay for the plane and everything. They just want you to tell them what your life is like. Is that all right?"

Danny didn't want to return but said he would if Killacky wanted him to. Killacky was a friend.

Collins then called the Bridges family, putting their minds at rest after the months they had spent asking people if they knew what had happened to the boy. His father had even carried a photo of Danny wherever he went and would show it to people on buses hoping that someone might recognize him.

The question was whether Killacky might have the authority to bring the boy back. He drove to the youth section headquarters at Halsted and Maxwell streets, the oldest police station in the city. His commander told him the department couldn't afford to fly in runaways as if the police were operating a Good Shepherd retrieval service.

The next day Collins and Killacky flew down to North Carolina on NBC's budget. The Chicago detective met High Point police and soon had a warrant for the green frame house where Danny was being kept. High Point is far from a typical Carolina town; it is one of the largest industrial centers of the South, and its highways are a parade of long-haul trucks.

Police had learned that a local man, Hal Hatten, used teenage boys in order to keep his lover from leaving. Sammy was involved, but the boy's mother claimed that conditions were better than in Chicago. Danny was given a room and food only as long as he performed oral sex on Joe, Hatten's boyfriend. The boy also dyed his hair and at least once dressed like a girl to satisfy Joe's fantasies.

When Killacky came through the door of the house, Danny was glad to see him but there was hesitancy in his voice. In the police car, he told of being ordered to have sex with Joe. "I didn't really want to," the boy said in his slow way, sometimes putting his tongue between his lips as he paused. "But if I didn't, I would have been thrown out." Danny told Killacky and Collins that he hated living the way he did, but he felt that if he were thrown out he would be picked up by police.

Danny kept talking about how he was glad he was leaving, and yet there was a need in his voice that might have explained why he didn't leave on his own. He said that what he disliked about Joe most was that the man "would go with girls and other guys as young as I am, and that wasn't nice."

The boy flew back to Chicago first-class with Collins and Killacky that Tuesday. An NBC crew waited at O'Hare Airport to cover Danny's arrival.

The crew then brought in the intruding eye of the camera to the cramped family home on North Spaulding as Augustine Bridges kissed her son, his quiet father cried, and his numerous brothers and sisters hugged him. Danny picked up the family's mongrel dog, smiling and crying. The boy was safe—that was all Killacky cared about. He wasn't living as a sex slave in a filthy apartment or selling himself to truckers.

During later interviews with Danny, Killacky and reporter Nykanen fell into the habit of treating the boy as a mascot. They fed his ego by telling him he was good-looking and intelligent, "a wonderful kid." But then there was virtually nothing of Danny left inside that shell. He moved slowly as if in a daze and there was no spark left in him; who knows where it was lost. Teased into what the detective and the reporter were hoping he would say, Danny told them of his future plans in his uncertain tone: "I would like to be a cop and work with children."

Danny really wished he could be like everyone else. On Sundays, Sharon took him to the First Baptist Church of Hammond, a fundamentalist church that had thousands of followers in other states as well as in Indiana. The boy found a girlfriend and made a little money doing errands for neighbors. He talked of going to public high school in the fall. But there was nothing in the mainstream for him—not enough money, not enough companionship, and no sense of being needed. He was a Pinocchio who wanted his strings back.

Chuck Collins felt good about being responsible for the reunion. He wanted to get Danny a job as a checker at a neighborhood supermarket. Collins and Nykanen even planned to pay for Danny's psychiatric care from their own pockets.

Then a strange thing happened. The Illinois Department of Children and Family Services, the guardian of troubled juveniles across the state, intervened and refused to let the boy have a job or undergo counseling. The department said the boy was not yet ready.

He went to Roosevelt High School a few days, but he didn't like the way other students looked at him. They didn't know about the Leavitt Street apartment or High Point, but they knew or guessed enough and called him "queer" and "faggot." He stopped going. Danny began slipping through the cracks in the system.

Somewhere along the line the person of Danny Bridges disappeared, like a bubble when it bursts. Sometimes he was the property of men; sometimes he was the property of the news media. The Department of Children and Family Services wouldn't let Danny have psychiatric counseling, but it encouraged him to talk to the *Chicago Tribune*. One of the reporters asked the boy, "Danny, do you know you're lucky to be alive?"

Even so, Danny drifted to the streets, the only world he felt comfortable in. He could be seen making the rounds near the Clark and Halsted gay bars wearing a shiny satin disco jacket and waiting to be used. His face was puffy now and he spoke in barely more than a mumble.

Danny would stand around and from time to time say something as unoriginal as "You got a cigarette, Mister?" It meant "I'm available." From then on, whatever the man told him to do, he did.

No one knows how many youngsters are on the streets. A U.S. subcommittee meeting in Chicago heard testimony that one in three runaways turns to prostitution within forty-eight hours of landing on the street. After two weeks, seventy-five percent survive by prostitution.

Danny was about to become the best-known teenager in Chicago through the interviews. His would be the voice of all runaways, the unwanteds trying to make do in a world that wasn't made for them.

Danny was just a small part of the "Silent Shame" TV news investigation. The crew had a lot of work left before the documentary would be shown nationally in late August.

On one of the raids the television reporter encouraged a boy named Bobby to talk about the oral sex he had been having with a man ever since he was ten. "You gonna take a bath, you think about it," Bobby said. "You go to bed, you think about it."

The crew filmed a business executive who boasted of all the little girls he had sex with. Photos of the girls were framed and neatly arranged on the wall over the couch, like hunting trophies. He kept their underwear in a locked closet.

This was the summer Larry Eyler tried to normalize his life. Everything was easier now that it seemed he would never be put on trial for murder. Schippers arranged for him to receive $4.50 an hour as a "resident technician" at the Augustana Group Home, a Lutheran service in a redbrick former private home on West Palmer Square.

Dr. Little gave Eyler a recommendation, and Schippers submitted Eyler's college transcripts. The lawyer reminded him that he didn't have to tell his interviewers anything they didn't request. With all truthfulness, Eyler signed a statement that he had never been convicted of a felony.

This was his kind of work, dealing with children. He was always good with his sister's and Sally's children. Eyler now worked with nine disturbed boys in need of a friend and a role model. He was part of a three-member team that stayed with them from 3 P.M. to 11 P.M., hoping to set their lives straight. He was good with children. He was part child, himself.

The staff was happy with Eyler in the two weeks he worked there, but he stopped showing up for work after he received his repaired truck. He disappeared from July 26 through 29. The staff double-checked his references and learned about the murder indictment. He was fired.

Jobless, living on the rim of depression, Eyler made trips to Uptown and drifted into the same circle as Danny Bridges.

Somewhere, somehow, they met.

17

August 17, 1984
Chicago

The air hung heavy with an impenetrable overcast as the temperature neared ninety. You almost felt electric charges passing from the sky to your fingertips. Throughout the Loop, workers were rushing through the afternoon to get ready for weekend vacations.

Dave Schippers already was in northern Wisconsin with his family, and Linda Holmes hoped to be on her way soon to her cabin in Minnesota. She dialed a number from her Rolodex file, and Larry Eyler picked up the phone on the second ring. He had been freed on bond for six months, but she and her boss continually checked on him. Not that they doubted he would stay out of trouble; they just wanted to have a complete whereabouts log should police try to charge him with another murder.

Larry was different from the way he had been the first few weeks after his release. It seemed that as soon as he received his truck back in late July, he became almost arrogant about his independence. He stopped calling in, and they had to check on him themselves even though they were doing this out of concern for him. It had nothing to do with his defense.

"Larry," Holmes said this early Friday evening, "can you keep your nose clean for ten days while I'm gone?"

"Yeah, no problem," he said.

She was not convinced. She was sure he was frequenting gay bars even after all she and Schippers had told him, but what could she do?

280

Shortly after Holmes' call, Larry dialed John Dobro-volskis' home a few miles away. The two men were to go out that Friday or Saturday, but now Larry was calling to say that Dr. Little was coming in for the weekend. Little didn't like John; the two perfectionists were insufferable together.

When Larry hung up, John made his own call. He talked to a mutual friend, Ray, who was not part of a sexual relationship with either man. Then they made the rounds of the Halsted Street bars until the last one closed at four o'clock Saturday morning.

The house was dark when the handsome blond man came in. He and Sally were now living in her mother's apartment on Rockwell Street. He tossed his keys onto a dresser, walked into the kitchen, turned on the light, and phoned Larry. He wanted to make plans, but Little was already in town. Maybe the two of them could get together Saturday night, John suggested. Larry said no, and the jealousies took over once more. John spoke of a party he was going to since Larry wouldn't be with him, and Larry begged him not to go. The pleading and refusals lasted until 5 A.M. as Sally slept. John finally hung up and went to bed.

He awoke shortly after noon. His two sons were watching television as he made his way to the kitchen and called Larry, only to reopen the wounds. John hung up and pretended he wasn't upset.

It was late on that pleasantly cool evening when he arrived at the party at 3500 North Lakewood. The apartment was crowded with fifty to seventy people, all gay. He laughed, talked, and drank with the many men. He ran into James Williams, Eyler's former lover, who had lived with Eyler and Little in Terre Haute. Now Williams lived in Rowley Towers in Indianapolis but had come up to Chicago for the weekend.

Around midnight, John made his way to the quiet of the host's bedroom and dialed Larry's number. "Hi, what are you doing?" he asked. Larry and Little were watching a rented tape of *Porky's II*. "I'm calling you from the party. I met some mutual friends of ours, James Williams.

When will we get together?'' Not until Monday, maybe late Sunday. ''I thought we were going to get together tonight. Tonight.'' Dr. Little—always Dr. Little. John hung up and joined the others, but he wasn't in a party mood.

Around 1 A.M. he left with five men. Four of them went to change their clothes at a house near Lakewood and Irving Park before they went to the bars. John stayed in the car with the other one, Dwayne, and decided to go with Dwayne to his apartment.

John called home late in the morning on Sunday and asked Sally if there were any calls. He sat drinking coffee with Dwayne as he spoke. Then he added, ''If Larry calls before I get home, tell him I had plans to meet with a couple of friends.'' He wanted to hurt.

He arrived home in the first-floor rear apartment and asked about calls. Sally didn't ask where her husband had spent the night. She felt it was none of her business. John was angry at missing Larry's call by ten minutes. He tried to reach him but there was no answer. Then he phoned Larry's apartment every half hour. The Dobrovolskises' phone rang about 8:45 P.M., and Larry was on the line apparently with a mind full of suspicion. Sally told him that John had come home shortly after he called before, and Larry accused her of lying.

John quickly took the receiver, happily assuming the call meant that Little had left and that they could go out soon. But Little was staying longer than usual, and John's voice raised in anger. ''We had plans this weekend, Larry. Yes, I'm mad. OK, then I'm going out again.'' He took little steps back and forth across the room like a wild animal in a cage. ''Yes, I am. I'm going out with Ray. He wanted to get together, so I'm going to meet with him. No, I'm not staying home. Yes, I went out Friday and Saturday, but you have Dr. Little there. What do you expect me to do? Look, when David leaves and if you want to spend some time with me, call. I'm staying here for half an hour only. That's just half an hour.''

John hung up, took a shower, and cleaned up the rooms in the small but tidy middle-class apartment. After half an hour went by, he called Ray. There seemed vengeance in his exact timing.

Some time between 10:30 and 11 P.M., Danny Bridges left his home on the Northwest Side after spending Sunday with his family.

Around 11 P.M., while John's son and foster son were still watching television with Sally and her mother, the phone rang and John answered it. Everyone knew it would be for him. He leaned against the doorframe of the kitchen and told Ray to pick him up in a few minutes.

Sally walked into the room as he hung up, but he told her nothing about his plans. He smiled his dashing smile— which was not always sincere—and walked out the door and down the carpeted steps on this mild summer evening. The phone rang again, and Sally called her husband back in.

Eyler was on the line, and John seemed reluctant to pick up the receiver. "Yes, I'm still going out," he said. "Don't try to talk me out of it. I don't have to stay in for you. You are yelling, Larry. I'm sorry. You are yelling at me, Larry, and I can't deal with this." At that, he slammed the receiver down.

He said a few words to Sally and combed his hair as if sculpting his own head, then Larry called back. The young woman gave a wan smile and once more handed the phone to John.

"Hello, Larry. No, I *said* no, I'm not staying in tonight." Larry said that Little was finally leaving. "Well, what time can you see me? You can't give me a time? I asked for a time all weekend."

After he hung up, John thought it odd that Little was still at Larry's apartment, since it's a long drive to Terre Haute.

Ray was going to pick up John between two gas stations at the corner of Western and Montrose avenues. Young people were leaving the beach at closing time. A stream of cars and trucks passed by. After about five minutes John saw Larry's pickup truck going south on Western. The driver's window was open, and he could see Larry's arm hanging down. He thought Larry might be heading for him, to stop by and say something, but the truck kept going. He called out Larry's name three times, knowing that Larry saw him standing at the corner. That was unlike him, no matter how angry he was.

Just then Ray pulled up in a car with a friend, and the three of them drove to Touché's, a leather bar. The three men listened to music and talked until the two o'clock closing time. Then they headed for Little Jim's, which had a later license.

The men watched the sex tapes that ran on the television set and left around 2:45 A.M. John talked with Ray for a few minutes in the deserted alley behind his mother-in-law's apartment.

When he walked in, the apartment was quiet. He kicked off his shoes and reached for the phone in the kitchen to call Larry.

"What are you doing?" Sleeping on the couch. "Why didn't you answer me when I called to you? You saw me, didn't you? Where were you going?" Larry said he was out to buy gas at the time and decided to take a ride. "You went out to buy gas?" John repeated suspiciously, since that didn't explain why Larry had pretended not to see him. "When did David leave? He's still there?" It was nearly three in the morning. "You don't sound like you were sleeping, you sound very awake." Larry told him he would have to hang up. "I can't believe that David is asleep; I thought he loved to go out with you."

John lit a cigarette to help him calm down. Then he told Larry he wanted him to come over and spend some time with him. After all, everyone was asleep. No one would know. "What do you mean, 'No you can't'?" he said. "I don't care if David is still over there."

He hung up and a moment later called again. This time the phone rang five times before Larry picked it up. John apologized for his rudeness and again asked him to come over. Larry repeated that he couldn't because of Little, and John slammed the receiver back onto its cradle.

He threw open the refrigerator door and angrily made a sandwich. The he dialed Larry once more. "I want a good reason why I can't be over there when David is around, if all you are doing is watching television or something."

Larry told him in a hushed tone, "I don't want to deal with this, you know how David gets."

"I don't like that answer, Larry. You come over here, now."

John listened to a few more words and threw the sandwich to the table. "OK, if you don't want to spend time with me, then I'm coming over there. Right now." Larry told him not to do that. "Why not? I'll be there in fifteen minutes. I'm going to get a cab. Don't tell me what I can't do."

"All right," Larry said. "I'll come over."

Nearly eighty minutes went by as John waited for him on the back porch where they usually meet. He walked back inside and called the apartment on Sherwin Avenue. He let it ring, upset at himself for letting the relationship deteriorate. This was no way to run a life.

He returned to the back porch and sat on the steps. Larry would normally park his truck behind the building, by the back steps or fence, and enter through the alley. But out of nowhere Larry emerged on the pavement in the false light of dawn. John got up, wondering why he hadn't heard the truck. Larry was wearing a black baseball cap, short-sleeve shirt, blue jeans, and a pair of hiking boots. The men hugged in greeting.

"What took you so long?" asked John.

"I had to clean up, get dressed, get together, and drive over," Larry said.

They talked for about twenty minutes, and Larry walked in for a drink of water. The kitchen was so small and narrow it was barely more than a pantry.

They talked by the sink, and John kissed Larry, then grabbed a blanket from another room and laid it on the floor. Larry lay with his cap over his face. He sighed; he kept still, as if exhausted. He raised a leg. "Untie my boots," he said. John knelt and untied the laces, and Larry kicked the boots off. They landed with a thud on the blanket. "You don't have any socks on, Larry?" John asked, surprised. Larry didn't even answer. "You take your own jeans off," John said. But Larry just lay there.

John undressed and had to take Larry's pants off. Larry was unresponsive—that wasn't like him—and he did not have much energy for sex. He even seemed to have his mind elsewhere.

John removed the baseball hat from over Larry's eyes and ran his finger across his lover's hair. "Your hair is wet," John said, still trying to understand. Everything they did and said was as they had done before, and yet a little different.

The two men were lying in each other's arms on the kitchen floor when the alarm went off at 5:30 A.M. in the mother-in-law's room. She awoke at this time every weekday morning to go to work. Since her room was next to the kitchen, Larry stood up first and got dressed in order to leave before she walked in. John put on a pair of gym shorts and folded the blanket.

Larry kissed him and whispered that he would call him in the afternoon. He then left the back way. John put the blanket away and went to bed. His wife was still sleeping.

He had just fallen asleep when Sally shook him, saying "Larry's on the phone." It was 6:15 A.M. In a sleepy daze, John picked up the receiver. "Yeah, what . . . where are your green goggles?" He had cleaned up Larry's apartment so often he knew it better than Larry did. "Do you know what time it is? What do you want them for?" Larry told him that he was going to paint his ceiling, and the paint would splash in his eyes. "They are in the closet on the shelf." He wondered how Larry could see out of those dark-tinted plastic goggles.

John slept till after noon, then he tried to return a call Larry had made to him but no one was home. He tried twice again after 3:30 P.M. Then at five o'clock Larry called.

"David has left now."

"I'm having dinner with another friend, but I could spend the night with you after I finish dinner," John said. "You can come over and wait for me to return. Then we'll go to your place, all right?"

John went to dinner with a man named Ralph and returned at 12:30 A.M. Tuesday. Eyler, Sally, and Mrs. Kyle were in the living room watching television. Sally's sons Matthew and Allen and Sally's sister were asleep in another room. John was wearing a suit and tie when he came in and quickly changed to blue jeans. He was happy because he was starting a new job the next day.

John thought it strange that Larry didn't say hello to him. He just sat there looking vacantly; he seemed troubled about something. They soon went to the Sherwin Avenue apartment in the pickup truck.

John walked in and could smell the fresh paint. The apartment was unusually clean. John noticed how the bathroom floors, walls, and even the chrome on the sink and tub had just been polished. When he came out, Larry was lying on the couch. John entered the kitchen to make macaroni and cheese. To speed the cooking, he decided to fill the pot with hot water. Larry came and stood in front of the sink.

"You can't run the water; the drain is plugged up," he said. "I have to call the landlord about it."

"I don't see any point in that; where's the plunger?"

"No, you can't do that," Larry said quickly. "I have to call the landlord."

"Larry, my God, where's the plunger?"

"In the closet," Larry answered, almost in a sigh of resignation.

John started to unplug the sink. As he applied pressure with the plunger, he saw a strange substance swirl into a pink fluid. "Larry, what is this? I have never seen anything like this before."

Larry looked at the debris going down the drain. "I don't know," he answered flatly. "What do you think it could be?"

Larry stood next to John, his thumbnail between his teeth. Finally the sink became unplugged and the mess started to flow down. Larry seemed relieved. In fact, he hugged John and said, "Thank you."

John tried to feed Larry, but Larry wasn't hungry; he just lay on the couch as they watched television until 3

A.M. John kept noticing how clean the house was. He usually had to straighten up after Larry.

They didn't make love that night, Larry was too tired. Both men went to bed—just to sleep. Lying in the bed, John saw how the new paint looked so even above the bed but then stopped. Who would paint only part of a room, and only as high as you could reach?

18

August 21, 1984
Chicago

Dawn brought color to the overflowing dumpsters behind Sherwin Avenue. As always, janitor Joseph Balla arrived in his 1975 Dodge van and hauled out a cardboard drum to carry the bags of garbage from the chute in the four-story brick apartment building at 1640 West.

Balla was a fifty-six-year-old Hungarian and liked things simple. He had parked alongside the white dumpster and was irked because some outsider had heaped a lot of gray double-ply trash bags into it. The scavenger company would haul everything away in an hour, but Balla didn't like the intrusion. Someone double-bagged most of the garbage, and one bag even had a clothesline around it; now who would do that?

Allen Budnick, the janitor from 1618 West, came rolling out his own barrel of garbage. "Your tenants are using my can," Balla called out and threw up his hands. "I have no room."

"I'm sorry," Budnick said on behalf of the tenants in his building. He was younger than many of the janitors in the area, and looked like a Viking with his reddish blond hair and beard.

Balla, a bear of a man, pushed back the heavy lid and lifted out the first bag with both hands, then the second one. They were heavier than the usual kitchen garbage. The heavy man swore in his thick accent as he dumped them into two green garbage cans across a parking alcove from his building.

His curiosity was aroused, and he held up one bag for a moment while deciding whether to let it go or look inside. He set the bag down in the alley and pulled it open only to see a yellow T-shirt and what appeared to be a hambone. He looked again and knew it was part of a human leg. "Why me?" he mumbled. "Why do I have to see these things?" He looked up at the building. Who am I going to call? he wondered.

He saw a light in the fourth floor apartment of Mr. and Mrs. Liptay. He didn't even close the bag. He left it in the alley and used his pass key to take the elevator to the top floor. He knocked on the door. "Joe Balla, Mrs. Liptay. May I use your phone? I got to make a call."

The middle-aged woman unlatched the door, her other hand holding together the robe over her nightgown. "Come on in," she said.

Walking to her phone, the stocky janitor told her, "Don't get scared, Mrs. Liptay, but I found a dead body out in my dumpster."

As he spoke her knees became weak and she began to fall to the floor. Quickly, Balla grabbed her and lowered the unconscious woman to the floor. He then looked around and saw the phone on the wall and called 911.

Balla next hung up and walked to the bedroom where Mr. Liptay was still sleeping, gently shook the small man, and said, "Take care of your wife."

Officer Michael Zacharski of the Rogers Park district had just finished an assignment on Farwell Avenue when the dispatcher called out his number and said "Check on a possible body in the trash can at 1640 West Sherwin."

The janitor introduced himself to Zacharski, then another squad car pulled up in the alley. Balla led the officers to the gray bag near the dumpster. As he was explaining how he found it, Nicholas Fritz, the janitor of 1648 West, came out with his trash before the 7 A.M. pickup.

Balla called him over. "Nick, I found a leg in the trash—a leg, a human leg!"

Fritz looked at the ripped bag without getting too close and stood back. "Wait a minute," he said with his German accent. "A guy came out yesterday afternoon from

Al's building. He was carrying bags like these, maybe these.''

Budnick was drawn out of his building at 1618 West by the sight of two police cars. Fritz said, ''You know anything about these bags? I seen a man he come from your building yesterday maybe 3, 3:30. Dark hair, mustache . . .''

Officer Zacharski called Fritz over to get details. Fritz told him he had just come from vacation yesterday and had been driving behind the row of apartment buildings when he saw a young man entering the alley carrying two heavy bags, just like the one Balla had ripped open. Fritz had pulled over to avoid hitting him. The young man bent down with the bags as he closed the door from a hallway to the alley. ''I was thinking, why he takes the bags out the back door. They got a chute in Joe's building. I stopped and he kinda looked funny.''

''Funny?'' the officer said.

''Like a stare; no, not a stare. Like a glassy look, you know. Glassy. I look back; he threw three bags on Al's dumpster. I got three mirrors in the jeep and I looked back when he threw the bags into there and then I took off.'' As Fritz spoke, Zacharski's supervisor, Capt. Francis Nolan, drove up and climbed out without interrupting him.

Budnick spoke up. ''Yesterday afternoon I saw one of my tenants putting bags into the dumpster.''

''A young man, the same one?'' Officer Zacharski asked.

''The guy in 106. Larry . . . keeps to himself. Larry Eyler.''

One of the officers who had just arrived, James Crooks, remembered the name from the newspapers. ''He's some kind of a serial killer, isn't he?''

Budnick continued. ''I saw him coming down the stairs with the bags. He said, 'I'm getting rid of some shit.' I told him to put them in other dumpsters, not ours.''

Nolan glanced at the other officers and asked the janitor, ''Do you think Mr. Eyler would be in the apartment at this time?''

"He sleeps late, that's all I know. He doesn't cause trouble."

"Do you have a pass key?"

The janitor reached into his pocket, and Nolan told the four officers around him, "Detain anyone occupying 106. I don't care who it is." The captain remained behind to make sure no one came near the bags in the alley.

The officers walked up a few narrow gray steps at the rear of the building. Quietly, Sergeant Jacobsen told Budnick, "When we go in, you stay in this hallway. Got it?" They had their guns near their faces, ready to spring. Budnick turned the key and stood back, and all four officers rushed in.

Jacobsen, Crooks, and Zacharski went straight through a narrow hallway into the bedroom. Officer Sharon Gatch split off and went to another room to see if there were any more people. The apartment was clean and reeked of new paint.

The officers who went to the first room off the hallway found two men lying on the bed, evidently awakened by the door opening. Dobrovolskis jumped out onto the floor, and Eyler pulled the sheet over his head, like a child caught in a shameful act.

"Get down on the floor, both of you, and put your hands behind your head," Zarcharski ordered. "Now!"

Budnick walked into the room as Dobrovolskis lay on the floor and an officer was putting handcuffs on him. "That's not Larry; that's his friend," Al said. "Over there—Larry—he's the man I saw with the bags."

At that, the sheet moved aside, and Eyler climbed out of bed in his boxer shorts and white T-shirt. He was shouting and flailing his arms, demanding to know why the police had barged into his home.

"Get away from that window," Sergeant Jacobsen ordered. Then he and another officer grabbed Eyler and laid him on the floor to get the handcuffs around him.

With all the excitement over Budnick, the janitor could look around. He noticed that the north and south walls of the apartment had been freshly painted. What an odd thing to do, since he had painted the entire apartment himself just last February, before the new tenant moved in.

Clothes were strewn on the floor, and there were pants across a small second-hand sofa. The officers helped the men with their trousers and shoes and led them to the door. Jacobsen told Officer Gatch to stay in front to make sure no one came in.

This was one of those arrests that police love to tell reporters about, even if the calls are anonymous. Larry Schreiner of WGN picked it up from his sources, and a police contact called Gera-Lind Kolarik at WLS. A television crew was able to get footage as the officers led the men outside and to the alley.

The men were held together long enough to hear their Miranda rights, then each was put into a patrol car. Nick Fritz hid behind an officer and pointed to Eyler. "That's him, the man I saw put the bags in the dumpster!"

When Zacharski returned, William O'Connor and his partner from the police crime laboratory at the downtown headquarters were distributing rubber surgical gloves to the officers on the scene. "Please put these on; don't touch anything, anything, until you've got these on. We must preserve evidence." His partner explained it in terms they could understand: "In other words, if you touch anything without gloves, we'll arrest you as a suspect."

It was now shortly after 7 A.M., and tenants leaving for work down the back stairs found police officers telling them to go back up and leave through the front door. A squad car and a police van blocked each end of the alley. Television crews were using rear porches in nearby buildings to tape the officers standing around the ripped-open bag and waiting for further instructions.

Area 6 commander Edward Wodnicki's pager went off while he was in an unmarked car on another case. For Wodnicki, this was the call he had been waiting for ever since February. The commander, one of the most streetwise detectives in Chicago, had actually taken charge of the investigation months before the murder occurred. He knew that Eyler wouldn't be able to stop himself even though police across the country knew about him. Wodnicki had decided that his officers would end the killings once and for all. In the meantime he left explicit orders for all shifts week after week that no one was to stop Eyler or touch anything belonging to him without a warrant or a damn good case of probable cause.

In Oak Park, Ralph Calise's mother, Carmen Pauli, was drinking coffee in her kitchen a little after 7 A.M. when she heard on WGN radio that a male body had been found dismembered in garbage bags and that police had taken two men into custody. She shuddered, reliving the murder of her own son nearly one year ago. She cried, and the coffee cup shook in her hand. She had to sit down. She found herself dialing the number for the Lake County sheriff's police. Perhaps if she could talk to Detective Colin she would feel better. She was told he wasn't in and she should call back.

At WLS, Kolarik phoned Smitty at the sheriff's police department. "Smitty, they've got Larry Eyler! Chicago police found the body of a boy cut up right in his dumpster. They've taken him and another man into Area 6."

"Great," Smitty said with one of his rare bursts of exuberance. "Dan's the expert on Eyler; I'll send him down there to help out. Chicago police usually know what they're doing, maybe this time the charge will stick."

A month ago Dan Colin had predicted that there would be another body by August 15. He was off by five days. Colin turned from the phone and told his wife, "Chicago's got Larry. There's been another one." He was leaving his home in Round Lake Beach when Smitty called and told him to go to the Area 6 police station.

"Don't worry, dinner will be here when you are," Pam said.

When Mrs. Pauli called the sheriff's police in Waukegan again, an investigator told her about Eyler's arrest and added, "We are dancing for joy. Please don't misunderstand us, Mrs. Pauli, but now we know he won't be on the loose."

For Mrs. Pauli, her son was not really dead. She had felt his presence more in the past year than she did after he had moved away from his family. Sometimes she talked to him, without making a sound. They've got him this time, Ralph, she thought. Let's hope they keep him.

Shortly after 9 A.M. Cook County Medical Examiner Robert Stein arrived in the alley in his office car. This little, wrinkled man was the one who lowered himself into the crawl space under John Wayne Gacy's home and saw the first skulls and bones in pits.

As Stein inspected the bulging garbage bags, Detective Fred Stone said, "I think we have to reconstruct the body." Some of the officers didn't understand. "We've got to know what's missing. I understand these guys sometimes keep parts of a body, and maybe we have more than just one body here."

"All right," Stein said, "let's do it."

Seven of the large gray bundles were double-bagged, but the one containing the torso was tied with clothesline and then covered over with plastic wrapping.

Crime laboratory technician William O'Connor took it upon himself to do the reconstructing. He brushed away the flies and bees as Stein watched wordlessly, with his hands halfway into his pockets and an occasional nod.

A housewife walked onto her back porch to watch the police and sip coffee.

The skin of the arms was almost white from having been drained of blood. O'Connor then lowered his hand slowly into another bag and a chill went through him when he felt human hair. The officer removed the head, and Danny's eyes seemed to be staring at him. Out of pity and respect, O'Connor closed the eyes before setting the head on the dirty alley.

The officers in their business suits stood around grimly for the fourteen minutes it took to make sure that the parts found in the dumpster belonged to a single person. There was complete silence except for the morning chirping of sparrows.

Some of the new officers arriving let out a few expletives, and a woman in one of the apartment buildings called out to make them stop their swearing. Finally letting out some of his feelings, Commander Wodnicki shook one of the arms and shouted back, "How could you let a nut like this live here?"

The woman answered by pulling down her shade.

The officers stared at the eight segments in position: the head, the two arms, a leg, a leg cut in two, the chest, and the abdomen. Crouching close to the ends, Stein said to Stone, "Looks like a saw-type instrument. Maybe a hacksaw. Look at this." He was pointing to cuts in the chest. "These weren't meant to kill."

Garbage men who had arrived for the 7 A.M. pickup were questioned about what they might have found in this alley in the past, but the workers told them to contact their supervisors before they would say anything, to the amusement of a transient who was watching the police work as he drank in the alley.

The gray plastic bags were being placed into evidence as Colin and Jim Rowley arrived at the station in the middle of Chicago's North Side to give Chicago police information for an affidavit needed for a search warrant. Stone and another officer went downstairs to one of the courtrooms and had a judge sign the warrant. Police were now authorized to seize practically everything but the walls themselves.

Information was so scanty coming into attorney Dave Schippers' office downtown that his secretary, Jerre, did not know whether the body found behind Eyler's home was Eyler or someone else.

The lawyer was in the yard of his family's cottage in Wisconsin when WGN reached him. He didn't want to think that the killer had been Eyler all along, and his first thought was "I hope it's Larry." Schippers had no other reaction; he was stunned.

Five minutes later his office called to say that WGN and WLS were requesting interviews and that Eyler had been taken to the police station.

"We don't know who the boy was that was killed," Jerre told him.

Schippers stood in the cabin with the receiver in his hand. He felt as if he had just been punched in the face.

All he could do was say "OK" and hang up. He called back a moment later and asked, "Are you sure?"

Jerre said yes and put him on to his law partner Jon Gilbert, who told him about the body parts and the search warrant. "All right, Jon, go down to Area 6 immediately. Tell Larry you're standing in for me. Tell him to keep his mouth shut. I'll talk to you later."

The impact was still settling in his brain. The fear that haunts every concerned defense attorney—that a person he had freed from jail would go out and kill again—had finally happened. He muttered, "My God, did I do that?" He glanced up and saw his sons looking at him, knowing that their father was in one of those moods when they shouldn't bother him.

He called his office again. "Jon? Go ahead and tell Larry to keep his mouth shut and tell him I'm through, and I don't want any part of the little son of a bitch, and I don't want ever to see him again. I've had it!"

He walked to the pier, not many thoughts penetrating. He was crying. "Christ," he thought, "did I become a lawyer for this?"

Judge William Block stepped down from his bench in Waukegan and entered his chambers. His bailiff came up with a message. It read that Eyler had been arrested for another murder and that the body had been found chopped up in a dumpster. Block closed the door of his chambers and sat in silence.

Twenty-one-year-old Sharon Faught was still looking for her brother Danny Bridges. She had been searching for him for two days. She went to a drugstore at Wilson and Magnolia avenues in Uptown to inquire about him when a squad car pulled up.

"Have you seen Danny?" asked the officer, who knew her from all the times Danny was involved with the police.

"No, that's why I'm here. No one knows where he's gone."

The policeman opened the car door for her and swerved around the corner to a restaurant, where other officers had already contacted Sharon's brother Michael Bridges as he was searching for Danny with a friend. When Sharon came out of the squad car, Michael handed her the photos and said with a vacant expression, "Please tell me this ain't Daniel."

Sharon saw a cut-up boy's chest with a heart tattoo. She screamed and pounded the hood of the squad car until her fists ached.

Whatever they are like to begin with, street reporters take on a flippant callousness toward death: they have to. Yet when editors in newsrooms at the Chicago newspapers announced that the victim had been identified as Danny Bridges, there was a hush. Not all reporters remembered the name, but for those who recalled the *Tribune* series or excerpts of the NBC special that had been aired in advance in Chicago, it seemed as if they had lost someone they knew. The newsrooms turned icy that August day.

Chicago police headquarters is in a modern building with the architecture of a cereal box in a blighted neighborhood just south of the Loop. Most people refer to it by its location, Eleventh and State. Two officers from the police van made their way up the stairs to the fourth-floor crime laboratory. A woman who worked in the finance department had just left the elevator on the fifth floor and needed to go down to the annex when she noticed the men carrying the body bag.

"Where are you going with that?" she asked.

"To the crime lab," one of the officers answered. "Wodnicki ordered it."

Watching them lug the bag, she said, "I never heard of a body being hauled through Eleventh and State before. I never."

Inside the crime lab, Marian Caporusso was running catalytic tests on a blood sample. Her job for twelve years had been to examine body fluids, residue, glass, paint, soil, fibers, and hairs. One of her supervisors, James Doran, came in and told her that body parts were coming in. Taking a pair of plastic gloves, tweezers, and some evidence containers, she followed Doran down the hallway to a side room. There on the floor was the open body bag, showing the eight pieces that had once been Danny Bridges. Caporusso stepped back quickly.

"We're going to try something new. We're going to laser the entire body for fingerprints." Commander Wodnicki had read about the procedure in a Florida rape-murder investigation.

Doran handed her a pair of goggles and put on the gloves. Next he checked the 35-millimeter camera that would photograph any print the laser beam brought out. The beam comes from an instrument that looks like a pen and is attached to a cord. The two of them stayed on their hands and knees for nearly two hours, going over every portion of the body with the laser. "Jim, there is glass on the body; and over here, what is that, dog hairs?"

"Would you believe they laid the parts out in an alley?"

She wished street officers would understand how they hampered lab work.

Despite their careful efforts, not one fingerprint was found. They ran the laser over the plastic bags that had held the body parts, and again they found nothing.

Doran was the new supervisor of the latent fingerprint identification unit, so he decided to attempt another modern technique: Supergluing. Six years earlier, a man assigned to U.S. Army intelligence and working with Tokyo police discovered that if an object is placed in a tank with Superglue, the strong fumes bring out ridge impressions that could not be found in any other way. The ingredient cyanoacrylate ether worked with the moisture of the print or the protein of the amino acids left behind in microscopic traces. The method could be used on all nonporous material.

Doran placed cotton pads of sodium hydroxide laced with Superglue on the bottom of an aquarium tank and lowered one of the bags inside. The heat to bring up the fumes was supplied by a light bulb. Then Doran covered the tank and went on to other work. Twenty minutes later he returned and was pleased to see a faint grayish white residue here and there on the plastic. They were still too faint for comparison work. These would be brought out further with fingerprint powder and laser light, then photographed.

In time the ridges and swirls were compared to Eyler's fingerprints. They matched.

The judge in the police station signed the search warrant at 12:20 P.M. A short time later the policewoman guarding apartment 106 stood aside for Commander Wodnicki and detectives Stone, Carroll, O'Connor, and Kajari, the man who had represented Chicago police at the Indiana summit in Crown Point in September 1983.

"Kind of spooky, isn't it," said Wodnicki.

The first room off the hallway was the bedroom. Then came the bathroom, kitchen, and living room. The men also searched the basement. They brought bags of clothing from the closet, a laundry basket of soiled clothing with brownish stains that could be blood, and a Duke University T-shirt. Danny Bridges had often worn a shirt like that. In the basement the officers found a hacksaw, and in the kitchen utility drawer were some hacksaw blades and an awl. In the garbage was a department store receipt from July for hacksaw blades, and there was a receipt for garbage bags. A partially empty box of gray garbage bags was under the sink. Wodnicki had his men measure the distance from the last bag to the top of the box to determine how many had been used. That would help ward off the defense's contention that practically everybody had bags like those.

To the untrained eye the apartment seemed spotless, but the officers knew where to look. They returned day after day, methodically taking ever more pieces of the place with them. The drain trap was removed to have its hair and slime analyzed. The threshold board in a doorway was pried up to reveal blood that had seeped under there before Eyler—or someone helping Eyler—could mop the floor clean.

Water samples were sucked from the sewer pipes to find traces of blood and flesh. Everything was placed in plastic evidence bags.

"Take your time," Wodnicki told the evidence technicians. "Larry's not going anywhere." Police questioned and requestioned everyone they could. One of the neighboring janitors, Nick Fritz, said he had seen Eyler quarreling with a short, heavy man in the alley the night before the body was discovered, and the heavy man shouted: *"You did it again!"* But, Fritz said, that's all he heard, and he couldn't identify the other man.

There were four men left in the Indiana task force now, and one of them, Frank Love, was vacationing with his wife in Dallas. She was watching Cable News Network in their hotel room and called to him when the newscaster said something about an arrest in a Chicago murder. He called his office, and Sam McPherson picked up the receiver.

"Sam, this is Frank—"

"You heard about it too?" McPherson drawled. "Hell, Frank, they got our boy good this time." There was no excitement in his voice. His tired tone seemed to say "The judge gave Larry enough rope and he's hanged himself."

John Bauer, the athletic older brother of victim Michael Bauer, learned from his father that Eyler had killed again. For months since he and his father watched Eyler walk free on television he wanted to kill Eyler as all those young men were murdered. He even called the phone company to learn Eyler's address but was told the number was unlisted. He stopped only at the urging of his mother. Now the young North Side man felt that police would want to know about Michael, since he had disappeared in Chicago but was found in Indiana. John drove to the Area 6 station that night and saw television crews setting up live shots. He thought of talking to the reporters about Michael, but what was the use? All they cared about was the one murder charge they had on Eyler. Bauer drove past the station filled with a rage deeper than his feelings about Eyler. He also hated Eyler's mother, attorney Schippers, and everyone who had ever been dear to him.

19

August 21, 1984
Chicago

William O'Connor of the crime lab and Detective Stone were examining the bathroom where Danny's body apparently had been dismembered. The window was open to relieve the smell of paint and to let in the cool air. O'Connor noticed something, then gestured for Stone to stay quiet although he himself kept talking as if nothing had changed. Reporters had placed microphones on the windowsill of the first-floor apartment to see what they could pick up. O'Connor went to the bedroom window facing the alley and pulled at the mikes, causing an immediate commotion as the tug disrupted tape recorders and television equipment.

"Hey, you guys, get these out of here!" O'Connor shouted. "This is a crime scene, not a press conference."

At Area 6 headquarters, Commander Wodnicki lamented that any fingerprints of the Bridges boy might be lost under the new paint in Eyler's apartment. Dan Colin was there to help advise the Chicago police, and he suggested that they try luminol, a chemical that can bring out prints that have been washed over. Colin wasn't sure of the details, so he called police in Georgia, where he had attended a seminar on the technique.

At the station, John Dobrovolskis was handcuffed to a ring on the wall of an interrogation room. There was a possibility that someone besides Eyler was involved in at least disposing of the body, and police were taking no chances. Detectives fired question after question at Eyler's lover, but it soon became clear that he was as much confused as he was frightened.

Wodnicki said, "Let's get him out of here."

Officers led Dobrovolskis out a back way and drove him to police headquarters, where he passed a lie test. Then they took him to a motel on the Southwest Side for questioning that would last as long as it took to learn everything he knew. He was being guarded twenty-four hours a day by Cook County sheriffs' police and felt he had no choice: either cooperate and turn state's witness or be charged with Eyler.

Nearly fifty police officers were working full-time on the case, many of them going door to door in the neighborhood and visiting places where Eyler and Danny might have gone. An assistant state's attorney was assigned to monitor the progress and determine when the information was sufficient.

At 8 P.M. the murder charge was approved, and Eyler was taken in handcuffs down the front stairs toward the lockup in full view of the television cameras and newspaper photographers. Instead of being placed in a cell, he was led to a side interrogation room. He wasn't paying much attention to the faces around him and heard an officer say, "He's all yours."

"Hi, Larry," came a familiar voice. Eyler looked up and was surprised to see Colin from the sheriff's office in Waukegan. "I told you I'd see you again. You're in Chicago, not Indiana. You're not going to get out of this one."

"Yeah," Eyler said.

"Larry, it's all over now. What happened?"

"You know I can't talk, Schippers' orders."

"I just wanted to see you before it all begins again," Colin said. "I'm always around, Larry; whenever you want to talk."

"I know, Dan. Thank you."

Colin sat on the desk and slipped his hands into his pockets and twisted his shoulders from side to side, as if he were physically as well as mentally winding down.

August 22, 1984

When Chuck Collins heard on the news that Danny had been killed, he screamed out loud in his North Side home, and he screamed inside far longer. He felt personally responsible and wished he had never put together the documentary. Outtakes from "Silent Shame," which were once discarded in a box in a cubicle near Collins' office, were now the most prized videotapes in Chicago. The newspapers and even the UPI and AP sent photographers to the station to obtain a still photo from the tape. The documentary that had taken months to put together eventually would win two local Emmys and a Peabody Award.

Police kept removing more possible evidence from the apartment. Some items eventually inventoried included jars of petroleum jelly, videotapes, a large latex dildo, and a black negligee. Prints were removed from the pickup truck. Dr. Stein performed an autopsy and determined that death was from a knife and an awl. There were up to sixteen "very small" cuts around the sternum, the apparent torture marks. In addition, there were five deep cuts, including one that caused the intestine to protrude—the highway killer's ghastly trademark.

The fingerprint work was going slowly because of the elimination process. Despite the rubber gloves that had been passed around, officers left their marks in the apartment. The prints of neighbors also had to be compared with ones found in the dumpster.

Doran and Caparusso from the crime laboratory began work on the apartment in the late afternoon. Doran removed the plug from the bathtub drain, and it was so slimy it slid across the floor. The drain was removed for study of whatever fatlike substance coated it. Doran and Caparusso also had police remove a mattress, a love seat, and a pair of painter's goggles for blood tests.

Next the two of them converted the apartment into a laboratory tank for Supergluing tests. They placed a number of sodium hydroxide pads in the bathroom and bedroom after officers sealed off the closed windows with plastic wrap to avoid weakening the fumes. The apartment was then locked up and guarded until the latent prints had a chance to appear.

Later that day, Area 6 violent crimes detective Fred Stone was walking to the back cell when he heard what sounded like, but could not possibly be, a child whimpering. The cell was off to the back, away from the other prisoners. Stone looked in and saw Eyler sitting with his head down against his knees, the fetal position. The muscular body was shaking as he sobbed.

"Larry, I want to talk to you," Stone said.

Eyler quickly uncoiled and gave the detective a cold stare. "What?" he asked.

"Do you want a sandwich or anything?"

"No, thank you," Eyler answered and turned to his bunk.

"Say, Larry," Stone said, "I want to show you something upstairs, all right?" He was holding a plastic bag that contained part of the bloodstained floorboard pried from the bathroom.

An officer opened the cell door, and Eyler went with him up the back elevator. Once in the interrogation room, Stone sat with another investigator and opened a yellow Chicago police envelope and removed some Polaroid shots of Danny's body. He placed them on the table in front of Eyler. "Look what we found in those garbage bags," he said.

Eyler pushed them away. "I don't want to see those; they make me sick."

Stone showed him the two-foot-long floorboard and said "This was just covered with blood. You think you cleaned up the apartment, but there was blood all over. Was that what the goggles were for, so you wouldn't get it in your eyes? What happened, Larry? Can you tell us?"

Stone moved the photos in front of Eyler again. The suspect turned away, gagging and coughing until vomit spilled on the floor. Stone and the other detective looked puzzled at each other, not knowing whether his retching was sincere or an act.

On Thursday morning the plastic sealing on the windows of the apartment was removed, and the fingerprints were lifted. None matched Danny's. At police headquarters a husky black officer, Theatrice Patterson, made the first physical link in the case. In the latent print identification section, he placed a photo take from the Superglued bags. Using two magnifying glasses he found what appeared to be the same markings as the fingerprints of Eyler. Even more telling, impressions of Eyler's right thumb and middle finger were found *inside* the eighth bag, the one that had contained Danny's right arm. He immediately called Doran, and Doran notified the state's attorney's office. Commander Wodnicki wanted still more evidence.

First Assistant State's Attorney Michael Angarola decided to go for the death penalty. Under Illinois law, that meant providing evidence that the murder had been committed in connection with another felony. The kidnapping of Danny Bridges could be construed as luring him to the apartment under a pretext, money for sex. He also drove to Indiana to pick up copies of the task force reports.

Eyler's family and friends no longer had money for his legal expenses. Dr. Little had taken out a second mortgage to help pay for the lawyers as well as a bed, color television set, and other things used to furnish the North Side apartment. The family was still trying to pay attorneys Kenneth Ditkowsky and David Schippers. After Chicago police tried to contact Little numerous times that day, the professor called to say he would issue a statement through his attorney.

At the motel near Midway Airport, police felt that Dobrovolskis was telling the truth as he saw it. He had a sharp memory and was able to reconstruct a good part of his days with Eyler. He recalled helping to get rid of a new mattress in April. He said he didn't know why Eyler wanted to throw it out, but he also remembered a red or brownish stain on the ceiling at the time. This was the closest police would ever come to linking Eyler to the disappearance of Cowboy in April, but they had no body to justify pursuing the case. When police and the prosecutors couldn't think of further questions, they released

Dobrovolskis to return to his family, though his marriage was collapsing.

Shortly after twilight Friday, Caporusso of the crime lab arrived at the Sherwin Avenue apartment with Area 6 commander Wodnicki, Colin, Allan Miller of the state's attorney's office, and five evidence technicians. By then the place was virtually bare because of all the possible evidence police had removed over the past few days. A camera on a tripod was set up on the hardwood floor. Newspapers had already been taped over the windows to keep out the light from street lamps. Caporusso carried with her a spray bottle of chemicals she had ordered days before and mixed at the laboratory. The room had already been gone over with saltwater in preparation.

Wodnicki was afraid this luminal test would be a waste of time. "This floor looks damn clean to me," he told Colin.

"Set up the camera over here; that's where we found some traces of blood," Caporusso said to a police photographer from the evidence section. She pointed to the floor near the closet. "We don't have much time when I spray, so keep shooting with the speed you have. This stuff only lasts a few minutes." She held the bottle a little away from her and said, "OK, ready." A policeman turned off the overhead light.

There was a hissing as she sprayed the floor and the walls in the dark. Soon a ghostly presence appeared as an eerie dark green glow above the floor. The camera snapped away. Not all the green marks were reemerging fingerprints. There was the print of a foot that had stepped in blood and smear marks that told where the body had been dragged to the bathroom. "Holy shit," Wodnicki muttered almost in respect. The dozen people in the room could even see where a rag had been used to sop up Danny's blood. The chemical was reacting with the iron oxide in the blood and shining in the dark like a luminescent watch hand.

Caporusso continued spraying, and the green glows appeared in her wake. They were on the bed and the ceiling and on the floor where the mattress had been. The luminol followed the trail of blood that flowed from the body across the floor. Near the bed was the bloodprint of a naked foot with a long middle toe, just like Larry's. In a moment the green marks disappeared, as if they had been no more than an illusion.

The dozen people moved to the bathroom, where jade green blots showed the horror of how the blood flowed and dripped over the side of the tub and worked its way across the floor to the cracks and under the floorboards. The same thought occurred to Colin and some of the Chicago police officers: it was as if Danny were helping them.

When the last of the green glows disappeared, a policeman turned on the light. There was an uneasiness among the officers looking at the black marks left by the chemical.

"Let's go downstairs," Wodnicki said. Technicians had found a pulpy whitish substance in the drain of the laundry room, and he wanted to see whether this residue had been human tissue.

They had just entered the basement when they heard sounds at the window. "Hey, you," Wodnicki called out. The black man trying to break in said, "Uh, just looking for Larry." Then he took off.

Wodnicki wasn't one of the youngest or lightest officers there, but he and Colin ran after him. They sprinted up the stairs and chased him down the alley. The commander laid him low with a tackle while Colin kept him down with the point of a gun. Nearby the thief's accomplice decided to start the car and get out of there, but Rowley drove his car to block the way. The driver was pulled out and thrown against the auto for frisking.

"All right, all right," said Wodnicki. "What are you two doing here? Come on, talk now."

The man who had just been pulled up from the ground answered, "Hey, I thought he was gone and there was no one home. How was I supposed to know half a police station'd be in there?"

About fifty boys from nearby Maryville Academy attended Danny's funeral on Saturday, August 25, in All Saints Cemetery in Des Plaines. The morning sun was already burning their necks. Father Smyth, in his black cassock and purple stole, tried to console the boys as they wept for themselves as well as Danny. This could have been any one of them. When the priest was called about Danny's murder he felt extreme rage, despite his vows and personal beliefs. But Smyth then put his hands together and prayed for the Bridges family and all the boys like Danny.

At the boy's funeral he went into the small, modern chapel just inside the entrance of the cemetery and let members of the Bridges family cry on his shoulder if they wanted to.

At least Danny was not being buried in potter's field. Oehler Funeral Home had donated its service, and a family that had read about the murder and Danny's life in poverty donated the plot. Maryville Academy provided the heart-shaped floral piece.

The funeral brought together the large family, including a brother who had been released from prison to attend while accompanied by a guard.

Brian Killacky and his partner, Sam Christian, were there along with Cathy Ryan. Priests, counselors, and social workers from Maryville helped bring the boys into the small chapel, which was designed to be as light as possible to relieve the grief that a graveside service can bring.

Father Smyth blessed the casket and said that Danny was now with God as one of His children. Looking into the faces of the abused boys standing behind the Bridges family, the priest added, "Where children see only despair in their hearts, help us plant the seeds of hope."

Schippers had reached the Gethsemane of his career. He was devastated by Danny's murder and for a moment even considered giving up law. When he was in church he prayed for guidance. He never wanted to see Eyler again, but now Mrs. DeKoff was asking him to take up her son's case. The unfortunate woman still believed he was innocent and that there might be some magic formula that would free him a second time.

The attorney did not doubt that Eyler was involved in

the murders, but he felt that Eyler could not be the only one. It didn't seem right that the state should try to send a man to death row when the responsibility for the act should be shared. Would he have killed one last time if he could not be sure of support?

Schippers began to feel that his outrage had just been the cry of wounded pride. Of course he felt as if he had been treated like garbage—he had been betrayed—but possibly stronger was the feeling that he would now be pointed out as an example of what could go wrong in the judicial system. It'll take guts to go in and defend him because everybody's going to say I'm an asshole and they hate my guts, he told himself.

The prosecution was going for the death penalty. If that's what Eyler gets, Schippers knew, everyone would say it was because Eyler had only public defenders. Maybe no one could save him, but perhaps someone should try. As Schippers saw it, more than just a life is judged in a capital case.

The prosecutors who would be handling the trial, Mark Rakoczy and Rick Stock, drove to Terre Haute to speak personally with Dr. Little at his lawyer's office. Juries become confused if they believe more than one person is involved in a crime, even tangentially, and yet only one is charged. Rakoczy and Stock needed Little to establish that Eyler was alone a short time before Danny was killed.

Little's attorney told the prosecutors that he would answer only questions pertaining to the case. Then the gray-haired professor methodically responded with precision; he would make a strong witness in court. But Rakoczy felt uneasy as Little answered the questions in the same way repeatedly over the next couple of hours. To Mark the professor's answers seemed rehearsed.

Six days after promising to make a statement, Little issued his account of that weekend.

The library science teacher said he and Eyler couldn't find a movie they both might want to see that Saturday night, so they watched television. They went to sleep, and on Sunday they watched wrestling until Eyler left to do a painting job at a doctor's home from 1 to 6 P.M. Eyler returned, and Little said he stayed until just after the ten o'clock news came on.

As with many murders, the prosecutors felt that the witness might know more than he was telling, but the state's attorney's office had to accept his account.

As Little accompanied them to the parking lot from the law office, Rakoczy stopped and asked casually, "Do you mind if we take some pictures for our files?" The lawyer accompanying Little shrugged, and the professor provided him with frontal and profile poses.

Copies of those pictures were sent to North Side police just in case someone might be able to place him with a victim or connect him to some other crime. No one could. Only then did prosecutors feel confident that Schippers wouldn't be able to impeach Little on the stand.

September 13, 1984

In the marble hallway of the criminal courts building, family members of several of the victims were waiting to see Eyler go on trial at last. Wilma McNeive, tired from her four-hour drive from Indianapolis, told the other mothers in her rolling accent that lay between Midwestern and Southern, "I just wanted to see what Eyler looked like. I don't care about the man one way or another; he can't give back what I have lost."

Assistant Public Defender Claire Hilliard was waiting inside Chief Judge Richard Fitzgerald's courtroom for her partner, Tom Allen, to show up for the plea hearing. He was being detained by another murder case.

A gray-haired man with a casual manner walked up to the defense table, put his large black notebook on the edge, and said, "Excuse me, my name is David Schippers. You're Claire?"

She extended her hand uncertainly, not sure why he was there.

He shook her hand. "I've been talking to Larry, and he wants me to get involved in this case, too. I don't want to be Larry's counsel; I really don't have the money and the time to get that involved again, but I'd like to help you as much as I can.

A well-known attorney assisting a public defender? "Larry is going to plead innocent today, you know that?" Hilliard asked.

"Yes, I do."

Hilliard took a breath and said, "Wait here, I'll be right back."

She went outside the courtroom and saw Allen down the hallway.

Hilliard hurried to him and explained what had just happened. Allen didn't know quite what to say either. "Nice to meet you," he greeted Schippers over a handshake. "We'll share with you anything we have."

"I don't know if I want to be the only lawyer in the case," Schippers explained. "Your office can take a lot of the expenses, and I'll give you my time and experience as a defense lawyer and as someone who knows Larry very well. I don't want to get paid."

Allen sat down. *"Pro bono?"*

Schippers laughed at the surprise. "Yes," he said. "The family still owes Ditkowsky, and I don't know when I'll ever be paid for the Lake County work I did. They're pretty well played out."

The three attorneys stood side by side as First Assistant State's Attorney Michael Angarolo walked in. Noting Schippers, he smiled and nodded at them. *Chicago Tribune* reporter Andy Knott didn't take Schippers' appearance so casually. As he walked into the courtroom he stopped in his tracks.

Soon the bailiff called the court to order. Schippers approached the bench and told Judge Fitzgerald, "My client pleads not guilty, Your Honor."

The process had to start all over again, but this time Schippers was in control from the beginning. His staff was not wholeheartedly behind him. Linda Holmes had let Eyler into her home often, and she drove him around the city while his pickup was impounded—only to have this happen. It was as if he were using her as a camouflage of normalcy, she thought.

Schippers knew that with her bitterness, Holmes could never be effective in working on Eyler's defense. Angry and yet understanding, he told her in the office shortly after the arraignment, "You're out. You can work on my other cases. You're not going to have a God damn thing to do with this one."

"Fine!" she shot back.

The prosecutors had amassed so much of what they considered evidence that Schippers believed he would need to show that their case had holes. That meant he needed to do a little sleuthing.

Schippers suspected that people in Eyler's neighborhood wouldn't talk to him if he wore a suit and explained why he was asking questions, so he decided to blend in. He drove to the far North Side with a bicycle in his car and pedaled down streets and alleys, wearing just a T-shirt and walking shorts. He would stop and talk to people as if he belonged to the neighborhood and eventually picked up a fair amount of information on cars that used the alley behind Sherwin Avenue.

One thing that caught his attention was a discarded couch behind an apartment building. He turned it over and saw a suspicious dark stain. If that turned out to be human blood, he could argue that Danny was killed in another apartment altogether. He removed a knife from the satchel he kept in the bike basket and cut out out a section in the alley, and the next day he gave it to Allen and Hilliard to be examined. But somewhere along the line the swatch was lost in that limbo where evidence sometimes disappears. Well, it was a long shot anyway.

Schippers was able to have a temporary gag order imposed on the case, but in December the judge assigned to the trial, Joseph Urso, held that impounding the files and issuing a gag order might force the media to rely "on less reliable sources," presenting a far greater damage to Eyler's rights.

There was another setback. The Cook County state's attorney's office was not as obliging as the prosecutors in Waukegan, and it wasn't until January that Schippers and the public defenders could examine all the reports the other side had compiled over the past five months. They discovered only then that Eyler's prints had been lifted from inside one of the bags.

In his heart, Schippers knew that no judge in Cook County would consider letting Eyler go, but in February he requested a hearing on whether to suppress the evidence. Judge Urso ruled in the only way he could—that all of the material seized be allowed into evidence during Eyler's trial.

A month later, state officials and Joseph Cardinal Bernardin attended a ceremony to open a shelter for runaway boys who could not be persuaded to return to school and their families. The shelter, open twenty-four hours a day in an old two-story building on Paulina Street, had only eighteen beds, but it was more than the city had before. The supervisor was Father John Smyth of Maryville Academy.

A large, forceful black man stepped forward. He was Gordon Johnson, the director of the Illinois Department of Children and Family Services. "If you can get kids off the street before they go too far and show them a better way, you can turn them around," he said. "If Paulina Home was open a year ago, I think we might have saved Danny."

Shortly before Christmas 1984, Frank Love was alone in the task force headquarters. A sprig of dried mistletoe from last year's party was still pinned to the wall. He took it down and threw it into the garbage can, feeling that this was happening to a year and a half of work done by a dozen officers. He was the last of them, and now he had been reassigned, too. Nothing the task force could come up with, even the Steven Agan case, could match what Chicago police had against Eyler now.

Love, the father-figure of the task force, thought about the parents and the brothers and sisters of all those Indiana victims. With frustration, the sergeant placed the floppy disks from Berner's computer and the investigation logs into one box, then on top of them put the inventory of evidence taken from Little's home. Phone records, maps, charts, everything went into one box after another. All those investigations had just been stopped as if someone had pulled out a plug. How do you tell all those parents that the murder of their son would remain unsolved forever? You don't. You just move twenty pounds of paper and tell them "We're doing everything we can."

He took the boxes by cart to his car as a light snow was blowing. After cramming the boxes into his trunk he drove to the Indianapolis police headquarters. Love watched as an officer went to the boxes and wrote in large letters in black marker: "Eyler . . . Eyler . . . Eyler . . ." The boxes were wheeled into a dark security room for storage, and Love felt that a part of himself went with them.

"Damn it," he muttered and walked back to his car.

20

July 1, 1986
Chicago

Dan Colin and Prosecutor Richard Stock rolled carts of evidence down the hall of the Criminal Courts Building, a massive square structure of ominous gray linked by a tunnel to the Cook county jail. In this building six years before, John Wayne Gacy made criminal history by being convicted of murdering thirty-three teenage boys and young men.

Most of the buildings at 26th Street and California Avenue have a 1930s look, but Judge Joseph Urso's high-security courtroom resembles a modern church. Bailiffs opened the doors, letting Colin and Stock push the gray carts past four rows of spectator benches. The benches face bulletproof glass half an inch thick. From the hip-high base, the glass slants inward.

Reporters joked among themselves that the inner courtroom reminded them of *Star Trek*. The inner doors admit only one person at a time, and then with a slow gasp. The courtroom beyond the bulletproof barrier is a horseshoe, with the defense table, judge's bench, witness stand, and jury box curving from right to left. Normally attorneys would speak at a lectern placed in the middle of the room, but so much evidence was being brought up the elevators that the podium and its microphone were moved to the back, near the two inner doors.

Carolyn Buddie of the Victims' Assistance Program in the state's attorney's office was the Good Shepherd for families who would be coming day after day into this antiseptic semicircle of a courtroom. She was a friendly, blonde woman who could easily imagine what these mothers were going through. Her own son had been murdered in a senseless shooting. She introduced Ralph Calise's mother, Carmen Pauli, to the prosecutors but kept closer to Augustine Bridges. This was her son the witnesses would be talking about and whose dismembered body would be shown in giant photographs.

The door opened and a bailiff in a black uniform announced, "Court is ready to begin."

Court artists from the television stations rushed in to be in the benches closest to the bulletproof glass, crowding out family members. Even Colin sat in the back row.

A back door in the courtroom opened and deputy sheriffs brought in Eyler, wearing brown pants and a short-sleeved yellow shirt. Schippers patted him on the shoulder as the young man eased into a chair. A moment later the court clerk asked all to rise, and Judge Urso entered, a broad and heavy man who seemed to belong to his black robe.

In a moment, Urso asked all the attorneys to come into his chambers for a conference on a procedural question. A deputy led Eyler to a holding cell nearby. As Schippers rose, a thought occurred to him and he stepped over to Linda Holmes in one of the benches behind the glass barrier. He motioned for her to talk to him in a corner where no one could hear them. Her face was as grim as those of the family members.

"Linda, I want you to go in there and say hello or something to Larry," Schippers said in an undertone.

"Me?" she replied, not as a question but as a refusal.

"He's a human being with an immortal soul; the least you can do is wish him luck."

After Schippers followed the two public defenders to the judge's chambers, Holmes stood for a moment. She was divided between what she felt she should do and what she wanted to do, which was never to speak to Eyler again. Then she went past the guards and saw Eyler handcuffed to a bar in the wall of a holding room.

"Hi, Linda," he said from his chair next to a small round table.

"Hello, Larry."

He looked up at her with fawn's eyes and asked, "Do you believe in me?"

What could she say, that she never hated anyone as much as she despised him now? She was supposed to wish him luck, but she couldn't lie. All she said was "I just wanted to say that I hope justice is done."

Eyler smiled. He really didn't understand, did he?

Jury selection had been easier for Schippers than if this had been in the 1950s, since most people today have a fairer attitude toward gays. The eldest juror was sixty-four years old, but the majority of them were rather young. The youngest was nineteen. There were seven women on the panel, most of them housewives, and five men.

The jurors were led in from a side room after the lawyers meeting in Urso's chambers agreed that the trial should not be held over the Fourth of July weekend. Assistant State's Attorney Mark Rakoczy faced the jury box and began.

"The evidence will show, ladies and gentlemen, that Danny Bridges worked the streets of Chicago in the Uptown neighborhood as a male prostitute to buy his own clothes and give a little whatever was extra to his mom and dad to help support his family."

One of the jurors, an athletic young man, looked not at Rakoczy but at Eyler during the opening arguments. The defendant saw him and turned a glance into a steady stare. The juror couldn't turn away, it seemed as if Eyler were challenging him.

Behind the glass partition, Mrs. Bridges seemed to sit in a daze. She was trying to hear and yet was blocking out the words. Carolyn Buddie, a plump woman in her forties, knew better than to let her be treated as if she were no more than a spectator. This trial was about to become a part of her that she could never escape from. "Remember, Mrs. Bridges, squeeze my hand if it gets too much for you and we will go down the hall for a cigarette or downstairs for a cup of coffee. Don't try to do it all alone."

"Why does the press take over?" Mrs. Bridges asked from the second row. "Danny was my son; I want to see everything. How come they come first and not the family?"

"I'm sorry," Buddie said. "I'll see what I can do, but not now. During the break."

As Rakoczy spoke, Schippers referred to his project notebook. Black ink was for routine notes, and red ink was for points he wanted to use in his cross-examination. The ruled pages were for exhibits, with blue tabs marking items for the defense. Schippers had a practiced informal manner in the courtroom, but his notebooks showed that he left nothing to inspiration.

Even the decision for Eyler to plead innocent to all counts against him had to be worked out through a consideration of all the factors. Schippers and the public defenders didn't agree on the strategy until just a couple of days before the trial. They were sitting around Claire Hilliard's desk with police reports and lists of witness questions in front of them.

Tom Allen, a tall, thin, balding man, sipped coffee and smoked a cigarette alternately as if reflecting the tension in the room. This was a tight case. Danny had even told the *Tribune* that he casually knew Larry Eyler. The boy had picked out Eyler's photo for Chuck Collins. This was still a circumstantial indictment, but it was almost as strong as if someone had actually seen the two together.

"Look," Allen said, "do we go for all the marbles, or do we focus our efforts and try to knock out one of the charges?" If Eyler were convicted of murder but not kidnapping, he would be sentenced to life in prison rather than death by lethal injection.

"This is a case where the facts are brutal," Hilliard said. "If the jury believes he did it, it'd be really hard to convince them to throw out one of the charges."

"We go for all the marbles," Schippers told them. He was the only one who was relaxed. "I will hit them good in the closing arguments. If that jury is convinced he did the big one, they are going to stray from their oath to follow the law and are going to tag the guy on everything.''

"But there is no evidence that Bridges got into his truck against his will," Allen brought up.

"We don't know that Eyler used his truck," said Hilliard.

"And we don't know, as a point of fact, that Larry was involved at all," Schippers said as a reminder.

"All right," Allen continued, "we have no evidence that Bridges entered that apartment against his will."

"The kidnapping statute is pretty broad; it doesn't have to be an abduction," Hilliard rebutted. Even so, she knew that a jury was not likely to accept a defense argument to scale down the allegations.

"Go for the marbles," Schippers repeated with finality. "Be on your toes on every witness. Everything they bring up, remember—they have to prove that Eyler actually, physically killed Bridges. Can they, really? They can prove Larry threw out the bags but not that he so much as ever touched Bridges. Just keep that in mind. Two friends of Larry's visited over that weekend, and at least one of them was in the apartment for a good part of the time.''

Thus the strategy was planned: innocent of murder and innocent of kidnapping. If they lost, Eyler would die.

All through opening arguments, Eyler sat unmoved by comments from either side. He made occasional notes and doodles on a legal pad. Mrs. Pauli and Mrs. McNeive were watching his every gesture from behind the glass, as if their concentration could affect the outcome.

During the lunch break, a stout Hispanic woman walked over to Mrs. DeKoff, Eyler's mother, as everyone around them waited for the trial to resume. "I am Carmen Pauli, Ralph Calise's mother," she said in a fragile tone. There was a pause, then the mother of the defendant and the mother of a victim extended their hands to one another with pity in their eyes.

A few minutes later Mrs. Pauli and Mrs. McNeive sat in the cafeteria with other family members and Gera-Lind

Kolarik, who was on leave from her television station. Mrs. McNeive looked at the reporter and asked, "Did my Danny suffer a lot? You would know. Did he suffer?"

"Your son felt very little pain. It was fast. I know, I read all the reports; I saw the photos." She looked at both mothers. "They died instantly." That may not have been what happened, but that was what mothers wanted to hear.

"My Ralph would never have gotten into that pickup truck," Mrs. Pauli said. "That man must have drugged him with something."

Mrs. McNeive sobbed, and her daughter comforted her.

Dr. Little was called as the first witness. Usually major testimony is held off until later in a trial, but the prosecutors wanted to establish quickly what sort of man Eyler was. They also wanted to defeat any attempt Schippers might make to cast suspicion on the professor.

Little told how he met Eyler at the university where he was the chairman of library science. That was in 1975. The professor said he had allowed Eyler and his friend James Williams to live with him rent free. Williams left the next year, but Eyler remained. Eyler sat biting his fingernail at this, something he did when he was uneasy.

Little told of helping Eyler get the Sherwin Avenue apartment and of coming up from Terre Haute on Friday, August 17, 1984. He said he had left around 10:15 that Sunday night and arrived home around 2:30 A.M., including a delay caused by a long freight train at the crossing in Dyer, Indiana. Later that morning, after a few hours' sleep, he paid a real estate tax bill and received a date stamp. The bill was entered into evidence.

Schippers picked up on this in cross-examination:

"When were your taxes due?" the lawyer asked.

"These were the fall taxes," Little answered.

"As you got up Monday morning, you decided to go in and pay your taxes that were due in October?" Schippers asked incredulously.

"I had some money then. I had been paid and I decided to pay my bills."

The jurors might not have guessed where this was leading until Little told Schippers a few minutes later that he did not know whether James Williams was homosexual or whether Williams and Larry had been lovers even though they had lived with Little for a year. Schippers was hoping that jurors would begin questioning the witness's veracity.

One of those jurors, Steve Wexler, later commented, "As I saw Dr. Little on the stand I felt that he knew more than he was saying. He looked nervous. I listened to every word he said. There was something there I just couldn't put my finger on."

Mrs. Bridges clasped Buddie's hand as her daughter Sharon took the stand on the left of the judge's bench. The blonde young woman, with a face like Danny's, answered questions so quietly that Judge Urso asked her to speak up. Prosecutor Richard Stock, with his fullback's build, eclipsed her as he paced across the stand. He showed her a photo of Danny, and Sharon said, "That is my brother." She then gasped when Stock was about to show her a blow-up of the pieced-together body.

"If the court please," said Schippers, "we will stipulate that the picture is as it purports to be and speaks for itself. There is no need to show this young lady the picture."

The following witness was Danny's closest friend other than his sister and the people of the street, his cousin Joyce Bunch. She described a troubled boy who had used drugs, run away from home, and sold his body as if he were no more than a bag of groceries. For all this, he had remained someone caring.

Behind the partition, Buddie whispered to Mrs. Bridges, "We can go now. Please don't do this to yourself."

The victim's mother shook her head, rubbed a Kleenex hard under her glasses, and said, "No."

Mrs. Bunch was the last witness of the day. The court-room artists cleared the front rows to rush their watercolor and ink sketches to the television cameras confined to the marble lobby in front of the ominous Babylonian columns.

Mrs. Bridges rose still holding Buddie's hand. This first day was not as bad as she had feared. But Mrs. Pauli's eyes were still fixed on Eyler, who was paler and leaner than he was at his arrest, as if trying to deny that he could have the power to stab a man so deeply. Detective Dan

Colin helped the prosecutors return the evidence to the cart and push it past the media wolves. The frail-looking press secretary for the state's attorney's office, Lisa Howard, was a former reporter and knew how to handle their questions. "Come on, you know that they can't tell you their case," Howard said. "We have a lot of witnesses, and tomorrow will bring new developments."

Buddie of the victims' assistance program drove the Bridges family to their Northwest Side home on Spaulding Avenue and returned there at 8 A.M. the next day, July 2, for what was bound to be the most difficult session of the trial for them. This was the day that the medical examiner would testify.

The short, gray-haired Dr. Stein spoke of his medical degree in Innsbruck, Austria, and how ten years before he became the first medical examiner in Cook County. Stein estimated that he had performed more than one thousand autopsies. He then told the jury of watching police assemble Danny's body in the alley.

Mrs. Bridges was aghast because no one had told her about this. But when Stein testified that he used one of the hacksaw blades found in the kitchen of Eyler's apartment to cut into the body and compare the marks, Buddie said to Danny's older sister, "Connie, we have to take your mother out."

Mrs. Bridges could barely stand as she cried into her hands. Mrs. Buddie helped her through the door and told a reporter, "Leave her alone, please."

In his raspy voice, Stein described the dismemberment at the neck, the arms below the shoulders, the hips, and the knees. There were no facial fractures, but the right eye was black and blue, and there were a number of small cuts across the face. Then there were fourteen puncture wounds on the chest made "with an ice-pick-like or an awllike instrument." Although Stein mentioned no other victims, the wounds were similar to all the bodies found along the highways and in ditches.

One wound was just to the left of the belly button. There was evisceration of the abdomen so that a part of the intestine protruded through the wound.

The three wounds in the back were so deep the blade had perforated the heart and the left lung. On both wrists were "round abrasions" as if they were bound with rope. He had gone to the funeral home in Des Plaines after the autopsy and compared the marks with the clothesline police seized. They matched.

"Were you able to determine what type of instrument may have been used to effect this dismemberment?" Stock asked.

"This type of cut through the bone was completely compatible with a hacksaw." He added that the serration cuts on the skin were "entirely compatible with the teeth of the hacksaw" such as the blades from Eyler's house.

Some of the jurors looked away as they were shown autopsy photographs. But they watched grimly as, one by one, the prosecutor asked the medical examiner to identify the pieces of evidence. Stock turned away for a second and picked up Exhibit #50: the awl. He placed it into the pathologist's bony fingers, and Stein testified that it was the one police had given him.

Defense lawyer Mark Allen then went into cross-examination, and Stein testified that there were cocaine and alcohol in Danny's blood. The testimony was important to bolster the contention that the boy wasn't kidnapped in the strict sense of the word, that he may have gone willingly with the killer.

When Stein finished his testimony he passed through one of the inner doors and walked by the rows of spectators. He turned to Kolarik—a friend from a number of investigations—and whispered in his rusty voice, "One of the worst cases I have ever seen."

After a break, Youth Officer Brian Killacky joined the spectators. He was the one who notified the NBC crew about Danny while the boy was in North Carolina, and he had taken the murder rather hard. He had just appeared in the building for a child molesting case, and now he wanted to see Eyler close up. Not only did the defendant sit at the table like a man without guilt, he looked as if he didn't know why he was there.

Sitting gravely in his dark suit, this officer with carrot-

orange hair looked around him and recognized two faces
from his undercover vice work. They were men he had
arrested for molesting Danny. They had abused him, but
now they felt a fondness for his memory.

Killacky nudged Kolarik and whispered, "They're the
ones who ought to be hung."

Yet how many others could take their turn in the defendant's chair? To Gera-Lind it seemed as if everyone who
ever had come in contact with Eyler or Danny took some
part in the boy's death, even men and women who were
only trying to do their best, from state officials and social
workers to family and friends. That was the saddest part.

Eyler had wielded the knife, but others might have
known of earlier crimes and kept silent.

Could blame be portioned out to the Indiana state
police, David Schippers, Judge Block? Didn't all of them
act to protect society? The police were concerned with
protecting the community; Schippers with the rights of the
individual within that community; Block with the constitution that guarantees those rights.

Killacky could look at the pedophiles in the spectator
rows and judge them, but in hindsight should he and television producer Chuck Collins have left Danny Bridges
alone? They had thought that by rescuing Danny from the
male prostitution ring in North Carolina they would be
giving the boy a second chance, as Schippers had felt he
was giving Eyler a second chance by finding him jobs.
The time for Larry Eyler and Danny to turn their lives
around had long since passed.

The state of Illinois had refused to let Danny get a job
or receive counseling. Then there was the 911 dispatcher
who paid no attention to the call about the human hand
found in the trash at Eyler's building four months before
the murder.

But Danny was not grabbed off the street. He had seen
Eyler around Uptown and had heard about him. The
actions of all the others would have meant nothing if the
boy had not been in the habit of going off with men who
offered him money.

The witness on the stand was an officer who testified

about the fingerprints. When Schippers rose to cross-examine him, a coldness ran through Carmen Pauli. Although Schippers was a friendly man, she knew him only as the lawyer who had set Eyler free so that no one would ever be convicted of murdering her son. Mrs. Pauli didn't want to see any more of him and went out to the fresh air of the corridor.

Schippers approached the bench and asked that all the fingerprint testimony be thrown out because Supergluing for latent prints "has yet to be developed to the extent that anybody can put a man's life on the line." Rakoczy assured the judge that the test had always stood up in court, and Urso said he would rule the next day on the request.

Mrs. Pauli feared the worst, and Colin told her and the other mothers, "Don't worry I don't think Eyler's going to win this time."

Indeed, Urso told the attorneys the next day, before the jurors were seated, that he determined the Supergluing technique was reliable and there was no reason to believe the crime laboratory experts had botched the tests.

One of the early witnesses that day was a biology student who had been an attendant at the Union 76 station at Ontario and La Salle streets in late August 1983. He told the jury he remembered Eyler pulling up between 11:45 P.M. and 1 A.M. because the pickup truck had an unusual feature—two gas tank covers. Killacky had spent weeks tracing the witness because he no longer worked at the station. His testimony did not place Eyler with Danny, but it showed that Eyler may have been on the prowl in an area of gay bars a little time before the boy was killed.

While waiting for his turn, janitor Al Burdicki sat in good clothes but his collar was open, showing the top of his undershirt, and his tie hung loosely below his throat. All that was fixed by the time he took the stand.

Over the objection of defense attorney Allen, Stock asked Burdicki about the ten or fifteen times he had seen young teenage boys enter Eyler's apartment. The janitor settled back in his chair and called them "street kids. They were dirty, unkempt, needed to be bathed, clothes were dirty—just looked like they lived off the street.''

Burdicki added that he had never seen any of the boys present while Little was visiting Eyler and that the last time he saw a boy with Eyler was a week before Danny's killing.

Stock asked Burdicki about the time he had seen Little and Eyler together at about one o'clock that Sunday morning. Burdicki was turning off the street to park behind the apartment building when he saw them standing directly in front of his garage door.

"And what did you see—did you notice anything about Dr. Little and Larry Eyler as they were standing in the alley?"

"Yes."

"What was that, sir?"

"Well, as I pulled up, my first impression was that there was a problem between the two of them, just by the way they were facing each other.'' He couldn't hear what they were saying because the air conditioner was humming in his auto. He waved to them and pulled into the garage, and the men walked down the alley for about one hundred feet. Larry had his back to a telephone pole, "and Dr. Little was, like, chastising him, you know; like you would wave your finger in someone's face.'' The vigorous-looking janitor with his Popeye arms shook a finger rapidly in front of his face as if gesturing in reprimand or warning.

After parking his car, he said, he had entered the building to make his nightly rounds. As usual, he took George, his one-hundred-and-forty-pound German shepherd, with him for companionship.

Burdicki said that on that Monday morning he had seen Eyler make "eight to ten" trips to the locker area. "In about the fifth or sixth trip I asked him what he was doing.''

"And what did he tell you he was doing?"

"He said he was getting tools for a job.''

Burdicki added that the dog hadn't acted in any unusual fashion at the time, but later, at 3 P.M., George became excited after the fire door slammed and there were footsteps coming down the stairs. This was Eyler carrying two heavy, silvery garbage bags while wearing leather gloves with finger holes.

"He got down about three more steps, and the dog started to growl."

"Now," Stock said, "why do you say they were heavy?"

"Larry's a healthy young man, and the way he was holding the bags, the material was stretched real tight. His shoulders were stooped over, just as if there was something heavy in those bags."

"What happened next?" Stock asked.

"Well," the janitor added, "the closer he got, the dog's growling got more vicious; as he came real close the dog started to go crazy on me. He was showing teeth, snapping, something he just doesn't do."

Stock asked, "Was he snapping at Mr. Eyler?"

"No."

"What was he snapping at?"

"The bags."

Prosecutor Mark Rakoczy could see that the jurors were riveted.

Burdicki said that to keep from creating a disturbance, he pushed the German shepherd into a tool closet, but the dog kept scraping at the door and barking. Eyler at this time had trouble opening the door because of the weight of the bag.

"He picked it up about midchest high with both hands, leaned back to support the weight of his shoulder, grabbed the door handle with his right hand, got his foot in between the door and the frame, pushed it [the door], caught it with his left foot, and just went through the door sideways."

When Eyler threw the heavy package into the dumpster he made "a 360-degree turn to get the momentum." Then, Burdicki said, "he looked at me and he got this startled look on his face."

During cross-examination, public defender Claire Hilliard decided to attack the graphic details the janitor had just given. She had gone to Eyler's apartment with an investigator a few days after the murder to pick up something for Eyler's family.

"August twenty-eighth, two people came into the apartment, one who represented Larry Eyler, is that correct?"

"Yes, ma'am."

"And you had a conversation with those two people, is that right? You recognize any of these people?"

"I only seen one of them at the time."

"Would the name Claire Hilliard mean anything to you?"

"Ma'am, it's eighteen months ago."

"So you don't always remember and recognize people, is that right?"

"The people I remember, generally, if they live there."

Hilliard made no further comment about his memory, and at midafternoon the jurors were excused for the long Fourth of July weekend.

On Monday, July 7, John Dobrovolskis walked to the witness stand, confident and handsome in a blue blazer. He sat down, and his stare locked into Eyler's. There was now a double betrayal between them.

Dobrovolskis' illusion of domesticity and life in the mainstream had collapsed in the last year and a half, and California was pulling at him like a magnet. But he wanted to see this thing through. He still loved his wife, in his emotionally complicated way, but Sally had left him shortly after Eyler's arrest. The day he took the stand was their seventh anniversary.

He calmly told the jury about the night he met Eyler. With his sharp memory he could recall the exact moment: 11 P.M., August 8, 1981. He had been at a gay bar on the North Side but felt ill and was going home. Eyler had seen him in the parking lot, then offered him a ride and some pills, Placidyls.

Eyler showed animation for what would be the only time in the trial, fidgeting in his seat and repeatedly whispering to Schippers.

Dobrovolskis said Eyler told him the pills were for headaches and things. The men had a few beers, and Eyler drove him somewhere in southern Cook County or in northwestern Indiana. Dobrovolskis was taken to a farm where Eyler handcuffed him from behind and tied his hands as well. But Dobrovolskis disliked bondage and asked Eyler to free him, which he did. Then Eyler drove him home, which was then in a South Side Lithuanian neighborhood.

The next day Eyler called to set up what might be considered a date, a meeting in Little's town house. The library professor was not home, and the two men had had their first sexual relations.

Assistant State's Attorney Mark Rakoczy privately admits he is a shy man, but he is something else when in front of a jury. The prosecutor was gradually leading Dobrovolskis through the ever-increasing tension between him and his lover since an incident that began in the Gold Coast bar—which had a small beer garden separated by a wall from public view—on a Tuesday night a little before the Danny Bridges murder.

"I was surprised to see him there, as I am sure he was surprised to see me," Dobrovolskis said. "I asked him where he was going from there; he said home. I went to order another beer. And when I went back outside, he had disappeared. He climbed over a wall and left. I decided to go straight for home. I had the bartender call a taxi."

But instead, Dobrovolskis had the cabbie take him to the apartment on Sherwin Avenue. "I wanted to see if he had made it home," he said. He claimed he rang the apartment buzzer for room 106 and no one answered. So he walked around the back of the building, where he had a clear view of the first-floor rear apartment. He stood on the concrete tire stop in the parking alcove next door and peered into Eyler's window.

"I saw Larry with another man, standing in the middle of the living room. Larry was about to remove the guy's shirt. And I called his name. He motioned for the person to be quiet, I assume." The other man was in his mid-twenties, "dirty looking, long hair; tattoos all over his arms, dirty T-shirt, dirty jeans; street-type person."

Dobrovolskis said he saw them go into another room. He went to a bedroom window and called out Eyler's name. No answer. So he walked to the front and knocked on the door and kicked it, and Eyler let him in. Eyler escorted the street person outside through the back way and gave him subway fare to go back where he came from.

"Larry and I argued and I spent the night; I wound up spending the night," Dobrovolskis said. He avoided looking at the heavy stare of his former lover. Eyler dug the tip of his pen into his yellow note pad. Dug and dug.

The jurors could not be given explanations. They would not be informed that Eyler often responded to jealousy by going off with a hustler and that he may have killed to stab out his anger. All the jury could be provided with were isolated incidents, and the prosecutors hoped the men and women would visualize the unspoken.

Rakoczy, in his deep, almost aggressive voice, now coaxed the witness to the weekend that led to the dismemberment of Danny Bridges. The prosecutor asked about the nature of Eyler's call to him at 11 P.M. that Sunday.

"He was trying to talk me into staying in that night. He told me I was out Friday and Saturday that weekend and that was plenty, and I should stay in Sunday night."

"How would you characterize the tone of voice he used at that time?"

"He was yelling. I was willing to get together with him. I wanted to; he was busy with David. So I decided to go out with my friends."

"Who hung up on who at that time?"

"He continued yelling, and I just didn't want to deal with it. I hung up the phone on him."

Dobrovolskis then told of waiting for his friend Ray to pick him up at Montrose and Western and of seeing Eyler drive by in his pickup. "I called out his name."

"How many times did you yell?"

"Three."

"Did Eyler respond to you at this time?"

"No. I was convinced he heard me and was ignoring me."

After the snub, Dobrovolskis went barhopping and made a predawn call to ask Eyler if they could get together that morning. Rakoczy had him specify that after each call with Eyler that weekend, it was Dobrovolskis who hung up in exasperation until Eyler finally agreed to come over.

"Could you characterize or tell us how Eyler sounded upon your calling him at that hour of the morning?"

"He was quiet," Dobrovolskis said. "He said he had been sleeping. He was extremely coherent. I don't believe him to be sleeping." And Eyler had said Dr. Little was there (even though Little testified that he had left around 10:15 the night before).

Dobrovolskis told the jurors he hadn't believed Little was still there at 2 A.M. "I was told it was a platonic relationship, and it made no sense to me, and I decided to confront him with it. He said something about 'You know how David gets,' and I didn't like that answer."

"Did you give Mr. Eyler an ultimatum at this time, Mr. Dobrovolskis?"

"Yes. I told him if he didn't come over to spend time with me I was coming up there. I told him I could be there, fifteen minutes by cab."

"What happened then?"

"He said, 'No, don't do that.' I said, 'I am going to.' He said, 'Fine, I will be over there to see you at your place.' "

And so Eyler, after making what should have been a twenty-minute trip, arrived about an hour and a half later and appeared exhausted. His hair was wet from a thorough washing, and he was too tired to take off his own boots. "He didn't respond; it was unusual."

In what way was he unusual? Rakoczy asked. "It was always mutual . . . even after a six-hour drive from Indiana or whatever." This particular time it was just a different kind of exhaustion. Dobrovolskis said he had assumed that his lover had been with another man that night. Another odd thing: unlike any other time in their three-year affair, Eyler wore no socks or underwear. (The unspoken suggested that there had been a sudden need to wash them or throw them away.)

When Dobrovolskis came home from a friend's house the next day, he found Eyler watching television with

Sally and her mother, but even then he seemed to be behaving strangely. Eyler ''was very worried about something'' but didn't elaborate. When Schippers asked if he knew why Eyler should have felt despondent and guilt stricken, Dobrovolskis said ''No.''

After they had made love on the floor in the Rockwell Street apartment, Dobrovolskis testified, he went with Eyler to his home on Sherwin Avenue. Usually he would straighten up the place ''just to get the mess out of the way,'' but on this Tuesday before dawn the apartment was ''sparkling clean.''

Rakoczy said, ''Tell the ladies and gentlemen of the jury what came out as you plunged that sink free.''

''Blood, like pieces of chicken fat; some kind of flesh; and black, gravel-type material or charcoal or something like that came up with it; and something pink and swirling that I thought was blood from the chicken fat or something.''

Rakoczy approached the shelf of evidence and handed Dobrovolskis Eyler's leather vest. Usually the vest was soft and supple, but now, Dobrovolskis told the jury, the leather was ''very stiff.''

''At one point of time did he tell you that 'I had wiped it off' or attempted to clean it?''

''He said he washed it.''

''Mr. Dobrovolskis, I am going to show you what has already been marked as People's Exhibit Number 120. Do you recognize them?''

Rakoczy lifted the goggles from the evidence shelf, and Dobrovolskis stiffened in his chair. Dan Colin, watching through the thick glass, leaned forward as he sensed the young man's uneasiness.

''Are those the goggles that you moved from the bottom portion of his closet to the shelf on his closet?''

''Yes.''

''And, how many times have you seen these goggles prior to that occasion?''

''Two or three.''

Rakoczy played upon the discomfiture of the usually self-possessed man, for Dobrovolskis had learned that the goggles were found with human blood on them, and he could imagine what they had been used for.

"How many times have you seen these goggles prior to that occasion?"

"Two or three."

Rakoczy had discovered a way to hint to the jury what the horror of Danny's death had been, and he milked it.

"Now, have you ever had occasion to look through these things, Mr. Dobrovolskis?"

"Yes."

"Why don't you put them in your hands?"

"*No,*" John snapped and moved his hands back.

"You have something against these?"

"I just don't want to."

"I will hold them up to your face."

The witness sat ramrod straight as Rakoczy lifted the goggles to his eye level. "Can you see anything through those?"

"A little bit of light."

"Would you use these goggles if you were going to paint something?"

Mark Allen spoke up. "Objection, Judge."

"The objection will be sustained," Urso ordered. "The jury will be instructed to disregard that question."

Having made his point, Rakoczy stepped back and lowered the goggles. He was through with the witness. His expression did not change, but he was smiling inside. No one had established who wore the goggles last or how they came to have blood on them, but he had made his point.

Schippers then stepped up to Dobrovolskis for the cross-examination and immediately tried to create a ripple effect in spreading out references to the gay world. In Schippers' first sentence, he repeated what he had already made clear, just to reintroduce a word into the juror's mind.

"Mr. Dobrovolskis, you were for a period of some three years Mr. Eyler's homosexual lover, is that correct?"

"Yes."

During his cross-examination Schippers apologized for having to ask a personal question, then referred to the three times Dobrovolskis had submitted to bondage. "Mr. Eyler in no way hurt you, did he? He did not try to hurt you or in any way attack you while you were in that condition, did he?"

Sitting back, Dobrovolskis muttered, "No, I think I was lucky."

Schippers was thrown off by the aside and turned to Judge Urso. "I ask that the last part of the statement be—"

Rakoczy jumped from his chair at the prosecution table and remarked, "*He* asked the question."

"I ask that the last part of the statement be stricken as nonresponsive," Schippers said, meaning unrelated to the question. During this spat, Dobrovolskis gave his one-time lover a smoldering glance as Eyler sat back and hung an arm over his chair.

Judge Urso responded, "It will be stricken."

The point of some of Schippers' other questions would not become clear until later in the trial. He asked Dobrovolskis whether Eyler climaxed during sex, and the former lover replied that he did. The question was intended to cast doubt about Eyler's guilt when technical testimony revealed that there was no semen on or in Danny's body.

Another question was about a man Eyler had lived with briefly, Bob Ciotta, after moving into the apartment on Sherwin Avenue. Then, mentioning again that Eyler had appeared "disinterested" in sex when he went to Dobrovolskis' apartment the morning of the murder, Schippers said, "You do not know whether or not he had just had a sexual encounter with another man, did you?"

"I assumed he had. I did not know that."

"As a matter of fact, he could have had another man up in his apartment at the time that you called and said that you were coming over."

"Could have."

"If he had reached a climax, he would be disinterested when he got to your house, would that be right?"

"I guess."

"Also that would be a good reason for him not to want

you to come to the house if he had another man with him,
isn't that right?"

"Yes."

Schippers immediately returned to the subject of Little
in a lawyer's way of casting aspersions by juxtaposition.

"Because of his coming between you and Larry, you
had an avid dislike for Mr. Little, isn't that correct?"

"No, I would not say I disliked him. I tried becoming
his friend several different times, but I would not say I
disliked him. I dislike him *now*, but I did not at the time."

"He hated you, though?"

"It appeared so."

Schippers let the subject hang in the air. Next he let
Dobrovolskis' matter-of-fact responses portray Eyler not
as a calculating killer but as an extremely immature, inef-
fectual man whose only interest seemed to be in his lover.

Referring to the weekend that Danny was killed, Schippers said, "You were constantly fighting with Larry. One
or the other was hanging up on the other one. There was
yelling. There was rancor and turbulence, isn't that
right?"

"Yes."

"Larry was very jealous of you, was he not, John?"

"What do you mean by jealous of me? Was he jealous
of other people's attention towards me?"

"That is correct. That is what I mean."

"Yes."

"Were you, in turn, sometimes jealous of the people's
attentions to Larry?"

"Sometimes, yes."

"You ended up in one of your screaming sessions over
the phone with Larry, isn't that right?"

"Screaming sessions?"

"How long was the longest you have had these arguments with Larry on the telephone?"

"As far as the screaming? As far as 'screaming session,' as you phrased it, a few minutes. The conversation
may have continued after that."

"And then it would escalate to screaming and then back
down to talking?"

"Sure."

"But sometimes you talked to him for an hour?"

"We have talked three hours."

"Wasn't it usually the way when Larry and you would argue, if one hung up on the other there would be a call back almost immediately?"

"Usually I would hang up on him and call back."

Schippers then eased toward his "sit-down" question designed to give jurors something to think about.

"Were you told that Mr. Little started a sabbatical that Friday so he did not have to be back at school on that Monday morning?"

Rakoczy interrupted. "How in the world would this witness know that?"

Dobrovolskis answered anyway. "I did not know that."

Judge Urso said in his tenor voice, "Objection will be sustained. Question and answer will be stricken. Jury will disregard that question and answer."

"I have no further questions," Schippers said.

The following session, July 8, would be Evidence Day, when testimony would be taken up by expert witnesses explaining how physical evidence was tested and its relevancy to the case. The man with the task of keeping track of everything was prosecution assistant Rick Pullano. His duties ranged from logging all the items when he removed them to going out for pizza when the prosecutors stayed late in the case. No one envied his job. The large unventilated "war room" where the evidence was kept reeked from the bags where Danny's body was found. The smell attached itself to everything in there, and Pullano closed his nose whenever he had to go inside.

A bailiff in a black uniform let Schippers into an unused jury room to do last-minute work on this leaden and drizzly Tuesday. The gray-bearded attorney looked over his notes and checked his textbooks, sometimes memorizing technical words. Schippers, who taught law at Loyola University, was no newcomer to lab tests. Now he was searching for a way to cast doubt on some of the circumstances that the prosecutors had piled one upon another. He had already looked up texts at Loyola, DePaul University, and the University of Chicago. Now he needed time to rehearse the plan of attack, whispering questions and answers to get the feel of how they might sound to the jury.

The massive gray building was filling up as cars parked along the parkway and people hurried across the street under umbrellas. Prisoners didn't have to worry about the weather; they were being brought in small groups from the jail through the underground tunnel.

Wilma McNeive and her family were staying in a motel rather than make the long drive from Indianapolis each day. She by now had lost the feeling of being intimidated by the block-square building, which belonged more to rain than to sunshine. On this morning, State's Attorney Rakoczy arranged for her family to meet Urso before the trial resumed. The bulky, black-haired judge, wearing a suit, smiled and greeted Mrs. McNeive's seven-year-old granddaughter and allowed the girl to sit in his big chair behind the bench in the churchlike courtroom. She, her mother, Martha Adams, and Mrs. McNeive then went behind the courtroom to the judge's comfortable chambers. There, the little girl saw diplomas and certificates on the wall and shelves of law books. Urso opened his closet and showed her his black robe. Mrs. Adams thanked him and escorted her daughter back up the steps to the courtroom.

Just then Schippers was passing through the inner doors. The girl couldn't restrain her thrill even though this gray-haired man was a stranger. "I met the judge, and I sat in his chair," she said.

Schippers, who had ten children of his own, knelt to her level, but Mrs. Adams jerked the girl away and said, "Don't talk to that man, he is *evil*." The entire McNeive family felt that the man responsible for freeing Eyler in the Calise case was a *de facto* accomplice in the Bridges murder.

The lawyer was hurt as he watched the girl being led away. He put his briefcase on the defense table. Hell, he thought, what is he supposed to do, crawl into a hole? He knew the country would be a lot worse if there weren't lawyers challenging capricious arrests and all the corners police and prosecutors cut when they aren't watched.

By then Colin and the assistant state's attorneys were wheeling in the evidence, some in plastic bags and police boxes. Eyler's mattress was brought in by itself. In all, the evidence was in a pile nearly six feet tall in addition to what was left on the two carts. Schippers knew that the sheer amount would sway any jury, and he needed to have some of it thrown out, beginning with anything touched by blood.

Out of the presence of the jurors, Schippers questioned the validity of the electrophoresis method the Chicago police used to analyze blood found at the scene. In the technique, blood proteins are made to migrate in an electric field. He went on for twenty minutes about this with Marion Caporusso from the crime lab.

Schippers noted that California serologist Benjamin Grunbaum had cast doubt on the process because blood deteriorates as soon as it is out of the body. Refusing to let the lawyer play cat and mouse with her, Caporusso countered that Grunbaum was the only expert "out of hundreds" who had negative feelings about the process. Schippers then badgered her about specific books and articles on blood analysis, and she admitted she was not familiar with them. Indeed, only an expert would be.

The defense attorney next asked whether there were a way to validate her findings. Caporusso, who had a master's degree in biology, replied, "We simply retest, by outside experts."

To every finding Schippers cited, Caporusso gave her explanation and once updated him in the latest procedures. His purpose was not to discredit the clearly knowledgeable lab chief but to let the back-and-forth exchange settle in Urso's mind the thought that blood analysis might not be certain under all conditions.

Prosecutor Rakoczy then walked up to Caporusso and had her simply close the gap by explaining that the procedures she used were those of crime labs across the country and that none had found electrophoresis unreliable.

Urso held that the tests were valid, and the jurors were

let in through the side door just past the spectators' partition.

For Rakoczy, Caporusso testified that she found no trace of semen in or on the body parts of Danny Bridges. The line of questioning was to bolster the prosecutor's contention that the boy was brought to the apartment to be murdered, not to have sex.

Caporusso testified about "reddish brown stains" that were found on virtually everything submitted for evidence: a bucket, a chair, a plastic stacking unit that had been painted white over the stains, and a sponge mop head that also contained a number of hairs. In addition, some green acrylic fibers from the mop head were found as "trace materials" between Danny's thighs. She also said that hairs in the bathroom trap matched Danny's.

"Mrs. Caporusso," Rakoczy said, "would you tell us how the bathroom in the defendant's apartment looked to you, to the naked eye?"

"It was relatively clean. There were no towels or anything on top of the toilet or anything."

"Were there any visible bloodstains?"

"There were very, very faint, almost yellowish-color, stains on the wall."

"What kind of tests did you perform around the wooden threshold?"

"I was in the bathroom on my hands and knees at the floor, and I was testing several stains that tested positive . . . The preliminary chemical tests for blood at the area of the threshold were becoming extremely strong. It's a color reaction. So, rather than getting a very light blue-green, the entire swab was going immediately a blue-green color. I then ran the swab along the threshold and came up with very strong preliminary chemicals tests for blood.

"At that point," she continued, "there were Area 6 detectives who were observing my preliminary chemical tests. One of them got a crowbar from someplace and assisted in lifting up the threshold and removing it from the floor. The area beneath the threshold had heavy, diffuse reddish brown deposits that extended at least an inch and a half. . . . Actually there were heavy brown flakes that were actually flaking off.'' The blood, she added, matched Danny's.

When it came to the green-tinted goggles that Eyler had been in such a hurry to find, Caporusso said that a visual examination had showed no blood. But tests under a stereobinocular microscope under high-intensity light had ''revealed that in the upper portion of the frame I found a minute reddish-brown stain that was present, with rust, in the well.''

''The sample of human blood you found was actually up in the well portion?'' Rakoczy asked, not for clarity but to let the jurors envision how it may have come to be there.

Caporusso also told of touching Eyler's mattress as she walked around his apartment and feeling ''bleach damage.'' This had led her to take samples through the stiff portion of the mattress and find stains of human blood.

Throughout the afternoon, Rakoczy moved along the shelf of evidence alongside the judge's bench. Exhibit #65, Exhibit #74—he referred to these tags with familiarity as if he were mentioning the names of relatives. Some items he held up for Mrs. Caporusso, and some he handed to her. One exhibit was a pillbox that held two samples of Danny's hair, which had been found in a plastic bag in Eyler's apartment.

One of the largest exhibits were blue jeans on which she had found that ''rivulets of blood'' had soaked through the fabric. Police had theorized that the killer had thrown Danny's body over his shoulder while wearing the jeans in order to carry it from the bed to the bathtub so that it could drain.

Two towels and a washcloth were found stained with human blood, but some stains near the tub were too diluted for tests. The diluting presumably came during the mopping up.

One of the jurors, Steve, had a difficult time keeping an open mind. Each time he looked at the defense table, Eyler would answer with a cold stare, until Steve turned away. Guilty or innocent, Steve felt that Larry Eyler seemed to be someone with a lot of built-up anger.

When Schippers took over the questioning of Mrs. Caporusso, he dropped the adversarial approach he had used before the jury was seated and questioned her about two nail clippings that had been found in an ashtray. They retained traces of blood and did not belong to Danny, but the crime lab had not taken samples from anyone else. Schippers was hoping the jury kept this in mind as he proposed in closing arguments that Eyler was not the killer.

"Were there any tests performed to the body of the defendant to ascertain whether there was a possibility of blood anywhere on his body?"

"No, sir."

Schippers moved away from this for a while, until it came to his "sit-down" question. With a deceptively soft tone he asked Caporusso, "Did you have any blood standards from any other being in the whole world to compare the blood found in the apartment?"

"No, sir, I did not."

"Thank you, I have no further questions." With this, Schippers sat down.

Judge Urso joked to the jury after the long day which lasted into the evening. "Ladies and gentlemen, again we missed most of the traffic because we worked later. There's a good likelihood the case will be completed tomorrow. As the case gets closer to conclusion, it'll become more difficult for you to avoid publicity in this case, but again I ask you to take those extra steps to avoid viewing any media coverage. Do not discuss this case with anyone, including your fellow jurors."

The morning session of the following day was devoted largely to evidence that both sides had agreed to beforehand. These items were outlined in court for the record. During the lunch break, word spread through the huge building that the closing would begin around 2 P.M. Secretaries, law students, and young attorneys crowded into the spectator section of room 201. An area intended to hold no more than seventy-five people shoulder to shoulder was now crowded with more than two hundred, some of them sitting in the aisles with their arms around their knees.

Others were standing in the back and out into the hall as summer heat came dripping down their faces.

There had been no disclosures, no conflicts during the trial, just the quiet horror of envisioning the dismemberment described by the medical examiner and the blood that Caporusso had found virtually everywhere.

Unable to contradict the testimony, public defender Tom Allen called two witnesses from his own side—Thomas Hickey of the public defender's office and Schippers' legal assistant, Diana Woznicki—to show that Eyler was cooperative and had done a good job of painting in Woznicki's house and the North Side home of a physician she knew. This ended the testimony, leaving the jurors, at best, with the feeling that Eyler was a nice guy most of the time.

Assistant State's Attorney Rick Stock led the closing statements.

"On Sunday, August 19, 1984, at eleven o'clock, Danny Bridges left his home. Had Danny Bridges stayed home that night, he would not have been deliberately tied, deliberately beaten, tortured, stabbed, and murdered."

No one ever took the stand to explain the "why" of Eyler. For Stock, in his closing statements, the murder was just an extension of bondage. "We know that Larry Eyler was always the dominant person in that bondage scene," the prosecutor said. "We know that John told you that he engaged in bondage with Larry Eyler on at least three, possibly more occasions. It was always Larry Eyler that tied up John. John didn't like to be tied up. He didn't like the bondage scene. It was always Larry Eyler's idea."

Stock reminded the jurors that Eyler was seen with street people in his home and that Danny Bridges would never talk to drivers if there was more than one person in the car. That meant he evidently had been picked up by just one person.

Stock repeated Dobrovolskis' account of how Eyler had seemed tired when they made love not long after Danny's murder and how his hair was wet and he wore no socks under his boots. (Caporusso had testified that a pair of socks were bloodstained.) Then, half an hour after Eyler had left, he called Dobrovolskis.

"Larry was asking about his goggles. 'Where are my goggles, John?' Well, John asked Larry, 'what do you need your goggles for?' And Larry said, 'well, because I'm painting and I need my goggles.'

"Well, now, that struck John as unusual because he had seen Larry Eyler paint before, and he's never seen Larry Eyler use goggles when he painted," Stock continued. "John Dobrovolskis told Larry Eyler where the goggles were, on a shelf, the same goggles recovered from Larry Eyler's apartment the next day with bloodstains."

Stock referred next to the injuries: the bruises, possibly from a fist, and the fourteen torture wounds from an awl, which he called an ice pick because of its harrowing connotations. "I don't think that any one of you can imagine the agony, the terror that had to have filled Danny Bridges in the last moments of his life."

The husky prosecutor looked into each face in the jury box. "Ladies and gentlemen, throughout this trial no one came into this courtroom to tell you, yes, I saw Larry Eyler tie and bind Danny Bridges' hands. . . . Larry Eyler didn't plan this crime that way, to permit eyewitnesses to the actual stabbing, murdering, and dismembering of Danny Bridges. But, ladies and gentlemen, Danny Bridges spoke to every one of you. He spoke to you through Dr. Stein. Through Dr. Stein, Danny Bridges told you of the agony and the torture that he—"

"Objection," public defender Tom Allen called out, but Judge Urso let Stock continue.

Eyler glanced over Schippers' arm as his lawyer made notations and underlined words. The clapping for Stock when he finished his summation was heard through the thick glass partition, and Judge Urso nodded.

When it came to Schippers' turn before the jury, he received permission to move the lectern closer. He paused a moment and started in.

"This is usually the time in a criminal case when the defense lawyer gets up and pounds the table, jumps around, screams, hollers, tries to convince you that his client is innocent and tries to overwhelm you with his own presence. I'm not going to do that.

"I want to stand here before you folks and I just want to talk to you. I just want to talk sense."

In a fatherly way he walked in front of Eyler, who sat with no hint of his former macho swagger. "What is the evidence beyond a reasonable doubt that Danny Bridges was kidnapped by anyone?" The lawyer slowly walked behind the defendant's chair, resting his hand on it.

As for the rope marks on Danny's arms, "I would hazard a guess that most of the people in this courtroom have a similar rope in their home, their automobile, or somewhere around," Schippers said.

"John Dobrovolskis told you what bondage is. It's tough for some of us to imagine this, but apparently these people consent to allow themselves to be bound, hands and sometimes feet, for some sexual gratification, which frankly is beyond my imagination." He continued his slow walking. "Homosexual prostitutes do this all the time. . . . Those rope marks might have been there for two or three days for all we know."

The prosecution had presented Eyler as a monster, and now Schippers tried to create an image of him as no more than a petty, overgrown adolescent.

"I think that you have probably ascertained also from what you have seen in this case that at least the individuals we're talking about—and with that I'm talking specifically of John Dobrovolskis, Larry and perhaps Dr. Little—that the homosexuals we are dealing with are vain. They are selfish. You can see through their testimony that each person seems to be more selfish than the other. They are emotionally immature. Indeed, their emotional immaturity ranks in the low teenagers and—probably most important—they are virtually insanely jealous."

Having introduced Little in connection with the homosexual world, Schippers reached the thrust of his reasoning and his tone was tinged with sarcasm. "The whole argument of the state has been, well, if Little says it, it must be true."

After an objection was overruled, Schippers compared the library science professor's report of being delayed by a freight train while driving home from Eyler's home that late Sunday evening to saying ''I killed a lion on the way in today with a stick and here's the stick to prove it.''

"Dr. Little, who never, never colors the truth, said 'I don't know that James Williams was homosexual,' '' the defense attorney remarked. ''The man lived with him in Indiana. 'No, sir, I don't know whether he's homosexual.' ''

Schippers went over all that could have been done by police but was neglected: sending fingerprints to the FBI lab, examining Eyler's nails for blood traces, determining the age of a bleach stain on Eyler's mattress, going over Little's TransAm for prints, even dusting for fingerprints the dishes Little said he washed for Eyler that weekend. Concerning the two fingernail clippings found in an ashtray, he said, ''They didn't check them against Dr. Little. They didn't check them against *any* of his friends that were up from Indiana that weekend.''

Urso admired the attorneys from both sides. Rakoczy and Stock were able to support more than two hundred items entered into evidence and some laboratory tests that took more than a year to run off and retest, and Schippers was doing the best he could with omissions and minor contradictions in the case rather than try to make things out of the air in hopes of confusing the jury.

Schippers personally believed his argument that Danny was killed by an acquaintance of Eyler's. He went over for the jurors some of the questions that he himself had been thinking about since the murder: Would the killer wear his own clothes while dismembering a victim? Would Eyler leave a body to drain in his bathtub on a hot summer day when the janitor had a pass key? Would the killer scrub his home spotlessly yet leave a pair of bloody pants hanging up ''for everyone to see, the pants that the murderer must have known were soaked with the blood of the victim? It doesn't make sense.

"If there had been knowledge in Larry Eyler's mind that that drain might contain damning material, he would have plunged that until he fell over in a dead faint,'' Schippers said.

He had finished his summation, but now he took a

moment and glanced up, as if grasping for a memory. As an aside he said one of his favorite plays was *A Man for All Seasons,* a story of conscience based on the life of St. Thomas More, chancellor of England. "He is the lawyer we would all like to be," Schippers remarked. More's son-in-law, Roper, tells him that a man should be arrested as a political expediency. "Thomas More said, 'Cut down the laws to get at him? . . . And then when all the safe-guards are down, sir, where would you hide when the wind blows?' "

To Sam McPherson, Eyler was sitting there as if he truly expected to be let go again; he was merely biding his time. Augustine Bridges grabbed Carolyn Buddie's hands in a silent gasp. Schippers stepped away from the jury box, and Eyler smiled.

No one in the crowded spectator section left during the break, for fear of losing a place. When the jury returned, Urso asked the other side if it wished to make a rebuttal argument. Mark Rakoczy rose, and there was an electric feeling as this shy family man transformed into an angry prosecutor.

"One of the many accidental misstatements that Mr. Schippers just got done making to you was that, jeez, the mattress could have been bleached a long time ago," Rakoczy said. He stepped over to the evidence cart, heaped high with items as if in a rummage sale, and pulled off the bloodstained mattress and lugged it a few feet to the jury box. "Well, look at this, ladies and gentlemen. Look at the size of that spot. Correspondingly, look what lies underneath that spot—blood. Yes, Mrs. Caporusso couldn't tell us that it was Danny Bridges' blood. How-ever, what Mr. Schippers failed to tell you a few minutes ago was the results of something that Officer O'Connor told us about the day before."

His voice harsh as if speaking with personal outrage, Rakoczy added, "This is the blood, the same blood type, the same enzymes as Danny Bridges'. This was not put on this mattress two months, three months, four months, or four days before the murder. This was put on when he killed Danny Bridges on this mattress. That's where he lay, ladies and gentlemen, right here. There's the blood.''

He threw the mattress onto the floor by the prosecution table. It landed with a quiet thump.

''No evidence? There's no evidence in this case putting Danny Bridges together with Larry Eyler? Oh my God, boy, that sounds great.''

The slender, dark-featured prosecutor returned to the heap on the evidence cart and grabbed the silver-gray plastic bag that Danny's head had been in. Rakoczy held the bag out to the jurors. ''What about Al Burdicki? Did we forget about Al Burdicki? Did we forget about him describing how the defendant carried these bags down to that dumpster? Good lord, ladies and gentlemen, no eye-witnesses to this case?

''Mr. Schippers, the defense, would have you believe that because this was August, in a non-air-conditioned apartment, and that several people had keys, that therefore Larry Eyler is not guilty. . . . I think he was trying to tell you something about what would have happened had the windows been open. Maybe Danny Bridges, quite possibly Danny Bridges would have been yelling . . .

''My God,'' Rakoczy added, ''the boy was killed in the bedroom and Little slept in the bedroom. Therefore he's guilty.''

''Objection, Your Honor,'' Schippers said and turned to the young prosecutor. ''I'm sorry, sir, I never said anyone else was guilty. I was giving an hypothesis.''

With the bite of sarcasm, Rakoczy said, *''Nobody* else was guilty, that's what I thought he meant. Now, I know what happened. Danny Bridges killed himself and then he dismembered himself. That's the logic to that, ladies and gentlemen. No one else killed Danny Bridges, so therefore Danny Bridges must have killed himself.

'' 'There should be more fingerprints.' Well, ladies and gentlemen, look at these bags. You know how fortunate it is to get *one* print off these things? Good Lord, you think you're going to get a hundred and fifty prints or something when you're just carrying the bag with your fingertips, when you're wearing gloves in the middle of

August?'' He threw the bag into the garbage can near the prosecution table.

Still with a sweep of anger, Rakoczy said that Eyler dragged the body from the bedroom to the bathroom to drain, then went to Dobrovolskis' house. '' 'Oh, John, could I stay for one more hour after we have had this great fun?' What's he got to lose? The body—that just gives the body time to drip some more. 'Let's get all the blood out before I go back and cut it up.' . . . You've got blood all over the threshold, ladies and gentlemen— the part that joined the bathroom and the hallway. That's where Danny Bridges bled. That's where he bled to death. That's where he bled to death while being dismembered in a very professional, calculating manner; the only way that he can get that body out of the apartment without being discovered.''

Rakoczy pointed to the enlarged photos, one by one. ''This, this is Danny Bridges''—the eight pieces that had once been human—''This is how he was carried out''— the plastic bags—''This is how he was buried by Larry Eyler, right here''—the picture of the garbage can.

''Danny Bridges cries out for justice,'' Rakoczy said. ''The evidence is overwhelming.''

Then he sat down.

Urso turned toward the jury and instructed them. ''It is your duty to determine the facts and to determine them only from the evidence in this case. Neither sympathy or prejudice should influence you.'' This was followed by the usual cautions against considering statements that had been stricken or from witnesses who may not have been in a position to comprehend what they said they observed.

Urso had told the jurors that evidence would be in their deliberations room for them to consider. Now that discussing the case was their responsibility, they hardly knew where to begin. The evidence virtually spoke for itself. Almost every item except for the photos had the blood of Danny Bridges on it.

After the juror Steve put the Polaroids of the body back onto the cart he began thinking over the case as a whole. That would have been easier if Schippers had put Eyler on the stand. As it was, there was nothing to offset all this evidence and the way Eyler showed no surprise or apprehension—nothing human.

A man's life was at stake and yet a trivial consideration entered Steve's head and wouldn't go away: Eyler never changed the yellow shirt he wore day after day in the trial. To the student, it seemed that this was a man who had no consideration for any life but his own.

One of the jurors was drawn to the goggles. Of all the items these had the least amount of blood—a single speck discovered amid the rust—and yet this was the one that haunted his thoughts. Someone wore these while methodically hacksawing through the body of a fifteen-year-old boy. The juror put the goggles back on the cart, and the deliberations began.

As the jurors waited for the bailiff to bring back pizza, the forewoman asked the others their feelings about the case and outlined the charges. No one questioned the murder count, but there was some doubt as to whether the kidnapping statute could apply. They were not lawyers or judges. Whatever the law stated, they could not rid their minds of a tied-up teenager undergoing fourteen torture wounds before being finished off with deep knife thrusts that went halfway through his body. That, they thought, was kidnapping.

Eyler was sitting out the deliberations while handcuffed to a chair in a holding cell. Schippers and assistant public defender Tom Allen visited him, showing more hope in their words than in their expressions. "Hang in there, Larry," Schippers said, with his large hand on Eyler's shoulder. "We have a fighting chance."

"Say a couple of prayers," Allen suggested. "It's in God's hands. We don't know how long it will take."

Eyler hardly said a word.

Outside, television vans were set up for live coverage on the stairs leading to the courthouse. Cables for electrical equipment snaked across the steps in the slow midsummer twilight.

Security was tighter than usual this evening. No one wanted to think about what some family member might do if the verdict turned out to be innocent. When Schippers started walking in the back of the courtroom, a guard in a black uniform grabbed him.

"Sir, we have deputies here to escort you out of the courthouse, just in case," he said.

"I don't need them."

"We have extra men to get you out of the back," the bailiff added in a tone that showed it didn't matter what Schippers thought. The escort had been ordered by Sheriff Richard Elrod.

Schippers turned to the glass partition. Most of the spectators had gone, but members of the Calise, McNeive, and Bridges families were still peering at him from their benches. At least one man among them had talked about killing Schippers if there were any verdict other than guilty.

Because Schippers had obtained Eyler's release before, some of these family members thought he had powers beyond just the law. Carmen Pauli admitted that when Schippers cross-examined a witness she would have to leave for a while. "I didn't want to hear the trickery he would use," she said.

Mark Rakoczy was complimented in the halls for his vigorous prosecution, but he was still dissatisfied. He had been hoping for a "nexus" (link) to open up in the testimony so he could present evidence in the other cases, but Schippers had been too careful for that.

The bailiffs had wheeled away all the evidence but overlooked the garbage bags that Rakoczy threw down in his final arguments. During the wait during deliberations, Danny's six-year-old nephew pointed to the garbage can in the courtroom and said, "See those bags? My uncle is in there." This brought his mother close to tears.

Usually prosecutors sit out a jury in Jean's, a restaurant and bar across from the criminal courts building. This case was so big that State's Attorney Richard Daley took Rakoczy and First Assistant Mike Angarola to dinner at Bruna's on South Oakley. Daley was beaming his Irish smile. Rakoczy's wife, Marianne, said she was on pins and needles waiting for the deliberations to end.

"What's the matter?" Daley asked over dinner.

"Maybe there's a loophole," Mrs. Rakoczy said. "Maybe they believed Schippers."

"Believe me, Marianne, it's not going to happen again," Daley said.

Angarola added, "You saw the jurors when Mark threw the mattress down and held up the bags? The jury was electrified! This case is buttoned up. I'm surprised the jury is still out."

Rakoczy had been allowed to concentrate on just this case for much of the time, but he still had to start on it early in the morning each day, work on it at his office area in his suburban home, and gain what he called "quality quiet time" by taking reports and notes with him to the Glenview Public Library while his wife contended with their three young children. She sat in on most of the trial, and so did Rakoczy's parents. They were as proud of his closing arguments as if he were giving a valedictorian address.

"The case gets to you," Rakoczy said as they ate. He would never forget Mrs. Bridges weeping throughout the testimony as if the trial were Danny's funeral or the cold indifference of Larry Eyler, who had had the look of someone just waiting for a train.

Rakoczy's beeper went off at 8:52 P.M., and everyone knew the jury was in.

"We've got him," Angarola said. Long deliberations would have hinted that the jurors were unsure whether to convict on one of the charges.

The prosecution team drove back to the somber courts building. Marianne Rakoczy took her place beside Carmen Pauli and held the older woman's hand to comfort her and relieve a little of her own nervousness. Eyler sat at the defense table reading a letter from a lover. When reporters saw the jurors file back in with downcast expressions, they rushed to phones in the corridor and said, "Eyler's guilty!"

Urso looked at the jury box and said, "Miss Foreperson, has the jury reached a verdict?"

"Yes, Your Honor, we have."

She handed the slips of paper to the clerk, who announced, "We, the jury, find the defendant Larry Eyler guilty of the offense of murder . . . guilty of the offense of aggravated kidnapping . . . guilty of the offense of unlawful restraint . . . guilty of the offense of concealment of a homicide."

Danny's father had been spared some of the details in testimony because he had lost much of his hearing, but now he rose and put his hand to his mouth. Eyler showed no emotion, but Mrs. Rakoczy pressed Mrs. Pauli's hand and felt depleted.

When the verdict forms were handed to the clerk, Eyler clamped a hand on the leg of each of the two attorneys sitting at each side of him, Schippers and Hilliard. He gripped their legs until the last guilty was pronounced.

Rakoczy went out to the corridor to speak to reporters. "One of the most dangerous people that ever set foot in this building is now behind bars for good," he said.

Colin walked over to Schippers and shook his hand. It hardly seemed that they were on opposite sides in the long, complex investigation. The older man gave the detective's hand an extra shake and told him, "Thanks, Dan, it's been a long three years. And it's not over yet."

"Yeah, I know." There were still the death hearing and the appeals.

Prosecutor Rick Stock hugged Mrs. Pauli and did a little dance with her around the table, saying in singsong, "He's guilty, he's guilty!" Stock hugged his wife, then ran to the empty jury room. He scooped out the crumpled jurors' ballots in the wastebasket and read one sheet after another. He bolted from the room and ran to where Rakoczy was kissing his wife and holding her hand.

"They all voted him guilty on the first ballot," Stock said. "The first ballot!"

For the television stations, the jury's timing couldn't have been better. The families were leaving just in time for live broadcasts on the ten o'clock news.

Carolyn Buddie of the state's attorney's office took the arm of Danny's mother, Augustina, and told her she didn't have to speak to the reporters they would be passing if she didn't want to.

"No, I want to be heard now," the woman said in her Missouri accent. Her voice quavered as she tried not to cry. Microphones protruded at her as she headed for the elevator.

"How do you feel about the verdict, Mrs. Bridges?" someone asked. Under the glare of the white lights it was hard to make out individual faces.

"It won't bring my son back, but it might save a lot of lives," she said. The murders at last had come to an end.

Danny's seventeen-year-old friend Ruth Pelz told the reporters, "I think he should get the death penalty, but even that's too good for him."

Schippers was walking behind them. A news producer tried to single him out in the corridor and asked, "Do you believe *now* that your client is innocent?"

Schippers answered in a clipped tone. "That, sir, is one of the dumbest questions I have ever heard." With that, he walked away.

21

September 30, 1986

The two sides of Larry Eyler were about to be paraded before Judge Urso, who had to decide whether Eyler should live or die.

Twenty-three victims could not speak, but the prosecutors had brought together three survivors of attacks to testify on this opening day of the death penalty hearing. The Illinois and Indiana police by now were familiar with these details, but they had not been brought out in the trial.

Mark Henry told of the night he was kidnapped at knifepoint and stabbed in the chest in 1978. He said he had been left for dead, but defense attorneys pointed out that Eyler immediately contacted help. Schippers questioned why an ex-Marine couldn't disarm someone who was holding a butcher knife on him while driving one-handed down country roads at more than fifty miles an hour. Repeatedly the innuendos were made: these were not rage attacks, just sexual games that got a little rough.

In the afternoon Fred Harte, now nineteen, told how Eyler had given him a beer and offered him some black pills in Greencastle, Indiana, in 1982. The boy awoke two days later in a hospital with patches on his chest and tubes in his arms because of severe dehydration. He had needed to be fed intravenously for a week and a half. There had been no sexual assault, but Schippers underscored the fact that Harte, then fourteen, had met Eyler after spending several hours in a game room at night.

Jim Griffin was called next. He told of the beating he

suffered while bound and lying facedown in his Chicago apartment in late 1981. He said Eyler had laid out some knives and an awl from what prosecutors called his "torture kit." Eyler told the short, balding young man that he was in no danger. Police attending the hearing felt that this time Eyler had been telling the truth: the assault may have involved self-hate, but it was not triggered by a quarrel with John Dobrovolskis. That may also have been why Henry was stabbed just once. The murders did not start until after August 8, 1981, the night Eyler met Dobrovolskis.

Public defender Tom Allen tried to put Eyler's mother at ease the next morning as they sat in a room of the criminal courts building while the rain fell hard on the county jail complex and the park across the street. Pulling up a chair to be closer to her, he said, "I am going to ask you to think of anything that shows your son in a good light. I don't care if it's helping an old lady across the street or Larry climbing a tree to save a cat."

"Larry was always doing good things, he was always helping people," Mrs. DeKoff said.

"Yes, I know. The judge, you see, he doesn't know Larry like you do. Shirley, remember, you may be the only one who can save Larry's life." Mrs. DeKoff cried as she nodded, but Allen wasn't sure how she would hold up. She had been undergoing professional counseling since the Calise arrest, but as soon as questions regarded her son she began to break up inside.

On October 1, testimony began with the fourth survivor of an assault, Ed Healy. Six years before, he had been blindfolded, beaten, and nicked several times across the chest with a razor-sharp knife. Healy said that Eyler removed the blindfold and took out a shotgun, saw that his captive wouldn't be aggressive with him, and put away the gun. Then methodically he placed the knife and handcuffs into something like a shaving pouch, the so-called "torture kit" that police were never able to find. "He threw it over the side of the truck as if he felt bad for what he had done," Healy said.

The prosecution ended its presentation, and the defense

began with the Catholic chaplain of the jail, the Reverend Edward Phillipski. Public defender Claire Hilliard asked, "How did he treat you, sir?"

"With a great deal of respect and kindness," the priest answered, and he added that Larry got along with the other prisoners.

"In fact, you could almost say he was a model prisoner?"

"In terms of being cooperative with the staff, I would."

Phillipski said Eyler would discuss church history with him and also read a number of books, largely biographies and modern history.

Calling a chaplain as a character witness is common enough, but Assistant State's Attorney Rick Stock sensed that this was part of Schippers' tactics to keep Urso uncomfortable about the death penalty. Schippers, Eyler, and Urso were all Roman Catholics, and the emphasis of the church is on redemption rather than punishment. Stock decided not to cross-examine the priest; that could just make Urso unconsciously side with the defense.

When Shirley DeKoff was called to the stand, she told of her 1955 divorce when Larry was two and a half years old. She had worked in a factory, then for the federal government, and on weekends and some nights in a bar. She had a "succession of babysitters" take care of the four children. "It was very difficult; very difficult financially, emotionally, because I couldn't be with them as much as I wanted to be."

"Now, did you eventually remarry, Mrs. DeKoff?" Allen asked.

"Yes, I remarried three times very briefly. I was obviously hunting for a husband and father for the children, somebody to help me with them." She seemed to be repeating the words of her counselor.

With the pain of memory, Mrs. DeKoff admitted that she had felt she could no longer handle the children even after putting Theresa and Larry in separate homes. She eventually tried to place them in an orphanage—the Soldiers' and Sailors' home in Knightstown, Indiana. She had to tell her three sons and her daughter that she still loved them but that this was just something that had to be done. "But when the lady visited me for the last time and told me I'd have to give custody of the children to the court, I said I couldn't do that. So I kept them, and we struggled."

"How would you describe or characterize your relationship then and now with your children?" Allen asked, and he saw that she was about to cry. "You want to take a minute, ma'am?"

"My children have always been the most important thing in my life," Mrs. DeKoff answered. "I love them very much and have done everything that I felt was possible to raise them, keep them together."

She couldn't continue. She wept uncontrollably even after a bailiff handed her a box of facial tissues. She wiped tears from her face over and over again. Her son fidgeted in his chair and grabbed Schippers' arm as if he wanted to halt the questioning. Only when the mother eased back into the chair did Allen resume his questions.

"Mrs. DeKoff, was there ever a period of time when Larry was removed from the family for any length of time?"

"Yes," she replied. "Larry was about, I guess, eleven or so and he was having problems with authority. He didn't want authority; he defied authority, my authority."

"He didn't want to do his chores, things like that?" Yes, she said. "So where did you send him?"

"I took him to the Riley Hospital in Indianapolis, and they suggested I take him to Fort Wayne—it's a Catholic home for emotionally disturbed children, and he was there for a period of six months."

"Was it like a boarding home?"

"Yes."

"And how did Larry react to that placement? Obviously it was difficult."

"He was very miserable. I talked with one of the sisters that were in charge of the cottage he was in, and she thought he was ready to come home, and I brought him home." He was never again a discipline problem. He had been raised in at least five homes and threatened with an orphanage by the time he was twelve. The unspoken testimony cried out that the boy would do anything to avoid the loss of love, of security.

Mrs. DeKoff told of how wonderful "Uncle Larry" was with her eight grandchildren and how he had called nearly every day he was in jail. When Allen asked her to tell the judge about her son's relationships with others, she said, "Larry, wherever we have lived, has been the only person I know of that everybody likes. . . . He always makes people feel good."

Urso listened, as usual, with detachment over his interlaced fingers.

Rakoczy chose to cross-examine her. "Did he ever tell you about any of the experiences he had in cruising around and picking up people?"

"Of course not," Mrs. DeKoff answered in a brittle tone.

"Were you aware that he was charged with the attack on a man by the name of Mark Henry a few years back?"

"Yes, I was. He said it was an accident at the time." Then, although the subject had not been mentioned, she second-guessed what Rakoczy was trying to imply. She immediately added, "I never delved into the sexual life of any of my children, and I didn't want to do that in this case either."

"I don't mean to ask you about any sexual connotations, ma'am; just did he ever tell you about the attack?"

"Yes, I told you he told me it was an accident."

"Mrs. DeKoff, did he ever tell you when he was charged with giving pills to a boy named Fred Harte?"

"Yes."

"Did he give you any details about that?"

"No, sir."

"Thank you, Judge," Rakoczy said, and the woman stepped down.

The time was 2:30 P.M., and Urso called a recess. Eyler's stepfather—his third—was called to the stand when the hearing resumed.

Irving DeKoff carried to the stand the authority of an administrator. He was the director of staff development at the state hospital in Richmond, Indiana, close to the Ohio border. He had known Eyler since the defendant was nineteen. "Larry has always been kind of the light in our eyes as a family," DeKoff told Urso. "Larry was always the one that was the most fun to be with, always the one that had good jokes, always the one that would be meeting people, and he seemed to be interested in everybody that he met. He was extremely intelligent."

The stepfather continued without a pause. "We always argued a great deal about politics. Being a Democrat, he and I did not see eye to eye, with his politics being relatively conservative, but I enjoyed that with Larry. Only thing I didn't like about Larry is that he beat me playing chess, and I thought I was good at it.

"I think the thing that probably characterizes him better than anybody I know is that the kids were crazy about Larry. Whenever he went out, Larry would be the one that would go to the nephews and nieces and play with them, and there was a joyfulness about him that all of us around Larry felt."

Referring to all the books the family had sent Eyler while he was in jail—including texts on algebra, geometry, and accounting—DeKoff said, "I think Larry had tremendous intellectual capacity far beyond what he's accomplished in his life up until now." *Until now:* two strong words in a death penalty hearing.

The final witness was Eyler's sister, Theresa, now remarried. She had been a friend and mother-figure to Eyler as he was growing up in home after home. "I just want to plead for my brother's life," she said. Looking into the judge's brown eyes, she added, "I just ask you to give me a part of him."

There was no cross-examination.

In his closing statements, Stock told Urso that "had it not been for Joseph Balla looking into that garbage dumpster, Larry Eyler would most probably be out on the streets today." Stock said Eyler tortured Danny Bridges until "he was finally put out of his misery."

"The tears and the agony that Mrs. DeKoff and Theresa Parrish suffer are real, Judge," Stock continued. "There's no question about that. They're as real as the tears and the

agony that's been suffered by Danny Bridges' sister. . . .
There is nothing, Your Honor, that can mitigate the tears
and the agony that Larry Eyler has caused his entire life,
thirty-three years, and he has caused more tears and agony
than one can imagine.'' This was the closest that anyone
in the trial and sentencing hearing had come to mentioning
the twenty-two other murders.

Pointing to Eyler, who was sitting as calmly as if he
wished he could be reading a magazine, Stock charged,
"Violence, torture, and death hang over this man like a
shadow. When Larry Eyler walks through those prison
gates, that shadow of death and torture are going to go
with him. . . . A sentence other than death will be giving
him his freedom.''

The word *freedom* had taken on a chilling aspect in this
case ever since Judge Block had thrown out the evidence
in the Calise murder, and Stock knew what effect it would
have on the judge.

Much of what Schippers was about to say had not been
planned; he had been writing down key words to hang on
Stock's thoughts. He stood now and delivered a rebuttal
that was aimed not at an abstract concept of justice but at
the judge's own religious beliefs.

"I am a Catholic," Schippers said, "but I feel there
are times when the death penalty may be appropriate.
There may be some wretch, there may be some monster,
who has no mitigating circumstances. This, in the name
of all that's holy, is not such a case.''

Schippers said that for a circumstantial evidence case
"the death penalty is never appropriate.'' Standing behind
Eyler, he added, "Some day, somewhere, God willing,
we may find we were wrong. We may find that the jury
was wrong and that Larry Eyler is not the murderer of
Danny Bridges. And Judge, what then?''

Schippers told Urso he knew from personal experience
that such things happen, citing a kidnapping case in which
all nine eyewitnesses were found to have been wrong.

The lawyer also worked on the judge's unfamiliarity
with the sexual underworld. Urso was an experienced
jurist, but when prosecutors had shown him some of the

items seized from Eyler's home they had to explain what they were used for, and Urso expressed amazement.

"This isn't criminal activity, Judge. Bizarre, yes; criminality, no. It's part of the subculture that neither of us will ever know except from what we hear in the courtroom. . . . The superficial marks on the chest that are now being called 'torture' apparently are part of the S & M culture that the hustlers have freely allowed to have happen to themselves for money."

A little later into his rebuttal, Schippers told Urso, "The newspapers, the television—they love to have a death penalty. The pressure is there. The pressure is there from some of your fellow judges, I don't doubt that. There's pressure all over, Judge, but I don't believe that you are the type of human being to subject, to give in to pressure. In fact, I know you're not." Once again, Schippers tried to make it seem that this arena of the law were just a conversation between two men about consciences.

Eyler, he continued, "reads, he studies, he learns. He's a feeling, caring human being. That's all you've heard from this. He's worked with retarded kids. He's helped the elderly. Is this some monster that should be taken out to the back of the lot and shot, or taken out and put out of his misery?" Schippers used Allen's phrase.

"This is someone who, whatever he has done in the past, is redeemable, even in the eyes of man. He can help to teach some of the others in our jail system. He can bring a little caring into that savage system. . . .

"The great men, the great events in the history of this nation, have been those that demonstrated mercy, not justice. I beg you, Judge, in the name of our common heritage, some day both of us will stand before the seat of God, and at that time I hope He can look at you and say 'You gave mercy and you shall have it.' "

The common heritage he referred to was the Roman Catholic Church. For many in that courtroom, the phrase and much of Schippers' argument were just rhetoric, but Urso knew better.

"Thank you," Schippers said and sat down.

Assistant State's Attorney Mark Rakoczy needed to dispel the impression Schippers had made. With a forceful, fast delivery, he began. "Do you think for one second, Your Honor, that Allen Burdicki was mistaken when Larry Eyler, the nice intellectual guy, said 'I'm just getting rid of some shit?' Do you think Allen Burdicki was mistaken when his dog went crazy when he [Eyler] walked by him with those bags?"

Point by point Rakoczy went over the solid evidence and the testimony of persons who knew Eyler. "There's no mistake, Your Honor. That is the killer right there in front of you. . . . You have heard, Judge, testimony showing a very definite common scheme of a man who is power hungry, who enjoyed the thrill of control and dominance over people." That, Rakoczy added, was despite a mother and a sister who always did their best for him.

"There hasn't been one bit of testimony that showed he was himself the victim of power or dominance or need to control. That was his conscious choice," Rakoczy said. "That was what he wanted. That's what makes him so dangerous.

"You do not learn this urge for power or dominance in a day; you don't learn it ten minutes before you kill Danny Bridges," Rakoczy insisted, once more drawing Urso closer to the other murders without being overt. "This is something that you [must] have a real lust for, a lust for that type of power, violence, dominance, and control. . . . Power and control, Your Honor. That is what he likes. That is what he loves. That is the only thing he knows.

"Think of the evil that is present in that man. This is the type of evil that has manifested itself over the years and years of that type of power-hungry urge. . . . That's the type of person that sits in front of Your Honor today."

Under an unusual agreement reached at the beginning of the proceedings, Schippers returned for a surrebuttal argument. Again, he chose careful simplicity over hammering away at minor discrepancies in the prosecution. "This is a man who will do anything for anyone when they ask him," the lawyer said. "I know; I've gotten to know this young man over a two-year period. I know what, how he thinks; I know what, how he feels. He feels deeply for other individuals and for other people.''

Now he turned away from the judge and looked at Rakoczy and Stock. ''I say to you gentlemen, in the words of Cromwell, 'I charge you in the name of Christ, think, man; you might be wrong.' I was a prosecutor, and I was wrong. Other prosecutors have been wrong, but thank God when they are wrong there's a living, breathing human being to go to and say I'm sorry—instead of a grave to cry over.''

Returning his look to Urso, Schippers acknowledged obliquely that everyone involved knew that this moment involved more than just the murder of Danny Bridges— that, in effect, they were speaking across two dozen graves. ''There's a great deal of pressure, there's a great deal of rumor, innuendo, hints, suggestions. You know that none of that counts. You decide on what you have heard in this courtroom. You have followed the law religiously. . . . You have followed the law and your conscience. There are mitigating factors, and unless you find there are no mitigating factors, you cannot sentence this young man to death. We beg for mercy; we ask that you follow the law.''

''Thank you, Mr. Schippers,'' Urso said as the lawyer sat at the defense table next to his client.

Urso ordered a ten-minute recess. When everyone returned, the judge said, ''Mr. Eyler, you wish to say anything to me to help me impose a correct sentence?''

In his first public statement since January 1984, Eyler said, ''I don't think it has anything to do with the sentence, Your Honor. I just want to publicly thank your staff over the last two years and month I have been in your courtroom. They all have been very nice to me despite all the circumstances surrounding myself.''

The judge said he would return his decision in two days; that is, at 10 A.M. on Friday, October 3. ''I have a lot to think about,'' he added.

Urso had sentenced only one man to death before. There is never anything clear-cut about such a decision. More than law and justice were involved. There was the sight of the Bridges family, Carmen Pauli showing up day after day ever since the trial began, and Wilma McNeive glaring at the back of Eyler's head for hours day in and day out during the murder trial. They represented the spirits of three sons and stood for all the others, even though legally Urso had to confine his decision solely to the Bridges case.

Like many jovial, popular men, Urso kept his serious side to himself. He had drifted away from the church, but ten years before, when his daughter Maria was born prematurely and was not expected to live, he made a pact with God. He would go to Mass at least once a week for the rest of his life if the child survived. In fact, he went to church every day for a month while Maria was in the neonatal unit. When the doctors said the girl would be fine, he had felt renewed.

"I have very strong feelings of the sanctity of life," he has said, "but my job is to follow the law."

When he arrived home in west suburban Melrose Park he blocked the case from his mind. Urso kept his life separate from his career. Talking over anything would tear down the wall that helped him think.

On Thursday he went to church before he drove to the courthouse for his usual calls, and he kept thinking about the decision he was putting off. The testimony of the men who survived attacks disturbed him, and so did Schippers' arguments of circumstantial evidence and how most of the survivors went with Eyler for money or, as with Fred Harte, for beer. If Danny Bridges wasn't kidnapped, Eyler could not be sentenced to execution.

Friday was cold and rainy. Urso entered St. Edmund's Church in the neighboring suburb of Oak Park and lit a votive candle. The heavy, dark-haired jurist knelt in a pew and prayed for guidance. He didn't want to feel alone in his decision.

Urso arrived in court at 8 A.M. and told his clerk he didn't want to be disturbed for two hours. Urso lowered himself to the chair behind his big desk, beside his wall of law books. Once or twice he glanced through his blue-grey notebook, more to have something to do than to go over his casual notes. No one should have the right to take anyone's life, not even the state, he thought, unless you make sure you're right. Urso had a Diet Coke, opened his closet door, removed a robe from its hanger, and was still working out his decision. He felt no pressure from the news media or other judges; Schippers had just thrown that in as lawyers do. No, the only pressure was from within. He remarked wryly to himself that some people have told him that he looks uncaring on the bench.

It was ten o'clock. Urso went up a few small steps, turned, and was at his judge's seat.

Reporters filled the jury box. Behind the glass partition, Carmen Pauli and Mark Rakoczy's wife, Marianne, held hands in the front row. Eyler's mother and sister were tense. Dan Colin, Ted Knorr of the Indiana state police, and Sam McPherson and Frank Love of the disbanded task force were near them, waiting for justice. Youth officer Brian Killacky sat with Gera-Lind Kolarik in the back row.

"I find the decision that I make today a difficult one. Difficult not only because of my personal belief. . . ."

McPherson relaxed and nudged Love. Eyler was about to be sentenced to die. Eyler looked coldly at the prosecutors a few yards away as the judge faced him and said, "The senseless and barbaric aggravated kidnapping and murder of a fifteen-year-old boy, a killing which was so brutal and heinous that it truly defies description, a killing that was accompanied by exceptionally brutal behavior. . . . shows me your complete disregard for this human life.

"The fact that you went over to John Dobrovolskis' apartment, to his home, had sexual relations with him on the kitchen floor while the body of your victim was lying dismembered or even draining of its blood is unbelievable.

"You have taken the only thing of value that Danny Bridges had. His life.

"You even tried to take the last bit of dignity from Danny Bridges after his death. That is to deny him a decent burial as a whole human being, not just discard him like bags of garbage just to disappear and never to be heard of or seen again by anyone."

Referring to the four men who had testified about their

attacks, Urso added that it was clear that this had not been "a one-time act," that Eyler committed violence against people weaker than he; not just because they were younger or not as strong, but because they were people "whose life society still does not accept or understand." Eyler knew, said the judge, that if they complained to authorities about the assaults, "people would laugh or snicker at them."

With his voice breaking with emotion, Urso said, "If there ever was a person or a situation for which the death penalty is appropriate, it's you. You are an evil person. You truly deserve to die for your acts. . . . I thereby sentence you, Mr. Larry Eyler, to death for the murder of Danny Bridges, committed during the course of his aggravated kidnapping."

Sharon Bridges rose and cried, and in a second everyone else in her family was embracing one another. Carmen Pauli glanced at Shirley DeKoff as if to extend a hand of sympathy. A woman's voice quietly said, "God, thank you," but there was too much emotion in the spectators' section to know who it was.

Urso resumed in a flatter tone. "The unlawful restraint, the kidnapping charge merge with the aggravated kidnapping charge, and I also sentence you to fifteen years in the Illinois Department of Corrections for the aggravated kidnapping and five years for the concealment of his homicide and death." The judge cleared his throat. "When you'll be put to death by lethal injection into your body, Mr. Eyler, I pray to God that he has mercy upon your soul."

Mrs. DeKoff approached Mrs. Pauli. For just a second they paused, uncertain what to do next, then they embraced. "Right now," Mrs. Pauli said, "I would rather be Ralph Calise's mother than Larry Eyler's mother."

Mrs. DeKoff stepped back and wiped away her tears. "Can I write to you?" she asked.

Schippers came through the inner doors and reached for Mrs. DeKoff and her daughter. As he led them to Eyler, Mrs. Pauli found a piece of paper and wrote out her address in Oak Park.

Detective Dan Colin smiled at her. During the last three years, each of them had to bolster the other when it appeared no one would be found guilty. Strange, but only now did it seem that Ralph Calise could, in spirit, be laid to rest. Love and McPherson shook her hand. They had had little contact with the woman, but they admired her determination.

Mrs. Pauli walked into the corridors, now brightened with the lights for television cameras. She almost froze as she heard Schippers tell the reporters "We are going to appeal this automatically to the Supreme Court and get the kidnapping charge and the death penalty overturned. We are not done yet."

22

"Mr. Eyler may have been proven guilty of concealing a homicide, but he should have been acquitted of murder and aggravated kidnapping," according to his appeal filed in May 1988. The appeal claimed that Danny Bridges was brought to the apartment on Sherwin Avenue by Little and killed by the professor while Eyler was away and that "this was not rebutted by the prosecution." Eyler's lawyer for the appeal, Steven Clark of the state appellate defender's office, added, "When a conviction for murder rests, as it does in this case, solely on circumstantial evidence, the guilt of the defendant must be so thoroughly established as to exclude every other reasonable hypothesis.

"Although there is a strong possibility that Mr. Little killed Danny Bridges, Mr. Eyler was wrongly convicted (only) because of the gruesome disposal of the body, and Mr. Little's carefully staged claim of innocence."

The appeal mentioned that Little's car had not been dusted for fingerprints and that his alibi of returning to Indiana at the time Danny was killed had not been corroborated.

"Little was in a position to intimidate Eyler and expect Eyler to cover up the crime," the appeal continued, because Eyler had been financially dependent on him and also would have been the immediate suspect if the body were found.

"As horrible as it may be to try to conceal a murder by cutting up a body, it does not prove Mr. Eyler guilty of murder beyond a reasonable doubt when the wholly circumstantial evidence points to the very real possibility that Mr. Little may be responsible for the murder.''

June 12, 1988

Larry was on Death Row in Pontiac Prison awaiting his appeal in the Illinois Supreme Court. For four years, ever since Judge Block threw out the evidence in the Calise case, the boxes of reports and other material that had been amassed against him lay in the basement of Colin's home. Now they were in the Lake County sheriff's office because Eyler's mother felt she should see what police had against her son. She had gone through counseling and believed she was ready to judge for herself.

While waiting for Mrs. DeKoff and her husband to arrive from Indiana, Colin thumbed through the papers in the five boxes. He removed surveillance photos of Eyler, photos of the tire tracks and boot marks, and a photocopy of the calendar police had made to log the whereabouts of Eyler at a number of the murders. That would be enough for the couple to see. Going over the record he was reminded of the frustrating investigation.

At 10 A.M. Colin left the building, crossed the street, and waited for the DeKoffs in the parking lot next to the morgue. When they arrived, Colin greeted them as a friend and made small talk about the weather. This summer was well on its way to an all-time record, with temperatures in the nineties nearly every afternoon since Memorial Day. He could tell that Mrs. DeKoff was emotionally stronger now than she had been during the trial in Chicago. She even no longer regarded him as an enemy.

Colin led the couple to the sheriff's office, which wasn't the same after the death of colorful Mickey Babcox that March. The new sheriff didn't invite reporters pheasant hunting or get carried away at news conferences.

There was no need to show the DeKoffs the photos of the victims or autopsy reports. Colin had made little piles of material that should be enough, especially after he showed them the calendar and explained the pattern as he had for Schippers.

Irving DeKoff sat silently. From time to time his wife would say quietly such things as "I believe Larry. He said he never killed any of these people." But there was no conviction in her voice. If psychiatrists cannot fully explain serial killings, how can mothers be expected to understand?

The couple rose to leave a little after noon. Irving DeKoff told his wife he'd be back in a moment, then he returned to the office. "I don't know how she thinks," he said to Colin, "but I can see how you guys think he killed all these boys. I understand now why you think the way you do."

DeKoff went back out and put his hand lightly on his wife's shoulder. They had a long drive to Richmond, Indiana. And Mrs. DeKoff had a much longer journey: from denial to acceptance and then the final phase—taking a little of the blame off herself by reinforcing the good memories, the special moments with Larry. There were lots of them.

May 10, 1989

The three-story, eighty-one-year-old courthouse seemed dwarfed by the domed Capitol building across the street in Springfield, Illinois. On the second level, floor-to-ceiling deep red curtains shadowed out the morning in the corridor leading to the state supreme court. Sharon Bridges, the McNeives, and Gera-Lind Kolarik met and hugged each other and walked to the state supreme court hearing room. As if this hearing on Eyler's case were a family reunion. Kolarik had left television for public relations work, but she continued to have an interest in the case and in the families.

Mrs. Pauli wanted to sit in at the hearing, but her son was coming in from college. Those who could make it down to central Illinois spoke quietly at a large oak table as they waited for the case to come up before the six justices. Eyler's attorney for the appeal, Steve Clark, a balding young man with an unlined face, arrived in a blue suit carrying a wide leather bag for his court notebooks.

In a mild voice he told the justices that Danny's finger-prints were not found in Eyler's truck. "I contend the victim was not in the truck. Eyler covered up a murder. *Little* picked up Danny."

As the spectators listened, it seemed that they were all a single family. Sharon Bridges, her yellow hair a floppy mass of ringlets, grabbed hold of Charles McNeive's arm. Charles' younger brother, also named Danny, could have been the victim the attorney was describing.

The representative of the state's attorney's office told the justices, in effect, that Clark was grasping at straws and that nothing new had been offered. The justices asked Clark whether there would be cause for reasonable doubt without Little, since there was no evidence to link him to the crime. "Eyler was out of the apartment, as the evidence shows," Clark answered, although the evidence was not all that certain. The justices had no further questions.

In the oak-paneled hallway as they were heading for the marble stairs, Mrs. McNeive asked under one of the globed chandeliers, "What does this all mean; what does it mean?"

The answer came suddenly, months earlier than expected. On the morning of October 25, 1989, Schippers was working in his Loop office when his receptionist buzzed him to say that Eyler was calling collect from prison. Since the Illinois Supreme Court had not been expected to rule until January, the lawyer wondered why Eyler might be on the line.

"Have you heard?" Eyler asked softly. "They're going to rule today. Do you know anything about it?"

"God, no, Larry. I'll see what I can find out. Call me back in an hour, all right?"

As soon as he pressed the disconnect button, Schippers dialed Steve Clark's office.

No more than half an hour later, a messenger arrived with a copy of the thirty-six page decision. Schippers flipped back all but the last page, and read "We affirm the defendant's convictions and sentence of death. We direct the clerk of this court to enter an order setting

Wednesday, March 14, 1990, as the date on which the sentence of death . . .''

The date was only a formality. Illinois had not executed anyone, even John Wayne Gacy, since reimposing its death penalty in the 1970s. The sentence might not be carried out for ten years or more. Schippers felt crushed. Later that day he and Linda Holmes walked a block from their office to St. Peter's Catholic Church. There they knelt and prayed for Eyler's soul.

EPILOGUE

Judge William Block knew the political consequences of his decision to set Eyler free, and he lost his effort to become an Illinois appellate and a federal judge. He continues hearing cases in the same courtroom at the end of the hallway in Waukegan. One of them was the final murder trial of serial killer Alton Coleman in July 1986.

Dan Colin still holds the rank of investigator in the Lake County sheriff's office. He is assigned to the state's attorney's office to investigate "white collar crimes," which involve multimillion-dollar fraud cases.

Willie "Smitty" Smith was promoted in the ranks and now serves as second-in-command in the sheriff's office as "under-sheriff."

Kurt Proschwitz was promoted to deputy chief of operations, where he is in charge of investigations in the highway patrol.

Ray McKoski and Pete Trobe are now associate judges in the Lake County Nineteenth Circuit Court judicial system. Fred Foreman was appointed by President Bush in April 1990 to serve as the U.S. Attorney for the Northern District of Illinois.

The horror of the Danny Bridges case never left one of the jurors, Brian. Several weeks after the trial he was driving to his North Side home from his printing job in suburban Winnetka when he glanced into the car that had just pulled up alongside his at the stoplight. He saw some wigs on mannequin heads, and a shudder passed through him as his mind flashed back to the photo of Danny's severed head.

Assistant State's Attorney Mark Rakoczy became chief of prosecutions for Cook County and later went into private practice. His former boss, Richard M. Daley, was elected mayor of Chicago in April 1989. Richard Stock went to the DuPage County, Illinois, state's attorney's office, where he heads prosecutions.

Award-winning NBC producer Chuck Collins gave up the news business soon after the Danny Bridges murder and settled down in Phoenix, Arizona. He suffered a breakdown, which he attributes to his involvement in bringing the boy back to Chicago. He has since recovered.

Sgt. Frank Love of the Indiana task force has retired, but the hefty man with the white beard teaches karate to young police officers and heads public relations for the Indiana Department of Corrections.

Sgt. Sam McPherson, who always hated the bureaucracy that he felt impeded officers in the Eyler case and others, quit the state police and opened a food store in a pleasant section of Putnam County, Indiana. McPherson couldn't stay away from law enforcement for long. He is now the chief investigator for grand jury cases in the Marion County Prosecutor's Office in Indianapolis.

The name of Sheriff Robert ''Mickey'' Babcox lives on at the new jail in Waukegan, which was dedicated in his memory.

Indiana State Trooper Kenneth Buehrle, who stopped Eyler because of suspicious activity, has been promoted to detective at the Lowell post. The other officers continue their duties there, from Sergeant Ezell to Sergeant Popplewell. Sgt. John Pavlakovic has retired.

John Dobrovolskis returned to Chicago from California and rejoined his wife, Sally. He died of AIDS in January 1990.

Dr. Little continues teaching library science at Indiana State University.

Carmen Calise Pauli feels her son Ralph lives, if only in a scrapbook on the Eyler case. The murder of her son stopped the serial killings for a while; at least that is some consolation for her.

In Blood Alley, the small curving alley near the Wilson Avenue elevated station, someone had written on the back

of an old brown building, "Danny Brydges Aug 21 84."
The misspelled inscription was still there in the summer
of 1988, but hard rains have since washed it away.

How many boys and young men were murdered by the
highway killer? No one knows except the killer himself.
There are a number of unsolved deaths of hustlers and
hitchhikers in northern Indiana that were not on the list,
and several more in Kentucky, Illinois, and Wisconsin.
Other bodies could still be out there.

Suspicions linger that more than one person was
involved in some of the killings. The FBI believed there
were two in the early series; the way Stephen Agan was
butchered suggests an accomplice; and police say two men
could have been involved in disposing of Danny Bridges'
body and cleaning up the apartment on Sherwin Avenue.

Eyler was freed to kill for six months. If there are
accomplices, they are still free.

AFTERWORD

October 1990
Newport, Indiana

The entire highway killer case exploded when Vermillion County Prosecutor Larry Thomas announced he was reopening the Steven Agan investigation. By his thinking, justice cried out for charges against Eyler. The evidence gathered for this book persuaded him that Eyler could be convicted despite the fact that eight years had elapsed since the murder.

Thomas was a tall man with a small mustache that distinguished his oval face. When he took office six years earlier, the Agan file was empty except for a list of people to be questioned. There was not even any indication whether they had been contacted. There was also no mention of Eyler even though, Thomas later learned, Dan Colin and others had pleaded with his predecessor to press charges.

Thomas had been meeting with Sheriff Perry Hollowell since late April for help in recreating the file. As the new sheriff, Hollowell could finally give him the manpower he needed in tracking down reports and evidence photos, even though the tax-conscious farmers and townspeople would not be happy about pursuing charges for someone already convicted of murder and awaiting execution in Illinois. After Thomas lost the primary in his re-election, he and Hollowell decided to bypass the grand jury and charge Eyler directly so that he would stand trial for at least one of the Indiana killings.

Thomas set up a meeting with Kolarik at the Villa Italian Restaurant in Terre Haute just after the first edition of this book was published. The meeting was so informal he wore blue jeans and a satin jacket over a flannel shirt.

"What good will it do you?" Kolarik asked when Thomas told her his plans. "All that evidence was suppressed by Judge Block. It has to stay in a vault somewhere."

"Hell with that," Thomas said in his soft, deliberate manner. "Block is from Illinois. Under Indiana law, I am bringing this evidence back. I can use Indiana case law to uphold that search as legal."

Eyler was no longer represented by Schippers. His appeal was taken on by attorney Kathleen Zellner from a new group called the Capital Resource Center in Evanston, Illinois, a publicly funded last resort for prisoners on death row. Zellner, a dark-haired woman with an attractive but severe face, was not deterred when the U.S. Appeals Court denied Eyler's request for a new trial based on the allegation that Little had bribed Dave Schippers to keep him out of the trial. Zellner had accepted Eyler's case just before this book was published and didn't know at first if she could believe everything her client was saying, especially in implicating Little in the Bridges murder. But after several visits she began to believe him and decided to use the material as a way of renegotiating his sentence.

Zellner drove her black BMW to Pontiac Correctional Center and talked to her client about the most difficult decision he would ever have to face, saving his life by pleading guilty to the Agan murder and implicating Little.

November 21, 1990
Waukegan

Vermillion County Prosecutor Thomas and Sheriff Hollowell arrived at the Lake County Sheriff's office on a warm, drizzly morning before Thanksgiving. Colin was waiting for them outside, smoking a cigar.

The visitors were led to a side room and looked over the transparent plastic bags of evidence laid out before them: maps, strands of hair, men's underwear, rope, boxes of plastic gloves, combs, surgical tape, a knife, and a small pillow with brownish bloodstains. Everything was as it had been when state police in Lowell searched Eyler's van.

A few minutes later the prosecutor and Hollowell solemnly went through the gas station receipts and phone bills. "With the key and all this, we've got enough," Thomas said. "More than enough."

"But it's not a lay-me-down case," Hollowell said.

The Indiana phrase seemed odd to Colin, but the detective understood from Hollowell's lowered tone what he meant. There was enough to convince police officers of Eyler's guilt, but possibly not a jury. They needed a clincher.

A few days later, Thomas was working in his office in the Vermillion County Courthouse when he received a call from attorney Zellner. Eyler was willing to confess, she said. That wasn't all. He was prepared to testify against Little—provided, however, that he would be given a fixed sentence of sixty years rather than the electric chair.

After Hollowell called Colin with the news, Colin dialed Schippers' number in Chicago. The attorney replied to the news with a drawn-out sigh. When he became involved in the case he had believed that Eyler was innocent. With the Bridges murder, Schippers convinced himself that his client had been only an accomplice and had not taken part in any other killings. Now he could fool himself no longer.

"I fought you tooth and nail, I fought you at every turn on this thing, and I always from day one thought you were totally out of your mind," Schippers told the detective. The bitter, cold feeling of betrayal was settling in. "God, after all these arguments we've had . . . You were dead right and I was dead wrong."

In Pontiac prison on December 4, Eyler gave his account of the Agan murder as Zellner wrote down his words, then he signed each of the seventeen pages. He ended with: "I ask God to forgive me because I can never forgive myself . . ."

December 8, 1990
Terre Haute, Indiana

Officers had a search warrant for possible evidence in Little's office in Room 336 of Reeve's Hall on the campus of Indiana State University. At the other end of the city, Colin accompanied sheriff's police at dawn as they once more raided Little's picture-perfect townhouse on Keane Lane.

Sheriff Hollowell was excited but tired. He was a moderately plump man with wisps of hair spread out across the top of his head. He had spent much of the night lying awake thinking about this case and was glad when 3 A.M. came around so he could get ready. Now, three hours later, and fortified by coffee, he joined Prosecutor Thomas at the door with plenty of backup.

Little answered the door in his flannel pajamas and was confused by the swarm of officers from the Terre Haute police department, Vigo County police, Vermillion County police, Indiana state police, and two detectives from Illinois.

Little was allowed to get dressed, and was taken in for questioning while the other officers loaded plastic trash bags with anything that might be evidence. The black sacks soon bulged with video tapes and a collection of more than three hundred photographs, many of them Polaroids. One photo was of Eyler posing in a jacket, jockey shorts, boots, and a riding crop.

The evidence was sorted out at the police office in City Hall. Colin, one of the two detectives from Illinois, was more than disappointed that they didn't find anything conclusive. Just photos of men, some of them in overtly sexual positions. None of the photos showed an assault and none of the faces were those of a known victim.

Back at police headquarters Hollowell questioned Dr. Little. One of the questions Hollowell wanted to ask Little was whether he had been in certain areas of western Ohio. There had been nine stranglings of young men near the Indiana border since 1980. The sheriff tried to provoke a reaction and said, "How is it, Dr. Little, that we have a witness that placed you in the car with Agan?'' The professor seemed visibly shaken and said he would answer no more questions without an attorney. The lawyer never showed up and Little demanded to be driven home. The police had to cooperate because Little was not considered under arrest, and they certainly did not want constitutional issues to surface as they had in Eyler's 1984 arrest.

After Little was driven home, he arranged for another professor to hand out finals the next week, then took an indefinite leave of absence. Rumor of his impending arrest spread rapidly among his students, some of them middle-aged like himself. Little was such a gentle, caring man that no one could believe the news.

December 13, 1990
Illinois Correctional Center, Pontiac

Sheriff Hollowell could never forget seeing Agan's body lying ravaged on the ground, unable to believe that any human would do this. Evidence technicians that day in 1982 found a Jack Daniels cigarette lighter next to the body and the tip of a yellow plastic glove under Agan's head. There were drag marks leading to the abandoned farm house, and the stains of splattered blood on the beam. What had really happened the night he died? Had someone taken this life during a ritual? Or a game? In looking at scene photos five days later, Hollowell saw what he thought was a brass key on the floor next to the beam. He returned to the shed, found that very key and carefully placed it in a plastic evidence bag, dismayed that it had been overlooked for so long.

But Hollowell could not hate Eyler when he met him in Pontiac prison this Thursday morning. Before him was a rugged-looking man so unusually polite that the sheriff could see why many people said they felt like parents toward him.

Eyler had been a model prisoner, working out with weights to keep his body trim and muscular. Despite his increasing baldness he had never looked handsomer. His dark hair was cut short and was showing a few strands of white. It gave him the appearance of a man who had just retired from the marines, until he spoke in his quiet halting way.

Still wearing a green jump suit, Eyler was kept in leg irons as he walked out of prison under the watchful eyes of guards on the ramparts. Authorities said that for a man to be transferred from Death Row to appear as a prosecution witness was unheard of at least in Illinois. This transfer was Hollowell's last official act as sheriff, and he was enjoying the moment. Kathleen Zellner met them in the parking lot with a briefcase and a pressed blue suit.

The midmorning sun glistened on the thin layer of snow as the convoy neared the end of its three-hour drive from Illinois to Indiana. Hollowell turned to the back seat in the middle of three cars and asked the prisoner, "Can you identify the place where Agan was killed?"

Eyler turned to Zellner and she nodded for him.

"Can you identify the Green Acres truck stop when we pass it?"

"Yes," Eyler said.

A few minutes later as they drove along the farmland, Eyler said softly: "That's the truck stop and, there, that is the hill to the house."

Well, Hollowell thought, at least he's not going to play games with us.

The town was quiet, with just the real estate office and the ma and pa grocery open this early. Newspaper reporters and broadcast crews decended on the food store, hungry for more than news. They pressed against one another for homemade deli sandwiches as a county salt truck lumbered by.

Every time a car passed by, reporters rushed out to ask the locals if that was the sheriff. Assignment editors at two Chicago television stations, WBBM and WMAQ, called Vermillion County police to say their crews were still enroute, as if the wheels of justice should be turned off until they arrived.

A dozen hands set down coffee cups and sandwiches at 9 A.M. when a cameraman from Indianapolis television station WTHI yelled into the grocery, "I see a convoy. He's here!"

As the cars approached, officers with hands on their guns rushed out and formed a human wall leading to the courthouse. Two deputies with shotguns ran up to the third floor, but they weren't afraid that Eyler might try to escape. Over the last few years, the families of several victims had threatened to kill him if they ever had the chance.

Newspaper cameras kept flashing as Eyler climbed out of the middle car. No longer in leg irons, he walked as if he didn't care about all the attention. But his eyes betrayed a nervousness under his black expression. A cameraman fell on the snowmelt of the worn marble stairs, but by then Eyler was out of view. Inside the courthouse he changed from his prison uniform to the suit and striped tie Zellner had brought for him.

Fourteen deputies kept reporters back as Eyler walked toward the judge's bench. This was an old courtroom with a white domed ceiling arching over plain oaken benches. Photos of past judges seemed to watch from the walls, and the room looked ready for Clarence Darrow.

"The defendant agrees to enter a plea of guilty to the offence of murder," Prosecutor Thomas told Judge Don Darnell. "The defendant also agrees to identify and give testimony against other persons who had knowledge of said murder or took part in said murder." The State of Indiana was recommending a sentence of sixty years.

Eyler became nervous when the young judge asked: "Do you understand that you will lose your right to remain silent and become a witness against yourself?" No answer. "Do you understand that?"

"Yes, yes. Yes, sir," Eyler replied. When asked how he pleaded, he said: "I'm guilty. Guilty."

"Tell me what happened back between the 19th of December and the 20th day of December of 1982," the judge said for the confession to be written into the record.

Eyler sipped water from a cup and placed his hands on the defense table. "If I break up a little, I'm nervous. So if I break up a little, I'm not . . ."

"I understand," the judge replied.

The defendant interlaced his fingers and began. "Dave Little and I were driving in my Ford pickup in an area by an old bus station . . . in an area where gays go cruising. Okay? It's a cruising area." The night, he recalled, was fairly warm for mid-December, perhaps thirty-eight or forty degrees. Little was in his middle forties then but already had graying hair, Eyler noted by way of suggesting that the professor needed him as a lure.

"Dave asked me, did I want to play a scene." Eyler claimed that he didn't know what Little meant by a "scene," and the professor told him he liked to photograph certain sexual situations "in sequences." They didn't pick up anyone in the area, but later they saw Agan walking by as they were driving away from downtown. Eyler said he had never seen the man before but nodded to him, and Agan nodded back. Agan then agreed to join them in the car and sat between them as they left Terre Haute. "I asked him if he would like to mess around with us, and he said yes." Eyler said he then offered Agan a beer.

Eyler testified that he told Agan "We're looking for something far out" and that it had to do with bondage. Agan reportedly said he had never been involved in anything like that but was willing to try. Eyler said he turned the truck around and drove to Little's home so the professor could get his cameras, a Polaroid and a Nikon "or something like that." Eyler picked up his own bag from the garage. Inside it were a rope, handcuffs, and a knife.

The men returned to the pickup truck and drove to a rural area near the National Guard airport, Eyler said. A guardsman pulled up in a jeep, shined a flashlight in their faces, and told them to drive off the airport grounds. They continued driving without a plan until Eyler remembered the abandoned shed off Route 63.

After pulling up, Eyler took everything out of his pockets and put them under the gas pedal. He didn't want to leave any evidence. The three men then walked toward the old house. Little reportedly said the parallel beams of the old house would make a good backdrop for the pictures, and Agan agreed to go in.

Sheriff Hollowell sat back in a chair near the judge's bench and grimly pressed his lips together.

"I cannot remember if I tied and handcuffed Mr. Agan's hands above the beams," Eyler continued. "I can't remember that. I just remember that I was the one that did tie his hands above the beam. I worked very fast and Dave Little started masturbating. And I got down and I tied Mr. Agan's feet and then Dave signalled me to tape his mouth. Mr. Agan never made any complaints. Never cried. Never said, 'What are you doing?' "

Eyler wrapped the duct tape four or five times around Agan's mouth and Little allegedly said, "Get his eyes!"

"I took the Ace bandage and wrapped it around his eyes, and Dave likes everything in sequence, so first he got his good camera, he got the Nikon . . . with its own flash and everything, and he took first a picture of me and Agan like that. Standing there. Then he took a picture of me starting to take off his shirt. And he took a picture of me, I had just unbuckled his pants and started taking them down."

The defendant raised his face to the judge, glanced at Zellner, and looked back at the judge. Eyler had the handprinted confession in front of him but seldom referred to it. "I'm sure it seems far-out, but you see—Dave likes to take everything in sequence and likes to control the events. Now, I'm not putting any of my responsibility off on him. I'm just telling you this so as these picture-things go along, so you'll know what is happening. Something, something, something in me feels a rage and a hatred, and I do not know what, and I have not come into contact with the feeling." It was obvious that Eyler was still trying to comprehend what he had done and how he felt about it.

Eyler was reluctant to go on, as if unnerved by his own silence.

"I've questioned myself a hundred times about it," he said after a pause. "A million times, perhaps. And at this point, I mean . . . I'm taking responsibilty for myself, too.''

Until now Eyler had done nothing worse with Agan than often happens in a bondage scene. But then, he said, Professor Little switched from the Nikon to the Polaroid and said to him: "Get out the knife."

Eyler testified that he raised the blade to the young man's naked abdomen. "I'm very aware of what's happening. I know that Mr. Agan isn't. And I told him to make his peace with God. . . . And after waiting those few minutes, then Dave said, 'Oh, kill the mother-fucker.' I then stabbed Mr. Agan and Dave took another snapshot. I stabbed Mr. Agan, then I stabbed Mr. Agan a couple or three times. I don't know how many times. I just did them very quickly. And then Dave came over and he took the knife from me and he stabbed Mr. Agan while he masturbated. And after he stabbed Mr. Agan a few times, then Mr. Agan went limp.''

Trying to make the judge understand, Eyler gestured with his arms in the air. "He was being held up like this, but he was still staying up on his own power. And then he just went limp, and I believe at this time that Mr. Agan was not alive anymore. And Dave had stopped and took another picture and then proceeded to masturbate. At this point in time I was scared and exhausted, and Dave said . . . 'This was too fast.' So we started talking for a few minutes, and the more that Dave and I started talking, he was still very hyper. He was still animated in his emotions, which is something. Because, you see, he's usually very calm when you see him, if you know him as a person. He's usually pretty controlled and calm.''

"Anyway," Eyler continued, "so, as we stood talking these few minutes, Dave wanted some more pictures and the rage in me was building again, and I picked up a piece of wood and I hit Mr. Agan with it. Beatin' Mr. Agan, although he was not alive any more, and Dave took a picture of that.''

The house-painter sounded less troubled as he continued. He said that Little told him "a very strange thing," to drag Agan behind the abandoned house and finish him off. "I still had felt this rage and I picked up the knife and I cut Mr. Agan open, and Dave Little took a picture of this and was masturbating."

Eyler said he felt exhausted after the murder and helped Little cover the body with leaves. He wanted to get away but Little, he said, told him to take Agan's wallet to make identification more difficult. Eyler, with his weightlifter strength, tore the wallet to pieces and threw them out the window of his pickup truck as they returned to Terre Haute.

Fidgeting, stumbling for words, Eyler tried to explain that there was no way he could have accidentally dropped evidence at the scene after putting his keys and lighter under the gas pedal. "I suspect, although I cannot be sure, I am at a complete loss, to me, in my mind, how, after doing this, how a key that could be connected to me and a particular lighter was found there. What I'm saying is, as I'm admitting to my guilt and you're hearing everything I'm saying, I am saying that there is no way that I could have put them there; so, I know, I'm not saying anyone from the law enforcement put them there, I know they're honest guys here." That was all he said about his suspicions concerning how the evidence was found.

They drove back to Little's immaculate house. "We washed our clothes. We cleaned everything. We didn't speak to each other. . . . There was just silence."

Now that he was nearing the end of his confession, Eyler explained that Little knew of a certain photo developing place. "They don't care what the pictures show, they just want to get paid. And I would like to say, then, when the Indiana State Police came to search the house at some point in time much later . . . they did not go into Dave Little's bedroom or his closet. And if they would have, we probably wouldn't even be here today. Because the pictures were there . . . they checked every place but the place they should have checked."

Further distancing himself from his former protector, Eyler assured the judge that he was not the one involved in voyeurism and souvenir-taking. "Once I have done this deed, I have no inclintion of ever wanting to look at it.

The pictures were for him, not for me. He also took one thing from the scene, Mr. Agan's shirt.'' He meant an undershirt.

Tired of having spoken without a rest for so long, Eyler slowly lifted his hands to gesture at his chest level. ''I guess when a person is in this position there is nothing left to do but just ask God to forgive you . . . you can't really forgive yourself. And you really can't expect forgiveness from anyone around you.''

Thomas called Sheriff Hollowell to testify that a former guardsman corroborated Eyler's account of stopping three men in the pickup truck that night. The judge took the case under advisement and said he would rule on December 28th.

Reporters flocked around Zellner in the hallway. She said her client was pleading guilty because he did not want to subject his family to a second trial. ''His mother stood by him. He did not want to subject his sister to this. He did not want to subject the Agan family. And he didn't want to waste taxpayers' money by coming in and proposing a defense that basically would have been a charade.''

The long investigation into the highway stabbings then completed its circle as Eyler was driven to the Vigo County Jail in Terre Haute, where security could be tighter than in the small Vermillion County jail. The man who led him to his cell was Sheriff James Jenkins, the officer to whom Eyler had turned over a handcuff key after Mark Henry was seriously wounded in a knife attack near a trailer park in 1978.

The sheriff said nothing about it to his prisoner, but for years he felt that the long series of murders would never have occurred if Henry had pressed charges instead of accepting money from Eyler's attorney. The money had come from Dr. Little.

When Sam McPherson saw Zellner's news conference on television in his home that night, he threw his sandwich down on a plate and said out loud: ''Damn 'charade' is what he is up to now. He ain't sorry for nothing!''

Sheriff Jenkins let Eyler meet his family in private at

the jail. As his mother and sister, Theresa, brought him a change of clothes they told him how proud they were that he was coming forward. Mrs. DeKoff had at last made the painful acknowledgment that her son was a murderer—and probably a serial murderer. The plump, white-haired woman seemed more at ease with herself than she had been during the Bridges trial.

On the afternoon of December 18, Eyler returned to the Vermillion County courthouse in Newport for a lie detection test in preparation for his appeal of the Bridges conviction. One of the witnesses sitting in was noted attorney Dennis Zahn, who was now representing Little. Zahn looked like a business executive but had an impishness about his expression as if to say he knew he could win this case.

The questioner at the lie test was noted polygraphist Fred Hunter of Hinsdale, Illinois. He repeatedly went over items in Eyler's confession about Little's supposed involvement in the Bridges murder. Hunter's conclusion was that Eyler was telling the truth or at least believed he was telling the truth when he said that Little took photos of the torture of Danny Bridges and inflicted the fatal wounds.

Also that Tuesday afternoon, Little surrendered to police after staying in hiding with a friend for nearly a week to avoid reporters. Wearing an unbuttoned trenchcoat over a sweatshirt and jogging pants, the rumpled looking library science professor was led away by a deputy at each arm. He turned away from newspaper photographers with a scowl.

With the arrest, police could release a few of the details along with their own inferences. Sheriff Hollowell told reporters that Little had paid rent for the Chicago apartment so that, in his opinion, Eyler would be "available to obtain victims for Little's desires." Zellner was not direct, saying the short, unattractive man had used his tall, handsome friend to lure victims to their deaths.

Professor Little pleaded innocent and was led away without a change of expression. His attorney kept assuring him that the trial would be the only way to clear his name and get life back to normal.

That same day, police from Preble County, Ohio, arrived with armloads of files for Prosecutor Thomas and Sheriff Hollowell. Maps of Cincinnati and Kentucky had been found in Little's home, and some of the strangling victims dumped in Ohio had frequented the Our Place gay bar in Indianapolis, where Eyler often went. Hollowell said Little was also familiar with the bar. Also on Tuesday, Indianapolis police arrived to pore over the evidence for four hours because some men found strangled in Shelby, Hamilton, and Hancock counties had disappeared from the state capital.

On December 28, exactly eight years after Agan's body was discovered, Eyler was sentenced to sixty years in prison. But the penalty was overshadowed by news that Eyler was giving an ultimatum to Cook County State's Attorney Jack O'Malley's office in Chicago. Eyler, Zellner announced, would provide information about more than twenty murders if his death sentence for the Bridges murder were reduced to life without the possibility of parole.

O'Malley's chief of the criminal bureau, Pat O'Brien, was put in charge of the case. The information he had was still a little unclear, and he set up a meeting in Chicago. Zellner claimed Eyler was just a member of a cult that killed for the "thrill of killing." She also told O'Brien that Eyler had no knowledge about cases in Wisconsin and Kentucky, but he could provide details about the more than twenty murders in Illinois and Indiana, including the disappearance of Cowboy, the teenage hustler in Uptown. She noted that forty percent of the pleas are bargained in this country and that the state would have nothing to lose, since Illinois death row inmates were more likely to die of old age than execution.

"Look," she said, "Eyler is never going to die anyway, so you all will be heroes. I believe in the death penalty, too. But you see all the details he gave on the Agan case. I can give you comparable information, name names, give you witnesses."

O'Brien took notes and asked some questions, but Zellner felt they were the wrong questions. "I'm a conservative, too," she said, "but we are talking about over twenty murders! Throw away the key on Eyler because you have a big problem in the Bridges case; and with the hearings and a new trial, this will cost hundreds of thousands of dollars. Believe me, this case will blow up in your face."

O'Brien didn't commit himself, but he felt she hadn't mentioned anything more than what the police had already. Zellner commented over a drink with a cousin in the western suburbs later in the day that she doubted whether Jack O'Malley would agree to deal. "It's politics," she said.

On December 30, O'Brien drove up to the Newport jail to meet Sheriff Hollowell. Over the jail's fax machine came letters from prosecutors in Putnam, Jasper, Newton, Hendricks and Lake counties, Indiana, offering sentences of sixty years if Eyler would confess to the murders in their communities. A total of twelve more cases would be solved.

Hollowell was sure O'Brien would see the importance of these offers. If the prosecutor in Chicago would overturn the death sentence, Eyler would be sentenced to serve seven hundred and twenty years in prison for these murders alone, and a dozen families would at last know how their sons and brothers had died.

O'Brien had a no-nonsense look about him in his tailored suit and well-trimmed hair. He listened to the sheriff without expression. He looked over each faxed letter one by one but resented what he felt was manipulation by these rural law officials. Whatever happened to their cases, he still had to close the Danny Bridges case.

When O'Brien returned to the city he drew up a chart of all the murders attributed to Eyler. "Let's be specific," his boss, Jack O'Malley, had told him. "How many cases are they saying we're going to solve?" But as the state's attorney saw it, the physical evidence just was not there. Nor was there any evidence against Little in the Bridges murder. As for the two friends Eyler was willing to name in other killings, Indiana investigators had looked into them and could find nothing to charge them with.

Zellner took her case to the news media. She insisted that if no arrangement could be made, Eyler would take his secrets to the grave. *Newsweek* magazine claimed the "deadly deal" might be unprecedented.

Jack O'Malley had just been sworn in on December 1 after waging a get-tough campaign, and he announced over the New Year's holiday weekend that he was still considering Eyler's offer. The story was in the newspapers and television newscasts in northern Illinois and Indiana nearly every day.

Mrs. Pauli was among the parents urging O'Malley to accept the deal so that the truth might finally be known, but the presecutor was concerned primarily with the Bridges family and his own concept of justice. The former Chicago policeman could not see this as a moment of conscience for Eyler, and felt that Zellner was treating the death sentence like a used car sale.

The new state's attorney even talked over the case with his wife, Terri, and came away as convinced as ever that the sentence was just and right. The fact that those additional Indiana counties were willing to reopen investigations only if the Illinois death penalty were overturned suggested that their cases weren't strong enough to stand on their own.

Once O'Malley made up his mind, he telephoned Danny's mother and told her his decision, then waited two days for her response. She had none. The reopening of the Agan case had just added to her grief.

On January 8, O'Malley announced that the offer was "quite repugnant" and would be "cheapening the death[s] of victims by using them as bargaining chips." He added that the proposal was "extortion of the most venal and gruesome nature."

This was a sad day for Mrs. Pauli. "There are a million things we don't know about these killings," she said.

Nevertheless, Zellner pressed on in her efforts to overturn the Bridges conviction. She persuaded Eyler to speak openly about the most painful periods of his life to forensic psychiatrist Lyle Rossiter, one of only two hundred and fifty board-certified forensic psychologists in the country and a man she had known for ten years. Rossiter, a tall, handsome man in his early fifties, was the son of a prominent attorney. He interviewed Eyler's relatives and put together all the documentation he could.

The psychiatrist was no stranger to the case. He had been following developments in the papers and in 1984 had been contacted by Schippers about a possible psychiatric evaluation. But the attorney canceled the strategy when he decided that Eyler should plead innocent.

Records at a child-guidance clinic showed Rossiter a five-year history of emotional and behavioral disorders before Eyler was ten. As Zellner sat in, the psychiatrist spoke to Eyler for hours in a soft but firm way and administered a battery of tests. To this information, he added interviews with relatives in Zellner's office.

From further visits with Eyler at Pontiac, Rossiter learned that Eyler had been the victim of extreme physical and mental abuse by his drunken father when he was two years old. Eyler also had seen his father beat his mother several times in their home. Rossiter also found an unusually strong history of alcoholism in blood relatives of both biological parents, suggesting a possible genetic disposition for irrational behavior.

The boy was abused by each of his first three stepfathers. And the second stepfather had sought to curb his rebelliousness by holding the boy's head under hot water. Larry—Dr. Rossiter found—also witnessed the hostility, indifference, alcoholism, and verbal or physical abuse directed against Eyler's brothers and sister by all three stepfathers.

Studies of abused children show that they try to block out their fear just to keep on living as normally as they can, which leads to chronic mistrust and insecurity. Sometimes, clinging to the illusion that they have normal and loving parents, they may split their image of the abusive one into good and bad parts, and then unconsciously identify with the bad. As adults, they may be aggressive and at times seem paranoid.

Somewhere in the frequent disruption of his life caused by his mother's marriages to four abusive men, Larry's needs for the steady love from a mother and a father became fused into a craving for a single love and then was sexualized, or at least so it seemed to Rossiter.

To Rossiter it was clear that Eyler had maintained two types of relationships. "The first of these consisted of an enduring homosexual love-affair with a hyper-masculine idealized young male," Rossiter said in a report for Eyler's post-conviction appeal. Eyler developed a pathological sensitivity to any hint of abandonment by this lover.

"Concurrent with this highly sexualized and conflicted love affair, Mr. Eyler maintained a non-sexual, childlike and intensely dependent relationship with an indulgent and fatherly older male with whom he lived for many years," Rossiter added in referring to Dr. Little. Rossiter, assuming that Eyler's confession was true, continued: "The most pathological aspect of this relationship was demonstrated by Mr. Eyler's surrender to the older man's perverse demand for destructive and violent action against Steven Agan."

Eyler, engaged at what he perceived as the rejection by his lover, had turned to the older man, who—so Rossiter believed—had responded by urging him to discharge his rage by killing Agan. Unlike many serial killers, who murder without a touch of conscience, the psychiatrist found no indication that Eyler was a sociopath. Instead, Dr. Rossiter concluded that Eyler had "a severe borderline personality disorder consisting of certain enduring and highly maladaptive patterns of perceiving, thinking, emoting and behaving in the world in general."

A "borderline disorder" is one of the newer classifications for psychiatrists. Generally such people are merely neurotic but may have "psychotic episodes" of rage when thwarted or abandoned. One disturbing feature is that they need to pull others into acts that live out their own fantasies, either as accomplices or victims.

Psychiatrist Richard Rappaport believes that serial killers commonly have a borderline personality. The general symptoms include emotional instability, chronic anger, a clinging or angry dependency, chronic boredom or restlessness, inability to tolerate solitude, and confusion about self-image and sexual identity.

* * *

In the Vermillion County jail at the time, a strange thing was happening. The presence of Robert David Little was civilizing the other inmates. The place wasn't much of a jail, anyway. Until a year before, inmates could drop strings outside the window for liquor and anything else they wanted. No one seems to have thought of smuggling up a gun, but the county built a fence around the building anyway. The jail repeatedly failed state inspections, but the state kept a few of its own inmates there because the prisons were overcrowded and Vermillion County never had much crime.

The twelve cells were never locked down because they had no running water. Prisoners—usually just people arrested for fights and drunken driving—were allowed to roam within the cell block. That was how Dr. Little's influence began to rub off on them. He clearly did not appear at home there, and so they began to feel they were invading his privacy. The inmates became more polite to the jail staff and started saying "Thank you" for small favors. When Eyler was at the jail a year before, the inmates were so afraid that they kept a twenty-four-hour watch on him.

April 11, 1991
Newport, Indiana

The big hill in town was once used by the Ford Motor Company to test drive its new cars. The hill continues to draw up to three thousand people every October for the annual Antique Car race, the Vermillion County version of the Indianapolis 500. But on this morning the hill was crossed by scores of autos for what promised to be one of the most lurid trials in the history of northern Indiana.

At 7 A.M. parishoners of the Church of God Community began setting up a table in the courthouse lobby to sell coffee, homemade bakery goods and chili. They always held one or two bake sales in the courthouse every year, and the trail of Dr. Little seemed like the best opportunity they would ever have. During the two days of jury selection the church made over a hundred dollars and that was without all the spectators and reporters they would have when the trial actually began.

Boxes of evidence that had been seized from Eyler's truck in Indiana and had been ordered suppressed by an Illinois judge were now stacked against a wall in the prosecutor's office on the third floor.

The new county prosecutor, Mark Greenwell, felt uneasy about this case, which he had inherited from Thomas almost as if his predecessor was burdening him out of spite for winning the election. Greenwell wasn't even sure whether Eyler would testify. Zellner had said her client might change his mind after O'Malley rejected a deal in the Bridges case. If so, Greenwell was ready to appear before Judge Darnell this morning and dismiss the charges against Little, however politically damaging that might be.

At last he heard people running up the stairs and knew that Little was being brought in. A short time later, Greenwell saw Zellner and knew only then that Eyler was going through with it. "Larry is very nervous this morning but he will be fine," she said. Greenwell wasn't entirely pleased. He was left in the position of having to present a major case without knowing what his principal witness would say on the stand.

The marble steps and floors were polished, and the courtroom smelled of lemon oil. Wilma McNeive and her son Charlie were among the first to pass through the metal detectors and take a seat. Then came Steven Agan's brother, Bob, with a yellow beard and his hands tanned from roofing jobs. Little walked in accompanied by his attorneys and two deputies, his nervous grimace looking almost like a smile.

The casually dressed jurors filing in included a truck driver, two nurses, a restaurant owner, and some factory workers. They took their places in an unusual arrangement. The jury box faced the witness stand and prosecutor's table so that they could see everything directly, even the spectators.

The court was called into session and Greenwell walked

over to the jurors. He was a man in his late thirties who kept a boyish look by parting his thick brown hair in the middle and preferring shirtsleeves to a suit jacket. He barely mentioned Little in his unfocused opening arguments. Then he said something strange for a prosecutor: "We will call Larry Eyler as a witness in this case. And it won't take a whole lot of thinking to figure out that without his testimony we don't have a case."

Zahn's partner in the defense, James Voyles, picked up on this in his own opening argument. Eyler, he said, had wanted to avoid the death penalty on the Agan murder. "The deal was, Larry was going to get sixty years and all Larry had to do was give up his friend, David Little." But testimony, Voyles said, would show that the professor was with his parents in Florida at the time of the killing. Voyles added that the jurors would hear from Eyler himself. "Listen to what he says. What he sounds like, and what he really is."

Then came Eyler, wearing a blue suit and not appearing to notice the lights of the television crews. He immediately stared at Little. This was the first time they had seen each other since July, 1986, when the professor took the stand against him in the Chicago trial. Now the tables were turned.

When Eyler was called to the stand, he must have remembered what Zellner had told him. "Don't let them upset you, you're doing the right thing."

April 11, 1991
Newport, Indiana

Eyler walked into the courthouse with the self-confidence of the marine he wished to be. But as the state's first witness he exposed himself as a rather unreliable witness and a man still grappling with his past and its consequences. He mumbled simple replies and took long pauses, even when Greenwell asked him to explain what he meant when he said Little wanted to do a "scene" the night they allegedly picked up Agan. "Well, a scene is when . . .'' Eyler shifted in his chair uneasily. "Well, I knew that he wanted to, ah . . .''

Greenwell could feel the case slipping away from him. "Well," he asked, "did you know what it meant to you?"

Eyler sat up straight now. "Yes, I did. I knew what a scene meant.''

"Do you think he knew what it meant?''

"Well, definitely he knew what a scene was. Yes.''

Walking closer to Eyler, Greenwell asked: "Did it have anything to do with someone dying? Yes or no?''

"Yes, yes,'' Eyler answered.

The man on the stand no longer seemed to know just who he was. He had problems speaking openly to the jurors about bondage even when repeating what he had said confidently in his court confession just four months before. He told of binding Agan to the beam and stabbing and beating him, but said that Little had wanted to see more.

"He said to take him to the back and finish him off and Mr. Agan was already dead so I really . . . didn't understand what that meant. I mean at the time . . . I was in such a—you know, high state of, you know, excitement at the time, you know, I really wasn't paying any attention. So then I took him back and while Mr. Little took a picture of it I took a knife and I just . . . Mr. Agan open.'' As he spoke, Eyler put his hand over his mouth as if denying the words were coming from him. If he said the word "cut,'' it came so softly that no one heard it.

"We then went around and sort of, you know, in a hurried course of frenzy, we both went around and tried to clean things up as best we could,'' Eyler continued.

Then a couple of days later, December 21, 1982, Little took him to a restaurant for his birthday.

When Zahn began the cross-examination, Eyler's responses became stronger and he even made a few light remarks to ease the tension. Zahn planned his questions so that Dr. Little was hardly mentioned, even when Eyler was asked to recount what happened to the body after Agan had been stabbed to death while suspended from the beam.

"Now, you didn't gut him until you took him down, did you?" the attorney asked.

"That did not happen until he was down."

"Did you get blood all over yourself?"

"As I remember, yes. There was blood on me. There was also blood on Mr. Little."

Zahn soon attacked the very nature of the witness, asking about Eyler's bag with the rope, a knife, a roll of duct tape and a pair of handcuffs. "And that was your little killing kit, wasn't it?" Zahn asked.

"I'm not going to call it a killing kit. You may choose to describe it like that," Eyler answered. He was beginning to get rattled.

"That's what you used it for, wasn't it?"

"You may describe it that way, if you choose, but I'm not going to be—I'm not going to . . ." Eyler's tone hung in mid-air as he stopped himself from completing his thought.

"Did you use that bag and the contents of that bag for killing?"

"The contents of that bag were used for killing, you're right, in the killing of Mr. Agan; yes, I must say they were."

"It was used in the killing of a lot of other people, too, wasn't it?"

"Those are your words, not mine."

"Well? I'm asking you."

"Well, I'm saying that I'm not going to answer that."

Eyler also didn't want to answer questions about whether he obtained placydil from Dr. Frank Smith, saying he didn't want the name to be "smirched with all this."

Zahn pressed harder, knowing what the answers would be. As to whether he obtained placydil from the physician, Eyler invoked the Fifth Amendment. As to whether he had been "into bondage for a long time," the witness again took the Fifth Amendment.

Judge Darnell cleared his throat and called for a break after he asked Eyler if he wanted to confer with his attorneys about the wisdom of refusing to answer. Robert Agan stood stiffly, his glare locking into Eyler's as men and women all around him headed for the door and the jury was led away.

Wilma McNeive introduced herself to Zahn in the back of the courtroom. ''I am Danny Scott McNeive's mother,'' she said, extending her hand. ''Please could you ask Eyler about my son's murder?''

''Yes, ma'am,'' he answered, shaking her hand. ''I plan to, you'll see.''

When the testimony resumed, it was as if there had been no break. The tension settled in immediately, and Zahn continued his line of attack. Eyler took the Fifth Amendment for each of the victims attributed to the highway killer—Crockett, Johnson, Roach, Reynold, Herrera, McNeive, Calise, Hanson . . .

For a moment, the defense attorney paused and said: ''Etcetera.''

''Etcetera, yes,'' Eyler answered back. ''I take the Fifth Amendment again.''

''Sort of casual, isn't it?'' Zahn asked.

''Well, you're asking the questions.''

The attorney resumed what he called Eyler's ''roll of carnage,'' asking if the witness knew the people on the police lists. Each name was answered with ''I take the Fifth Amendment'': Bartlett, Bauer, Richard Wayne, and Block. But when Zahn asked ''Who is Danny Bridges?'' Eyler reacted strangely.

''Someone that—'' Then silence.

''Someone, what?''

''Someone that I was accused of killing in Chicago.''

''But you didn't do it,'' Zahn asked sarcastically.

''No, I did not.''

''Did you kill all those other people that I just mentioned?''

''Not saying that I did. Those are your words, sir.''

''No, not my words,'' Zahn replied. ''It's a question. Did you?''

''I'm not answering. I did not, no. How's that?''

Zahn next referred to early questioning by Greenwell, in which the prosecutor had asked if Eyler knew the meaning of doing a "scene." Zahn added: "And then I think you said that you knew that meant . . . someone dying."

"I don't remember actually saying that, no," Eyler answered.

"Is that what it means?"

"Ask Mr. Little."

"Are you answering it?"

"No."

Before Zahn was through, Eyler had invoked the Fifth Amendment twenty-four times. The hammering away at what Eyler refused to answer had, in effect, put the witness on trial and took attention away from the short, dour defendent who looked so insignificant watching through squinting eyes and thick glasses.

On re-direct questioning, Greenwell wanted to bring the case back to Little. His first words were: "Mr. Eyler, you were shocked when Robert David Little didn't give you money back on your birthday in 1982. Do you remember that?"

"Yes."

"Why were you shocked that he wouldn't give you money?"

"Because after the event—this event had taken place between us [the Agan murder] and I was generally used to getting money from Dave anyway, because he basically supported me. I was just shocked that after an event like this that he would tell me no."

Under further questioning from the prosecution, Eyler gave the first public account—true or not—of how he had become involved in killing. He said Little had talked to him about murders after James Williams moved out of the house and "asked me if I thought I could go through with it on several occasions."

He also said that he posed for pictures for Little "in different positions and things like that. With different things on." The photos, he explained, were not individual shots but more like a striptease "so that when he looks back over them, then it's almost like a slide reel when he can see the events taking place on the camera."

"Is that similar to the fashion as you described him taking the pictures at the murder of Steven Agan?"

"Yes, it is."

Greenwell also asked Eyler about Little's supposed involvement in the Danny Bridges murder. "You indicated that you disposed of the Bridges body," the prosecutor said.

"Yes, I did."

"Where was the Bridges body?"

"The Bridges body was left by Mr. Little dead beside my bed in the apartment in Chicago."

Kathleen Zellner smiled as Eyler's statements were now made public and part of an official court record, but the professor just slowly shook his head. With that Eyler was finished testifying and was then taken back to death row in Illinois.

One question hung in the air as Eyler was excused from the stand, on the exact day that Agan was murdered. The autopsy had not been specific, and in repeated questioning Eyler would say only that it was around December 19 or 20.

Greenwell wished he could have the man put on the stand who said earlier that he saw Eyler and Little in a car with Agan, but the man on later questioning was less sure of himself, and there were no reports to back him up. That left the prosecution the only option of attacking Little's character.

Mark Miller of Tennessee, appearing embarrassed as he faced the spectators, testified that he would get drunk at the professor's house and then be photographed in various stages of undress for five or ten dollars. Miller added that Little told him to change a pose or remove more clothing by saying, "Let's do the next scene."

Another witness called, Keith Hagelmeyer, nervously said he lived with Little for two years before joining the army, and that the professor would become sexually aroused taking pictures of him. Hagelmeyer said Little even paid for his airfare to Terre Haute and for his divorce, but that they were not lovers and there was never any bondage. The former soldier reddened as photos of his poses were shown to the jury, and he stared down at the rail of the witness stand rather than watch those twelve faces.

On the morning of the next session—Friday, April 12—four sheriff's deputies used the elevator to bring a seven-foot-tall section of the murder shed to the third floor courtroom. Two large nails were still protruding from the beam. The beam and bloodstained crossboards created a menacing presence as they leaned behind the witness chair.

Medical pathologist Robert Pless showed half a dozen slides of the autopsy on Agan, and one juror pressed her hand to her mouth. For an instant as Wilma McNeive sat among the spectators, she did not see Steven Agan in the photos; that was her own son's face, until she turned away, shaking. Little lowered his head and squeezed his eyes shut until after the final slide was shown. By then, Agan's brother had slipped out of the courtroom. As he said later, "I wanted to keep my sanity."

Pless, who had been the first professional to realize a serial killer was roaming the highways, detailed the beating and slashing injuries—most of them inflicted after Steven Agan was already dead. The tall, lean professional sat firmly back in his seat and testified that there was no indication that the victim had struggled against his bounds. Some of the slashing while Agan was alive had sliced into the scrotum and penis, and other cuts went through the veins in the neck, the carotid artery, and down through the front of the spine.

"This is the worst that I've seen without the body being cut into pieces," Pless told the jurors. But he admitted he could not pinpoint the time of death. Bacterial infection increases with gaping wounds, and he needed to use sunburn on the dead skin to make an estimate. His conclusion was that Agan was killed "sometime prior" to December 21, 1982. But later he conceded that it could have been as late as December 25.

Sam McPherson took the stand that afternoon, and he thought he would be able to close the case on Dr. Little. The former detective didn't need photos to remind himself of the body, and he didn't need an autopsy report to feel sure that two men had taken turns hacking at it. But every time the boyish Mark Greenwell asked a question about the professor, Zahn would object.

Come on, come on, McPherson thought, ask me about the studded "dog collar" found in Little's home; ask me about the video tapes of S & M, and the phone calls to Little's house on the murder nights and the photos you guys found of Eyler undressing. Introduce these photos now; ask me, ask me.

He was frustrated as he sat in the witness chair. He felt this murder trial was being treated like show and tell day. He hadn't realized until now that the Vermillion County budget was so modest that the case had been prepared by just one state police investigator, an ex-sheriff, and one assistant. McPherson stewed at being treated as if he had been just a cop who had looked at a crime scene, not as one of the leading members of a task force that had been following every lead as the bodies turned up one by one.

But there was still the prosecution's most importance piece of physical evidence, the key. A state police sergeant held up the front door lock to Eyler's former office, inserted the key, and turned the tumblers. But nothing was said to link the key to Dr. Little.

The prosecutor tried to shore this up by calling witnesses to suggest that Little must have been in Indiana at the time of the murder. Someone took the professor's 1980 Pontiac Trans Am to Clinton, Indiana, for repairs on December 21. There was a one-hundred-dollar deposit made through an automatic teller machine for Little's account that day; and, also on the 21st, someone called from Little's house to Tampa, Florida. In addition, a check was deposited on the 22nd. But no one said yes, he or she saw Little in Indiana on December 19, 20, 21, or 22.

And so Greenwell ended his case, and everyone in his office knew he had not come up with anything decisive. That afternoon, his people came and went slamming doors. But the prosecutor thought that perhaps he would have a chance the next morning, when Little would be called by the defense.

Zellner, whose main concern was finding a way of taking Eyler off Death Row for the Bridges murder, had contributed a list of seventy-six questions geared to unnerve the library science professor. She and Greenwell's staff members waited for hours for the prosecutor to show up at a boardroom in a Danville hotel so they could go over the attack. But Greenwell felt stifled with everyone telling him how to question people or what do to on his case. He ordered everyone out of his office so he could be alone with his wife and two young daughters for a few hours to ease the tension.

He showed up at the Danville hotel at 9 P.M. From then to midnight Zellner, dressed in a silk jogging outfit, grilled Greenwell on her list of questions, stressing words that she was sure would prove reactions from Little:

"How many men have you had sex with? You were aware that Larry Eyler had four stepfathers, weren't you? You associated with Larry Eyler because you had something in common with him, didn't you? On a number of occasions you asked Larry Eyler if he could kill someone, didn't you? Professor Little, do you make it a habit of associating with violent and dangerous people who commit crimes? In fact you helped unleash the violence in Larry Eyler, didn't you, Dr. Little? You encouraged and preyed upon Larry Eyler's sickness, didn't you? Did you know that Danny Bridges was a police informant? Did you know that Danny Bridges was under police surveillance? Your car was never dusted for fingerprints after the Bridges murder, was it Dr. Little?"

At the same time, Zahn and Voyles were mulling over their game plan. The graphic testimony of Eyler, however halting, had been disturbing but the prosecution had not produced anything else directly related to Little. There was a possibility that the appearance of their client on the stand might weaken their case.

Also that night, one of the jurymen got drunk out of frustration and went to the home of one of the investigators. The drunken juror said that unless the prosecutors produced someone who saw Little with Agan, they would lose their case.

The next morning, April 16, Judge Darnell dismissed the juror and let the defense begin. Greenwell's nervousness showed, and his eyes were bloodshot from his late-night preparations with Zellner.

Defense attorney Zahn, energetic as usual, presented evidence that no juror could fail to respond to—a videotape deposition by Little's eighty-three-year-old mother, Grace, who was living in a Wisconsin nursing home with her ailing husband. In a loving tone she told how "Bob," the younger of her two sons, "never missed a Christmas" with her when she lived in Tampa from 1958 to 1989. He always flew down about a week before, decorated his parents' tree, had a holiday meal with them, and would stay until New Year's Day. As the tape played, Greenwell blew on his perspiring hands and rubbed them against his pants.

There also was a tape of a former neighbor who said Little usually arrived on December 18 or 19, but another Tampa woman said into the camera that he sometimes arrived just a couple of days before Christmas. No one on the tapes could be sure where the professor was on December 18, 19, 20, or 21, 1982.

Little was to be the next witness, but his attorneys spoke to him in a side room during a break. "You know," Zahn said, "the jury has that image of your mother in their minds. I don't think if we put you on the stand that you would be on trial. I think homosexuality would be on trial, your lifestyle."

Little was prepared to testify, but he trusted his counsel. The small, gray-haired professor returned to his chair, nervously twisting a pen in his hands. Zahn faced Greenwell and said, "The defense rests."

Zellner was still in the hall when an assistant ran out with news that Little was not going to take the stand. She returned to the courtroom and suggested to Greenwell that having Eyler's mother testify might help the case. Zahn argued in sidebar conference with the judge that it was too late for this tactic, since the prosecution had rested without listing her as a witness. But Judge Darnell allowed Greenwell to bring her to the stand after lunch.

Shirley DeKoff walked through the courtroom and was sworn in. Greenwell had never conducted practice questioning with her and did not know what to expect. She told the jurors she clearly remembered calling her son at Little's home on December 21, 1982, because that was his birthday. But she did not know whether Little was also in the house.

Closing arguments began Wednesday morning, April 17. The two defense lawyers divided their presentation. Voyles portrayed Little as a man victimized by the justice system because of his lifestyle, and questioned whether anyone would make a phone call to his mother "in the middle of a killing."

In contrast, Zahn attacked the prosecution's case point by point. In his argument, there were only two men on that abandoned farm that night, the killer and his victim, and he reminded the jury about Eyler's nature.

"I suspect that in no time in your life before, and God forbid no time in your life yet to remain, will you ever be so close to pure evil," Zahn said. "Larry is a monster. He is an aberration of humanity. But he is a clever monster. Make no mistake. Larry knows exactly what he is doing. He doesn't want to die. He wants to beat the death penalty. That is the single motivating force in his life. It's no coincidence that he suddenly gives up Bob Little for the killing of Steve Agan. It's no coincidence that happened within a couple of months of the Supreme Court of the United States' turning down his appeal. Larry Eyler is manipulating the court system and the court procedures to save his life. . . . Just like he's now manipulating the system or attempting to, God forbid you let him, to get out from under the death penalty. . . . Can you convict Bob Little on the word of a sadistic killer? Like Larry William Eyler?"

Next Zahn read off the names of killings attributed to Eyler, reminding the jurors that Eyler took the Fifth Amendment twenty-four times. Then, quietly, he added: "Can you convince Bob Little on the word of this monster? This manipulator? Oh, no, make no mistake. Larry can be very charming, if it suits his purpose."

Zahn took off his glasses and often raised his voice in repeating every point against Larry Eyler. When he grabbed the knife from the evidence box, two jurors instinctively pulled back in their seats. Placing Agan's slashed blue jacket onto the top of an evidence easel, he made it take the form of a body. Zahn next portrayed Eyler slashing at it with the knife. "How are you going to get his shirt off? You can't. The blood. Blood. Blood. More blood." He pointed, and pointed again. "Knife wound. Knife wound." Finally he stood under the shed beam to suggest Steven Agan suspended helplessly by his wrists.

The defense attorney became even more energetic as he moved back and forth across the jury box. "This animal, this monster, this evil thing called Larry Eyler has killed so often, so much, so brutally that he has trouble distinguishing one victim from another. . . . Look at the hate. Look at the violence. Look at the act of a madman."

Speaking calmly now, Zahn returned to the jurors. "Here's what you've got. You got Larry Eyler. He tells you that Bob Little was there and participated in the killing of Steven Agan. Nothing fits the facts. . . . [It] Wasn't Bob Little's key. Wasn't Bob Little's lighter. Can you be sure what Larry Eyler says? Would you risk anything that Larry Eyler says? Would you convict an honorable man on the word of Larry Eyler? . . . Don't give him a conviction on the strength of this monster."

The jury went out to deliberate shortly after noon. Wilma McNeive gave Zellner her phone number on a blank bank deposit slip, should Eyler ever confess to killing her son Danny. Larry's mother remained in a motel room near the Pontiac prison, waiting for Zellner's phone call with the verdict. She wanted to tell her son personally what the outcome was.

Spectators passed the time by walking outside the courthouse in the mild spring day or buying cake and coffee from the church women in the lobby.

At 7:30 P.M., after nearly seven hours, the court clerk informed Judge Darnell that a verdict had been reached. All the spectators rushing back into the courtroom were searched for weapons again, and Little was surrounded by deputies as he sat between his two lawyers.

The clerk handed Darnell the verdict sheet. The judge raised his head and announced, "Not guilty."

Little's secretary and longtime friend Pat Gunther sighed a "Thank God." The professor jumped up and hugged his lawyers. But Robert Agan called out "Freed to kill!" as he rushed for the door with his father and stepmother.

Little broke into a smile, and it made him look friendlier and even younger. He glowed even under the intimidating stare of news cameras and microphones set up for a news conference in the basement auditorium of the courthouse.

"I'm sorry that the Agan family had to be put through the awful ordeal," Little told the reporters. He still looked rumpled in his gray suit and slightly tousled hair. "I know it was difficult for them. It's difficult enough without something like this happening. My sympathy goes out to them. Obviously, I'm very happy it's over."

The professor announced that he would take a few weeks to relax before returning to teach summer courses at Indiana State University. When a newsman asked about Eyler's charges on the Danny Bridges case, Little just smiled again and one of his attorneys responded: "What case?"

That night a panicking woman juror called Greenwell, saying she might have allowed a guilty man to go free. After the juror spent a sleepless night she met with Greenwell in her home at ten o'clock the next morning, saying "my mind is so boggled" that she couldn't remember her reasons for voting innocent. The prosecutor said there was nothing he could do.

Zellner did not give up in her attempt to reduce Eyler's death penalty to life by implicating the professor. Her staff continued inquiries into the whereabouts of the supposed Agan murder photos. Police privately said they expected the killings to continue.

Within two weeks of the trial the name of Dr. Little returned to the news. He had visited the Vermillion County Jail to see his former cellmate, James Byrnes, who had a record of thirty-two arrests including assault, armed robbery, and weapons charges. Little handed a deputy an envelope with one thousand dollars in various bills to pass on to him, saying it was to hire an attorney.

Within hours, Byrnes escaped by climbing into a waiting car as he was working outside. Police were able to trace him to Chicago, then notified Kathleen Zellner and Gera-Lind Kolarik that they might be in danger. Byrnes then passed out of sight.

One week later, officials at Indiana State University announced that Little was no longer suspended from his job as chairman of the library science department.

Police continue investigating the murders in Ohio and have never given up hope that someone will come forward in the unsolved murders linked to Eyler. At this hour he remains in prison, keeping with him secrets that can only be guessed at while twenty families grieve and long for justice.

GERA-LIND KOLARIK, *August 1991*

CONSTITUTIONAL
COMMENT

I.

The heroes of this book are dedicated law enforcement authorities: the police and prosecutors in several Illinois and Indiana jurisdictions.

The principal facts developed in the cases referred to here do not seem to be seriously disputed so far as they bear upon the career of Larry Eyler. All parties involved in those cases assume that the police testified truthfully about their encounters with Eyler. The mistakes of the Indiana police in dealing with him are evident in their own testimony. They do not pretend to have themselves done or said, or to have heard him concede, anything of importance that Eyler himself disputes.

Several of our rules for securing the rights of defendants are condemned by some critics as unduly burdening law enforcement efforts in this country. If police forces in the United States could generally be depended on to act with the integrity of the Illinois police forces in the Eyler case, there probably would be less need for the rules complained of. Still, the desperate situations and questionable people that the police must routinely cope with move them to sometimes cut corners in the interest of efficiency and justice.

The police forces seen in this book may conduct themselves as well as they do in large part because they have been disciplined for decades by the rules in question. The

See pages 422–3 for an identification of the law professor who wrote this constitutional comment and for citations to the litigation described in this book.

prospect of having evidence suppressed if it is not properly gathered no doubt inhibits some police. Even with these rules hanging over them, however, the Indiana police force did slip up in such a way as to permit Eyler to secure his release from an incarceration on a murder charge in Lake County, Illinois that, if it had led to a conviction, would have kept him from involvement in a subsequent murder in Chicago.

It is this Lake County release, believed by a trial judge (sitting in Waukegan, Illinois) to be required by the rules governing the proper mode of gathering evidence, which led to the rare if not even unprecedented situation described in this book: the release of a man suspected by the authorities of being a serial killer who then went on to be arrested, charged, and convicted for a subsequent murder.

II.

The decisive facts of the Eyler cases, as set forth in Illinois judicial opinions in 1985 and 1989, are as follows:

Larry Eyler, a longtime resident of Indiana, was arrested in October 1983 for the August 1983 murder of Ralph Calise in Lake County, Illinois. Vital to the case against Eyler in the Lake County hearings was evidence collected in Indiana on September 30, 1983 independent of the investigation of the Calise murder in Illinois. That evidence, gathered by Indiana state police in the course of investigating a series of murders in their state, was challenged in Lake County, Illinois on the basis of the Exclusionary Rule to be discussed below.

In April 1985 the Illinois Appellate Court reviewing the 1984 Lake County hearings described the 1983 Indiana police activity in this way:

The key to all of the suppression motions [in Waukegan, Illinois] was the warrantless search and seizure conducted by the Indiana state police . . . on September 30, 1983. The defendant was travelling south on Interstate Highway 65 in northern Indiana when he was stopped by an Indiana state trooper for a traffic vioiation. The initial stop extended to a 12-hour station house detention of the defendant regarding his involvement with homosexual murders in Indiana. The defendant's truck and a bag inside the truck were searched and the defendant's boots were seized.

The inner sole of one of those boots, it eventually turned out, had blood stains which were said by the authorities to be connected with the Lake County, Illinois victim, Ralph Calise. It is evident from other legal documents that Eyler had been for some time a suspect in the investigation of a series of more than twenty unsolved murders committed in Indiana and Illinois in 1982 and 1983. The bodies of the victims had been dumped in fields near principal highways.

A tipster, one of the many who named suspects, had first called the attention of the Indiana police to Eyler. But since the police did not believe they had enough evidence to charge Eyler, they were reduced to keeping him under surveillance. A routine surveillance alert distributed among Indiana police was evidently mistaken for a detention order by the police sergeant in charge—and so a casual and itself proper traffic-violation investigation escalated into a premature, day-long murder interrogation of Eyler. It was the evidence collected on that occasion that the Lake County, Illinois sheriff's police and prosecutors principally relied upon in charging Eyler for the Calise murder. But it was that evidence that an Illinois trial judge came to believe that he should rule to be inadmissible.

The Illinois Appellate Court confirmed the propriety of the February 1984 release of Eyler in Lake County, Illinois. By the time the Illinois Appellate Court made its ruling, in April 1985, Eyler was known to be again in custody, this time in Cook County, Illinois for the murder of Danny Bridges, whose dismembered body had been found on August 21, 1984 in eight garbage bags in a dumpster outside an apartment rented by Eyler in Chicago. The evidence was overwhelming that Bridges had died in the Eyler apartment and that Eyler had deposited the bags in the dumpster. A curious janitor happened to open one of the bags shortly before they were scheduled to be hauled away.

Eyler was convicted of murder, aggravated kidnaping, and concealment of a homicidal death. In October 1986, a trial judge, sitting in Chicago, "finding no mitigating factors sufficient to preclude imposition of the death penalty," imposed the sentence of death. The conviction and the death sentence were unanimously affirmed by the Illinois Supreme Court in October 1989. It is not unusual in this country for a decade to elapse between a sentence of death and an execution. In Illinois, where more than one hundred inmates are currently on death row, the last execution was in 1962, except for one in 1990 after a condemned man refused to continue press appeals that would have delayed further his execution.

III.

Citizens concerned about the efficiency of law enforcement in this country are naturally disturbed upon learning of the release of apparently dangerous men who then commit horrendous crimes. The Eyler case can be cited as a particularly disturbing instance of such folly, especially by those who suspect that he was responsible for a series of murders before and after his aborted 1983 detention in Lake County, Illinois.

Even so, the Indiana police work, however flawed, did not go to waste. We should recognize that Eyler, whether or not involved in earlier killings, may have been forced back into the community by the Indiana police more than he had been for years. That is, he could not continue to conduct himself as he had before his 1983 exposure.

It does not seem that Eyler was followed by any police after his February 1984 release from the Lake County jail in Waukegan, Illinois. But was there an alert out to chronicle the movements of his pickup truck? He evidently believed there was, and that sufficed to restrain him, changing his mode of operations, if only out of fear of being "framed" for some offense on the highway. Thus, a body that might once have been casually dumped in a lonely Midwestern farm field had to be disposed of in garbage bags out of a Chicago apartment building. Perhaps this could be done now and then without detection, but the risks were much higher than they would have been earlier. It is somewhat reassuring to be reminded of how difficult it is to dispose of corpses in a modern city.

To notice that Eyler, whether or not personally guilty of multiple murders, was forced back into the community is to recognize why we can have the mass murderers of whom we hear so much these days. They are largely unsupervised marauders, moving in circles where there are potential victims that no community keeps track of.

A critical problem evident throughout this book is that there is truly no enduring community for all too many Americans, victims and victimizers alike. This can sometimes make it seem that things are out of control, that one monster after another is free to kill, restrained neither by social supervision nor by personal inhibitions.

IV.

There was, therefore, a salutary effect resulting from the initial efforts of the authorities against Larry Eyler, even though he, in the opinion of some, "got away with it" the first time he was jailed on a murder charge, which was in Waukegan in 1983.

Eyler, we have noticed, "had" to change somewhat his way of life once he knew the police suspected him of multiple murders. But, one might well wonder, why did he, once he was suspected, go on to do anything at all, and so soon and so near thereafter, to get himself into the trouble he did in Chicago?

It seems that he could be deterred by his exposure, but only in how he operated. Whatever "drove" him to kill, assuming he did commit a series of murders (something that has yet to be proven about him or about anyone else referred to in this book), evidently kept asserting itself. There is about such compulsion both a desperation and an arrogance that smack of the irrational. The same can be said of respectable people, in other times or places, who continue to associate intimately with and rely upon someone known to have been exposed as destructive.

How *does* one deal with such irrational people, people who somehow feel not only compelled but even entitled to do what they please in satisfying themselves? Their victims may even seem to such victimizers to "ask" for it.

It is often difficult even for those closest to these people, victims and victimizers alike, to know what they are like. It can be difficult to detect compulsive but still crafty murderers or to know what to do with them once identified. Both victims and victimizers do have to be brought more into the community, thereby creating conditions that reduce the tempting vulnerability of one group and the seeming immunity of the other.

Even so, the bulk of our population would consider itself grievously imposed upon if serious efforts were made to create more of a community for everyone. More intensive mutual supervision would likely be seen as an unwarranted burdening of our everyday life. The occasional madman is free to kill again and again in various parts of this country partly because we are all as free as we are day in and day out. We can see in Eastern Europe a rise in violent crime as the powers of the secret police are curbed. We have seen also the past year a high-ranking official of the Government of the United States publicly identified as a suspected spy for the Soviet Union, followed around for months by the FBI, the television networks, and the press, and yet not formally accused, indicted, or brought to trial. There are edifying as well as troubling aspects of that episode.

V.

Who *are* likely to be the victims of a serial killer? One model is provided by the female prostitutes who were the victims of Jack the Ripper in nineteenth-century London. This very pattern may be seen as well in the recently solved Rochester, New York serial murders. Most of the Indiana victims investigated by the police in 1982–83 were young males evidently available for homosexual prostitution.

Such victims are often drifters or otherwise outcasts, misguided if not even self-destructive people that no one really cares much for, except perhaps for their immediate families. Young male homosexuals are particularly vulnerable, since they usually do not have the opportunity to set up conventional families or to move in "regular channels."

Can anything be done for these potential victims, aside from trying to persuade the sometimes hostile police to be more concerned for their welfare? We can see in this book the way a highly mobile society contributes to criminal homicidal epidemics. We can also see that the things described here can go on in part because of an ever-growing emphasis among us upon sexual gratification. We have even come to insist upon the "principle" that one is entitled to live one's life pretty much as one pleases, that the community has no right to interfere, and that what consenting adults do between themselves is usually no one else's business, making it almost inevitable that more and more bizarre experiments will be resorted to.

This permissive approach to disciplining human beings affects what appetites people have, who the consumers are of purchased indulgences, and how victims are recruited and exploited.

VI.

We have learned in recent years how these developments bear upon the problem of drug control in our society. The limitations of recourse to the criminal law as the principal way to handle the drug problem or to reduce its damage are becoming evident.

We can also see in the drug problem the considerable role of the middle-class consumer who helps sustain vigorous markets in immoral, if not illicit, commodities. Such consumers also help keep the multitude of hustlers on the street, the vulnerable youngsters that an occasional madman can "safely" kill.

Murders aside, should we not reconsider the notion of "victimless crimes," especially when youngsters are corrupted, questionable appetites are heightened, and disturbed people are left to sordid devices? It should be evident that all of us are likely to be affected by those free choices that are said to "harm only oneself."

Many citizens are tempted to see these developments as

due primarily to the rules "coddling criminals" that have been developed by judges. If only a few changes were made, it is often said, we would be safe from the criminal. But the problems we have been surveying are much deeper in their origins: fundamental changes in our way of life may be called for, changes that we simply may not be prepared to make.

It hardly seems likely that building and filling more and more prisons will help much. Indeed, considering the corrupting effect of much of prison life, increased reliance on prisons can make matters even worse. Besides, it should be noticed, out of the more than thirty million serious crimes against persons or property committed annually in the United States, only several hundred thousand result in felony convictions and imprisonments. Vital to making the law more effective in curbing such crimes is the shaping of a sound public opinion about how we should all act. At the least, certain crimes should be made practically unthinkable.

VII.

Even so, one can wonder, upon reviewing the disastrous effect of the Exclusionary Rule in the Eyler case, "What ever happened to common sense?"

The Exclusionary Rule is grounded in the Fourth Amendment to the Constitution, which provides, "The right of the people to be secure in their persons, houses, papers, and effects, against unreasonable searches and seizures, shall not be violated, and no warrant shall issue, but upon probable cause, supported by Oath of affirmation, and particularly describing the place to be searched, and the persons or things to be seized." The Exclusionary Rule, which forbids governmental use in court of any evidence improperly seized, is a possible but not a necessary implication of the Fourth Amendment guarantee. This implication, developed by American judges, is rarely resorted to elsewhere in the world. For example, it is not the rule in Great Britain.

What is the genesis of the American rule? It is considered unbecoming for the State to depend on evidence that is tainted. Judges sometimes say that the honor of the community requires that only lawful means be used to secure convictions. Even more is made of the need to discipline not only the police but also the community at large. Various rules are defended as serving the development and maintenance of a moral sense in the community: this is a way of teaching that human relations are not to be merely the result of the random play of forces.

Many older lawyers and judges believe that the Exclusionary Rule and other such rules have had, despite occasional injustices in their application, a generally salutary effect upon the police. The police, they remember, were all too often a law to themselves before these judicial curbs were imposed upon them.

Even today, some police are notorious for using supposed or minor traffic violations to stop, search, interrogate, and otherwise harass many people, especially members of minority groups, who are innocent of any crime. Our automobiles have become so important to us that they are, in important respects, like the houses we have traditionally considered privileged places.

Law enforcement authorities frequently testify that a well-disciplined police force is not likely to be adversely affected by the Exclusionary Rule, once the rule is properly publicized. In the Eyler situation, for example, the Lake County, Illinois police force, which proudly considers itself well-disciplined, had to try to work around a critical and probably avoidable mistake by the Indiana state police.

Be that as it may, surprisingly few indictments, except perhaps in "the war against drugs" where the volume of offenses encourages even more official shortcuts than hard-pressed police routinely resort to, are dismissed because of the Exclusionary Rule. It is hard to determine, however, how many prosecutions are *not* initiated because of the Exclusionary Rule. Still, it should be noticed that criminal law specialists generally believe that, contrary to a widespread public perception, the Exclusionary Rule has had relatively little adverse effect on the criminal justice system and no discernible effect on the crime rate or on law enforcement's ability to control crime in this country.

VIII.

The Exclusionary Rule, it should be noticed, is a relatively minor offender among the various legal provisions that routinely deny courts access to the truth and protect guilty people. Far more important are such traditional immunities as the right against self-incrimination, the right of a defendant to remain silent at his or her trial, the right not to testify against one's spouse in most situations, and the right of clients to speak in total confidence to their attorneys. Even more pervasive in liberating our everyday life is the law of private property, which leaves a wide scope for unsupervised activity.

Do we really want our lives organized in any other way? After all, the police are sometimes rather confident about who the criminals are that are at large in the community. What do we want done about the people thus suspected, when there is no solid evidence available with which to prosecute them? Should torture be permitted? More lie detector use? Universal surveillance, including systematic eavesdropping on all telephone conversations? Official monitoring of all financial transactions, travel activities, and even social relations?

However reluctant we may be to go this far, we can still wonder what should have been done in the Eyler case in Waukegan. The sensitive Lake County trial judge in the case evidently believed he could, without fear of being reversed on appeal, have ruled either way on the issue of the admission of the evidence seized in Indiana. Why, then, should he not have admitted the evidence seized after the extended traffic-violation stop in Indiana? What injustice would have been done to a defendant of whom the judge himself has since said that he was ''sure'' at the time was guilty? It is hardly likely that anyone in Eyler's alleged circumstances ever conducts himself with the expectation that he would be entitled to the evidence-suppression ruling made here.

The disciplining effect of the Exclusionary Rule is much more likely to be achieved when the prosecutors in a jurisdiction are spurred by a local judicial reprimand to insist upon proper conduct by the police they routinely depend on. On the other hand, it should not be expected that prosecutors and the police in one state will usually pay much attention to what is said about them by judges in another state.

Ordinarily, however, the rules of evidence do encourage the professionalization of the police force. Considerable effort is devoted to these rules in the training sessions of the Federal Bureau of Investigation and other well-trained police forces. It is probably good for the morale, self-confidence, and hence competence of police forces and prosecutorial staffs to recognize that there are plausible rules that they should respect, rules that are more than mere technicalities. It can at least have the effect that intensive close-order drill has for military recruits.

IX.

Larry Eyler exploited the system—not only the legal system but also the social system (including its network of lonely highways). He was able thereby to get extra opportunities to do mischief, to the grief of additional families, including his own.

But eventually the legal system itself tripped him up. We can see here that one cannot always predict the consequences of trial stratagems. The simply prudent thing to do, therefore, is to behave oneself, rather than depend on lawyers to salvage one's life. Thus, Eyler was his own final victim. Had he been put away in Lake County, Illinois in 1984, or better still after a non-fatal knifing he evidently admitted in Indiana back in 1978, he probably would be far better off today—better off not only in the sense that he probably would not have been sentenced to death, but also in the sense that he would not have hurt still more people. (It would also have helped him with both judge and jury if he had simply left Danny Bridges in one piece, however it happened that he had his corpse to deal with in his apartment.)

Eyler's lawyer is presented in this book as conscientious, humane, and competent. That he permitted himself to be swept along so long by his faith in Eyler reflects the not-unnatural tendency of dedicated defense attorneys to get caught up in their clients' cases. Eyler's lawyer did not really know what was good for his client.

But, then, it must be a rare criminal-defense attorney who understands his client well enough to know what he truly needs. If Eyler's lawyer had believed what the Lake County police in Waukegan believed about his client, he would have wanted him locked up indefinitely for his own good as well as for the good of the community. Had Eyler admitted to a series of killings, an insanity plea might also have made sense. How should such insanity be dealt with by the community?

We can see that those who live by the rules of the law, whether defense attorneys, judges, or law-enforcement authorities, cannot avoid running risks if they conscientiously try to do their duty. Still, everyone is better off if the parties can indeed rely upon the others whom they contend with to "play by the rules," especially if the rules both make sense and appear to do so. It is particularly important for everyone, including potential criminals, to observe that the authorities try to abide by the rules even when they are severely hampered in doing so. This at least teaches the useful lesson that law-abidingness is worthwhile, contributing to the moral ascendancy of those who do stand for the law.

The community at large is thereby reassured, as by the story told in this book, that justice is not only something imposed upon the weak by the strong but is also something that the strong do themselves the honor of respecting.

George Anastaplo

George Anastaplo is professor of law, Loyola University of Chicago; professor emeritus of political science and of philosophy, Rosary College; and lecturer in the liberal arts, University of Chicago. He has published several books, including *The Artist As Thinker: From Shakespeare to Joyce* (1983). His most recent book, *The Constitution of 1787* (1989), is the first section-by-section commentary ever published on the text of the Constitution of the United States.

Judicial statements recorded in the course of the Larry Eyler litigation in Illinois include the following:

1. Opinion by Judge James B. Moran, in *Larry Eyler* v. *Robert Babcox et al.*, 582 F. Supp. 981 (United States District Court, Northern District of Illinois, Chicago, Illinois, December 19, 1983).

2. Memorandum by Judge William Block, in *People of the State of Illinois* v. *Larry Eyler*, 83 CF 1585 (Circuit Court of Lake County, Waukegan, Illinois, February 3, 1984).

3. Opinion for the Court by Justice George W. Unverzagt and Dissenting Opinion by Justice George W. Lindberg, in *People of the State of Illinois* v. *Larry W. Eyler*, 132 Ill. App.3d. 792, 87 Ill. Dec. 648, 477 N.E.2d 774 (Appellate Court of Illinois, Second Division, Chicago, Illinois, April 26, 1985).

4. Opinion for the Court by Justice John J. Stamos, in *People of the State of Illinois* v. *Larry Eyler*, 133 Ill.2d 173, 139 Ill. Dec. 756, 549 N.E.2d 268 (Supreme Court of Illinois, Springfield, Illinois, October 25, 1989).

Compelling True Crime Thrillers
From Avon Books

BADGE OF BETRAYAL
by Joe Cantlupe and Lisa Petrillo

76009-6/$4.99 US/$5.99 Can

THE BLUEGRASS CONSPIRACY
by Sally Denton   76441-8/$4.95 US/$5.95 Can

A KILLING IN THE FAMILY:
A TRUE STORY OF
LOVE, LIES AND MURDER
by Stephen Singular with Tim and Danielle Hill

76413-X/$4.95 US/$5.95 Can

LOSS OF INNOCENCE:
A TRUE STORY OF JUVENILE MURDER
by Eric J. Adams   75987-X/$4.95 US/$5.95 Can

RUBOUTS: MOB MURDERS IN AMERICA
by Richard Monaco and Lionel Bascom

75938-1/$4.50 US/$5.50 Can